Jung and the Postmodern

The psychological writing of Jung and the post-Jungians is all too often ignored as anachronistic, archaic and mystic. In *Jung and the Postmodern*, Christopher Hauke challenges this, arguing that Jungian psychology is more relevant now than ever before – not only can it be a response to modernity, but it can offer a critique of modernity and Enlightenment values which brings it in line with the postmodern critique of contemporary culture.

After introducing Jungians to postmodern themes in Jameson, Baudrillard, Jencks and Foucault, the author introduces postmodernists to Jung's cultural critique and post-Jungian discussions of representation, individuation, consciousness and the alternatives to Enlightenment rationality. He also takes a totally fresh approach to topics such as hysteria and the body, Jung and Nietzsche, architecture and affect, Princess Diana and the 'death' of the subject, postmodern science and synchronicity, and to psychosis and alternative 'rationalities'.

Jung and the Postmodern is vital reading for everyone interested in contemporary culture, not only Jungians and other psychotherapists who want to explore the social relevance of their discipline, but anyone who shares a passionate concern for where we are heading in postmodern times.

Christopher Hauke is a lecturer in Psychoanalytic Studies at Goldsmiths College, University of London, and an I.A.A.P. Jungian analyst in private practice.

Jung and the Postmodern
The Interpretation of Realities

Christopher Hauke

Brunner-Routledge
Taylor & Francis Group

HOVE AND NEW YORK

33.95

First published 2000 by Routledge
11 New Fetter Lane, London EC4P 4EE

Simultaneously published in the USA and Canada
by Taylor & Francis Inc
325 Chestnut Street, Philadelphia PA 19106

Reprinted 2003
by Brunner-Routledge
27 Church Road, Hove, East Sussex, BN3 2FA
29 West 35th Street, New York, NY 10001

Brunner-Routledge is an imprint of the Taylor & Francis Group

Typeset in Times by Keystroke, Jacaranda Lodge, Wolverhampton
Printed and bound in Great Britain by TJ International Ltd,
Padstow, Cornwall

British Library Cataloguing in Publication Data
A catalogue record for this book is available from the British Library

Library of Congress Cataloging in Publication Data
Hauke, Christopher, 1953–
    Jung and the postmodern : the interpretation of realities /
Christopher Hauke.
        p.   cm.
    Includes bibliographical references and index.
    1. Psychoanalysis and culture. 2. Postmodernism—Psychological
aspects. 3. Jungian psychology. 4. Jung, C. G. (Carl Gustav),
1875–1961. I. Title.
    BF175.4.C84H38 2000
    150.19′54—dc21   99–41262
                                                              CIP

ISBN 0–415–16385–4 (hbk)
ISBN 0–415–16386–2 (pbk)

For Joseph, Matthew and Ben.

Man has awakened in a world that he does not understand, and this is why he tries to interpret it.

(Jung, 1940: 81)

Contents

x *Contents*

Foreword

Andrew Samuels

Over the last fifteen years, I have been involved in the publication of around fifty-five volumes for Routledge which, it is generally agreed, cluster at the 'academic', 'demanding' and 'critical' end of the range of analytical psychology and Jungian analysis. Of all these, I have never believed in a book as much as I believe in this one. Over the same period, observers of the Jungian analytic and psychoanalytic scenes have noted in academic quarters and in intellectual life in general what has been termed Jung's return from banishment. Some of this re-examination of Jung and his work rests in a clearer understanding of the globally damning way in which it was dealt with by the psychoanalytic establishment. Some of it is due to the quiet penetration of a number of academic fields by those with knowledge of Jungian ideas and a desire to apply these ideas in their fields of interest and expertise. Some has come from the growing recognition that Jungian analysis is not only as effective as any other kind of psychotherapy, but that it also has interesting features, some of which are unique to its approach. Further re-examination stems from a recognition that comparisons between Jung's work and that of other writers or movements are much more substantial and important than we thought before and can no longer be disregarded if we are to retain any sort of academic and intellectual openness.

We should not overlook the role played in these developments by courses in Jungian Studies in universities – often in centres dealing with psychoanalysis and psychotherapy, but sometimes to be found in departments of literature or religious studies. Evidence from the Internet too suggests that the 'Jungians' – to use a shorthand term – are changing their nature. Anyway, all of this has been going on since the early 1980s and gradually a new field has been emerging. There is no readily agreed name for it but I still like the tag 'post-Jungian' and it is often used.

Having said all this, there remains, in some quarters, an elitist attempt to imitate Jung's spirit, his thought, clinical style and even his manner of life.

In spite of the massive amount of revisionary work that goes on with ever-greater energy, 'Jungians' often say things about gender, 'race' and economics that reflect a social insouciance and an unwarranted privileging of an 'internal' perspective over all others, as if adherence to this viewpoint is the only way into what remains, in tone at least, a Brotherhood. Hence, there is still some raw material left for those who wish to claim that Jungian analysts are like 'cult' leaders, or that Jungian scholars are not scholars (by definition).

Then, along comes Christopher Hauke's book which pulls so much of this re-reading of Jung together. And, if it is absorbed in the way it deserves, this volume will not only establish the claims I have just sketched, but it will push the case for the serious treatment of Jung and Jungian psychology to a point where it is irresistible.

In this foreword I wish to offer my personal reading of the book which will inevitably compete with other different and varied responses it is going to generate. As Lacan said, 'style is the person you are talking to'. The first thing I have discovered about the book is that it taught me something new about Jung. Hauke's concern is not only with Jung as a critic of modernity, but also as an apostle of what came after. Time and again as I was reading, the more radical Jung came to mind and, as the deliteralisations flowed into each other, I came to see Jung and his heritage as perhaps one of the finest healing commentaries on the social and cultural world that we in the West inhabit and will continue to inhabit long into the twenty-first century.

Jung's interest in gender, in subjectivity and rationality, in the body, in the sublime, can all be seen, not only as cries of pain in an angst-ridden world, but also as an on-going challenge to that world to change its ways. Hauke's perspective is one which names Jung as the healing therapist of modernity. And, just as the contemporary therapist or scientist or political thinker or artist cannot remain outside the world with which they engaged, so too Jung's personal dis-ease is the *sine qua non* of his strange authority to hold up a mirror before us.

Reading Jung is one thing; studying Jung is another, and I find in Hauke a stimulating teacher of depth psychology. This teacher helps the student to focus his reading ('his' because I am talking about myself), so as to align the student's interests and needs with what is to be found in the massive contents of the *Collected Works*. For me, two themes that emerged quite powerfully were 'nature' and 'body'. In the case of nature, my speculations ran to the ways in which the manufactured environment makes people ill, and, in the case of body, to ways in which it is possible to listen to our bodies without essentialising or idealising them as sources of ineffable wisdom. (I refer the reader to Chapters 4 and 7 respectively if he or she wishes to follow my fingerprints.)

Studying is different from reading but neither goes in a vacuum. The need to 'locate' Jung is as pressing as ever. Last week I went to the launch party for an important new feminist book. I was introduced by one professor to another as 'This is Andrew. He's a Jungian – but we love him anyway!' What was happening was an exercise in compressed cultural locationism. 'Jungian' tells you most of what you need to know. Now, for whatever reason, conventional works of intellectual history, with the stated aim of positioning Jung in the flowchart of European ideas, really have missed something. Succinctly I think that what has got overlooked – and what Hauke keeps pointing out – is Jung's encouragement to us to translate into *action* the epistemology he develops in his works.

It is so hard to word this epistemology and, arguably, Christopher Hauke spends a whole book doing it. Some elements I can write about easily: closing the subject–object divide, emphasising that relativity is not equivalent to no values, perceiving how phenomena at the margins of discourses strongly define phenomena that seem more central and consensually accepted. Then there are words like 'soft' knowledge, or tacit, implicit, intuitive knowledge. I do not like the word 'feminine' that often gets used here because it is so hard to disentangle 'women' from 'feminine' (as Jung said he wanted to but I do not believe him!) and we end up denying women access to and usage of 'hard' knowledge. (See Christopher Hauke's innovative treatment of these issues in Chapter 5.)

To make my point clearer, I would draw the reader's attention to Jung's extraordinary statements regarding two kinds of thinking first published in 1911–1912. (I will quote from the initial 1916 translation into English rather than the better known but less radical-sounding 1956 translation):

> [Directed, rational] thinking creates innovations, adaptations, initiates reality and seeks to act upon it. [Undirected thinking], on the contrary, turns away from reality, sets free subjective wishes, and is, in regard to adaptation, wholly unproductive.
>
> (Jung, 1911–1912: 20)

To call both 'thinking' is to valorise Enlightenment ways of doing things and to critique them at the same time. It is a hard act to pull off and, central as this topic is to the Jung–Hauke enterprise, the younger partner may be said to have come to the rescue – or at least the assistance – of the older.

Continuing to try to convey my experience of reading this work, I have been struck by the subtlety with which Hauke addresses the questions of opposites and oppositionalisms – in our minds, language and societies. On occasions Hauke is the consummate Jungian: opposites either blend with each other, transcend their illusory oppositionalism, and a new, third, mediating product will emerge. On the other hand, if something gets too extreme, then what will emerge is its extreme opposite (*enantiodromia*, following Heraclitus). On other occasions, Hauke does things with 'the opposites' that take the breath away. He can ignore them and just let things shake down the way they want to; or he allows the oppositeness to linger, sometimes even celebrating it. Moreover, at any one time he will be doing more than one of these things with the opposites.

In all the time I have spent reading (and writing) about the question of 'the opposites', I have never come across so satisfying and stimulating a treatment of the problem.

But the theme of 'the opposites' might take time to emerge if the reader is not one who (like me) had almost despaired of finding anything new to be said about the matter. Hauke's book is a portmanteau volume (he likens it to the work of a *bricoleur*, after Lévi-Strauss) and, if you think about it, this has to be so. He is not parading knowledge, not stuffing everything in, nor being a maddening amateur in fields where there are real pros. It is essential to his project that he engages with subjectivity, the physical environment, gender, science, philosophy, symbolism, affect (a masterly chapter, Chapter 9) and post-modern critical theory. To begin with, as the book is a challenge to the thinking world to wake up to Jungian ideas and drop the off-hand slurs often used to neutralise such ideas, Hauke has to make sure he says something that will reach as many groupings as possible. (It will.) In addition, as he wants his book to become a standard text for Jungian Studies courses (it will) and in clinical trainings (it will) he cannot run the risk of confining himself to any one field. This is because Hauke is teaching us – inspiring us, actually – to change the way we 'do' Jung. If this involves changing the Jung we do, then this can be accepted as a further 'interpretation of realities'.

I want to end on as direct a note as I can. This is the book some of us have been waiting for for quite a while, but it will shake up even those of us who have anticipated it eagerly. However, it will disturb even more profoundly those who have supinely let the location of Jung be settled for them by so-called authorities, none of whom have dared to engage as extensively with the issues as this book does. It is up to us to make that engagement in return.

Acknowledgements

I would like to thank all my friends and colleagues, and the students at Goldsmiths College, the Laban Centre, Centre for Psychoanalytic Studies, University of Kent, and elsewhere, who I have shared these ideas with over the last four years – not only for their support and encouragement but especially for their arguments and criticism which always helped me to sharpen my focus and extend what I had to say.

I would especially like to thank Andrew Samuels, Martin Stanton, Anastasios Gaitanidis and Larry O'Carroll for their belief in me and in this project over several years, and for reading and commenting on earlier drafts. I am also grateful to David Peat for his support and special help with the chapter on 'Jung and postmodern science'. Others who have been generous with their time and their comments are Tessa Adams, Ian Alister, John Beebe, Petruska Clarkson, David Hewison (for lending me the out-of-print books), Sean Homer, Vincent Keter, Ian Marshall, David Reason, Joy Schaverien, Peter Tatham, Michael Whan and Mary Wilson (for the leaping boy). My deepest gratitude goes to Michael Vannoy Adams who, despite a distance of four thousand miles, helped me get this whole caboodle into shape and pointed me in directions I did not even know I needed to go, who sent me material I was unaware of, and who was my guide throughout the completion of the book. Thanks.

Although all the material is published here for the first time, many themes of this book and earlier versions of some chapters have been given as talks and seminars and I would also like to thank all those participants at the Association of Group and Individual Psychology; the Association of Jungian Analysts; Department of Anthropology, Goldsmiths College; University of Cork; University of Essex; Limbus, Devon; Middlesex University; T.H.E.R.I.P.; the Universities Association for Psychoanalytic Studies; the Society of Analytical Psychology; West Midlands Institute of Psychotherapy; United Kingdom Council for Psychotherapy; for their kind invitations and lively responses.

Finally, my greatest thanks goes to Susan Holden for her interest in this book, her focus on keeping things clear, her forebearance at my absences up the garden for hours at a time, her energy when I needed it, and her all round love and support. I could not have done it without her.

Permissions

The author and publishers wish to gratefully thank the following for granting permission to quote from their work:

Nick Hornby, *High Fidelity*, published by Victor Gollancz. Thomas Merton, *The Way of Chuang Tzu*, published by Search Press Ltd. and reproduced by permission of Laurence Pollinger Ltd. For the same extracts by Thomas Merton, from *The Way of Chuang Tzu*, copyright © 1965 by The Abbey of Gethsemani. Reprinted by permission of New Directions Publishing Corp. For extracts (pp. 67, 91) from *Lao Tzu: Tao Te Ching* translated by D.C. Lau (Penguin Books, 1963) copyright © D.C. Lau, 1963. Reproduced by permission of Penguin Books Ltd. Umberto Eco, *Reflections on the Name of the Rose*, published by Minerva, Random House and Gruppo Editoriale Fabbri Bompiani. *The Collected Works of C.G. Jung*, edited by Sir Herbert Read, Dr Michael Fordham and Dr Gerhard Adler, translated in the main by R.F.C. Hull, published by Routledge, and for the same extracts, copyright Bollingen Foundation NY © PUP, reprinted by permission of Princeton University Press. And special thanks to Frank O. Gehry and to Charles Jencks.

Every effort has been made to trace copyright holders and obtain permissions. Any omissions brought to our attention will be remedied in future editions.

Introduction

Nowadays, the world hangs by a thin thread, and that thread is the psyche of man.

(C. G. Jung, 6 August, 1957)

GETTING RE-HOUSED

I will come straight to the point: I regard Jung's psychology, and that of many post-Jungians, as *a response to modernity*. To put this more strongly, Jung's psychology constitutes a critique of modernity and of Enlightenment rationality and values that, to my mind, brings it in line with many aspects of the postmodern critique of contemporary culture. This implies, therefore, that I regard Jung as not so much a theorist and practitioner of the treatment of mental pathologies along the lines of the medical model emphasised in psychoanalysis, but far more a theorist of culture as a whole who still retains the psychotherapeutic aim of *healing*. Unlike other cultural theorists, Jung writes from a background of the psychoanalytic treatment of the *individual* in a way that valorises subjective experience as a legitimate approach to concerns of the wider, collective culture and to 'scientific' investigation in general. Such an approach addresses the gap between contemporary collective norms, values and Truths on the one hand, and the variety of beliefs, desires, experiences and 'rationalities' individual subjects encounter, on the other.

By extending a theory of the unconscious to embrace a vast historical and cultural range of human actuality and human potential, Jung found that, in spite of several hundred years of 'liberal' Enlightenment, the citizen-subject of the industrialised West was only a human being as far as the dominant culture would allow. The cultural conditions of modernity had set a limit upon the permitted scope of the human psyche. At the start of the twentieth century, Freud's theory of psychoanalysis had asserted that the subject was no longer 'master in his own house', there was now the unconscious to consider, but with psychoanalytic tools and insights, stability could be re-established. Jung's analytical psychology goes further than this. It is not so much a case of no longer being master of the house – a sublimely modernist concept itself – but the fact that *we need to do something about the house itself.* The culture of modernity, the product of five hundred years of Enlightenment, no longer feels like home. If we take Newton as emblematic – although David Hume or Adam Smith would do – this is the house that Isaac built, constructed on certainties, facts and heirarchies of Truth about the material world which extended to the social world and the individual subject's place within it. Jung's phenomenological approach to the unconscious revealed not just the irrationality and instinctual in 'man' – as it had for Freud – thus deposing the arrogance of human 'rationality' to provide a fuller description of ourselves; the rediscovery of the unconscious meant more than this for Jung. It implied that there are aspects to our humanity which contemporary cultural conditions of modernity have seen fit to ignore as irrelevant, untrue, 'primitive', of no use and, above all, unprofitable (in every sense). Jung applied his psychology – the method of the individual – as an overall cultural tool to critique not only the modern psyche but its cultural setting as well. In doing so, Jung's psychology challenges the splitting tendency of modernity: the splitting of the 'rational' and 'irrational', the splitting of the social, collective norm and individual, subjective experience, the splitting of the Human and the Natural, of mind and matter, and, perhaps above all, the splitting of the conscious and unconscious psyche itself.

Reflecting upon such a bold and assertive opening statement – ironically, so typical of the over-confident style of rationality addressed in Jung's psychology – I am prompted to recall a dream I had in the middle of writing the first draft of this book. The scene was the outer stone facade and steps of a large Victorian building like a university college. A middle-aged, grey-suited man stood at the top of the steps while his son sat below near the bottom of the steps. While the father was an educated professorial type, his son was a slobbering young man with obvious 'learning difficulties', thus making the contrast between them even greater. The man was viewing the wall of the building and watching as these chalked words appeared or faded (or both):

> *The relationship between the ordinate and the inordinate is achieved via the square root of the formula for a straight line.*

I woke immediately after the dream and wrote it down. The writing was on the wall but I reckoned I needed some knowledge of the maths involved before I could begin to fathom what it might be signifying. I rang a friend who I thought might help – the physicist and writer F. David Peat whose work crops up later in this book. He pointed out that, in mathematical terms, square roots are 'irrational' while the formula for a straight line is 'rational'. This opposition appeared to resonate with other aspects of the dream: the professorial father and the 'idiot' son, and the other 'relationship' referred to – the one between the ordinate and the inordinate.

But the opposition ordinate/inordinate is not simply one of rational measurement versus the irrational unmeasured. Inordinate also refers to an excess, a super-abundance or a *superfluous* amount; and while ordinate does refer to measure, it is also connected with *ordination* into a doctrine and with *rites*. On a personal level, perhaps the dream was referring to the overwhelming amount of material I had gathered and to my need to get it all into some sort of cohesive order in the form of a conventional and coordinated book. In a parallel way, there could be a reference here to the excess of Nature which Enlightenment thinking attempted to tame and corral into a rational Human Order. How some crazy maths formula was meant to 'achieve' this was anyone's guess.

But what if the 'relationship' to be 'achieved' is not referring to any sort of *resolution* (or *solution*) at all but is functioning more like a Zen koan? In other words, rather than trying to coordinate the inordinate amount of material into a book, or, put another way, to rationalise the gap between the rational and the irrational – the educated father and the simpleton son (both 'me' of course) – the dream was indicating something rather different. In an attempt to restore the full speech of the unconscious (as Lacan would have it), the dream proposed a way forward (*via*) in the foreign language of mathematics, an *other* language and not my *mother* tongue. Additionally, the proposition – *the square root of the formula for a straight line* – is itself 'irrational' like that famous sound of one hand clapping. What the dream seems to be proposing is the limitation of any critique that may only be expressed in the same language as that which it seeks to criticise.

Neither is there is a transcendent 'Jungian' solution to this. What the dream proposes does not *transcend* the irrational/rational, disorder/order difficulty that dogs both my writing and modernity itself. *Books* are Enlightenment projects *par excellence*; there can be no *transcendence* of Enlightenment oppositions in books alone. This is the point, I believe, which Jung arrives at when he asserts that,

'Life is crazy and meaningful at once . . . When you come to think about it, nothing has any meaning, for when there was nobody to think about it, there was nobody to interpret what happened. Interpretations are only for those who don't understand; it is only the things we don't understand that have any meaning.' (Jung, 1954, CW 9, I: para. 65)

But when he poses the question, 'how do we assign meaning? From what source, in the last analysis, do we derive meaning?' he comes back with an answer that points beyond modern conscious formulations back to the depths of the unconscious itself.

> The forms we use for assigning meaning are historical categories that reach back into the mists of time – a fact we do not take sufficiently into account. Interpretations make use of certain linguistic matrices that are themselves derived from primordial images. From whatever side we approach this question, everywhere we find ourselves confronted with the history of language, with images and motifs that lead straight back to the primitive wonder-world. (ibid.: para. 67)

What Jung points out is that the meaning we make, although limited by the language available, rests on a base more profound than modernity ordinarily allows or recognises. It is possible to address the limitations of conscious language through our attention to the unconscious – the 'primitive wonder-world' with its polyvalent, pluralistic imagery which is as inordinate and untidy as Nature itself and is thus rejected and ignored by modernity. Nietzsche got there before him when he asserted that what moderns of his time needed was not more History but *more psychology*. In doing so he ushers in our contemporary need for the radical questioning and deconstruction of the assumptions of modernity – in Nietzsche's words, *the transvaluation of all values*. This is the shift from modernity to the postmodern we also find in Jung's psychology and which this book will be describing. As the unconscious implied in 'my' dream, we walk a fine line between the meaningful and the meaningless. As we proceed with such an 'impossible' task it is possible that our self-imposed limits will be exceeded; for, as A. N. Whitehead said: 'A clash of docrines is not a disaster, it is an opportunity'.

COMING HOME

A more extensive, if not precise, definition of what I mean by Enlightenment, modernity and the postmodern will follow in Chapter 1, but I wish to use the rest of this introduction to sketch the significance of psychoanalysis and analytical psychology – which I will refer to jointly as depth psychology – for the beginning of the twenty-first century. I will then describe how Jungian psychology in particular has reponded to the post-modern condition in a creative and critical way by introducing some of the main players and significant moments in this post-Jungian development. I will conclude with a summary of the chapters to follow.

As Ernest Gellner argues in *The Psychoanalytic Movement* (1985), Nietzsche's critique of modernity produced an alternative vision to that of the social idealising of Enlightenment figures such as David Hume and Adam Smith. Confident in its unitary vision of man and nature, the Enlightenment depicted its human subjects much as any other natural phenomena: subjects knew themselves, just as they knew the rest of the world, through the senses. Hume's assertion of Man as a 'bundle of perceptions' brought with it the mechanistic corollary that human behaviour was simply the response to the accumulation of feelings and sensations which constituted the 'stimulus'. This view bred the Stimulus-Response model that matured in later years as the Behaviourist Theory of empirical, experimental psychology. For many years Hume's was the 'official' perspective or *pays légal* of Enlightenment Europe. But the *pays légal* of Enlightenment's vision of humanity was far less convincing by the end of the nineteenth century due to the fact that, as Gellner notes, 'anyone who has the least sense of what it is like to be a human being knows perfectly well . . . that the Hume/Stimulus-Response account of man bears no relation whatsoever to the facts' (Gellner, 1985: 16). Nietzsche's deconstructive critique spoke for the alternative, clamorous voice of the *pays réel* – those whose experience did not correspond to the simplistic official view. But it was not until the birth of Freud's psychoanalysis that the *pays réel* was more fully provided with an idiom and a doctrine. Freud's psychoanalysis became heir to this reactive need of Europeans in the twentieth century in the way that it offered a fresh understanding of human nature – one that accounted for the contradictions, desires and symptoms of human experience – as well as a *method* of individual treatment. Although there are some exceptions, on the whole, psychoanalysis has proved less successful as a critique of culture in general for several reasons: the oligarchic style of leadership, its establishment in private institutions and refusal to join in the debate of the University, its attempts to stay linked with the medical, and scientific, establishment, and, perhaps most importantly, its eventually exclusive focus on the mental pathology of individuals and theorising restricted to treatment aims within a medical model.

Jung began his career immersed deeper in psychiatry than did Freud, but, after breaking from Freud, he also developed his thinking in the direction of cultural concerns as a whole. Such views were always present with Jung as *The Zofingia Lectures* (1896–1898, 1983, CW Supp. Vol. A) of his youth reveal and it may be surmised that psychoanalysis, the cultural re-emergence of the individual subject at the start of the twentieth century, provided Jung with a vehicle by which his interest in the relationship between the individual psyche and the social collective might be understood in a new way.

Now, at the beginning of the twenty-first century – one hundred years since Freud came to the attention of the public at large with *The Interpretation of Dreams* (1900) – psychoanalysis and Jungian analytical psychology are both firmly established in Western culture at the level of popular discourse and in specialist discussions in a variety of fields. Equally they both attract a great deal of ambivalence and criticism, such as recent works by Malcolm (1982), Masson (1990, 1992), Crews et al. (1997), Sulloway (1979, 1992), Grünbaum (1984), Shamdasani (1995), Noll (1996) and Gellner (1985) reveal. The publication of, and interest in, texts critical of Freud and Jung appears to reinforce the importance and significance of their views for many in the industrialised nations of the West. And now countries recently freed from the restriction of Communist ideology also wish to catch up on depth psychology, too, judging by the teaching invitations being sent to Western analysts. Concepts and theories explaining and distinguishing functions of individual psychology have become part of common discourse. Words such as repression, projection, sublimation, splitting, complex, ego, super-ego, narcissism and archetype – coined early in the days of depth psychology – are used as aids to subjective and interpersonal understanding by people of varying levels of educational attainment, as equally as they are used by psychotherapy practitioners themselves. The language and concepts of depth psychology, for all their much debated value as 'scientific truth' or as an 'hermeneutic approach', have stuck around because there is clearly a need for the type of under-standing of ourselves that such ideas provide. The most recent development of establishing the teaching of psychoanalytic studies in the University (in the broad sense of the depth psychologies, post-Freud and post-Jung as well) further reinforces the cultural relevance and application, not to mention the long awaited public debate and testing, of such ideas. In the UK, there is a Chair of Analytical Psychology at the University of Essex and a Chair in Psychoanalysis at the University of London. Psychoanalytic Studies are, or have been, taught at post-graduate and PhD level at the University of Kent, Goldsmiths College and UCL, University of London, Middlesex University, the University of North London, University of Hertfordshire, Leeds Metropolitan University, University of Sheffield and in Dublin (where they also offer the only undergraduate degree in this part of the world). What is new about these institutions is that, unlike previously, the aim is not the clinical training of students but the academic study and debate of depth psychological ideas alongside other disciplines in the University such as cultural studies, history, sociology, anthropology, but with the notable absence of academic psychology which is still tied too unforgivingly to its experimental, statistical methods and models which eschew psychoanalytic discourse – although this may be changing too.

The arrival of psychoanalytic studies in the University has both an aetiology and a teleology, so to speak. In recent years, psychoanalytic theory has influenced and been employed by various other disciplines as a useful tool. Feminist scholars, especially, have turned to psychoanalytic theorising to elucidate the social position of women, and in their analysis of contemporary art, film and other media, and literature. Elsewhere, studies of culture and society use psychoanalytic ideas – not only Freud's but also Kleinian and object relations – in an effort to apply theories derived from clinical work with individuals to society as a whole (e.g. Alford, 1989; Elliott and Frosh, 1995; Elliott, 1998; Richards, 1984, 1989, 1994; Frosh, 1987, 1991; Kovel, 1988; and, earlier, Fromm, 1942, 1968; Marcuse, 1955; Adorno, 1950) and I deal with some of the problems of the psychoanalytic theorising of culture that arise from this in Chapter 2. If the employment of psychoanalytic ideas in other disciplines has opened the door to psycho-analytic studies in the University, the teleological result of this is the generation of a dialogue between these disciplines and their various theoretical bases. At last psychoanalysis is potentially in a position to contribute from an equivalent academic point of view rather than from the 'clinical' – a position of 'privilege' for previous generations of psycho-analytic thinkers, but one which in fact kept psychoanalysis away from serious and useful dialogue with other perspectives and disciplines.

On the other hand, there are many who criticise psychoanalytic theorising from the postmodern point of view – that is, one that sees psychoanalysis as a universalising theory, steeped in the racist and sexist assumptions of patriarchy, oblivious to difference and thus typical of the modernist theorising that the postmodern seeks to challenge. However, I have come across a particular defence of the contemporary value of psychoanalysis from the well-known feminist and psychotherapist, Susie Orbach which sheds light on the concerns of this present book. Orbach admits that psychoanalysis has been employed in both reactionary and progressive ways. She agrees that psychoanalysis constituted part of the modernist project those in the West have used to understand themselves and how, 'The failure of the modernist project to achieve a world of justice and plenty has led some to argue that the understandings offered by modernist disciplines are either inadequate, impossible in principle, or wrong' (Orbach, 1997: 154). Unlike myself, she has no confidence in the alternative perspective of the postmodern which she says mimics what it sees rather than offering understanding, 'it is a shopping basket of possibilities rather than a deeply thought through understanding of ourselves and our predicament (ibid.: 155). As you will notice in the chapters that follow, I do not have a problem with this view and, given the recency of its development, I do not see how the postmodern could be

– leaving aside Orbach's consumerist slur – anything but 'possibilities' at present. Is this not preferable to 'certainties' that are harmful and misleading?

However, my main point in quoting Susie Orbach is not to deny her preference for a continuance of the modernist solution but to show how the very terms in which she values psychoanalysis as a preferred modernist enterprise, in fact constitute *postmodern values and not modernist values at all*. It is astonishing that she falls into the trap of having to defend useful aspects of psychoanalytic thinking as if they are modernist, instead of realising they now constitute aspects of the postmodern challenge to modernity. As she says quite correctly,

> Political discourse is unused to managing complexity, ambiguity and contradiction. While such a way of thinking is not exclusive to psycho-analysis, nevertheless the management, containment and expression of complexity, ambiguity and contradiction is one of the hallmarks of contemporary psychoanalytic thought and practice.
>
> (ibid.: 159)

Exactly! And complexity, ambiguity and contradiction are also 'hallmarks' of the postmodern as the following chapters will elucidate. And is it coincidental that the only person she refers to as envisioning the contribution that depth psychology could make to political culture is Andrew Samuels – who we will also hear more about in the following pages – who is not a 'psychoanalyst' (which, in the UK, indicates a Freudian training) as Orbach calls him, but who is in fact an internationally known Jungian analyst?

What I am hinting at here is how, when it comes to the postmodern applications and contemporary relevance of depth psychology, the Jungian perspective is where the action is. Of all the recent applied psychoanalytic work, some is useful and some of it rather inadequate, but all of it tends to ignore the contribution that Jungian and post-Jungian thinking has made to these themes. This is more true for the UK than the USA where post-Jungian developments and applications have been established and taken seriously over the last thirty years – largely due to the work of the American Jungian analyst James Hillman who trained in Zurich, but also, more recently, due to Andrew Samuels (from a UK Jungian background), Michael Vannoy Adams (USA), Adolf Guggenbuhl-Craig (Zurich) and others. This present book aims to serve as a continuation of this re-reading of Jung and *a repositioning of Jungian thinking within current debates around culture, epistemology, politics, representation, and the life of society*. Such 'current debates', and experiences, of human life in the contemporary West have become collectivised under the term 'postmodern' – the postmodern condition, the postmodern problematic, postmodern debate, postmodern attitude, being some of its extensions. This book seeks to articulate Jung and the post-Jungians with these debates.

POST-JUNGIANS AND THE POSTMODERN: THE STORY SO FAR

The relationship between Jung and the postmodern has an important history and genealogy that goes back as far as the late 1960s when a number of post-Jungian analysts and theorists began tackling aspects of Jungian thinking from what we would now regard as a postmodern position. For some, their interest stems from ongoing debates in sociology, anthropology and the analysis of contemporary culture. Others are approaching Jung and the postmodern from the point of view of post-structuralist linguistics and theories of representation, while yet others are interested in aspects of Jung that resonate with the new physics and biology, and the study of the brain and the phenomenon of consciousness. Some brave souls traverse a number of these disciplines! Many of these views will be presented in detail throughout this book but I think it is important to make space here for a name check and a genealogy of what is clearly an important project, maybe even a movement, that has gained considerable momentum during the last decade. I propose to tackle this initially by mapping the occasions – conferences, publications, meetings and the contributors – that have been significant for this movement. In this way I hope to show how the post-Jungian postmodern debate is a local force now revealing its potential for powerful influence in academic and clinical spheres on both sides of the Atlantic and elsewhere.

Throughout this survey, and, indeed, throughout this book, certain questions will arise which, although impossible to answer fully, should be borne in mind. One will be: Is Jung's psychology itself postmodern? Or, is it more that part of it is postmodern while other parts are clearly not? Another will be: Is it perhaps not more the case that Jungians are now reading Jung in a postmodern frame? But given that such 'reading' is an authentic postmodern position, does this not make the project all the more legitimate? As Michael Vannoy Adams has put it: 'Is Jung postmodern, or are we "postmodern" about him?' (Adams, 1998, personal communication). Why is Jung regarded by so many as a 'premodern', a 'mystic' and anachronistic? When it comes to the absence of references to, or the denigration of, Jung in texts concerning the postmodern, are these writers prejudiced against Jung or are they simply unaware of what he wrote? Why is Jung regarded as conservative and reactionary by some when postmodern Jungians are clearly able to make the case for his radical critique of modernity and for Jungian psychology as a critical method helpful for both individuals and the social collective alike?

The 1960s were a watershed in the century for the revaluation of values we now call the postmodern. Although Jung's ideas were influential in this, in the late 1960s many of the new generation Jungian therapists and trainees – that is, those in their late twenties or early thirties – were starting to question some of the Jungian concepts and attitudes that had tended towards a rigidity sometimes amounting to dogma after fifty years of Jungian psychology. Jung had died in 1961 and his psychology and the training of therapists was well established in America, in London and especially in Zurich where Jung had lived. Many young people were attracted to Zurich from the USA where radical protest movements – such as those concerning civil rights, women's liberation and the Vietnam war – had contributed to mobilising a generation. In Europe, young people sought to address prevailing social and individual values in a comparable way – the events in Paris in 1968 being the most obvious example. It is no coincidence that such radical movements sought a way of expressing the voice of individuals through psychological means alongside the social-political voices more typical of movements earlier in the century. This seeking of the personal and psychological side-by-side with the collective and socio-political may be regarded as what was so original and radical about this period. In France the psychological voice was supplied by a fresh reading of Freudian psychoanalysis led initially by the writings of Marcuse, the Marxist Louis Althusser and the psychoanalyst Jacques Lacan. In the UK there was R. D. Laing and the Radical Psychiatry movement. Jung's psychology became linked for many with the growing interest in Eastern philosophy and religion which had begun in earnest after the Second World War on the West coast of America. Jung had been involved in the earlier, more esoteric European history of this which had centred on German writers and artists such as Herman Hesse, Paul Klee and Richard Wilhelm. The young Americans who arrived in Zurich in the 1960s brought with them radical expectations from both fields of influence and, naturally, this energy generated fresh discussions and arguments about Jung's ideas. Eventually, owing much to the inspiration, articulateness and energy of one of them – James Hillman – this energy manifested itself as Archetypal Psychology – a new emphasis in Jungian thinking that can now be regarded as the initial stirring of a postmodern Jungian psychology.

Patricia Berry was also part of the group in Zurich at the time and in a controversial talk 'Reminiscences and Reflections' given in 1992, she has described the events that led to the beginning of archetypal psychology around the figure of James Hillman. In fact, Berry places the inception of archetypal psychology in a London pub in 1968 where Hillman made the statement that 'The problem in psychology and in Western thought in general is *Monotheism*' – the remedy for which lay in the restoration of a more pagan, polytheistic world. This was the call for a pluralistic society uttered in psychological language of the individual – the language of Jung's psychology being read by a new generation keen on transforming both society and individuals.

The international journal *Spring*, which has long been the mouthpiece for archetypal psychology, began its life in Patricia Berry's bedroom and Guggenbühl-Craig's bathroom, Berry tells us. She describes how the *Spring* seminars began at this time as Dionysian events quite in contrast to more Apollonian conversations about Jung's psychology happening elsewhere. Among those present with James Hillman, Patricia Berry lists: Rafael Lopez-Pedraza, John Johnston, Paul Kugler, Bob Hinshaw, Bill Walker, Nathan Schwartz-Salant, Sid Handel, Jeffrey Satinover and herself. Although intellectual, these passionate and inspired conversations focused on Jungian and esoteric texts where the aim, above all, was a sharpening of intuition and of the imagination. Berry characterises the creation of archetypal psychology as a *via negativa* and she provides a list of negatives which expressed this. Archetypal psychology was *not* . . .

> . . . *monotheistic*
> . . . *ego personal*
> . . . *transcendent*
> . . . *structural*
> . . . *linear*
> . . . *Christian*
> . . . *normal*
> . . . *mediocre*
> . . . *about getting better*
> . . . *balanced*

We might compare this series of 'nots' with the qualities and concepts of the postmodern listed in Chapter 1. In addition, a more complex comparison may be made with Jung's and Freud's concepts I list in Chapter 2. In this we can already see that some of Jung's concepts do not qualify as postmodern, thus making a clearer case for the argument that, in part, postmodern Jungian psychology is a post-Jungian development of Jung's thinking. As Andrew Samuels wrote when he coined the term post-Jungian, 'I have used the term *post-Jungian* in preference to *Jungian* to indicate both connectedness to Jung and distance from him' (Samuels, 1985: 19);

archetypal psychology was a post-Jungian departure in the same way. Equally, *the term postmodern indicates a connectedness to the modern and a distance from it.*

Chronologically, a second major event to further the postmodern post-Jungian project was the conference on 'C. G. Jung and the Humanities' co-convened by the C. G. Jung foundation of New York, and held at Hofstra University in 1986. At this, James Hillman, Paul Kugler, Edward S. Casey and David L. Miller got together to discuss Jung and the postmodern in a conversation now published along with many other essays in *C. G. Jung and the Humanities: Towards a Hermeneutics of Culture* (Barnaby and D'Acierno, 1990). Many of the ideas aired at this conference are represented throughout the present book (especially in Chapters 4, 5 and 8), so there is no need for detail here except to say this was the first conference to directly address aspects of Jung that resonate with postmodern concerns, and the first to bring together those who had been writing about these topics for the previous ten years. As the fly-leaf of the book states:

> The essays reveal dimensions of (Jung's) work that extend far beyond psychoanalytical theory and that show his hermeneutics to be a much more subtle and sophisticated methodology than previously allowed by his critics. *The methodology appears, in fact, to have anticipated significant aspects of contemporary critical principles and practice.*
>
> (ibid., italics added)

Patricia Berry's talk referred to earlier was given on a further occasion that marks the expansion in postmodern Jungian psychology: the 'Festival of Archetypal Psychology in Honour of James Hillman' held at Notre Dame University in 1992. This festival included several papers, performances and lots of discussion of the postmodern including a session 'Brains unleashed: practices in lifting mental repression' which featured Patricia Berry, Ed Casey, W. Geigerich, Paul Kugler, David Miller, Sonu Shamdasani and Michael Vannoy Adams.

Finally, there have been a series of bi-annual 'Jung Studies Days' held at the University of Kent, England, by Dr Martin Stanton, Dr David Reason and Dr Leon Schlamm between 1991 and 1996. In these, scholars and analysts with an interest in Jung – including Michael Vannoy Adams, Tessa Adams, Marie Angelo, Nick Battye, Alan Bleakly, Petruska Clarkson, Andrea Duncan, myself, David Maclagen, Kate Newton, Renos Papadopoulos, Andrew Samuels, Joy Schaverien, Peter Tatham, Molly Tuby and others – have all contributed papers and discussions now published as the Proceedings of the Jung Studies Days held by the Centre for Psychoanalytic Studies in the Faculty of Humanities, University of Kent at Canterbury. The value of these occasions was the way in which Jung and post-Jungian discourse was discussed on the most contemporary level. The themes – which included 'Masculinity', 'The Child', 'Imagination', 'Alchemy' and 'The Sublime' – brought in aspects of the postmodern as the debates proceeded and introduced a foothold for this perspective into the Jungian field in the UK. Inspired by one such occasion, Dr Petruska Clarkson recently edited a collection of papers by US and UK authors now published as *On The Sublime in Psychoanalysis, Archetypal Psychology and Psychotherapy* (Clarkson, 1997). Andrew Samuels and Renos Papadopoulos are now joint Professors of Analytical Psychology at the University of Essex which is becoming a new home for Jungian MA and doctoral studies and continuing debates in a similar spirit. Yet other degrees such as the MA in Psychoanalytic Studies and MA in Psychotherapy and Society at Goldsmiths College, University of London also have a critical post-Jungian postmodern element.

As far as all these names and details go, this is by no means an exhaustive list; the same applies to the texts that I cite throughout this book and I apologise in advance for those names and works that have been left out. Such is the growth in this field, that even as this book goes to press there will be further publications appearing that could easily have been included had they been available beforehand.

(HOME ON) THE POSTMODERN RANGE

By now, if not before, the question must arise: Surely, neither does Jungian thought encompass *all* the varieties of postmodern debate, nor do the post-Jungians have something to say about every niche of the postmodern, do they? The answer to both parts is: No, of course not, but they *do* have a great deal in common. It is these areas, themes and perspectives they have in common that have been hitherto uninvestigated within psychoanalytic and cultural studies and it is these that comprise the themes of this book. The first three chapters will go into a selection of postmodern thinking in detail, all the while pointing out the corresponding emphases and views within Jungian thinking, as well as beginning to tackle the disjunctions that appear. The remaining nine chapters pick up on other themes that, in themselves, are strictly more adjacent to both Jungian and postmodern thought, but, from my point of view, offer further themes which, from a psychological perspective, are able to deepen the debate further beyond initial expectations of a book on Jung and the postmodern.

I intend to summarise these chapters in this introduction, but before I do so I am aware of an Authorial need to offer you the Reader some form of orientation. In doing so it is not my intention to limit your own expectations of such a book, but rather to be frank about the limitations arising from my own personality, experience, background and taste. In other words, I do not intend to say everything there is to be said about postmodern thinking or about Jung for that matter. There will be omissions that you will know far more about than me. There will also be inclusions which, I hope, will surprise you, interest you and justify your time and money. Reading any book – especially one which is doing something new as I intend this one to do – is an exploration and therefore needs a map and a way of orientating oneself to it so that, on the one hand, not too much is missed along the way, and, on the other hand of course, so you do not get lost. If I lost Readers along the way I would have to send out a search party in the form of another book, and I really do not have time for that. Here's the map.

I have chosen to restrict myself to the word postmodern throughout the book rather than exchange this term with its parallel forms such as post-modernist, Post-Modernism, postmodernity or post-modern. This is because I wish the word to cover several aspects of contemporary life and the psychology that goes with it: both cultural movements and social conditions, the new economy and space-time of globalisation, but also the deconstructive aspect and critique that accompanies these. In this I differ from Charles Jencks who divides his usage of terms into post-modern for the cultural movement, the elided postmodern for the Deconstructive movement, and Post-Modernists – which derives from post-modernisation, that is, the global, electronic civilisation we inhabit (Jencks, 1996). Similarly, I have chosen to use the single word modernity to refer to a range of individual, cultural, social and psychological values that have persisted since the Enlightenment but which now are being revised in the way this book describes.

My use of upper case for some words, and quotation marks or italics for others requires a mention. The use of upper case to start a word, or the use of lower case and quotation marks has become a signifier of the contrast between positivistic assertions, on the one hand, and critical, deconstructive discourse on the other. The feminist, black writer bell hooks always publishes her name in lower case, I have always thought, to draw our attention to her positioning as other to dominant, white, patriarchal discourse. Thus, one side may assert Truth or Reality, while the other indicates 'truth' or 'reality'. The shift denotes an attitude both to the concept being referred to – that is, it is under scrutiny as a concept and not to be taken for granted as a fixed term – and also to the word and language itself. The quote marks are there to point up the attitude that *this is a word and there are other words which might replace it; the transparency of language is being brought to our attention.* A further example comes from Umberto Eco who offers a succinct illustration of this aspect of the postmodern – reference to the outworn forms of 'the already said' – in his book *Reflections On The Name of the Rose* (1985). For Eco, the postmodern attitude is that of a man,

> who loves a very cultivated woman and knows he cannot say to her 'I love you madly', because he knows that she knows (and that she knows that he knows) that these words have already been written by Barbara Cartland. Still there is a solution. He can say, 'As Barbara Cartland would put it, I love you madly' . . . having said clearly that it is no longer possible to speak innocently, he will nevertheless have said . . . that he loves her; but he loves her in an age of lost innocence. If the woman goes along with this . . . both will have accepted the challenge of the past, of the already said which cannot be eliminated; both will consciously and with pleasure play the game of irony . . . But both will have succeeded, once again, in speaking of love.
>
> (Eco, 1985: 67–68)

My own use of italics is intended, I confess, to promote my old-fashioned Authorial intentions. When the italics appear I am seeking to make a particular point that I wish you to attend to. If I was speaking these I would *slow down to add my emphasis and look straight into the camera.* Granted, it is a bit of a positivistic trick, but, on the other hand, it is also a way marker on this journey to help with the orientation.

As for the particular characteristics of the postmodern which are the focus of this book, the aspect most frequently encountered is: a critical questioning of the values, 'truths' and belief systems held by Modernity since the Enlightenment; mainly a critique of the promotion of a certain style of Rationality above any other version of understanding ourselves and the world. This critique brings with it a pluralistic attitude to 'truths' that sees these as various perspectives of equivalent validity, and consequently forms an attitude which is not supportive of the heirarchising of views and knowledge but welcomes the celebration of their difference and multiplicity. The postmodern aspects featured in this text, therefore, are those that become so defined due to their *context: that is, psychological and cultural phenomena that are discontinuous with Enlightenment assertions and values and the epistemological values of modernity.* This means that we will come across concepts and perspectives that have been supported in other times but which have tended to be neglected or denied through five hundred years of Enlightenment. One such concept might be the 'ineffable', that which is beyond representation or language. In Chapter 8 this is discussed in terms of Bion's 'O' and Lacan's Real. This does not mean that I am asserting that either Bion or Lacan are postmodern in their thinking in general – many have pointed out how Lacan and Derrida, for example, retain Enlightenment roots – but that there are elements in contemporary theory that are disjunctive with modernity and, when viewed in parallel with Jungian psychology, these elements constitute part of a postmodern critique of knowledge and culture. The postmodern attack on essentialist positions, and Lyotard's assertion of the disappearance of master-narratives, are recognised and discussed as postmodern concerns that are often in tension with some of the claims, and the style, of Jungian psychology. (I discuss the tension between the views that claim the postmodern to be a continuation of modernity, on the one hand, or a break from modernity, on the other, in Chapters 1 and 2.)

Through examining the postmodern side-by-side with Jungian thinking, other elements emerge such as the use of *reference* to past forms of expression and knowledge and *double-coding* or contradiction which constitute further characteristics of the postmodern. When it comes to the psyche we also cannot avoid the 'already said'; we cannot avoid both the past and our difference from it and Jung's psychology, with its personal and collective unconscious and awareness of cultural change and limitations throughout human history, I believe, observes the same spirit of this postmodern attitude. I have a personal example of the relationship between present and past that pushes conceptualising even further by the inclusion of modern technology and its ambivalent relationship with previous forms. The singer Bjork's second album was called *Post* which, of course, led me to look out for aspects of its presentation and content I might find ironic and deconstructive. At the end of one song on the CD, a repetitive click occurs as when a record player has reached the end of an analogue, vinyl record and the needle is stuck as the disc continues going round. I thought this a neat trick which might fool some the first time but, in my postmodern sophistication, or so I thought, I caught on immediately with a wry smile. I was very disappointed however, when, further into the CD, I noticed an annoying scratchy sound appearing in the middle of the song called 'Possibly Maybe' which, despite careful cleaning of the CD disc, would not go away. I took the CD back to the shop where the assistant played it and informed me it was a sample (a form of digital sound recording) being used on the production and was integral to the song. The producers and Bjork had sampled a second or two of deep bass thud for the drum track from a scratchy old vinyl record – it could have been James Brown or Led Zeppelin – and synchronised it in time with the rest of the drum track recorded in the present, resulting in not only a deep thud desired for the track, but also the extraneous surface noise of the original analogue recording. In this way, what starts as a deliberate joke with the technology – the inclusion of a sound as if it is a vinyl record that is on the turntable – ends up with an unavoidable inclusion of the limitations of the old technology at the same time it is being integrated in a fresh way into the new. Moreover, the imperfect sound is retained self-consciously (it could easily have been 'cleaned up' using the same digital technology) rather than attempting to disguise its source. This is the irony of the postmodern both at its most self-conscious and witty and in its inevitably pluralistic combination of the old and the new. My mistaken reaction to the second instance was simply the result of me thinking I was too clever by half. As it has been said elsewhere – the postmodern always knocks twice.

In parts of the book, I also pay attention to aspects of the postmodern that are not so much to do with knowledge – 'what can be said' and 'how' – but more to do with the products and phenomena of contemporary culture as it surrounds us. Postmodern culture is accused of being superficial, insubstantial and transient; it relies on surface images and interchangeable meanings in a practice which is regarded, from the point of view of modernity, as destructive and nihilistic. Our present condition is arising out of the political and economic conditions of life that have grown more and more sophisticated over the last five hundred years, and so it is a matter of debate whether contemporary cultural conditions mark a 'wrong turning' in the otherwise 'progressive' onward march of the Enlightenment project, or whether they mark the 'end' of modernity and the start of something 'new' which consciousness and cultural expectations have to recognise and take on board. Perhaps such postmodern conditions are only problematic to those who cling to the values of modernity without recognising that their 'modernity' is over and done with. The 'modernity' still longed for has now spawned this postmodern present, and it is from this position – which is truly the result of a paradigm shift – that culture and the individual now must be 'judged'. For modernity, such judgement ends in a guilty verdict and a condemnation, while for others more accepting of this revaluing of values, postmodern qualities have much to add, and indeed *to restore*, to human life. Given that Jung and psychoanalysis has its roots in modernity while at the same time Jungian and post-Jungian thought also critiques the values and shortcomings of modernity, such contradictions of the present time – and the sense of these being 'beyond good and evil', as Nietzsche affirmed – will appear frequently throughout this book.

Aspects of the postmodern which I do not attend to in detail are its manifestation in avant garde and general artistic practices (see, for example, Foster, 1985) or the more detailed philosophical discussion of the postmodern such as that undertaken by Jane Flax (1990: 187–221). There is excellent work available on these areas which I have not felt the need to summarise here. This book is not an introduction to postmodern ideas nor is it an introduction to Jung's and post-Jungian ideas. What it does introduce is a comparative view of *some* ideas from both these fields. I have gathered my material, rather like Lévi-Strauss once said of his own work, in the manner of a *bricoleur*. If there is an Author's voice to be found in this book it lies mainly within the selection and combination of the voices I have chosen to illuminate and expand my overall theme. I have sought to frame its contents around various sub-themes that seem important to both the Jungian psychological and the postmodern cultural approaches to human life as it is lived in the West. The metaphor is one in which we are gazing through *a Jungian transparency or filter being held up against the postmodern while, from the other side, we are also able to look through a transparency or filter of the postmodern to gaze at Jung. From either direction, I suggest, there will be a new and surprising vision.*

READING THIS BOOK

Although the following chapters have been written so that ideas build up and previous chapters prepare the way for subsequent ones, it is not necessary to read them in sequential order at all. In fact, if you are new to Jung or the postmodern I suggest that this path is avoided. Chapter 1 is important for a general orientation to the book, but from here the reader may leap to Chapter 4 and then Chapter 8 where similar themes are followed up in two particular directions. From there, the reader can go forward and backwards through the other chapters gradually amplifying various themes or following up specialist areas – the significance of Nietzsche (Chapters 6 and 7) or the feminine (Chapters 5 and 7), for example – as they need. Moreover, the chapter titles and sub-headings give a good indication of what to expect and these may also be used to link up a thematic – as opposed to a sequential – reading of the book according to the reader's needs.

Chapter 1 introduces my position on the postmodern in more detail. Here I follow up the themes of meaning, knowledge and power in a discussion of modernity and the postmodern from twin points of view. These involve a comparison of modernity-postmodern from an historical, time-oriented perspective on the one hand, and an evaluative, good/bad perspective on the other, which involves the work of Daniel Bell on *The Cultural Contradictions of Capitalism* (1979) and commentary from Peter Homans's book, *Jung in Context. Modernity and the Making of a Psychology* (1979). I discuss how the shift from modernity to the postmodern involves changes in, and a challenge to, the psychological *attitude* of contemporary individuals – a theme common in Jung's work. The ideas of Fredric Jameson, Baudrillard and Barthes on globalisation, the image, simulacra and hyperspace are discussed towards the end of the chapter before it zooms into a final close-up on the postmodern significance of the photographic image.

Chapter 2 begins with a comparison of the views of Habermas and Foucault, the former asserting his reasons for the 'incomplete project of modernity' with its possibility for Truth, while the latter counters that each age brings with it its own 'truth' which is based on the power interests of the dominant group who proclaim it. In other words, human Knowledge is not a neutral entity, it is a powerful commodity. The chapter continues with a discussion of the use of psychoanalytic Knowledge as employed by Freudian thinkers, especially in the context of social and cultural analysis. In his interesting book *Identity Crisis. Modernity, Psychoanalysis and the Self* (1991), Stephen Frosh maintains that Freudian psychoanalysis, and its Kleinian spin-off, have much to offer the crisis of modernity, but in doing so, I believe, falls into a conformity similar to Habermas. I argue for the advantage that Jungian concepts offer to a depth pychological analysis of culture, and use Andrew Samuels' arguments against the reactionary tone of the 'object relations consensus' which he sets out in *The Political Psyche* (1993).

Chapter 3 expands on themes of Fredric Jameson encountered earlier – the 'death' of the subject and the 'loss of affect' – as they relate to Jung's analysis of the fate of the individual subject in mass culture. Jameson's ideas on the need for individual reorientation under postmodern conditions are compared with the Jungian idea of individuation and the phenomena of mass-man; these are discussed against the background of the mass reaction to the death of Princess Diana and the individual differences this reveals. I then bring these ideas, and those of Nietzsche and Deleuze, together with my own thoughts about the meaning of individuation in postmodern times, and what hyper-reflexivity may mean for *consciousness* itself. I discuss Nietzsche's perspective on consciousness and the will to power both as a reflection of what postmodern consciousness *implies*, and what our conscious psychological attitude *requires* – something I call *consciousness consciousing itself.*

Chapter 4 brings a lighter touch to the comparison of postmodern and Jungian themes with a focus on the contribution offered by architectural criticism, especially the work of Charles Jencks, to the postmodern 'debate'. Themes revealed in postmodern architecture – such as the use of reference, double-coding, and deconstruction in the work of Frank Gehry – are compared to similar themes expressed in the psychology of C. G. Jung. The chapter considers the way metaphors of buildings and structure are used in depth psychology, and how psychoanalytic metaphors are employed in the analysis of postmodern architecture. The way that the use of past forms is regarded as 'essentialist' or, alternatively, as 'reference' is discussed using the 'case examples' of Frank Gehry's house and Jung's own Tower at Bollingen to survey how these concepts appear in both analytical psychology and architecture. In doing so, the theme of periodising modernity and the postmodern, and the theme of individuation are revisited from another direction.

The essentialism of modernity is hardly more evident than in the way that women have been treated and written about, or ignored, by Enlightenment. A variety of feminist challenges to the grand-narratives of patriarchy are discussed in Chapter 5, where Jung's own essentialist views come in for criticism. The efforts of post-Jungians such as Zabriskie, Wehr and Samuels, to re-theorise the 'feminine' in Jungian psychology are discussed within the context of postmodern feminist theory – especially that of Julia Kristeva. Her concept of the *abject* is compared with the function of Jung's alchemical *lapis*, and the shadow, all of which involve what is marginal and excluded. The concept of the goddess and the use of myth is critically discussed and the chapter ends with an example of clinical work with a client whose struggles with her identity as a woman were expressed in aspects of the Ariadne myth.

Chapter 6 is a vehicle for several Jungian themes and concepts which have been influenced by Friedrich Nietzsche's critique of modernity and which are also central to postmodern debate. Those I have selected for such a linkage here are: the deposing of the subject in Nietzsche and the ego-self relationship in Jung; Nietzsche's perspective theory of affect and Jung's complex theory and pluralism; the use of the past as a genealogy along the lines of Foucault and Nietzsche which is compared with Jung's inclusion of pre-modern beliefs – such as alchemy and Gnosticism – in his psychological and cultural discourse. Finally, an important comparison is made between Nietzsche's *Ubermensch* or Overman and the Last Man, with Jung's emphasis on the self-overcoming of individuation and the 'mass man', respectively.

Chapter 7 is mainly about the body which has been somewhat neglected in depth psychology. Here I refer to the Nietzschean themes of the Will to Power, the fragmented body and consciousness in the context of the symptoms of hysteria which were seminal to the beginnings of psychoanalysis. These themes are analysed along postmodern lines with, on the one hand, the body as an expression of the psychic 'inside' while, on the other hand, using the work of Elizabeth Grösz, the body is theorised as also inscribed on its surface from the *outside*. The chapter continues with a discussion of Jung's revision of Freud's theory of trauma and hysteria, a perspective which criticises one-way, linear theories of 'past causes' and offers us Jung's alternative focus on the situation in the present and what the 'symptoms' are trying to achieve for the 'hysteric'.

Chapter 8 is as central to the book as its themes of representation and symbolising are to both post-Jungian and postmodern thinking. After introducing the concepts of the semiotic, structuralism, post-structuralism and deconstruction, the chapter brings together several post-Jungians and discusses what they have to say about the semiotic, and the symbolic, Jung's '#1' and '#2' personalities, and the known and unknown – leading to a discussion about the limits of what can be said or can be represented. A comparison is made between the 'unknown' in ancient Taoist texts, with which Jung was familiar, and other expressions of the ineffable as they are to be found in modern psychoanalysis.

Chapter 9 suggests how 'affect' as a discrete object is the result of modernity's tendency to divide the world into discrete parts then to mediate these parts according to its power and knowledge interests. 'Affect' as an object of psychology is briefly discussed through theories of emotion in Darwin, James and Lange with the eventual focus on psychoanalysis and especially analytical psychology as psychologies of a specifically *modern* consciousness or psyche, and its modern pathologies. Chapter 10 extends this critical theme to consider the relationship, and the bifurcation, of matter and mind within the context of the critique of classical science. Jung's relationship with the theorists and discoveries of sub-atomic science reveals his position with regard to the postmodern critique of classical science and the 'myth of objectivity'. A need to radically revise our ideas of mind, matter and the apparent separateness between individuals is introduced with Jung's theory of synchronicity where I offer several personal examples. The implications of these ideas for psychotherapy practice – especially counter-transference and projective imagination – are discussed in terms of the *mundus imaginalis*, and Nathan Field's and Steven Rosen's ideas about the interactive field in psychotherapy.

Critical approaches to the dominant rationality of modernity have often focused on the concept of *psychosis* as we find in the work of R. D. Laing (1959, 1967) and it is in this spirit, that I ask in Chapter 11, 'What is the Other to rationality, and who says so?' The idea of *multiple rationalities* emerges through the work of the critical anthropologist Stanley Tambiah and his approach to the question of rationality, relativity and pluralism. The chapter continues with James Hillman's archetypal perspective on the *necessity* of abnormal psychology, and finishes with an anthropological example of psychotic breakdown in a non-Western young woman. Her community's response to her breakdown offers us in the West an opportunity to revalue what we mean by 'deviance', on the one hand, and the 'rationality' of cultural dominants on the other. Finally, Chapter 12 concludes the book with a briefly sketched comparison of Jung's psychology and the postmodern paintings of David Salle. In this

I summarise not so much the content of what I have been saying, but more the spirit in which I would like it to be understood. Understanding the relationship between Jung and the postmodern can offer us new perspectives where, as in dreams, 'That which was meaningless becomes meaningful; that which was full of meaning becomes free of sense' (Mulder, 1999: 27) – themes we will encounter many times over as we explore Jung and the postmodern: the interpretation of realities.

1 Why postmodern?

> History is a strong myth, perhaps, along with the unconscious, the last great myth.
>
> (Baudrillard, 1994: 47)

MODERN AND POSTMODERN

Not so long ago, the well known anthropologist Clifford Geertz returned from Japan with a fascinating report (Shweder, 1996); as a response to their customers' interest in the European festival of Christmas, a Japanese store had come up with something that seemed to incorporate all the important elements. They exhibited a display of Santa Claus nailed to a cross. With its pluralistic combination of plundered symbolism, consumerism and globalised economics, and its surreal juxtaposition of the sacred and secular, the ancient and the recent, Santa Claus on the Cross is a sublimely postmodern image.

What does this word 'postmodern' mean? It seems to free-float across texts as a qualifier or an adjective for most things you care to name – postmodern culture, postmodern thought, postmodern science, postmodern medicine, postmodern art, -cinema, -novels, -music, -economics, -politics, -psychology and so on. While having been embedded and discussed for the last two decades within academic discourses around philosophy and the theory of culture and aesthetics, the term postmodern (let us drop the scare quotes from now on) pops up in various media in reference to anything vaguely wry, ironic, askance – or merely topical and of the moment. I believe there is far more precision in the concept of postmodern than this ubiquity of usage, and misuse, seems to suggest. But, at the same time, this great plurality of applications and the slippery refusal of the concept to be precise remains, for reasons I will discuss, an important aspect of the postmodern condition itself.

First, what is useful about this initial problem of the meaning of *the word postmodern* is that it serves as a signpost to the postmodern problematic. By being forced to wonder about a 'concept', its 'word' and its 'meaning' – what it refers to in 'reality' – we are already living within what the postmodern draws our attention to. That is: the relationship between the so-called 'real world', our representation of this in concepts (the *signified*) and the words and images (*signifiers*) in which these are registered to ourselves and transmitted between us. All in all, these are the assumptions we live with in contemporary Western society; they constitute the consciousness – some would call it the 'common sense' – of urbanised humanity. It is our assumptions about scientific 'truth' as well as social truths and values that postmodern thinking now critically addresses. The postmodern labels a point of view that refuses to take such 'truths' for granted any more. As the post-Jungian Paul Kugler points out, all systems of knowledge, and especially depth psychology, rely on an 'originary, explanatory principle' which is intended to give meaning to phenomena – such as clinical material or dreams – but to do so it has to stand outside, or beyond, 'meaning' itself. In Jung's psychology the 'self' stands as the 'origin' but, as Kugler points out, this begs the question of not only the origin of this posited origin but, ultimately, how it is language itself that has 'trapped us inside the logic of the "origins" metaphor' (Kugler, 1990a: 314). This issue will be explored in Chapter 7 where we will come across an approach to the postmodern 'meaning of meaning' in which post-Jungian psychologists contribute to a deconstruction of our systems of representation. It is a central postmodern concern that the relationship between things, ideas and words may no longer be taken for granted in an uncritical fashion. Such a relationship – the baseline of both scientific and social 'truth' – is not a 'given', and yet, to put it another way, it *has* been given to us: by which I mean that the way we consciously experience the world has been imposed upon us by several hundred years of a certain style of rationality. For Jung, this style of rationality – initiated in the Enlightenment – was distinguished by 'masculine' values: the rationality of patriarchal society. Jungian analyst Beverley Zabriskie sums them up as, 'authority and dominance within hierarchical structures, penetrating and focused assertion and aggression, superiority of linear cognition and detached rationality' (Zabriskie, 1990: 272).

My second point is this: postmodern is a compound word which appears to refer to the dimension of *time*. A simple analogy is that other well-known pm – the post meridian or after noon. There is a seductive subtlety in this comparison that appeals to me: the double reference to pm draws our attention to an 'after the high point' of something. This adds a qualitative tone to postmodern suggesting not only 'after the modern'

(I'll say what I think the modern is in a moment) but also 'after we've scaled the heights and are now going down the other side'. I could push this further to make the chain: postmodern . . . postmeridian . . . Greenwich Meridian . . . Millennium . . . postmillennium and all the additional sense of the *fin de siècle*. This shapes the postmodern as both history and anti-history: history in the sense of it being 'about' contemporary human life as distinct from what went 'before', and anti-history in also suggesting that the postmodern did 'happen before' (at the end of the nineteenth century, for example) and probably not once but many times before. This contradictory sense of postmodern as a word referring to history and time, on the one hand, and to the revaluing of values at *any* moment in history, on the other, does not necessarily have to be resolved. By staying with the tension between these two views, a further aspect of the postmodern comes to light.

The postmodern is not solely or necessarily a temporal or historical concept at all, although it can be used this way and it very often is. However, nearly every time, I think you will find, this strictly chronological application of the concept tends to end up in a wrangle about what came first and the piling on of qualifiers to create 'late modern', 'pre-postmodern', 'early postmodern', 'pre-modern' and so on. It creates more hierarchies and essentialisms just when it is trying to break these down. It strikes me that this tendency arises from the over-rigid imposition of an historical grid on human life as if there were not many other ways of thinking about what is going on in contemporary society to which the postmodern also refers. In fact, the over-rigidity found in this understanding of postmodern is another aspect that the postmodern seeks to draw our attention to – not by deleting any such singular view (in this case the 'historical') but by *favouring a plurality of positions and understandings* so that claims for essentiality are questioned and singularities keep their place beside other singularities in a pluralistic fashion. The tension between essentials and pluralities in Jung's thinking will emerge as a repeating feature of this book.

Sticking with recent history for a moment, however, Jung died in 1961 at the beginning of a decade which witnessed the most radical challenge to the values of the two previous generations. The 1960s were a time of rapid change when social and cultural values came under particular scrutiny that had originally had its roots far earlier in the century. (I am thinking here of the challenge to class divisions brought about by the the experience of mass mobilisation for the First World War, and of the success of women's voting rights in the 1920s.) As 1960's icon Marianne Faithfull writes of her youth in the period,

The distinctions were getting blurred between upper and lower classes, male and female, recreation and work, politics and life. The uniforms were disappearing, along with the idea that you were meant to look like who you were – doctors were meant to look like doctors, call girls were meant to look like call girls. In the sixties all these things blurred.

(Faithfull, 1995: 22)

Although Jung might not have approved of many of the changes, his psychology was highly influential in the challenge to prevailing values. It is true that Jung's writing was misinterpreted by elements of the sixties counter-culture (see pp. 25–26 of Marianne Faithfull's biography, 1995, for a grotesque example) but it is also true that Jung's thinking, as much as Nietzsche's from the end of the nineteenth century, grew in popularity and in readership as a result of the new generation's need to find a critical perspective and a voice. Jung's face was chosen as one of many significant influences used for Peter Blake's iconic record cover photograph for the Beatles' 'Sergeant Pepper' album in 1967. Marie-Louise von Franz predicted in 1972, 'Today, interest in Jung is growing year by year, especially among the younger generation. Accordingly, the growth of his influence is still in its early stages; thirty years from now we will, in all probability, be able to discuss his work in very different terms than we do today' (von-Franz, 1972: 3). By the late 1970s, the critical perspective and voice of a new generation was becoming legitimised within intellectual circles through the conceptual terminology of the postmodern. Somewhere along the way C. G. Jung's contribution to the postmodern critique of contemporary life has been neglected, an omission that many today wish to see reversed.

If the postmodern is not necessarily a quasi-historical concept what else might it be? When we think about ourselves – individual subjects and social collectives – in terms of chronological history, what we seem to be grasping for is contrast and change, differences and disjunctions. From this perspective, time as history appears more a 'formal' knowledge; that is, historical knowledge viewed not as the content of what we are seeking but more as *a way of structuring, or of 'forming', our 'knowledge'* – and then only one way among many. Similarly, human urges towards making meaning may be viewed as *information* – not as a passive translation of something else (i.e. the phenomena under analysis or interpretation) but rather as in-*form*ation. This emphasis draws our attention to the very process of forming and constructing 'meaning': which is, ultimately, the process of validating or legitimising what is to be regarded as meaningful or rational or legitimate or 'real' – in a similar way that historical knowledge 'forms' reality. This ushers in an important sub-theme of postmodern critical thinking – that of the relationship between power and knowledge. In other words, the realm of Reason and Non-Reason, Truth and Untruth and, above all, *who says it is so*? Questioning these seemingly transparent categories which, especially in the discourse of scientific rationality, present themselves as 'facts of nature', often reveals their profound 'unnaturalness'. In social science and psychology, the categories of 'madness' and 'sanity' can come under a similar scrutiny and this theme will be explored in a later chapter. In doing so, we will come across contexts where the line which divides such categories will be found to be more fuzzy than modernist thinking allows – as, indeed, Jung himself concluded through his extensive psychiatric work.

The structuring power of meaning, and the faith in a particular style of human reason – instrumental scientific rationality – has provided the energy for the West's apparent scientific and social progress from the dawn of the Enlightenment until very recently. Scientific research, and classical psychoanalysis, share the paradigm of the detective narrative and archaeologist in which hidden fragments of meaning get unearthed and put back together through the 'objective' private eye of the detached scientific observer. Since the Enlightenment, meaning has been formed out of Nature's chaotic secrets by the genius of human scientific rationality. By selecting phenomena and then combining selected observations into rules, science believes it has 'understood the meaning' – but this position has resulted all too often in the discovery of an infinite regression of further 'puzzles of Nature' – or are they puzzles of meaning? The nineteenth century delighted in unearthing hidden meaning of a more human sort: the 'other', not-us humanity hidden in archaeological remains which led to a search for, discovery, reassembly and translation of human ancestry. I talk about this in later chapters but it is worth noting here how this reflexive twist in Western civilisation's meaning-making activity, grew apace and professionalised itself at the same time as the emergence of psychoanalysis which was swift to take up archaeology as metaphor for its own search for the hidden – or latent, as Freud called it – meaning of dreams and symptoms. At one time, the aquisition of knowledge was regarded as a good enough end in itself. Since this time, concerns about the status of scientific rationality – both as a *method* and as a *benchmark* for Truth and Reality – have formed part of the growth of greater and greater reflexivity in human affairs which questions the validity of such an aim.

The postmodern is often characterised as a period or a state of *hyper-reflexivity*. The emergence of the new 'science' of psychology and more importantly, the depth psychology of psychoanalysis, towards the end of the nineteenth century might thus be regarded as the initial stirrings of the postmodern in general. Here for the first time was modern rational science turning in on itself, the human observer, in a reflexivity never previously attempted in the same way. We are not in a position to turn back. As Jung puts it,

To the man of the twentieth century this is a matter of the highest importance and the very foundation of his reality, because he has recognised once and for all that without an observer there is no world and consequently no truth, for there would be nobody to register it . . . Significantly enough, the most unpsychological of all the sciences, physics, comes up against the observer at the decisive point. This knowledge sets its stamp on our century.

(Jung, 1952, CW 11, para. 465)

Out of this reflexivity a new 'object' emerged – one that paradoxically belonged to the Subject and was Other at the same time. This was the Unconscious, and much of this book will follow up the implications of this for Jung's thought and postmodern concerns. Throughout we will see how the unconscious through Jung, Freud, Lacan, structuralists, post-structuralists and others involves many of the postmodern vertices of concern such as the Other, the Subject, language, the Sublime, rationality, fragmentation, plurality, meaning, knowledge, power and the image.

Throughout the rest of this chapter I see it as my task to map the trajectory of modernity-postmodern, or, putting it in another frame which is non-temporal, to oversee modernity-postmodern in a gestalt ground/field sense of the relationship between the two. This is far from unproblematic as any survey of collections of readings titled 'modernity and postmodernity' will reveal. Such a field consists of a great number of competing descriptions and ideas. The territory is still so unclear, or, more accurately so complex, that there are no longer sufficient tools to grasp what we may wish to discuss. We need some sort of map to orientate us through, however, and so it will have to be the case, as Baudrillard notes, where 'the map precedes the territory'. Each commentator on this subject draws his or her map according to the grid of their preferences, experience and interests which themselves are dependent on their own psychology and I, of course, am no exception to this. Jung never underestimated the importance of what he called the 'personal equation' and he noted how the competing psychological theories of Freud, Adler and Jung himself arose out of the personal psychology of each writer and thus none could claim to be a final truth. In this Jung was expressing a pluralism many now regard as postmodern although, of course, when he was writing, the term had not yet been coined. Here are three examples from *The Aims Of Psychotherapy* (1929):

Both truths [the Freudian and the Adlerian viewpoints] correspond to psychic realities. There are in fact some cases which by and large can best be described and explained by one theory, and some by the other.

(Jung, 1929, CW 16: para. 68)

It is in applied psychology, if anywhere, that we must be modest today and bear with an apparent plurality of contradictory opinions.

(ibid.: para. 71)

I hope I shall not be misunderstood. I am not advertising a novel truth, still less am I announcing a final gospel. I can only speak of attempts to throw light on psychic facts that are obscure to me.

(ibid.: para. 72)

Just as Jung notes when he is explaining his own psychology against the background and language of Freud's psychoanalysis (ibid.: paras 69 and 74), a particular difficulty that applies to much of what can be said about modernity and the postmodern is that, by and large, talking about the postmodern still relies on the assumptions, concepts and language of modernity itself. Perhaps more than anything else, it is this that leads to confusion – especially in the writing of Freud and Jung. I wish what I have to say here to serve as a contribution to untangling the net, or net-works, of postmodern thinking. I think this is, in part, one of Jung's own aims in his thinking through of analytical psychology as a critique of modernity and modern consciousness. But analytical psychology is also a *method*, the living practice of Jungian psychotherapy in which I am also engaged and which offers a form of this untangling at the level of individuals which, I believe, is complementary to the academic study of the postmodern in sociology and critical theory. Faced with such competing discourses I have had to place my grid in such a way that will make sense to me and reflect the aims of this book. I begin with the historical perspective of modernity-postmodernity and follow this with an evaluative view which presents both in differentiating positive and negative lights. The postmodern has also been discussed from a social-political perspective and I will show how this is differentiated from a mass- and popular-culture perspective. Sometimes these different perspectives on modernity-postmodernity – the historical, the evaluative, the political and the cultural – may link up according to the net or grid being applied. The potential for them to do so, however, does not imply such connections will necessarily occur. The 'connection' may be an antithetical one like the repulsion between two positive poles. Perhaps the way the points connect in agreement or in disagreement is less important than the gap between each. *It is often in the gap that something happens and the spark is revealed.*

Before proceeding with this overview, I present a table illustrating comparative terms and concepts that distinguish the postmodern from the modern. I am familiar with a variety of similar attempts at dichotomising the two concepts – such as those of Ihab Hassan (1985) and Charles Jencks (1996) for example – but rather than repeat one of these here I decided to compile one of my own as it arose from the synthesis of my own thinking and reading around modernity-postmodernity, Jung and psychoanalysis. The table is far from exhaustive of course and it is certainly not definitive. Even at a first glance, it is clear that we seldom live on one side or the other but move between the poles. It is offered largely to the reader who may be familiar with Jung but unfamiliar with what the postmodern is all about.

MODERN	POSTMODERN
Truth	perspectives
Knowledge	information
God	gods
Science	myths
Character/personality	complexes/sub-personalities
One	many
Culture	multi-cultural
Nation	multi-national
War	conflict resolution
Central	regional
Global	local
Man	humanity
Centre	margin
Rationality	rationalities
Objective	subjective
Complete	fragmented
Universal	individual
Concrete	abstract
Progress	nostalgia
Evolution	regression
Future	present

JUNG AND THE LIMITATIONS OF ENLIGHTENMENT RATIONALITY

Jung wrote:

The activation of the unconscious is a phenomenon peculiar to our day. All through the Middle Ages people's psychology was entirely different from what it is now; they had no realisation of anything outside of consciousness. Even the psychological science of the eighteenth century completely identified the psyche with consciousness. If . . . you could observe the state of the unconscious in a man of two or three thousand years ago and compare it with that in a modern man, you would see an enormous difference. In the first man it would be quiescent; in the modern man, tremendously aroused and active. Formerly men did not even feel they had a psychology as we do now. The unconscious was contained and held dormant in Christian theology.

(Jung, 1937: 106)

Central to postmodern concern is the dominant rationality through which we represent ourselves to ourselves, as a society and as individuals. In making his historical comparison, Jung was writing from the point of view of the psychology of the unconscious. From a social-political perspective there persisted a situation in which the dominant rationality of medieval times ordered the cosmos into a hierarchy, with God at its apex. From this stemmed an earthly order descending from Kings ruling by Divine Right, through Lords and Bishops down to their servants and serfs – an heirarchical order which arose by analogy to, and was held in place through the legitimating power of the greater cosmology. Secular human urges towards territoriality, expansion and aggression could be subsumed within the legitimating order of God and the King as in the case of the Crusades. Human urges towards an animistic relationship between subjects and the living world, and other views which fell outside the sanction of the Church's dominant rationality – the so-called pagan or heretical – were dealt with by the oppression of identifiable 'others' such as women persecuted as witches or marginal groups such as the Cathars.

The Enlightenment sought to replace the order of medieval rationality. The Dark Ages were to be illuminated, not by the light of God, but by the brilliant searchlight of human scientific reason. Out went belief, blind faith and trust in the God-given order of things, and in came objective observation, measurement, the generation of rules and experimentation. The Enlightenment sought to replace a representation of humanity and the world that relied on the will of God, on the one hand, and on an animistic natural world, on the other, with a singular, universal rationality – one that could be derived from and, above all, *serve* human intellect and concerns. This movement from the medieval world order to Enlightenment values is the fundamental shift that ushers in our modern frame of representation – this is what I refer to as modernity – although, strictly, we should admit there have been several 'modernities' – each characterised by the progressive crossing-out of God and an accelerating emphasis on instrumental rationality: that is, reasoning aimed not at metaphysical speculation ('How many angels can you get to dance on the end of a pin?' 'Why was Christ not born as a pea?'), but reasoning aimed at the unmasking and control of nature for human purposes and, inevitably, for financial reward.

From a contemporary perspective, there are certain ironies to be detected in this shift from a gods-centred universe of the Ancients or pagans to the medieval God-centred Universe and, eventually, to a Human-centred Universe. We should not lose sight of the fact that this apparent genealogy has been fabricated by the final 'rationality' – modernity itself. It is well documented, for example, how nineteenth century Enlightened Europeans rewrote their roots in terms of polytheistic ancestors such as the Greeks, not to mention the 'clans' of Scotland which was an economic reinvention conducted by Victorian textile manufacturers seeking a market for their wide range of tartan designs. We should bear this in mind when we consider Jung's apparent 'regression' to Greek polytheism as an expression of 'our' psychology in his work. Is this evidence of an anti-modern tendency in Jung, a conservative reversion to abandoned positions, or is it a postmodern *looking backwards in order to look forward*? Viewing Jung's thought in this way brings it in line with some of the retro- and nostalgic tendencies in the postmodern which the cultural theorist Fredric Jameson regards as a 'reinvention of the past whereon . . . (to) fantasise about a healthier age of deeper historical sense' (Jameson in Stephanson, 1988: 20).

A further irony may be spotted in what is possibly *the* paradigmatic shift from the Medieval into Enlightenment rationality – the one brought about by the work of Copernicus and Galileo (published in 1543). This succeeded in reversing the assertion that the Earth was the centre around which revolved the sun and the planets. This paradigm of Enlightenment thought was coined by Freud as analogous to his own de-centring of human autonomy with his concept of the unconscious. The irony lies in how shifts in a world-view deriving from human efforts to rationally grasp the world and reality according to the power of human intellect – and thereby gain control and understanding – seem to result in a greater and greater realisation of human *insignificance*. The negation of the human Subject arising from the privileging of a certain form of rationality, again illustrates a postmodern concern expressed by Jung who often cites our contemporary over-emphasis on scientific rationalism, 'Scientific education is based in the main on statistical truths and abstract knowledge and therefore imparts an unrealistic, rational picture of the world, in which the individual, as merely marginal phenomenon, plays no role' (Jung, 1957, CW 10: para. 498). Using a military metaphor derived from notions of 'conquering nature', Jung acknowledges the achievments of Enlightenment but reminds us how these have come about at some cost to the human psyche,

> Although at the time of the Renaissance . . . the newly won rational and intellectual stability of the human mind nevertheless managed to hold its own and to penetrate further and further into the depths of nature that earlier ages had hardly suspected. The more successful the penetration and advance of the new scientific spirit proved to be, the more the latter – as is usually the case with the victor – became the prisoner of the world it had conquered.
>
> (Jung, 1912/1952, CW 5: para. 113)

There is also a social and political discourse that runs in parallel to the symbolic and the scientific which, despite Enlightenment's idealisation of the objective observer, shows us how interests, power and knowledge are in fact entwined. 'Biblical Truth', which, up till the Copernican revolution was the 'true order of things', was legitimated and held in place through the power of the Church and the forces of the State. Copernican teaching was forbidden by Rome and thus Galileo's scientific assertions were also *political acts which critically addressed political power as well as a scientific and symbolic image of the order of reality.* This 'science' has far more implications than the Enlightenment image of scientific investigation as an 'objective', rational approach to phenomena which has persisted throughout centuries of modernity.

It has been a postmodern concern to point out and deconstruct, the variety of assumptions held within such a discourse of 'Truth'. As Thomas Docherty notes, 'The Enlightenment aimed at human emancipation from myth, superstition and enthralled enchantment to mysterious powers and forces of nature through the progressive operations of a critical reason' (Docherty, 1993: 5). In effect this meant a re-thinking of the natural world in abstract concepts. The Copernican example is paradigmatic for the way in which the common sense impression of the sun's movement over the earth was denied and reversed through the activity of a certain form of reason. But most importantly, the particular style of reason initiated by the Enlightenment took a hegemonic hold and became presented as if it were the only valid form of rational thinking. What had begun as a radical challenge and an emancipation of knowledge from the strictures of the Church and superstition resulted in new hegemonic 'Truth'. Now power might be held not solely by physical force but more subtly as 'a power over the consciousness of others who may be less fluent in the language of reason' (ibid.: 6).

Jung reflects upon the relationship between knowledge in the form of scientific rationalism and the individual in many of his later writings. He is often critical of the contemporary tendency towards collective thinking and behaviour, the psychology of the 'mass-mindedness' which overrides and eclipses the individual and individual consciousness and experience. Here, five years before his death, Jung expresses a passionate concern for the survival of the individual subject who is under threat from more than one direction, 'Apart from the agglomeration of huge masses in which the individual disappears anyway, one of the chief factors responsible for psychological mass-mindedness is scientific rationalism, which robs the individual of his foundations and his dignity.' (Jung, 1957, CW 10: para. 501). In Jung's view, individuals become more and more uncertain of their own judgement; thus leading to the collectivisation of individual responsibility. The real 'life carrier', the individual subject, is usurped by an 'abstract idea' – society and the State. 'The State in particular is turned into a quasi-animate personality from whom everything is expected' (ibid.: para. 504). Jung's grasp of the relationship between scientific rationalism and the fate of the individual subject in modern society will surprise many who have not been aware of how, as early as 1956, Jung was arguing in the same vein as current postmodern concerns.

In much of his later work from 1928 onwards, Jung's psychological writing emphasised the social and historical context of what he called the modern psyche. He was not only interested in the content and treatment of neurotic and psychotic disturbances in the patients he saw, but was also focused on how the psyche of twentieth-century Western men and women was very much a product and development of a general evolution in human conconsciousness. In *The Meaning of Psychology for Modern Man* (Jung, 1935, CW 10) he emphasises how the development of individual consciousness arises out of the indispensable condition of the difference between consciousnesses. The universal similarity of the psyche is a fallacy as the evolution of consciousness is one of progressive and profound differentiation. 'One could liken the progress of conscious development to a rocket that rises up from the darkness and dissolves in a shower of multicoloured stars', he writes (ibid.: para. 283). He maintains that the premise of the equality of the psyche has until very recently prevented psychology from being born. Differentiated consciousness – which then requires and makes possible the empirical science of psychology – is very young: no more than 50 years old (in 1935). In fact, Jung affirms, 'Our present-day consciousness is a mere child that is just beginning to say "I"' (ibid.: para. 284). Nowadays, any psychotherapist knows what Jung discovered – how enormously different people's psyches are. In this affirmation of both the nature of modern consciousness and the arrival of psychology, Jung emphasises how both of these challenge previous assumptions of unity with a pluralistic point of view with the recognition of difference at its core. Not one homogenous Psychology modelled on the grand single theories of the Natural Sciences, but a plurality of psychologies. It strikes me that in this way, the arrival of psychology signals the end of the single big ideas of the Enlightenment. The postmodern theorist Jean-François Lyotard is well known for his view that a key distinguishing feature of postmodern culture is the end of master-narratives or discourses in favour of the plural and the local (Lyotard, 1984). Reading Jung from 50 years before we find that he was already coming to the same conclusion – he was noting aspects of what we now call the postmodern condition through his psychological insights. Moreover, it was psychology itself, consciousness at its most reflexive, that made this possible.

Jung goes on to point out that the degree of differentiation, separation and opposition manifested by contemporary consciousness results in a degree of dissociation and of sickness that goes beyond the individual. Writing in a way that is strikingly up-to-date Jung notes,

> The political and social conditions, the fragmentation of religion and philosophy, the contending schools of modern art and modern psychology all have one meaning in this respect . . . we must admit that no one feels quite comfortable in the present-day world; indeed it becomes increasingly uncomfortable.
>
> (Jung, 1935, CW 10: para. 290)

The question then arises for us: Is this development 'bad' and in need of correction or is it an inevitable result of the development of a highly differentiated consciousness which, otherwise, has many benefits and simply has to be gone along with? The first point of view is that of those who regard the postmodern condition as undesirable and a loss as we shall see in the work of Daniel Bell below. The second point of view strikes us as too *laisser-faire* and perhaps irresponsible. Is there another, third, perspective? Jung seems to supply one that is typical of his psychological point of view that emphasises how, in the individual as in society, *les extrêmes se touchent* – the compensatory quality of the psyche pushes extreme positions towards their opposite. This allows Jung to affirm the positive side of our condition which, for the contemporary reader, coincides with a positive postmodernism, 'thus the sickness of dissociation in our world is at the same time a process of recovery, or rather, the climax of a period of pregnancy which heralds the throes of birth' (ibid.: para. 293). Jung makes historical comparisons with the dissolution and malaise that spread throughout the Roman world in the first centuries after Christ which also ushered in a new era and rebirth. Similarly, the dissociation which arose out of the dissolution of Church authority during the Reformation eventually gave birth to the Enlightenment. Jung makes the point that our own time – which we in the 2000s call the postmodern – is a similar period of rebirth and an opportunity for humanity.

A seminal critique of Enlightenment reason which has informed the postmodern is Adorno and Horkheimer's *The Dialectic of Enlightenment* which was first published in 1944. Their work stemmed from the Frankfurt School whose theorists, among whom were Erich Fromm and Jürgen Habermas, were influenced by Marx and psychoanalysis. It is to be regretted how this radical branch of psychoanalytically influenced critical theory lost impetus through its enforced dispersal due to the Nazis. Its members settled across the USA where the loss of a collective focus and American hostility to the Left resulted in a failure of its critical thrust and the growth of a conservative psychoanalysis within the medical establishment (Jacoby, 1975). It would be good to regard postmodern depth psychology as the return of the prodigal heir to the Frankfurt School late in the century. Adorno and Horkheimer point out how Enlightenment's aim of power over 'nature' was mere illusion as the concepts and practices legitimated by Enlightenment were limited to its abstract and utilitarian aims thus producing 'success' purely within the terms of Enlightenment itself. 'The very myths from which Enlightenment claims the capacity to disenchant humanity are themselves the product of Enlightenment, constructed and produced in order to be unmasked by Enlightenment, and hence to legitimise the utilitarian activity of an Enlightenment epistemology' (Docherty, 1993: 6). As Adorno and Horkheimer put it, 'Enlightenment behaves towards things as a dictator toward man. He knows them in so far as he can manipulate them. The man of science knows things in so far as he can make them' (Adorno and Horkheimer, 1944: 9). Fifty years before this, and almost exactly one hundred years ago today, we find the young Carl Jung, twenty-one years old, expressing similar criticisms now published in his Zofingia Lectures of 1898,

> in today's world people are inclined to pursue scientific work for the sake of success . . . They evaluate their field of study in terms of its future income . . . Strictly speaking, no science is the least bit useful . . . man can survive perfectly well without science. Science is not

useful until it abandons its exalted status as a goal in itself and sinks to the level of an industry.

(Jung, 1898: CW Supp. Vol. A: para. 166)

From Plato through to Kant, human thought has long struggled with the problem of the relationship between a 'real world out there' and the image of reality as apprehended by human consciousness. In its attempt to close this gap, Enlightenment reason is accused of promoting a one-sided style of consciousness that then sets the standard for all other ways of seeing the world and of measuring what is 'true'. We become trapped within this 'iron cage' of instrumental rationality, as Weber called it. The seamless articulation between Enlightenment reason and Capitalist economic expansion and exploitation made the Enlightenment approach to knowledge and reality an ultimately social and political question – far more so than philosophical considerations of previous eras. Adorno and Horkheimer wrote *Dialectic* in full knowledge of the Nazi atrocities and the genocide of European Jews between 1936 and 1945. Writing on the Holocaust, Baumann brings the postmodern perspective to this, perhaps the most horrifying result of Enlightenment rationality: 'every "ingredient" of the Holocaust . . . was normal, 'normal' not in the sense of the familiar . . . but in the sense of being fully in keeping with everything we know about our civilisation, its guiding spirit, its priorities, its immanent vision of the world' (Baumann, 1989: 8). Both of the Great Wars of the twentieth century, begun in 1914 and 1939 respectively, can be viewed as progressive postmodern breaks with an old order that have successively ushered in the postmodern period and the contemporary postmodern 'mood'. It is within such periods that the actions of men and women and the development of new technologies and a new language – the words 'machine' and 'gun' were not linked until the Great War, for example – have forever shaped the spirit of the times and the civilisation we experience now.

Jung's inner life and his understanding of modern consciousness were closely tied up with these periods. In *Memories, Dreams, Reflections* he describes his prophetic vision, in 1913, of Europe being engulfed by rivers of blood and,

a thrice-repeated dream that in the middle of summer . . . the whole of Lorraine and its canals [were] frozen and the entire region totally deserted by human beings. All living green things were killed by frost . . . On 1st August the world war broke out . . . my task was clear: I had to try to understand what had happened and to what extent my own experience coincided with that of man in general.

(Jung, 1963/1983: 200)

After the war he wrote:

> It may justly be maintained that the acquisition of reason is the greatest achievement of humanity; but that is not to say that things must or will always continue in that direction. The frightful catastrophe of the first World War drew a very thick line through the calculations of even the most optimistic rationalizers of culture . . . . . . as is the psychology of humanity so also is the psychology of the individual. The World War brought a terrible reckoning with the rational intentions of civilisation.
>
> (Jung, 1917/1942, CW 7: paras 72,74)

It is Arnold Toynbee who is often cited as the first to coin the term 'post-modern' (*sic*) in the context of political and social history in his vast work *A Study Of History* (1954). In earlier volumes (1934), he regards the 'modern' period as ending sometime between 1850 and 1875. He revises his view in a later volume (1939) where he regards the end of the modern as stemming from 1914, with the gradual confluence of the postmodern proceeding from various elements in the period 1918–1939 to eventually produce the present postmodern era. Toynbee dates the 'Modern Age of Western History' from the last quarter of the fifteenth century. He connects this with the European expansion of colonial exploitation across the Atlantic which was made possible by the 'technological conquest of the ocean' (Toynbee, 1954: 144). As far as a periodisation of the modern and the postmodern goes I have already indicated that I am in sympathy with the first view – the 'roots' of the postmodern, and equally have no quarrel with the second – the inception of the modern. I have written elsewhere about how I regard the 'Colombian moment' as seminal to an analysis of modern Western consciousness along lines similar to Jung's. In this paper (Hauke, 1996b) I suggest how the inception of a 'racist' consciousness arises from the objectifying consciousness of modernity which creates its own Other, coinciding with, and sustained by the growth of European capitalist expansion and the exploitation of lands and people that began in earnest around 1492.

Originally, the Latin term *modernus* had been used to distinguish the official Christian era from the pagan or Ancient that went before. After the Enlightenment the term 'modern' gradually took on an evaluative quality resulting in the concept of 'modernity as a distinctive and superior period in the history of humanity. In relation to reason, religion and aesthetic appreciation it was argued that the moderns were more advanced, more refined and in possession of more profound truths than the ancients' (Smart, 1990: 17). Scott Lash, however, proposes that our age, the 'modern', should be understood in terms of the fissure that appeared between modernity and modernism, 'a paradigm change in the arts which began at the end of the nineteenth century' (Lash, 1987: 355) and which may be 'extended to encompass contemporary social practices' (Smart, 1990: 18). This requires us to shift our focus from a more or less overlapping of the discourses of the aesthetic-cultural and the socio-political, to their splitting – an historical moment of critical reflexivity which, for a number of commentators, marks the end of the modern era or modernity. The challenge *to* modernity, yet from *within* modernity, provided by the rise of a radical artistic *avant garde* between 1890 and 1930, with its power to shock, disturb and produce fresh perspectives exhausted itself, however, and failed to produce in culture the wider changes once promised. By this time – the early twentieth century – capitalist forces of production and consumption had developed to such an extent that the new art and music was rapidly absorbed and legitimated within the greater culture. Beginning initially as the possession of a privileged class elite, the *avant garde* rapidly became absorbed within the cultural mass as reproductive techniques of photography and recording developed; ending up as cheap possessions for mass consumption, as Walter Benjamin analysed. Nowadays, since the sixties, it is the establishment norm – transmitted through the glossy, disposable pages of the Sunday colour supplement, giant street posters and the fleeting film images of the advertising industry.

DANIEL BELL AND PETER HOMANS: MODERNITY, CAPITALISM AND THE PROTESTANT PSYCHOLOGIC

The work of Daniel Bell, especially in *The Cultural Contradictions of Capitalism* (Bell, 1979), provides a specific analysis of modernity, modernism and postmodernity which moves us towards an evaluative stance on the postmodern while remaining within a discourse of historical periodisation. For Bell – who describes himself as 'a socialist in economics, a liberal in politics, and a conservative in culture' (Bell, 1979: xi) – modernism is the cultural contradiction not only of capitalism, but, more specifically, of a bourgeois or middle-class society. Bell points out how the bourgeoisie revolutionised modern society after the sixteenth century by making economic activity, rather than military or religious concerns, central to society. Moreover, this singular new mode of operation, capitalism,

> was fused with a distinctive culture and character structure. In culture, this was the idea of self-realization, the release of the individual from traditional restraints and ascriptive ties (family and birth) so that he could 'make' of himself what he willed. In character structure, this

was the norm of self-control and delayed gratification, of purposeful behaviour in the pursuit of well-defined goals. It is the interrelationship of this economic system, culture and character structure which comprised bourgeois civilisation.

(ibid.: xvi)

Bell's linkage of cultural and psychological qualities in his discussion of modernity bears a comparison with Peter Homans's analysis of Jung's articulation of the individual and the cultural in his book *Jung in Context. Modernity and the Making of a Psychology* (Homans, 1979).

For Homans, the era of 'psychological man' (Rieff, 1959, 1966) arose out of three specific conditions. First is the decline of the power of traditional religion to organise personal and social life; second, the development of a new diffuse and heightened sense of personal self-consciousness; and thirdly, the split which arose between personal self-consciousness and the social order which led to a devaluing of the social structure. As people become less and less able to relate to impersonal social structures there follows a collapse of the public sphere of life. We see this these days quite clearly when politicians, especially, come under media scrutiny which leads to calls for their resignation, not for duplicity in government but for extra-marital shenanigans conducted privately out of the public gaze as thousands of national figures from Catherine the Great to John Kennedy have always done. The difference nowadays seems to be an attitude, fostered within the validating power of the media industry, that profoundly blurs distinctions between the public and the private spheres.

Along Jungian lines, what Homans adds to this picture is how, as religion wanes a 'meaning vacuum' arises and this empty epistemological space is then filled by psychology – what Homans calls the 'the Protestant psychologic'. This may be characterised as an aspect of modernity. But then Homans explains how Jung's thinking interrupted the Protestant psychologic and ushers in a further radical approach characterised by aspects of narcissism – idealisation and grandiosity – not all negative by any means and this may be characterised, in my own view, as coinciding with the postmodern.

Homans points out that Jung's originality was the admission into psychology of the inevitability of modernity. He also notes how aspects of Jung's own experience and personality – namely his disillusionment with his pastor father and the sterility of the Christian church, and a narcissistic valuation of the subjective, individual inner world over the outer social world – coincided with cultural and social changes in the wider world and led Jung towards a therapeutic cure inscribed in psychological concepts. Jung could not accept Christianity but neither could he let it pass him by and so his psychology developed a religious quality conceived this time in terms of the individual and the inner world of the psyche. Religion afforded a personal experience as an antidote to modernity and 'mass-man' but the Christian church had itself become rationalistic and futile, losing, for Jung, the transformative power its symbols once held. The solution lay in self-understanding and self-knowledge, the path to which analytical psychology and its methods could offer. As Homans summarises, 'In all this, Jung rendered normative a lack of meaning in the public sphere. He spoke against the institutional structuring of the personal sector of life, creating in effect a doctrine of the private self' (Homans, 1979: 200). Later in this present book we will return to the implications of this statement in terms of the concepts of individuation and the collective unconscious which provide a more sophisticated psychological approach, thus adding a further dimension to any simple, sociological polarisation of the individual subject and the social collective.

Clearly, in Jung, modernity is regarded in a fully psychological perspective as an aspect of the evolution of consciousness itself. This is in contrast to Bell, for whom modernism, as a whole, parallels the social science assumptions of Marx, Freud and Pareto where 'the irrationality of the substructures of reality belied the surface rationality of appearances' (Bell, 1979: 47). This is especially so for Freud where the civilised organisation of the ego has to keep a tight rein on the impulsive instincts of the id. Modernism arises as a response to two social changes in the late nineteenth century: changes in both the sense perception of the social environment and in the consciousness of self. The revolutions in communications and transport arising from the railway, the telegraph, piped gas and eventually electricity led to disorientation in sense perceptions of speed, time, atmosphere, light and noise. At the same time, the loss of religious certainties such as God's creation of Man and the existence of an afterlife contributed to the crisis in self-consciousness, or, as Peter Homans refers to it, a 'meaning vacuum' which gets filled by psychology at the turn of the century. According to Bell, modernism 'dirempts' the long-prevailing hierarchy in Western consciousness that had placed rational judgement over and superior to the will or desire. Bell also notes how, 'The emphasis of modernism is on the present or on the future, but never on the past. Yet when one is cut off from the past, one cannot escape the final sense of nothingness that the future then holds' (ibid.: 50). Modernism – at this point Bell suddenly calls it 'traditional modernism', probably to make a point about his version of 'post-modernism' which follows swiftly – employs art, the aesthetic, as a substitute for religion or morality as the means for man to transcend himself. Nietzsche conceived his *Ubermensch* as a self-overcoming to make oneself into a work of art – a concept which influenced Jung's notion of individuation (see Chapter 6).

Indeed, as Bell notes without making this precise connection himself, 'the very search for the roots of self moves the quest of modernism from art to psychology; from the product to the producer, from the object to the psyche' (ibid.: 51).

The 'culturally conservative' Bell then asserts a simplistic linear progression with: 'In the 1960s a powerful current of post-modernism carried the logic of modernism to its farthest reaches' (ibid.). Calling it the 'post-modern mood' or 'post-modern temper' (echoing the psychoanalytic infantalising of a variety of radical protests), the postmodern is berated for 'acting out', for substituting the instinctual – meaning 'impulse and pleasure' – against the aesthetic justification for life, and, sin of sins, for undermining 'the social structure itself by striking at the motivational and psychic-reward system which has sustained it' (ibid.: 54), that is, the Protestant work ethic. Bell not only refers to the 'porn-pop' (ibid.: 51) and 'drug-rock' (ibid.: 54) culture at this stage in his argument, but he also cites Foucault, Burroughs, Mailer, Genet and Norman O. Brown as the carriers of his version of post-modernism. Common to both Toynbee and Bell are their ideas that the crisis in Western civilisation stems from three things: the loss of the Puritan work ethic – the 'zest for work' – the demise of 'high' culture due to new forms of cultural production and consumption associated with economic and technological innovation and, perhaps above all, the loss of belief.

Citing the same crisis, Peter Homans points out how Jung's psychology arises as a response to this crisis in modernity but offers a different way forward – one that has the distinctive quality of looking to past values and non-Western ways of thinking, qualities that have brought on accusations of anti-modernist and 'mystical'. For some, Jung has been too closely associated with the 'drug-rock' explorations of the Woodstock generation, but to dismiss his critique of modern consciousness and culture through such an association would be a mistake. Just as Bell is wrong in his negative evaluation of the postmodern as a simple rejection of all standards and values, it is also short-sighted to regard Jung's thinking as purely regressive and rejecting of modernity. Common to Jung's thought and postmodern critique is a sincere wish to restore to humanity that which five hundred years of Enlightenment 'progress', despite many gains, has robbed. Of course this will involve criticising contemporary values, but, just as for Nietzsche, this is not simply nihilistic and destructive but *deconstructive*, not leading to death but to *rebirth*, not the loss of values but the *revaluation of all values*.

The *Cultural Contradictions of Capitalism* was first published in 1976 which explains Bell's somewhat dated examples and a narrowness in the defining of postmodern as hardly more than a negative result of late modernism or late capitalism. By aligning the postmodern too closely with aspects of modernism, the paradigm shift of postmodern culture, its radical deconstructing of old values to allow space for something new and its celebration of the individual Subject gets completely missed in Bell's analysis. I believe it is this different, radical progressive sense that Nietzsche was referring to in his prophetic way, and it is also the vision contained in Jung's psychology and his perspective on the needs of modern Western civilisation. Bell's contrasting attitude is useful to note, however, for the way that Marxist and post-Marxist political theories about capitalist society have been influential in discussions of the postmodern. These are missing in Jung's perspective which is focused on the individual and on psychology as much as on history. I see as one of my tasks in this book to bring these divergent paths – those of the political, social and historical subject and the personal, individual, psychological subject – together.

FREDRIC JAMESON: 'HISTORY' AND NOSTALGIA

As I have been indicating, one aspect of the debate around modernity, modernism and the postmodern contains specific, opposing positions. On the one hand, the postmodern is viewed as merely a continuation, a 'late stage' of modernism or of modernity; on the other hand, the postmodern represents a break with modernity, a radical shift into something different. Consequently, a further pair of views arises which questions whether we are either to value the postmodern as degenerate, regressive and a loss, or, alternatively, to value the postmodern as representing rebirth, regeneration and hope for the future. Fredric Jameson draws the distinction between ideological theorising about social realities and the realities themselves, 'I am not willing to engage this matter of pessimism and optimism about postmodernism, since we are actually referring to capitalism itself: one must know the worst and then see what can be done. I am much more polemical about postmodernist theories. Theories which either exalt this or deal with it in moral ways are not productive' (Jameson quoted by Stephanson, 1988: 29).

Jameson is in disagreement with the influential views of Lyotard (1984) which emphasise how a major characteristic of postmodernism is the abandonment of 'master narratives' such as those of Marx and Freud which attempt to interpret humanity in terms of universal, globalising theories and 'rules' along the lines of Enlightenment rationality of which both are the offspring. For Jameson, narratives or stories are the form in which we represent the world to ourselves and it would be hard to imagine ourselves doing without them. The idea that we have done so really becomes part of another narrative itself. In the post-Jungian field, James Hillman has detailed how depth psychology employs its own narratives or 'healing fictions' (Hillman, 1983) to treat both individuals and culture therapeutically – a topic that will be addressed further in later chapters. Jameson defends Marx's concept of 'modes of production' not as a literal story of successive economic stages but as an heuristic, a way of viewing the relationship between various social phenomena within an historical framework. The aim has similarities with the 'genealogy' of Nietzsche and Foucault which elicits the unexpressed text existing in the gaps of a cultural text – in other words: the 'small print' or, rather, the 'missing print' not conveyed in conventional explanations of economic and social norms in contemporary culture that we are expected to accept. This emphasis on the importance of retaining an historical perspective in the face of its denial can be similarly found in Jung's thinking which frequently cites historical comparisons to point out gaps and differences of which modern consciousness is unaware. Some may criticise Jung's idealism and his use of material derived from myths, medieval alchemy and Gnosticism to grasp the unexpressed text modern consciousness omits but, in doing so, Jung does seem to demonstrate an heuristic approach which compares with contemporary postmodern methods.

The promotion of an historical perspective is vital for Jameson precisely because he sees postmodern culture as an effect of, and shaped by, the historically-late stage of international consumer capitalism. As Sean Homer points out, this late stage – which constitutes contemporary social experience in the industrialised West – is characterised by an illusion of increasing diversity of experience which disguises what is in fact an accelerating *homogeneity*. As with modernity in Marshall Berman's vision (Berman, 1983), rapid transformations accelerate the pace of life, resulting not in greater diversity but in a greater standardisation and *lack of differentiation* (Homer, 1998: 147). To put it more vividly, the faster we are able to travel between cities and continents in our BMWs, or Fords, or Boeing 747s, the quicker we arrive to find the same Safeway, Sainsbury's, Ikea or Marks and Spencer stocking identical goods, or the faster we are able to eat a Big Mac served up with an accent from Manchester, Minneapolis, Moscow or Milan.

Jameson's theorising links the arrival of a global international capitalist world with other cultural, social and psychological phenomena that have emerged at the same time and together constitute the postmodern dominant. These include the dominance of *images* – led initially by the photographic image – which work to promote pastiche and nostalgia with, in his view, a resultant loss of a sense of history and loss of a critical distance. In a great deal of cultural production, in the UK particularly, there appears a powerful tendency to revise the present by promoting a neo-Utopian future conceived of in terms of an idealised or reproduced 'past'. The resulting simulacra have a powerful influence and range from the political urges of Margaret Thatcher to return to 'Victorian values' or John Major's romantic valorisation of Englishness condensed into the image of warm beer, bicycles and cricket on the village green, through to Noel Gallagher's open borrowing of melodies from the Beatles and songs of the 1960s to create the hugely popular music of Oasis, and numerous TV advertisements, like those for Hovis and Irish beer, set in a 'past' which never existed. When it comes to 'history' there seems to be a distinct difference between the employment of nostalgic, historical *details*, on the one hand, and the use of history as a *genealogy* with which to trace the present, on the other. The first can lead to a Romantic blindness or Totalitarian tunnel vision, while the latter – the genealogical or historical *method* – offers opportunities for insight and for an understanding of the postmodern condition. This topic will be dealt with in detail later, especially in Chapters 4 and 7.

Jameson focuses on literature, film and architecture which, through their employment of pastiche and nostalgia, express, for him, a postmodern loss of history and, indeed, loss of the individual subject,

> Pastiche is, like parody, the imitation of a peculiar mask, speech in a dead language: but it is a neutral practice of such mimicry, without any of parody's ulterior motives, amputated of the satirical impulse, devoid of laughter and of any conviction that alongside the abnormal tongue you have momentarily borrowed, some healthy linguistic normality still exists. Pastiche is thus blank parody, a statue with blind eyeballs.
>
> (Jameson, 1991: 17)

Jung's use of past historical forms is clearly not in the service of pastiche nor parody. In *this* sense he is not postmodern. That is, if pastiche is a postmodern technique we will not find this in Jung's use of past forms. However, Jung does use past forms to gain a perspective on contemporary phenomena, and thus his use of history as genealogy may be classified along with the 'revealing' tendency of postmodern epistemological approaches. As Jung states in his foreword to *The Psychology of the Transference* (1946),

> The reader who approaches this book more or less unprepared will perhaps be astonished at the amount of historical material I bring to bear on my investigation. *The reason and inner necessity for this lie in the fact that it is only possible to come to a right understanding and*

appreciation of a contemporary psychological problem when we can reach a point outside our own time from which to observe it. This point can only be some past epoch that was concerned with the same problems, although under different conditions and in other forms.

(Jung, 1946, CW 16: 165–166. Italics added)

This postmodern use of history is a deconstructive approach – in this case Jung's method of understanding the psychological phenomena of the transference in a fashion quite outside the terms in which it is conventionally described in Freudian psychoanalysis.

JEAN BAUDRILLARD: IMAGE AND SIMULACRUM

The aspect of the postmodern condition most frequently slated or celebrated is its reliance on the surface image. In contemporary culture we are surrounded by a fast-moving stream of images – the street posters that come and go through the windscreens of our cars, or the rapid, barely discriminated TV images where 'News' follows advertisements which follow fictional drama in a confusion of 'realities' that all demand interpretation. (Research has shown that children under eleven are not particularly aware that advertisements are carrying images of products that advertisers wish us to buy. What aspect of life and reality, then, one might ask, do children believe TV ads to be representing?) The photographic image dominates in the determination of reality for the contemporary urban psyche. So much so that images which start out as representations of reality end up as representations without any 'reality' 'behind' them at all. This is the *simulacrum* found in Baudrillard's analysis of the postmodern condition which he sums up in four stages:

Such would be the successive phases of the image:
it is the reflection of a profound reality;
it masks and denatures a profound reality;
it masks the *absence* of a profound reality;
it has no relation to reality whatsoever: it is its own pure simulacrum.

(Baudrillard, 1994: 6)

Hollywood films, themselves imitations of 'reality', come to mind, but even more so do Disneyland and the Hollywood or Granada Studio tours. With their re-enacting of the already enacted – from Indiana Jones to Coronation Street, and, especially in the case of the cartoon- and fantasy-characters of Disney World – they are examples of the 'bringing to life' of what was never alive in the first place. Or, as Jameson says after Baudrillard: the representing of that for which no original has ever existed. In fact, Baudrillard points out how the spectacle and simulacra that is Disneyland serves to distract our attention from the simulacra quality of the rest of the USA itself:

> Disneyland is a perfect model of all the entangled orders of simulacra
> . . . Disneyland exists in order to hide that it is the 'real' country, all
> of 'real' America that *is* Disneyland (a bit like prisons are there to hide
> that it is the social in its entirety, in its banal omnipresence, that is
> carceral). Disneyland is presented as imaginary in order to make
> us believe that the rest is real, whereas all of Los Angeles and the
> America that surrounds it are no longer real, but belong to the hyperreal
> order and to the order of simulation. It is no longer a question of a false
> representation of reality (ideology) but of concealing the fact that the
> real is no longer real, and thus of saving the reality principle.
>
> (Baudrillard, 1994: 12–13)

Baudrillard's reference to 'saving the reality principle' may be read as a concious noting of Freud's ego-aim, enshrined within the ego-psychology of US psychoanalysis, but also, in Baudrillard's analysis, trapped within social imagery which masks the insubstantiality of such 'reality' and, most importantly, prevents its availability for criticism. If the real is no longer real, what does the future hold for the Freudian ego's urge towards adapting to 'reality'? Consider the times you have been told of, or witnessed, some dramatic scene in daily life which then gets summed up with 'It was just like something out of *Eastenders* (or *Friends* or *Roseanne*)'. It is as if the reference to a fictional TV soap guarantees the authenticity of the real life event – rather than the other way round.

Jameson cites the 'nostalgia film', such as *American Graffiti* (1973), to demonstrate how, far from an indifference to history, 'the remarkable current intensification of an addiction to the photographic image is itself a tangible symptom of an omnipresent, omnivorous and well-nigh libidinal historicism' (Jameson 1991: 18). These films 'restructure the whole issue of pastiche and project it onto a collective and social level, where the desperate attempt to appropriate a missing past is now refracted through the iron law of fashion change and the emergent ideology of the "generation"' (ibid.: 19). I would like to push this view further to claim that different films mine history through particular signifiers, signs and degrees of 'realism' in different ways. In his book *Mythologies*, first published back in 1957, Roland Barthes discusses Mankiewicz's film version of *Julius Caesar*, pointing out the significance of all the male characters wearing fringes. For

Barthes this is, 'Quite simply the label of Roman-ness. We therefore see the mainspring of the Spectacle – the sign – operating in the open. The frontal lock overwhelms one with evidence . . . everyone is reassured, installed in the quiet certainty of a universe without duplicity, where Romans are Romans thanks to the most legible of signs: hair on the forehead' (Barthes, 1973: 26). In the same film, Barthes points out how (Vaseline) sweat on the faces of labourers, soldiers and conspirators is also a sign, this time a sign of moral feeling. These characters are sweating because they are debating something horrible within themselves; only the object of their crime, Caesar himself, 'remains dry since he does not know, he does not think' (ibid.: 28).

By today's cinematic standards, as an attempt at 'historical realism' these signs are crude and simplistic; but as Barthes is saying, reality is not the point. It may be harder for us to grasp the more subtle significance of a new muddy, ruralised 'historical realism' found in the new generation of Westerns, in adaptations of eighteenth century novels such as Jane Austen's, in historical epics like *Braveheart* and in colonial stories set in the nineteenth century such as Jane Campion's *The Piano*. Here, the ubiquity of mud, dust and stained faces and clothing serves to convey the 'past' itself, that is, an Other to the urban, clean, modern present of the spectator in the cinema. It is a general overarching sign that structures an image of our – idealised – modernity as much as it indicates a 'past' – far more effectively than can the hooped skirts or the prevalence of horses for transport. As Barthes points out, 'the sign is ambiguous: it remains on the surface, yet does not for all that give up the attempt to pass itself off as depth' (ibid.: 28). One perspective sees this as a deception, a confusing of history with 'style', promoting a false consciousness. From another point of view, though, perhaps the escalation of this sort of simulacra is rather a sincere attempt on the part of the culture to reconnect with certain human values – often of a spiritual and psychological nature – thought to have been lost and therefore needing to be explored in a 'past' that is 'authentically' reconstructed from a consciousness of the present – a modern present which is self-conscious of both its achievements and its losses.

Other films like David Lynch's *Blue Velvet* differ in using generic styles – in this case Hollywood's idealisation of the small American town as in *It's a Wonderful Life*, for example – against the darkness of the narrative to deconstruct the whole process of what it is to watch a modern film, thus making it a self-consciously postmodern product. Oliver Stone's *Natural Born Killers*, despite the censorship fuss over its 'violence', goes even further by using photographic and editing techniques not to enhance the realism of the movie in the conventional Hollywood fashion, but, on the contrary, to distance the viewer from the violence of the characters and the narrative. A similar contra-realism is achieved by Tarantino in *Pulp Fiction*

– this time by chopping up the linear sequence of a conventional narrative which is otherwise used by conventional movies to promote the viewer's involvement and suspension of thinking. (David Lynch reports how, during a recent screening of one of his films, the reels were shown in the wrong order without any complaint from the cinema audience). These deconstructive techniques would seem to address Adorno and Horkheimer's critique of the 'culture industry' in the late 1940s where they despair at the effect of the Hollywood film:

> The more intensely and flawlessly [the filmmaker's] techniques duplicate empirical objects, the easier it is today for the illusion to prevail that the outside world is a straightforward continuation of that presented on the screen . . . Real life is becoming indistinguishable from the movies. The . . . film . . . leaves no room for imagination or reflection on the part of the audience . . . the stunting of the mass-media's consumer's powers of imagination and spontaneity does not have to be traced back to any psychological mechanisms; he must ascribe the loss of those attributes to the objective nature of the products themselves . . . They are designed so that quickness, powers of observation, and experience are undeniably needed to apprehend them at all; yet sustained thought is out of the question if the spectator is not to miss the relentless rush of facts.
>
> (Adorno and Horkheimer, 1944: 126–127)

Adorno and Horkheimer are referring to an art-style – in this case the cinema film epitomised by the Hollywood style – that has predominated until recently. When it comes to the wider culture, this style, which tends to minimise the critical role of the viewer, is analogous to modernity and the transparency of its values in general. The critical, deconstructive styles I mention may be termed postmodern for the way in which they challenge the techniques of the modern cinema and reveal its tricks. They require the subject, the viewer, to take a position that restores an individual relationship to, and conscious reflection upon, their experience. It is the same shift, I believe, that Jung's psychology is able to offer.

The contradictory qualities of the postmodern are in evidence with 'the nostalgia mode' just as they are with the apparent 'death of the subject' which I will deal with in Chapter 3. It is unwise to evaluate or judge the postmodern in any moral sense precisely because postmodern culture – for all the accusations of its addiction to the image, its losses of history, the subject and a critical distance – is also expressing passionate concern for the refinding of human values, for *rebirth*: not in terms of modernity and 'what went before' (despite appearances!), but in terms as yet unknown, in language as yet unspoken. Pastiche and nostalgia are the fumblings in the dark or, to put it another way, attempts to see through a glass darkly. There is a spiritual purpose around, a *resacralisation* as Andrew Samuels calls it (Samuels, 1993) which makes Jungian perspectives highly relevant even if, at the moment, they do not appear obvious. It is only from the point of view of modernity itself that the postmodern appears solely as an empty, superficial condition and evidence of a decline in civilisation. From a different perspective, one that is only gradually emerging and is still constrained by having to express itself in the foreign language of modernity, the postmodern may be viewed as a radical break and a beginning.

2 Freud and Jung: the analysis of the individual and the collective

What is truth but a mobile army of metaphors.

(Friedrich Nietzsche)

HABERMAS AND THE INCOMPLETE PROJECT OF MODERNITY

There is a further view on the varieties of postmodern experience and analysis I wish to introduce here which contrasts with perspectives that depict the postmodern as a break with modernity. Much of what I have said up until now, especially in my use of Jameson, lies within such a model, but when we examine the work of Jürgen Habermas we find a perspective that claims the postmodern holds a possibility for completing the project of modernity – that is, that the postmodern constitutes not a break with modernity but that it constitutes a continuation: the extension of Enlightenment reason. In this, Habermas has his most powerful critic in Michel Foucault and this section is an opportunity to bring this pair of arguments to light so we may refer to them at later stages in the present book. After summarising Habermas's position on modernity and the postmodern in which he employs a version of psychoanalytic theory, I turn to a different, more recent theorising of the individual and society. Stephen Frosh's use of the psychoanalytic theory of object relations is discussed together with a critique from the post-Jungian writer Andrew Samuels. In this we may see the success and the limitations of psychoanalytic attempts to analyse the social collective and the possible advantages that the Jungian perspective offers.

A psychoanalytic critique of society has been attempted by several Freudian writers in recent years and psychoanalytic theorising about society has had a significant presence since the heyday of the Frankfurt School. In general, the advantage offered by psychoanalytic theory is a description of how, on the one hand, the inner world and dynamics of the individual is structured by the environmental conditions he or she encounters, and, on the other hand, how these inner dynamics also tend to structure, through projections and through activities, the outer world of social relations which the individual inhabits. Freud's theory of the individual and what he called civilisation, however, differs from the perspective we find in Jung. For Freud, self-hood, the ego, is formed at some cost to the whole organism in that ego develops through a series of losses and sacrifices – largely consisting of the repression and sublimation of instinctual urges. Civilised social life becomes possible through the management of the instincts but this process leaves in its wake a range of repressed contents which then constitute the unconscious psyche.

As a younger representative of the Frankfurt School, in his earlier work, Jürgen Habermas was a contributor to the project which sought to wed psychoanalysis to Marxist thinking in an effort to construct a more complete analysis of the subject in capitalist society. The failure of European Marxism after the events of May 1968 in France led Marcuse to declare the obsolescence of the Freudian concept of man because the (Freudian) ego was now collectivised in modern industrial society. The equation of individual repression of sexual libido and successive historical forms of surplus repression generated by the inequality and domination inherent in the structure of class society was no longer a tenable idea. In France, Marxists like Althusser found a new approach through their use of Lacanian psychoanalysis, but Habermas clarified what it was that linked the individual and society in their illusory web in a different way. Habermas rejected the Freudian formula that viewed culture as arising directly out of instinctual drives or out of conflicts between them, and he emphasised how the human shift into culture is made possible only through the unique action of a consciousness characterised by its ability to produce symbolic representations. Habermas was separating out the two spheres that Marcuse had compounded: the economic and the symbolic are both mediations between human society and nature, but, for Habermas, it is only through the symbolic that the individual can form ego identities appropriate for handling the conflict between instinctual aims and social constraints. Pushing this idea further, Habermas's emphasis on the importance of human social interaction led to his giving prime importance to *communicative* action and to his ideas of *repressive communication*. Despite the fact that there are many forms of social interaction – war for example – that are not communication (Anderson, 1983: 61), Habermas goes on to refine his idea down to one where communication becomes increasingly identified with language as if these two were also interchangeable. In *Knowledge and Human Interests* (1972) Habermas declared 'what raises us out of nature is the only thing whose nature we can know: language' (ibid.: 314). As Anderson summarises,

> Psychoanalysis becomes, in this reconstruction, a theory of the 'deformation of ordinary language inter-subjectivity', whose aim is to restore to the individual the capacity for undistorted linguistic communication. At the level of the collectivity (*sic*) . . . democracy can be defined as the institutionalisation of conditions for the practice of ideal – that is, domination-free – speech.
>
> (Anderson, 1983: 64)

Comparisons between Habermas's emphasis on language and the views of the French structuralists is seductive – and, indeed, it is Habermas who pushes hardest at 'sustained attempts to erect language into the final architect and arbiter of all sociability' (ibid.). But while Lacanian psychoanalysis seeks to restore to the patient the 'full word' of the unconscious against the claims of an alienated and artificial ego,

> Habermas views psychoanalysis as a therapy whose goal is to repair the subject's capacity for the 'ordinary language of inter-subjectivity', with a much more traditional estimate of the positive instance of the ego, closer to that of Freud. In either case, however, a dematerialization of Freud's theory has occurred, in which instinctual drives are alternately effaced or resolved into linguistic mechanisms.
>
> (ibid: 65–66)

How, then, does Habermas's theorising on communication link up with the 'project for modernity' that is still to be completed, and how does this involve the possibility of still pursuing the Enlightenment ideal of Reason? And, second, how does Habermas come up against the postmodernists who argue that this project is over and cannot be resuscitated? For Habermas, the 'pathologies' of modernism stem from the underdevelopment of our system of inter-subjective communicative action compared with the more complete rationalisation of the social systems we inhabit. In other words, our ability to understand and communicate to each other our experience is out of step with – and far less sophisticated than – the structures that maintain both the economic and political social order. Habermas disagrees with how the philosophy of the subject – as propounded especially by Foucault and by Baudrillard – replaces Enlightenment rationality with a subject-centred reason which, 'undermines the very basis for the existence of rational, relatively self-contained individuals and fosters a regressive Dionysian and ecstatic impulse . . . "a merging with amorphous nature within and without" [Habermas, 1987: 94]' (Ashley, 1990: 92). For Habermas,

> this structure of a subjective reason that is socially divided and thereby torn away from nature is peculiarly de-differentiated . . . it is the sorts of phenomena rediscovered by Romanticism – dreams, fantasies, madness, orgiastic excitement, ecstasy – it is the aesthetic, body-centred experiences of a decentred subjectivity that function as the placeholders for the other of reason.
>
> (Habermas, 1987: 306)

Against this, Habermas recommends a paradigm of mutual understanding and 'an analysis of formal procedural principles of *communicative* rationality as these evolve within differentiated, but heteronomous (*sic*), spheres of communicative action' (Ashley, 1990: 92).

Habermas's accusations could be directed at a range of critical thinkers from Nietzsche onwards and Jung would, no doubt, easily fall into the firing line with his own emphasis on the subject's unconscious as a particular sphere of otherness specifically opposed to the particular rationality that is Enlightenment reason. This comparison will be picked up later, but for now it is to Foucault that the argument turns. Foucault views Habermas's theory of communicative action as basically 'utopian': for Foucault, there are no 'universal processes of reaching understanding' – there are no transcendent grounds for truth.

> Instead of being entrapped by the philosophy of the subject, Foucault demonstrated how the subject is produced by power. Rather than seeking a romantic (de-differentiated) solution to the anarchy of modernism, Foucault (tries) . . . 'to create a history of the different modes by which, in our culture, human beings are made subjects'.
>
> (Foucault, 1982: 208 quoted in Ashley, 1990: 94)

It is naive to believe, as Habermas does, in the possibility of human communication without constraints and coercive efforts.

The core of Foucault's critique lies in the fact that Habermas is unable to ensure a sufficient critical distance from his object – modernity itself – incidentally thus confirming an aspect of the postmodern indicated above by Jameson. Habermas's aim is a rationalisation of the division and fragmentation of contemporary life – to include this as a logical and rational extension of modernity. To do this, Habermas documents, in *Legitimation Crisis* (1975), how the class power of the bourgeoisie rooted in the morality of the Protestant work-ethic 'enabled commodity relations to displace already existing social relations, and to do so without political authorisation from above' (Ashley, 1990: 95), thus creating the 'truth' of bourgeois economics legitimated for use against a subordinate class. Thus, ironically, Habermas illustrates how, in fact, 'truth' is dependent upon power – as in Foucault – rather than power dependent upon 'truth'.

Foucault's thinking is more pluralistic and less subject to modernist restrictions on thought and in this we might wish to compare him to the pluralistic perspectives we find in Jung. For Foucault, 'truth' is a human invention, and each society or 'mode of domination' – has its own 'regime of truth' upon which that society's 'knowledge' depends. That is – no knowledge stands independent of such a regime. This is why he can assert that it is precisely the yearning for truth which is so ahistorical and depoliti- cised due to its having been fostered and given direction, historically, by the first class to claim universality – the bourgeoisie. In countering Habermas with Foucault we are back to the position of one of the key features of the postmodern problematic: the idea – also featured in so much of Jung's psychology – that the type of reason which gets promoted within modernity has failed to deliver the goods. The inadequate rationality of Enlightenment persists alongside the cultural contradictions it continues to produce. Humanity's shelves are stripped as bare as a Soviet supermarket while the hologram of McDonald's golden arches glows from across the street.

FREUD AND MODERNITY: POST-FREUDIAN SOCIAL ANALYSIS AND POST-JUNGIAN CRITIQUE

Since 1989 and the demise of Eastern bloc communism, Marxist theorising has diminished in popularity as a tool of social analysis. But psychoanalytic social theorists still aim for the rationalisation of the division and frag- mentation of contemporary life, and, like Habermas, wish to include this as a logical and rational extension of modernity. Their current technique is to promote a specific field of psychoanalytic theorising – object relations theory – into first place as the analytic tool of choice, and offer hope within modernity along these lines. This psychoanalytic paradigm has achieved greatest popularity in the UK where recent theorists, largely influenced by Melanie Klein, Bion, Winnicott and other post-Freudians, tend to pay more attention to the earliest months of infant development and to place emphasis on the inner object relations of the individual. This theoretical development has been used in an attempt to theorise linkages between the inner subjective worlds of the psyche and the outer world of society. There are considerable problems with such a linkage that I will briefly enumerate. In doing so, three important distinctions are revealed. First, the difference between Freud and Jung in their conception of the psyche; second, the difference between Freud and Jung in their respective attitudes to modern consciousness and modern social forms; and third, the difference between post-Freudian theorists and post-Jungian counterparts in their attitude to, and use of, Freud's and Jung's formulations.

From his biological-evolutionary standpoint, Freud theorised that what made civilised society and modern ego-consciousness possible was the repression of primal instincts, notably those aimed towards sexual reproduction and survival. 'The ego represents what may be called reason and common sense, in contrast to the id, which contains the passions' (Freud, 1923). Mental health consists of a successful adaptation to 'reality' as achieved by the ego:

> The functional importance of the ego is manifested in the fact that normally control over the approaches to motility devolves upon it. Thus in its relation to the id it is like a man on horseback, who has to hold in check the superior strength of the horse . . . The analogy may be carried a little further. Often a rider, if he is not to be parted from his horse, is obliged to guide it where it wants to go; so in the same way the ego is in the habit of transforming the id's will into actions as if it were its own.
>
> (ibid.: 25)

There are significant differences in Jung's formulation of the psyche. First, he did not place such emphasis on the primacy of the sexual instinct and instead conceived of a generalised psychic energy which might be channelled, differentially, in many ways. Second, although he retained a concept of the ego which he regarded as the centre of the conscious part of the psyche similar to Freud, Jung conceived of the relationship between the conscious and the unconscious part in terms quite unlike the antagonistic ego-id relationship of Freud's formulation. Jung called the whole of the conscious-unconscious psyche the *self*, of which the ego was but a small part that the psyche as a whole uses to conciously relate to itself and the outer world. Moreover, rather than the ego being in charge of this process, Jung reverses the priority and regards the relationship of the ego to the self as that of the 'moved to the mover'. In addition, for Jung, the unconscious psyche consists not only of a personal unconscious as it did for Freud, but it also contains the collective unconscious – a phylogenetic inheritance of the human psyche amassed over aeons of human evolution. Thus the portion of our human potential available at any one time would depend not only on the personal environmental and family conditions of the individual, but also on the conditions and values of the wider culture that the individual finds themselves in – conditions that vary across cultures and across history. Jung emphasised that by no means does the collective unconscious manifest itself in its entirety *but only insofar as historical, cultural and personal conditions will permit.*

The differences between Freud and Jung on the structure and dynamics of the psyche arose from a very different attitude to the individual and to modern society, which then had consequences for what each regarded as the task of psychology. These differences became reinforced by a third difference in emphasis. While for Freud, mental pathology consisted of the ego's failure to adapt to 'reality' – by which he meant modern social conditions – for Jung, as we have seen above, there was something about the modern condition itself, and the type of consciousness it supported and fostered, that needed to be addressed. Put simply, what we find in Jung is a critical attitude to modernity and modern consciousness where a challenge by the ego (informed by the bigger self) is regarded as healthy although it may struggle against the prevailing values of 'civilisation' – meaning, modernity. This is in contrast to the psychoanalytic attitude where the aim of treatment was once summed up by Freud himself as the transformation of neurotic misery into common unhappiness. It it the 'common unhappiness', the struggles of modernity itself that Jung and the post-Jungians, in a broader way, seek to address. This difference in emphasis is not to particularly criticise Freud or Jung; indeed, it seems as if after their fall-out, they proceeded to differentiate and specialise their own theories of the unconscious in complementary and useful ways. What I would like to suggest, however, is that the Freudian psychoanalytic theorising of society comes under some strain which certain approaches from the Jungian perspective are able to avoid. This is partly due to the Freudians' less critical attitude to prevailing consciousness and an overvaluing of the ego-function, but, connected with this, it is also due to a further major difference between the Freudian and Jungian perspective. Whereas in the former there is an emphasis on past causes – the reductive point of view – the Jungian position emphasises the understanding of phenenomena – including social conditions – by asking 'Where is this heading? What are these conditions – or 'symptoms' – leading us *towards?'*

I have supplied a further table – this time placing concepts from Freud and Jung side-by-side-at the end of this chapter; I think it might pay to compare this with the table of modern-postmodern above.

In his book *Identity Crisis. Modernity, Psychoanalysis and the Self* (Frosh, 1991), the British academic and clinician Stephen Frosh shows how a certain form of psychoanalytic thinking – Kleinian object relations – can be used analyse modernity. Here, I will summarise Frosh's position and follow this with a critique of the 'object relations consensus' as a basis from which to analyse society as expressed by the post-Jungian academic and analyst, Andrew Samuels in *The Political Psyche* (Samuels, 1993). Frosh follows Marshall Berman, author of *All That Is Solid Melts Into Air* (Berman, 1983) who supplies this classic description of modernity and its drawbacks,

> To be modern is to find ourselves in an environment that promises us adventure, power, joy, growth, transformation of ourselves and the world – and, at the same time, that threatens to destroy everything we have, everything we know, everything we are . . . a maelstrom of perpetual disintegration and renewal, of struggle and contradiction, of ambiguity and anguish. To be modern is to be part of a universe in which, as Marx said, 'all that is solid melts into air'.
>
> (Berman, 1983: 15)

Frosh finds in Berman an essentially optimistic vision of the possibilities offered by modernity and *modernism* – which Frosh defines as 'the human and cultural response to modernisation and the experience of modernity' (Frosh, 1991: 16). But how is the apparent contradiction between an optimistic view of a creative modernity and the pessimism around its destructive qualities to be resolved? Frosh maintains that, psychoanalytically, it is the *ego* that offers the possibility for either outcome. The concept of the ego, he maintains, separates the individual and the social; 'the ego may be swamped by the forces of modernity, but it can also be a bulwark against them' (ibid.: 19). Through the ego, despite the ravages of modernity, the individual can form constructive and reparative object relationships – if all goes well. For many psychoanalytic theorists, the experience of modernity – the speed, confusion and depersonalisation of contemporary urban experience – produces a tendency in the ego towards alienation and illusion, a tendency to escape from the 'realities' of existence, or, 'the human condition' as they call it. This is the pathology of the everyday life of modernity.

But what is this ego that we find to be so central to the Freudian viewpoint and at the core of both Habermas's and Frosh's use of psycho-analysis? Differing from Habermas's emphasis on inter-subjectivity based on language communication, Frosh points out how both Freud and post-Freudian formulations track the formation of the ego (which Frosh consistently calls self and self-hood, something that merits comment shortly) from early life as introjections of lost loved objects (often people, usually the mother) so that it barely has an identity of its own. In the culmi-nation of such theorising of how the outside comes inside, as expounded by Melanie Klein, reality is only ever perceived through the phantasising tendency of the unconscious mind and so all experience is one step back from objective reality. The inside can be experienced through projection and projective identification as outside, while the outside, whether it was originally projected or not, can be internalised and introjected. So far, this general dynamic of projection and introjection bears a similarity to the Jungian view. The devil, however, is in the detail. Following the Kleinian point of view, Frosh argues that such a dynamic is characterised by inherent, destructive rage on the part of the infant which is met in its environment by the 'containing' mother with her capacity to accept these attacks without retaliation, thus promoting the infant's sense of being 'held' and avoiding a devastation of its fragile ego. When the 'strong' view of the effects of early psychic life and infant–mother determinism is subscribed to by Kleinian oriented thinkers there is a good deal of pessimism when it comes to considering humanity's ability to make any radical changes. Elliot Jaques suggests in his paper 'Social Systems as a Defence Against Persecutory Depressive Anxiety' (1955),

> it may become more clear why social change is so difficult to achieve, and why so many social problems are intractable. From the point of view here elaborated, changes in social relationships and procedures call for a restructuring of relationships on the phantasy level, with a consequent demand upon individuals to accept and tolerate changes in their existing patterns of defences against psychotic anxiety.
>
> (ibid.: 498)

Frosh extends his own psychoanalytic inference from the infant–mother relationship to the formation of self under the conditions of modernity in general:

> everyone engages with the conditions of their own time and place; they are exposed to the world and their self forms in response to it. Everything that happens resonates on the subjective level; if it happens consistently enough, it becomes an element of structuration; that is, the inner world is formed along the axes which it provides. So it is with class, gender and race, the great structuring dominations of western society.
>
> (Frosh, 1991: 73)

Put this way, Frosh seems to be contradicting his earlier emphasis on the complementary structuring power of the inner world. This seems to arise out of the difficulty Freudians encounter through having only one term for self-hood: the ego that forms in each individual. Jungian theory also has an ego formed in a similar fashion out of the encounter with the environment – although the aggressive, destructive aspect is not made a feature – but, in addition, it has a highly developed theory of the Jungian self: the larger 'personality' which is not restricted to current or local conditions for its formation. In fact this self is an *a priori* – just as, but different to, the phantasising tendency of the mind is for Klein – and so constitutes another 'environment' if you like. The self is also in a position to 'structure' our experience. It is for this reason that Jung refers not only to the objective environment but also to the *objective psyche*. When it comes to theorising society from a psychological point of view, Jungian theory has an advantage in its inclusion of a *collective* unconscious aspect of the psyche in each *individual*. What this concept implies is that our potential for changing the paths of both our individual personalities and our social–environmental conditions lies deeper within us than any individual experience in the first months of life – or even a complete single life – might determine. The individual–society dynamic does not need to be reduced to the infant–mother dynamic.

In Jung's later thought, the core process of Jungian psychology is regarded as a therapy for the ills of modernity which, on the level of the individual, was conceived of as a rigid persona characterised by extra-version and excessive rationality. For Freudians, narcissism is a popular concept for the psychoanalytic theorising of society because it appears to bridge several behavioural elements found in both the modern psyche and in modern society. In its original Freudian and later post-Freudian formulation, narcissistic pathology is closely connected to a withdrawal from the world of reality, a return to an idyllic, non-differentiated 'Eden' characterised by illusion, the avoidance of relationship (in favour of fusion), and omnipotence and grandiosity of the individual subject. Frosh follows Kernberg in linking narcissistic personalities with a failure to deal with the Kleinian dynamic sketched above, where the aggressive rage leaves the individual with a split, depleted inner world not capable of achieving the 'depressive position' of successful object relationships. At the individual level, 'the lack of dependency on, and closeness to, others, is a defence against this agonising rage, a rage that, once mobilised, threatens to devour the fragile self' (ibid.: 76). Frosh then makes a direct comparison with society which is worth quoting at length:

> So there is a mode of functioning, arguably characteristic of many individuals in the contemporary western world, designated by mirroring, concern with surfaces, self-aggrandisement, manipulation of others, control. This mode of functioning reflects, feeds into, and is reciprocally produced by, those cultural conditions that emphasise the image, the

superficiality of things (including relationships) and the interchange-ability of objects of all kinds. *Behind this mode of functioning, however, lies a different reality: of a dissolving self characterised by splitting, projected aggression and violence, and all-consuming rage.*

(ibid., italics added)

For Frosh, and several other psychoanalytic theorists, the Kleinian version of object relations offers a sufficient analysis of the relationship between modernity and the contemporary psyche: either modern conditions fail to supply the contemporary subject with sufficient conditions for the optimising of the subject's inherent tendencies towards full and intimate relationships with others (a Winnicottian position), or human subjects are more fully constructed by society in its own image (whatever that means). One apparently specific effect of modernity for Frosh is racism – and this too is explained as arising in a world where

> the continued existence of the self can only be supported through constant buttressing involving denigration of the other – that is, by way of a phantasised expulsion of one's despair into the object . . . projecting one's weakness into the other and then denying the link. This is a possible model for a general defence against the terrifying fluidity of the modern world.
>
> (ibid.: 77)

I have written elsewhere (Hauke, 1995, 1996b) offering a contrasting perspective on both narcissism, from a clinical perspective, and on racism from a socio-psychological and historical point of view and I refer the reader to these publications which are too lengthy to summarise here. The Jungian Michael Vannoy Adams also offers a very different view of contemporary issues of 'race' in his book *The Multicultural Imagination. 'Race', Color and the Unconscious* (1996a). But what needs to be pointed out immediately is how the psychoanalytic–Kleinian–object relations perspective, for all its attractions, fails to include a vital step in its trajectory between the individual and society – a vital step that we have already noted to be present in the Jungian version of events. *The vital step is the consciousness of humankind; it is not the vicissitude of the dynamics of early mother–infant relationships (which are probably more benign in these times than in most) which offers an explanation of the modern experience, but the very fact that the development of a highly differentiated consciousness, rather split off from the rest of the psyche, now dominates both individul and social functioning and behaviour.* We have no 'choice' about our consciousness – to us it constitutes our experience as human beings in present times – but it is the highly differentiated nature of modern human consciousness that constitutes both the illness and the 'cure'. When it comes to the big question, 'Why are we living like this and creating the world in this way?', the specifics of early mother–baby relationships are just froth on the surface. When they are not attempting to act as anachronistic grand narratives, such individualised analyses seem more typical of the superficiality of modern life that the psychoanalytic arguments on modernity and the postmodern seek to criticise.

The post-Jungian Andrew Samuels offers a succinct critique of the biases and assumptions that the object relations approach brings into any theorising about society, politics and culture – assumptions which indicate the conservative, even reactionary, tendencies of the theory. His critique involves the general problems found with using individual clinical psychology to engage with social and collective themes – a position also criticised by sociologists and anthropologists. He notes that what constitutes a consensus between all the object relations positions is the interplay between unconscious phantasy and potential and the good-enough, personal, facilitating environment – as we have seen in the example from Frosh above. This point of view – an assumption around *the relationship between the given (the innate) and the discovered (that which is experienced in the environment)* – is all very well for thinking about how people individualistically relate to society, up to a point, but what, Samuels asks, might we consider as *society's* 'innate aspects' or *society's* 'environmental factors'? He notes how, in fact, 'well-being may not be achievable in a society characterised by alienation' (Samuels, 1993: 271).

Samuels also draws our attention to the bias towards the developmental time-frame, towards diachrony and towards causality. A heirarchy is imposed in which earliest experiences are regarded as a template for later ones – thus the mother–infant relationship gets priority over other relationships such as those with the father, siblings, spouse, rival and so on. This search for a psychologically fundamental relation is itself a flawed project for Samuels: why should the psyche be best expressed through the metaphor of a house built up from strong foundations? He notes how the idea of 'foundations' supports a conservative politics – as does the essentiality of women's role as mothers which the object relations view also implies. Samuels points out how the idea of 'development' – an assumption that runs even deeper – is not a 'natural' approach to psychology, it is an artifice as Freud himself noted when he wrote to Fleiss in 1898, 'the mirror image of the present is seen in a fantasised past, which then prophetically becomes the present'. Linked to this is Samuels's criticism of the bias toward diachrony found in the object relations consensus: changes over time are purported to unfold in a linear, causal and chronological sequence from specific origins. Samuels asks why should the time-frame of an individual be applicable to whole societies and cultures? In the object relations model where development is always 'going somewhere', 'Features of modernity – fragmentation, stasis, discontinuity – are overlooked. Diachrony avoids the integrity of the now. No matter how polished the use of object relations becomes, diachronic and causal models of development dominate it' (ibid.: 273).

In prioritising the 'baby' – even if it is 'only' a metaphor as some theorists claim – the metaphor gets literalised with the result that adults and whole societies get treated as if they were babies. 'Regression', also, is taken to mean only one thing – the return to infantile states, whereas if this were taken more symbolically, Samuels argues, regressions would refer as much to regeneration and psychological deepening. We have seen above how Jung's perspective on modernity emphasises a crisis that is not simply a dissolution or regression in values, *but one that manifests itself as such in order to make way for something new*. This is a conception of the term regression in the sense of something – psyche, ego, society, whatever – *becoming less organised* so that space may be created and structures dismantled so that a new order might emerge. This conception is an alternative to the developmental emphasis on regression to infancy and one which is used by post-Jungians, myself included, both in their clinical work and their thinking about society (see Hauke, 1996a).

Lastly, Samuels points out the object relations bias towards complementarity and towards wholeness. In this, the so-called developmental Jungians come in for equal criticism. Samuels criticises the key concept of container–contained asking why this has become the main idea of what relationships are for and what they are about. 'What about exchange, bargaining, negotiation, equality – or even torture?' he asks, 'Does society 'contain' its individual members? Should it? Or is the notion of containment just not adequate to depict the huge range of social relations that exist?' (ibid.: 274).

As in his other writings, Andrew Samuels offers a deconstructive approach to many issues in depth psychology which, elsewhere, are transparent and taken as givens – regularly going unseen. Both Jungians and Freudians come under fire for the unexamined fundamentals their theories contain and so, to my mind, Samuels's work qualifies as part of the postmodern critical tendency in post-Jungian thought:

> it is the numinous image of mother and infant that object relations theory set out to explicate which now tyrannizes it. The professionals have become fascinated, even hypnotized, by the very images that their

professional skills uncovered. The numinosity of sex has become replaced by the numinosity of feeding. This leads directly to the tendency, which becomes unavoidable, to treat society and its institutions as if they were babies.

(ibid.: 274)

The bias towards wholeness results in a pathologising of sub-personalities as part-objects which are regarded as insufficient or a sign of immaturity: 'scanning part-objects for signs of movement toward whole objects suggests that the object relations paradigm is in the grip of a maturation morality and a fantasy of wholeness, and is just as normative as Freud's strictures on love and work or about genitality' (ibid.). It is the normative tendencies in depth psychology that Samuels (and I include myself here) most objects to. Freud's original theorising of the unconscious and Jung's development of a psychology that constitutes a response to modernity are radical bodies of thought that the medical professionalisation of analysis and psychotherapy has tended to obscure for much of the last fifty years. In doing so they are no more to blame than any other institution and body of knowledge that succumbs under the tendency within modernity and late capitalism to flatten out what is different, radical and challenging, and then to refashion such ideas within its own image – thus simultaneously legitimating such ideas and stripping them of power in order to maintain the status quo.

The version of personality that object relations theory presents, with its accent on the decisive part played by early experiences, maternal containment, and the move toward the depressive position or stage of concern, is, in many senses, little more than a reproduction of the kind of personality that the culture which surrounds object relations theory already valorises. If we want to apprehend personality, we have to consider the historical context in which personality exists.

(ibid.: 275–276)

The emergence of theories of postmodern society over the last twenty years has offered an opportunity for post-Jungian writers both to restore and to develop the critical aspect of Jung's thinking. This is not so much a 'return to Jung' but more a recognition that the social and intellectual context and conditions are now ripe for the contribution that a postmodern Jungian psychology can make.

A COMPARISON OF SOME OF THE CONCEPTS OF FREUD AND JUNG

FREUD	JUNG
Id	self
instinct	archetype
sexual libido	generalised psychic energy
Oedipal crisis	incest–rebirth myth
God the father	father the god
unconscious psyche	personal unconscious (the shadow)
phylogenetic fantasy	collective unconscious
interpretation	amplification
reductive	synthetic
past causes (aetiology)	future causes (teleology)
uncovering	linking
personal history	personal myth
analytic treatment	analytic relationship
object relations	imagos
analytic cure	self healing
symptoms	signposts
unconscious bisexuality/ anatomy as destiny	anima/animus
reality principle	psyche in the world
common unhappiness	mass-mindedness

3 Consciousness Consciousing: Individuation and/under Postmodern Conditions

It is not I who create myself, rather I happen to myself.

(Jung, 1938, CW 11: para. 391)

Following on from the discussion of the Freudian ego and the Jungian self in the last chapter, I want to pursue the relationship between these concepts and one of the more fashionable themes in contemporary theory: the 'death' of the subject. I begin with Jameson's ideas around the significance of this theme and his conclusion that within the postmodern condition the death of the ego also entails the end, or 'death', of the psychopathologies of that ego. Jameson characterises this as the 'loss of affect' individual subjects suffer and I take up this idea in terms of the Jungian concept of the relationship between the individual and the mass we have come across earlier. The manifestation of public and private emotions in reaction to the death of Princess Diana in August 1997 is used to illustrate some of these concepts at work in the 'life-world' (as Habermas calls it). Jung's recommendation for modern individuals at risk of being subsumed within the psychology of the mass, or of renouncing all responsibility onto the State, was that subjects needed to resist these processes by attending to the psychological urge towards individuation inherent in every human being: I compare Jung's concept of individuation with Jameson's theory of how the postmodern subject might address their condition. Finally, I return to the Jungian theme of modern consciousness itself and reconceptualise a postmodern individuation using Nietzsche's imagery and his concepts of affirmation, being and will. In doing so, I restore the emphasis on modern consciousness found in Jung and I suggest that, under postmodern conditions, it is human consciousness that both constitutes and enacts affirmation of our being – a reflexive process of individuation that I term 'consciousness consciousing itself'.

PRINCESS DIANA AND THE 'DEATH' OF THE SUBJECT

In his consideration of the 'death' of the subject, or, the end of the autonomous bourgeois monad or ego or individual, and the *decentring* of that formerly centred subject or psyche (Jameson, 1991: 14–15), Jameson makes some links that are useful for our purposes here in analysing the relationship between the postmodern subject, individual psychology, 'pathology' and the Jungian development of psychoanalysis. Jameson points out how postmodern culture demonstrates a particular 'waning of affect' (ibid.: 10) and that this 'waning of affect' corresponds to the depthlessness and play of surfaces, the dominance of the photographic image and simulacra that have been mentioned earlier as characteristic of the postmodern condition. If the period of high modernism – the last half of the nineteenth century or thereabouts – was about the subject's experience of anxiety and alienation – 'those canonical experiences of radical isolation and solitude, anomie, private revolt, Van Gogh-type madness' (ibid.: 14) which are epitomised for Jameson in Munch's painting 'The Scream' – these now seem no longer appropriate in the postmodern world. Although, Jameson asserts, 'it would be inaccurate to suggest that all affect, all feeling or emotion, all subjectivity, has vanished from the newer image' (ibid.: 10), he does point out its waning and replacement by 'a strange compensatory decorative exhilaration' (ibid.) which is different from it and far from equivalent. Citing the subjects of the great artist of the 'surface' Andy Warhol – Marilyn Monroe and Edie Sedgwick – Jameson feels the dominance of burn-out, self-destruction, drugs and schizophrenia of the late 1960s has little in common with the hysterics and neurotics of Freud's own day or with the pathology of high modernism just mentioned. Most succinctly, Jameson states, 'The shift in the dynamics of culture pathology can be characterised as one in which the alienation of the subject is displaced by the fragmentation of the subject' (ibid.: 14).

The decentring of the formerly centred subject or psyche or individual, produces new stresses in a postmodern age but also new opportunities. Jameson notes how Munch's painting conveys the complicated situation of the (modernist) centred subject – 'the unhappy paradox that when you constitute your individual subjectivity as a self-sufficient field and a closed realm in its own right, you thereby also shut yourself off from everything else and condemn yourself to the windless solitude of the monad, buried alive and condemned to a prison-cell without egress' (ibid.: 15). The 'death' of the subject or ego means the end of this dilemma as it also entails the death of the *psychopathologies of that ego*. This is what Jameson refers to as the 'waning of affect' – but it also means the end of individual style, the end of individuality as something unique and personal; and along with the liberation from anxiety comes a release from every other kind of feeling as well, since there is no longer a self present to do the feeling (ibid.). Jameson does not claim that all feeling is absent from postmodern cultural products, 'but rather that such feelings – which it may be . . . more accurate to call "intensities" – are now free-floating and impersonal, and tend to be dominated by a peculiar kind of euphoria' (ibid.: 16).

I believe a recent example of this may be the mass euphoric adoration and mourning which swept Britain and the world after the death of Princess Diana, in the first two weeks of September 1997. There is perhaps a way of understanding this phenomenon which uses both Fredric Jameson's ideas and those found in Jung's psychology. Diana, the epitome of a postmodern cultural icon enshrined and known almost entirely through the photographic image, seems to have attracted to her image aspects of the human self (not in Jung's sense, but self as in the subject's sense of selfhood) which became embodied and personalised, in the individual known as 'Princess Diana'. These aspects of self range from her kindness and love towards unfortunate others, her challenging of taboos around 'contamination' such as those towards leprosy and AIDS, her exposure of personal vulnerability in revealing her bulimia and low self-esteem, her willingness to maintain her individuality against a background of establishment protocol, and her public valuing of her role as a mother being the first that come to mind. Facilitated – to use a neutral term – by the vast media and broadcasting coverage of her life and death, a huge number of people suddenly found a range of human qualities condensed in Princess Diana which had been, and still are, lost to their own fragmented sense of themselves, and ambiguously valued, if not lost entirely, in the culture at large. Under the legitimating influence of Diana's tragic death and the mourning which followed, deeply felt personal emotion became expressed through the image of Diana and the actually *impersonal* event that was her sudden death at still a young age.

The high theatricality of Diana's death, which focused further its chances of serving as a cathartic dramatic work, were enhanced by the way Diana – the goddess of the hunt – was herself hunted to her death, according to the early accounts, by a pack of paparazzi on motorbikes. This involvement of the image makers in the moment of her death is no small irony and adds further depth to its grand operatic – or should I say mythic? – quality. And, as if the personalised human response was not already ensured, Diana was finishing a highly publicised and photographed holiday with a new man who it seems had just bought her a huge diamond engagement ring and who died in the car with her. The mass expression of mourning which followed suggests how feeling and affects not readily available to the fragmented, decentred subject were able to free-float across to the impersonal surface image that was Princess Diana to return as subjective experiences of personal emotion. In psychoanalytic terms, this was a dynamic of projection followed by a re-introjection of the projected affect: 'I never met her, but I felt I knew her', people queuing to write condolences would say to TV cameras. Despite appearances – that word again – this was never any real 'knowing' but rather the experience of another simulacrum. No original had ever existed but the postmodern subject 'discovers' affect through the image, imagining they are feeling for a person 'behind' the image. In fact, this *person* does not exist, only the *image* exists; moreover, the image functions as a *location* for affects unavailable to the postmodern subject or individual.

In addition, we need look no further for evidence of the tendency within postmodern culture for signifiers to free-float between objects to create affect than this final irony. Elton John's song 'Candle in the Wind', originally written to 'mourn' the loss of an earlier surface icon of vulnerable young femininity, Marilyn Monroe, was performed with slightly changed lyrics at Diana's state funeral – not only to generate emotion as with every popular song, but also, through its connection with Marilyn, as if this was a deeply resonant statement about the meaning of Diana. It was of course nothing of the sort but merely more Disneyland. The fact that people were moved by its performance does not contradict this, either – after all, the audience cried in *Bambi* too.

I am aware how cynical this type of theorising sounds as if I, too, am confirming my own postmodern waning of affect and loss of human feeling. But I think the point to remember is that critical cultural theory is not there only to deconstruct and destroy, but also to point out disjunctions so as to stimulate reflection and the desire for something else to arise within ourselves and our culture. In terms of a mass reaction that seemed to unite a huge range of different people in a shared experience that conveyed their shared sense of humanity, the response to Diana's death – no matter how shallow and manipulated through its signifiers it was – stirred a communal solidarity of feeling that, in other circumstances, is often the basis for political action and change. The 'Diana effect' will not result in anything like this, however, precisely because the human qualities and desires involved, tied as they are to the image of Diana, remain, by definition, not owned by any of the subjects themselves.

I wrote these thoughts just after the events, having heard many comments from individuals interviewed on TV, from conversations with patients in my consulting room, and friends and colleagues, some of whom are psychotherapists. As one said, Jung is useful in understanding such events as he had much to say about the behaviour and psychology of masses. Jung's idea was that when aspects of the collective psyche – human qualities we share despite the complexity of our differentiated individual subjectivities – are repressed and unexpressed due to the cultural and historical bias of the era, these aspects tend to be projected as fantasies and beliefs about the world in general. Often, through historical circumstances, these projections find a charismatic individual to which they can attach themselves. Jung's frequent example from his own times was the figure of Adolf Hitler who managed to sweep the German people up into a euphoria of belief about themselves and their destiny to produce such a devastating effect on Europe and the Jews. Psychologically similar to the figure of Christ, such a charismatic figure has the archetypal qualities of a saviour whose presence promises to heal our imperfect humanness – experienced in one era as profound alienation, in another as decentred fragmentation. The mass response to Diana's death might be viewed in this Jungian way as an opportunity for a mass cultural healing of the fragmented subject by linking up with aspects of its 'lost' humanity in the projected form of 'Diana's qualities' as I listed a few paragraphs above.

This view allows us to revise the contemporary idea of the 'death' of the subject into one where the Unconscious features in the explanation. Important for cultural theorists to note, this is not the modernist personal unconscious of Freud's original formulations. That indeed did sound the death knell of the 'bourgeois ego or monad or subject' while at the same time promising its cure through psychoanalysis. No, in a rather more sophisticated way, Jung's development of the concept of a collective unconscious, and ultimately Jung's collective 'subject' which he called the self, helps us with understanding the postmodern subject in a contemporary way less dependent on modernist formulations.

What Jung termed 'internationalism' and 'mass man' are the 'global capitalism' and the culture of mass consumerism and communications of the cultural theorists. Jameson's idea of affects as free-floating 'intensities', and others' ideas of 'sliding signifiers', may be viewed as elements expressed in Jung's psychology as the projection of aspects of the collective psyche – aspects denied to the individual by the way contemporary culture denies the individual subject a range of human potentials, notably those that do not accord with cultural dominants which are themselves dictated by the requirements of global consumer capitalism. The fragmentation and 'schizophrenia' of the postmodern subject can be viewed as arising out of the fragmentation of human qualities beyond any choice or control of the individual; the result is a fractured psyche, internally competing between its parts and seeking resolution and healing through projection onto such objects the culture offers. It is not incidental that the very thinness of the images offered by photography make this an energy consuming activity – one which saps and detracts the subject's efforts in the opposite direction

– that is, towards an unprojected, more 'inner healing' through self knowledge. I would argue that this view of the postmodern subject restores the concept of the unconscious – as conceived in Jung's wider, collective sense – to contemporary cultural debate in a way that moves it on from Freud's personalistic, modernist formulations. In doing so, psychology – especially depth psychology, post-Jung and post-Freud – holds a radical importance through its valuing of subjective experience. Potentially, this provides a challenge to the cultural dominants and structures which deny or devalue aspects of our humanity.

The Jungian concept of individuation becomes relevant here. Jung wrote of this, 'I use the term "individuation" to denote the process by which a person becomes a psychological "in-dividual", that is, a separate, indivisible unity or "whole"' (Jung, 1939, CW 9i: para. 490). In my conversations about the reaction to the death of Princess Diana I detected a consistent difference between people: on the one hand there were those who felt sincerely swept up in a tide of feeling for Diana, the sense of her being 'one of us'. There seemed to be an irrational identity with the Princess, as though a closely known and loved relative, or even *part of themselves*, had died. These seemed to be individuals who through lack of investigation or lack of confidence, or both, were not so aware of their own natures or their own potential to any great extent. They seemed more oriented to others' reactions, external to themselves, and to understanding themselves in relation to the wider culture – more explicitly, the 'culture' presented to them through the mass media.

On the other hand there were those who did not feel at all touched by the reaction to the Princess's death but remained fascinated by the mass reaction and, to some extent, felt left out. (These were different again to another group who were critical of the mass reaction and denied their interest, and their shared human feeling, with a disparaging of the mass emotion in a way that seemed defensive of their own projective tendencies.) No, those not swept away by identification with the feelings but nonetheless empathic with others' need to express themselves – of which I count myself one – tended to be individuals, either as therapists or patients in the ones I came across, who had gone some way in confronting and integrating aspects of themselves and seemed less – although far from entirely – entangled in cultural expectations and significations. Their relationship with different aspects of themselves, and with historically and culturally different expressions of humanness, seemed to result in less of a tendency to search for their sense of self or 'subjecthood' through projections alone. These people did not fail to identify or project entirely – that would have equally been missing something – but the identifications took on a more personal meaning according to their present concerns: in one case, a pending divorce, an involvement with mentally ill women in another, or an awareness of a son's loss of a mother in a further case. In these individuals, the tendency for the culture to drive impersonal projections was ameliorated by a more *personally chosen identification* with the cultural object which retained much more of the subject's sense of self. The path of individuation recommended by Jung and fostered in the psychotherapeutic relationship seems to be, as with much contemporary cultural phenomena, both an expression of the postmodern 'death' of the subject and also its opportunity for rebirth. Similarly, the Princess Diana spectacle itself offers a similar contradiction. This is another reason why I have to endorse Jameson's view that postmodern culture is neither 'good' nor 'bad' but simply *is*.

TEMPORALITY, SPATIALITY AND OUR NEED FOR MAPS – JAMESON'S ROUTE TOWARDS INDIVIDUATION?

From his own political-cultural point of view what does Jameson recommend to counter the dehumanising effects of contemporary culture? Let us return to the discussion of the homogenising effects of international capitalism featured some pages ago, delineate the contradictions Jameson detects and note how he uses Marxist ideas from Althusser and psycho-analytic ideas from Lacan in combination with the notion of 'cognitive mapping' derived from urban planner Kevin Lynch. Once we have followed Jameson's thinking I will reintroduce Jung's idea of individuation as a parallel, or even a replacement, concept and practice for postmodern subjects faced with their own extinction within what Jung called 'mass man'. Sean Homer summarises the difficulties well:

> The overriding problem with postmodern hyperspace, for Jameson, is our inability to conceive . . . of our situation as individual subjects within this new global network of multinational capital. This space has become unrepresentable and we are left with the ability to grasp only our most immediate surroundings.
>
> (Homer, 1998: 138)

The most important effect of this, for Jameson, is our loss of 'critical distance' in the present era: 'distance in general (including "critical distance" in particular) has very precisely been abolished in the new space of postmodernism . . . our now postmodern bodies are bereft of spatial co-ordinates and practically (let alone theoretically) incapable of distantiation'

(Jameson, 1991: 48–49). Significantly for my argument, he claims how the expansion of multinational capital has penetrated previously 'extraterritorial' enclaves such as Nature and the Unconscious thus removing the last Archimedean points outside at a distance from which to operate an effective critical leverage.

But, as has been noted, Jameson refuses to stay with the split, moralising analysis of the postmodern we have seen in Bell. Instead, a particular contradiction is noted which, for me, is reminiscent of Jung's perspective on the operation of opposites as much as it is Marxist for Jameson – which is not surprising given Jung's and Marx's shared Hegelian influences.

> The distorted and unreflexive attempts of newer cultural production to explore and express this new space must then also, in their own fashion, be considered as so many approaches to the representation of (a new) reality . . . As paradoxical as the terms may seem, they may thus, following a classical interpretative option, be read as peculiar new forms of realism (or at least of the mimesis of reality).
>
> (ibid.: 49)

On the other hand, says Jameson, the products of postmodern culture 'can equally be analysed as so many attempts to distract and divert us from that reality or to disguise its contradictions and resolve them in the guise of various formal mystifications' (ibid.). Although paradoxical, both views are of course 'right'. Marx detected hope for world-wide socialism emerging precisely out of the newly unified space of the international markets. Nowadays, we can detect the potential for humanity's extension, both collectively and individually, through the technology that links us into an electronic network of information exchange via instantaneous global communication and the Internet, for example. With the electronic shrinking of world space arises the paradox that, on the one hand, humanity suffers mass homogenisation (where the international ownership of PCs emerges as no different to the 'internationalism' of a Coca-Cola in every fridge), while, on the other hand, there opens up opportunities for communications on a scale hitherto undreamed of. After all, buying and consuming Coca-Cola is of a different order to PC and Internet consumers being able to communicate with each other across the globe for the price of a local phone call. In both cases there is an homogenous consumption with profit being made by someone else, but the qualitative difference between the activities – and the implications for the individual subject – is vast. There is a thrust in the opposite direction to that of homogenisation – the restoration of the individual subject, of difference and of plurality. (This is not a new position, or contradiction, either, as I believe we may detect parallel contradictory effects which arose from the technologies of earlier eras such as the railways and the telephone. It is in this sense that the postmodern is more a *phase of the modern* that emerges from time to time, rather than a discrete 'stage' in some linear, developmental process.)

I would not be the first to remark on how this phenomena of globalisation is strikingly similar to what Teilhard de Chardin, in his book *The Phenomenon of Man* (1965) refers to as the *noosphere*. De Chardin traces global evolution from *geogenesis* through *biogenesis* to the *psychogenesis* of self-conscious *Homo sapiens*, until, finally, 'Now it effaces itself, relieved or absorbed by another and a higher function – the engendering and the subsequent development of the mind, in one word *noogenesis*' (Teilhard de Chardin, 1965: 201). It is important to point out how de Chardin's apparent tendency towards holism, which contemporary postmodern views would reject, is consistently contextualised within his awareness of paradox. This suggests an inherent postmodern pluralism running through de Chardin's ideas which will be useful to bear in mind when we consider the tension in Jung between holistic and pluralistic views. De Chardin is fully conscious of our ambivalence towards the results of modernity,

> this perspective is at first sight disconcerting, running counter as it does to the illusion and habits which incline us to measure events by their material face. It also seems extravagant because, steeped as we are in what is human like a fish in the sea, we have difficulty in emerging from it in our minds so as to appreciate its specificness and breadth. But let us look round us a little more carefully. This sudden deluge of cerebralisation, this biological invasion of a new animal type which gradually eliminates or subjects all forms of life that are not human, this irresistible tide of fields and factories, this immense and growing edifice of matter and ideas – all these signs that we look at, for days on end – to proclaim that there has been a change on the earth and a change of planetary magnitude.
>
> (ibid.: 203)

(The image of ourselves as fish who are aware, for the first time, of the water they inhabit, is now a common metaphor for our postmodern hyper-reflexivity.)

For Jung, the tension and the contradiction lies between universal mass culture and its denial of the individual, on the one hand, and, on the other hand, the contemporary subject's unrealised access to a conscious relationship or dialectic with the collective psyche which is the potential of each individual. Through the process of individuation, attention is not simply paid to making conscious the repressed elements of the personal unconscious as in Freud's 'where id was there ego shall be' – as Jameson says, that Unconscious has been colonised in the period of late modernity where the classical Freud is located. In addition to this, what is aimed for in Jung's psychology is a consciousness of the collective unconscious, not only through its 'inner' imagery but precisely in its projection in the form of mass phenomena. This view acknowledges both the inevitability and the importance of globalisation and the mass but at the same time suggests a method for humanity to gain (not even 'regain' as some conventional views would have it) further human qualities as opposed to the losing of them which the notion of the 'death' of the subject suggests. As in de Chardin's ideas, what arises is a new individual–collective dialectic which neither collapses into the mass man, nor into the individual monad. The Unconscious as trapped in modernity is lost as a point which may offer any critical distance. It has been commodified and absorbed and has no radical edge left. But the Unconscious as conceived by Jung retains the radical challenge by the way it is conceptually maintained at a greater distance from ego-consciousness by Jung's consistent emphasis on its unalterable Otherness. For example,

> Always, therefore, there is something in the psyche that takes possession and limits or suppresses our moral freedom. In order to hide this undeniable but exceedingly unpleasant fact from ourselves and at the same time pay lip service to freedom, we have got accustomed to saying . . . , 'I *have* such and such a desire or habit or feeling of resentment,' instead of the more veracious 'Such and such a desire or habit or feeling of resentment *has me*' . . . we immediately identify with every impulse instead of giving it the name of the 'other', which would at least hold it at arm's length and prevent it from storming the citadel of the ego. 'Principalities and powers' are always with us; we have no need to create them even if we could. It is merely incumbent upon us to *choose* the master we wish to serve, so that his service shall be our safeguard against being mastered by the 'other' whom we have not chosen.
>
> (Jung, 1940, CW 11: para. 143)

Instead of 'where id was there ego shall be' which expresses a temporal dynamic, in Jung's psychology there is the notion of choice and of movement, of travel between ego and self, and between conscious and unconscious. There is a spatial dynamic where consciousness or ego can never fill the place ('there ego shall be') of the other, the unconscious or id, but where they remain at a distance and in a dialogue. In this formulation there *is* a chance for 'critical distance', the creation of an Archimedean point of leverage, to be rediscovered. The dialogue that arises through the individuation of the subject can then itself live dialectically with the instantaneous de-spatialising globalisation of the lived world – the so-called 'outer world'. There is a chance for the individual subject to make conscious choices about their relationship to globalisation – whether it is in the form of space-shrinking communications by Internet, fax or TV news or the flattening of difference through the totalising duplication of commodities – without being absorbed into the unconsciousness of the mass. Discovering a 'space within', as psychotherapists call it, acts in both directions. Not only does it critique the 'lack of space out there' in the world, but through the activation of an 'inner' choice and dialectic it also provides a subjective quality of distance and of space which, as Jameson asserts, is otherwise absent within the de-spatialising 'moment of truth' of postmodern culture.

Jameson's own recommendation for tackling the loss of distance is also psychological but restricts itself to cognitive psychology. Taking as his inspiration the work of Kevin Lynch who, in *The Image of the City* (n.d.), 'taught us that the alienated city is above all a space in which people are unable to map (in their minds) either their own positions or the urban totality in which they find themselves', Jameson concludes that, 'Disalienation in the traditional city, then, involves the practical reconquest of a sense of place, and the construction or the reconstruction of an articulated ensemble which can be retained in memory and which the individual subject can map and remap along the moments of mobile, alternative trajectories' (Jameson, 1991: 51). To my mind, this view compares well with Jung's ideas about the need for individuation as defined as an internal registering of an inner–outer relationship that would otherwise remain unknown or unconsciously projected.

It is more the pity that Jameson does not refer to Jung but, it seems to me, he is heading in the same direction when he refers to the work of Althusser who develops his ideas on ideology through the psychoanalytic concepts of Jacques Lacan. Jameson points out how his own idea of the cognitive map the subject requires to navigate between a sense of him- or herself and the greater totality, coincides with the

> Althusserian (and Lacanian) redefinition of ideology as 'the representation of the subject's *Imaginary* relationship to his or her *Real* conditions of existence'. Surely this is exactly what the cognitive map is called upon to do . . . to enable a situational representation on the part of the individual subject to that vaster and properly unrepresentable totality which is the ensemble of the city's structure as a whole.
>
> (ibid.)

Jameson pushes his analogy of the city further when he compares it to the relationship between the subject and the totality as encountered in ocean navigation, where, through techniques of compass, triangulation, the stars and, finally, Mercator's projection and the invention of the globe itself (around 1490), 'cognitive mapping in the broader sense comes to require the co-ordination of existential data (the empirical position of the subject) with unlived, abstract conceptions of the geographic totality' (ibid.: 52). To those familiar with Jung's formulations this sounds highly reminiscent of the 'coordination' of the conscious ego with the 'abstract unlived' unconscious collective or self.

Jameson points out how, 'The existential – the positioning of the individual subject, the experience of daily life, the monadic "point of view" on the world to which we are necessarily, as biological subjects, restricted – is in Althusser's formula implicitly opposed to the realm of abstract knowledge' (ibid.: 53). In other words, Althusser detects a yawning gap between experience and scientific knowledge which ideology then functions as a way of articulating these with each other. Different historical situations will produce different functioning and living ideologies, but in some eras this may not be possible at all and Jameson suggests that this absence of a functioning ideology is what is happening in the current crisis. Contemporary human experience is quite disconnected from contemporary scientific knowledge.

He then points out how Althusser's opposition of ideology and science corresponds to Lacan's Imaginary and the Real, respectively, and that 'Our digression on cartography . . . a properly representable dialectic of the codes and capacities of individual languages and media, reminds us that what until now has been omitted was the dimension of the Lacanian Symbolic itself' (ibid.: 54). Jameson's idea, then, is that what he calls cognitive mapping will have the power to serve as a new Symbolic by which we may orientate ourselves in the world space of multinational capital. My idea is that much of Jung's psychology and the lived task of individuation – a three-way 'dialectical' task, between the subject and the 'inner' world mapping, the subject and the 'outer' world mapping, and, thirdly, between these 'inner' and 'outer' mappings themselves – may supply what Jameson seems to be after: 'a breakthrough to some as yet unimaginable new mode of representing this [world space] . . . in which we may again begin to grasp our positioning as individual and collective subjects and regain a capacity to act and struggle which is at present neutralised by our spatial as well as our social confusion' (ibid.).

To summarise so far, what has been under discussion is the postmodern theme of the 'death' of the subject – the loss of individuality and together with this, the projection of individual affects and qualities into the mass, into social collective images and entities. Jameson suggests a new cognitive mapping is required – one that might create a new Symbolic that restores the link between individuals' experience of the world and the otherwise alien dimension of scientific knowledge and social forms individuals are required to inhabit. I suggest that the Jungian concepts of individuation and an ego–self dialogue provide a comparable, psychological, way forward. The final section of this chapter now directs us towards a *psychological attitude* and towards a *transcendence* of the terms that have been employed up till now by introducing imagery that focuses and illuminates the function of *conciousness itself* – an approach to the subject which derives from the perspectives offered by Jung, Gilles Deleuze, the Nietzschean scholar and Nietzsche himself.

AFFIRMING CONSCIOUSNESS: BEYOND GOOD AND EVIL POSTMODERNS

Central to the crisis of postmodernism is the ever-present tension between, on the one hand, the fully constructed subject – the 'mass man' – the 'puppet' not in charge of him or herself, or his or her conditions of life, and, on the other, the *will* of the individual to improve or change their conditions. In the present context, *will* may be represented as the *fact of consciousness itself* which, from time to time and from individual to individual, may be thin and weak or it may be full and strong. I am not talking about ego or 'ego strength' here – although I can see how the concepts may be confused in the discourse of psychotherapy – because I regard ego in the Lacanian sense as itself an imposed construct, an operating system for the individual which is contingent upon differing historical conditions, alien to the subject and a fictional expression of the self. Jung notes how in recent times, 'inflation and man's hybris between them have elected to make the ego, in all its ridiculous paltriness, lord of the universe' (Jung, 1940, CW 11: para. 144). It seems to me that the more the subject is conscious of the degree to which they are constructed – including how they are constructed *as an ego* – by forces 'other' to them, the less they remain a victim of these 'forces'. At first sight this implies that something is freed, or that something is 'regained', through achieving such 'greater' consciousness. This view derives from Freud's original model where psychoanalysis removed symptoms by bringing repressed unconscious contents to consciousness. My particular view is that perhaps this account is not necessary in this case. Perhaps there is no 'something else', something lost or unconscious, that is 'freed' or 'recovered' or 'discovered' by the process of fostering greater consciousness. Perhaps this *process of greater consciousness*, implied by the Jungian concept of individuation, is the 'freed' thing itself. In other words, there is no separation between the *process* (freeing) and something it is *acting upon* (the freed). The process is *it*: conscious awareness's 'aim' is the 'achievement' of itself: consciousness expressing itself or even *consciousness 'consciousing' itself*.

So far this is in line with Jung's recommendation that individual consciousness may provide an antidote to unconsciousness absorption in the mass and the dangerous social and political effects of unconscious collective projections. Ironically, critics of the postmodern echo the criticism of modernity we find in Jung when he argues how contemporary culture and recent history reveals a catalogue of mistakes, wrong moves, and great losses which are dangerous for humanity and the psyche. From this view arises the idea of refinding lost parts of ourselves of which we are unconscious – and lodged elsewhere in the ancients or in other cultures where a greater part of our humanity may be discovered. Although there is insight to be gained by revalidating our 'other', in another sense perhaps this point of view is surplus to what is required when addressing the postmodern condition. What if we were to view the apparent restrictions or pathologies of postmodern life, mass homogenisation, superficiality, and loss of affect, distance and selfhood that are felt to be problematic and which consciousness has to struggle 'against', as not so much a 'mistake' but more as a *necessity and essential to the manifestation of consciousness itself*? What if we viewed these not as if we are correcting or overcoming a 'mistake' in human life, but more that we are finding in this particular epoch, this particular opportunity for the psyche to *be* – *the opportunity for consciousness to celebrate itself as it always has done and always desires to*? That there is no 'symptom' to be got rid of or cured does not mean we can be complacent, though, but it does mean that the postmodern 'crisis' that makes such demands on reflexive, conscious activity is, as crises go, more a useful fiction, or a set of fictions, but nevertheless *vital* in the way it draws our attention to psyche's urge towards self-overcoming, which although always present, is impressed upon us, in these times, as an *unavoidable necessity*. To put it another way, it is not that there is nothing to worry about ('the postmodern's just all right by me'), but that the postmodern 'concern', or 'issue', or 'problematic', is not the issue, but *our psychological activity in response to it, is*.

This perspective also begins to address those arguments which regard the postmodern as nihilistic, destructive and empty of any redeeming creativity – as the location of the 'Last Man' rather than the 'Overman' of Nietzsche's vision. This sort of dichotomisation is a mistake, however, and it is Nietzsche who supplies the perspective by which we may transcend the dialectic of good or bad when it comes to our present condition – that is, transcend the opposites of negation *or* affirmation which form the conventional response to the postmodern. In Gilles Deleuze's analysis, affirmation and negation are both qualities of the will to power which for our purposes may be regarded as the will of consciousness referred to above. But these apparent oppositions are not equivalent: negation is opposed to affirmation but affirmation *differs* in that it stands outside and apart from negation and opposition. In fact, as Deleuze asserts, 'Opposition is not only the relation of negation with affirmation but the essence of the negative as such' (Deleuze, 1986: 188). Deleuze offers an understanding of Nietzsche's thinking on being and nothingness, becoming and affirmation that may help us with our psychological *attitude* to the postmodern and to modern consciousness. Moreover, he does so by way of imagery that is resonant of Jung's expression and so this perspective also contributes towards countering any oversimplification of Jung's own critique of modernity in the terms of analytical psychology. Nietzsche uses the mytho-logical imagery of Zarathustra's two animals, the eagle and the serpent, and the myth of Ariadne, Theseus, Dionysus and the labyrinth to express his meaning.

First, Nietzsche proposes a new conception of being, that is, affirmation *as* being: 'Affirmation is not the power of being, on the contrary. Affirmation is itself being, being is solely affirmation in all its power' (ibid.: 186). For Nietzsche, '*Being and nothingness are merely the abstract expression of affirmation and negation as qualities (qualia) of the will to power*' (ibid., italics in original). Affirmation is being in that it has no object other than itself. Doubleness – a concept we will encounter frequently in this book – comes in here:

> In itself and as primary affirmation, it is becoming. But it is being insofar as it is the object of another affirmation which raises becoming to being . . . this is why affirmation in all its power is double: affirmation is affirmed. It is primary affirmation (becoming) which is being, but only as the object of the second affirmation.
>
> (ibid.)

What Nietzsche affirms is that our being, our conscious existence 'is' affirmation itself. Affirmation does not 'act upon' being to make it something more. Affirmation (Nietzsche called himself a 'Yes sayer!') is life itself. How might we understand this idea of primary and secondary affirmation? Is it perhaps something like the primary and secondary processes of the psyche in Freud's formulation – that is, spontaneous instinct on the one hand and conscious reflection on the other? Is it to be grasped through a similar, but not identical, idea of 'two kinds of thinking' which Jung describes: undirected fantasy thinking as experienced in dreams or day-dreaming, on the one hand, and directed, goal-oriented thinking on the other? In the first position – in the instinctual or in pure fantasising – psyche is 'becoming'; that is, it is affirmation as life but without the self-consciousness of knowing its 'being'. When the second affirmation of psyche's life – conscious reflection or directed thinking – acts upon the first, primary affirmation is transcended beyond its status of 'unaware' becoming to one of being itself. The life of human 'beings' is characterised by this doubleness of the human psyche where its life – conscious life – is the affirmation of an affirmation.

One image and interpretation of this understanding of affirmation is the relationship between Zarathustra's two animals, the eagle and the serpent:

> the eagle is like the great cycle, the cosmic period, and the serpent is like the individual destiny inserted into this great period . . . The eagle flies in wide circles, a serpent wound round its neck, 'not like a prey but like a friend' [Nietzsche, 1883–1885, *Zarathustra* Prologue 10: 53]: we see here the necessity for the proudest affirmation to be accompanied, paralleled, by a second affirmation which it takes as its object.
>
> (ibid.: 186–187)

The Jungian scholar might also reflect upon the way this imagery parallels the relationship between the collective unconscious and the self, on the one hand, and the personal unconscious and ego-consciousness, on the other, in the process of individuation. Here, individuation may be realised in Nietzschean terms as 'the power of affirming as a whole'.

The second image is that of the divine couple, Dionysus–Ariadne. Ariadne loves Theseus who is a representation of the higher man – he is heroic, he takes up burdens and he defeats monsters. But, Deleuze continues, as long as woman loves man, even a higher man, 'as long as she is mother, sister, wife of man . . . she is only the feminine image of man: the feminine power remains fettered in man' (ibid.: 187). However, when Ariadne gets abandoned by Theseus (the event which leads to her encounter with Dionysus) her transmutation is imminent: 'the feminine power emancipated, become[s] beneficient and affirmative, the Anima' (ibid.). Deleuze fails to relate this vital concept, the Anima, to Jung's extensive analysis of the function of the Anima in his psychology. For Jung the Anima or feminine principle acts as a bridge between the conscious and the unconscious psyche; it is the 'other' to the 'masculinity' of rational ego-consciousness that dominates the modern psyche and is thus vital in the transformative process of individuation. Moreover, Ariadne-Anima in her relation to Dionysus (the god, as opposed to the mortal male, Theseus) is like a second affirmation,

> Dionysus is the first affirmation, becoming and being, more precisely the becoming which is only being as the object of a second affirmation; Ariadne is this second affirmation, Ariadne is the fiancee, the loving feminine power.
>
> (ibid.: 187–188)

The third image, that of the labyrinth, designates, first of all, the unconscious, the self. For Deleuze, just as for Jung, we need the Anima to link us with the unconscious, to give us the guiding *thread* for its exploration. Second, the labyrinth is becoming and as such is affirmation; the secondary affirmation of the labyrinth is the affirmation of Ariadne's thread.

> As long as Ariadne remained with Theseus the labyrinth was interpreted the wrong way round, it opened on to higher values, the thread was the thread of the negative and *ressentiment*, the moral thread . . . But Dionysus teaches Ariadne his secret: the true labyrinth is Dionysus himself, the true thread is the thread of affirmation.
>
> (ibid.: 188)

Finally, Ariadne affirms Dionysus in return (the secondary affirmation) by putting a *shrewd word* into Dionysus's – labyrinthine – ear: 'having herself heard Dionysian affirmation, she makes it the object of a second affirmation heard by Dionysus' (ibid.). Here, expressed in mythological imagery, is the 'relationship' that is beyond relationship, but one that can only be expressed in terms of 'relationship'. In Deleuze's terms, 'Affirmation is the enjoyment and play of its own difference, just as negation is the suffering and labour of the opposition that belongs to it. But what is this play of difference in affirmation? Affirmation is posited for the first time as multiplicity, becoming and chance' (ibid.: 188–189). In other words, the opposing categories of being and becoming, of multiplicity and unity, and chance and necessity and, perhaps conscious and unconscious, individual and collective are transcended in this formulation. This, then, may imply that the 'problem' of postmodern and modern may also be subject to transcendence.

The conclusion Deleuze reaches in his interpretation of Nietzsche's text constitutes a difficult, philosophical and imagistic version of what Jung asserts about consciousness and the psyche which we first encountered in Chapter 1. In Jung's simpler psychological terms he emphasises that the greatness and the difficulty with modern consciousness lies in its capacity for vast differentiation.

It has been my strategy to take 'the affirmation of affirmation' Deleuze refers to throughout, as an activity which is vital for the conscious–unconscious psyche and which is expressed in Jung's psychology as the process of individuation. My preferred phrase for this process is *conciousness consciousing itself*. It is consciousness itself which makes all the difference for the modern psyche; a consciousness aware of and willing to engage with and affirm, not only the unconscious in which it is embedded (the Freudian position) but, vitally, to engage the affirmation of consciousness itself: the affirmation of the differentiating factor that consciousness both 'is' and 'expresses'. For Nietzsche the 'will to power' is the carrier of this differentiating consciousness, a concept that will be explored further in Chapter 6, 'The will to power as the differential element that produces and develops difference in affirmation, that reflects difference in the affirmation of affirmation and makes it return to the affirmation which is itself affirmed' (ibid.: 188–189). It is consciousness that differentiates both itself and an unconscious; we have no alternative but to engage with *both of these* with the fullness of our being. This has never been more true than it is for our hyper-reflexive, postmodern present.

4   Frank Gehry's house and Carl Jung's Tower

Gehry: I'm not sure if it is finished.
Diamonstein: You're not sure?
Gehry: No.
Diamonstein: Is one ever sure?
Gehry: It's confusing. I was wondering the other day what effect this had on my family. I've noticed my wife leaves papers and stuff around on the table so there's a kind of chaos in the organization of how we live in the house. I was beginning to think that it had something to do with her not knowing whether I'm finished or not.

(Diamonstein, 1980: 46)

In this chapter I want to explore Jung's relationship with the postmodern in a playful way by considering an element in his own myth; an element that belongs to his own individual character and personality and so also belongs to his personal psychology and the psychological and cultural analysis he has provided us with. On the one hand, I am referring to Jung's metaphorical use of the 'building' as an image of the psyche; but on the other hand, I am thinking of Jung's literal affinity for stone, for constructing and for building – an affinity that expressed itself in the Tower he built and added to over many years beside the lake at Bollingen, Switzerland. The design and the construction of the Tower were clearly important to Jung and, as he tells us, deeply expressive of his inner world and what it meant to be a human being. He devotes a whole chapter to it in his autobiography *Memories, Dreams, Reflections* (1983/1963) and spent many of his later years living and working there. It was a newly-built construction but he tells us how he had many older and ancient structures in mind as he tackled its design and construction at different stages in his life. It is not a public building and even now it is kept closed to general visitors by the Jung family. The Tower is a private, modern construction built for its architect's personal and intimately private use. And although Jung was a psychologist and not an architect (interestingly one of his sons did become an architect), he found it necessary and fulfilling to express himself not only in his writing, his scholarly research, his painting and carving and his work with patients, but also in the building called the Tower. Because Jung is not coming from a culture and a training in architecture like, say, Frank Lloyd Wright or Frank Gehry, Jung's Tower does not self-consciously conform to any particular direction in twentieth century architecture, nor does it present itself as an 'answer' to any architectural theme, or desire or paradigm. However, as a contemporary building I believe it is legitimate to view it beside other contemporary examples of architecture, especially those built as private dwellings for and by the architects themselves. There is a two-way resonance in making such a comparison that will shed light on Jung and the postmodern, and on the relationship between the general and the particular, and especially the relationship between the individual personality and the general experience of the subject in the wider culture. It seems evident that every building designed by an architect who is in a position to have a free hand must express something of the individual personality of the architect as well as something of their relationship with the wider culture, and so in that sense constitutes a self-expressive work of 'art'. Such buildings are, as with Jung's Tower, expressions of their designer's inner world. Equally, however, for all the individuality involved – and Jung's building appears quintessentially individual – I believe, as do those who theorise about architecture, that every building also conveys something of the collective *zeitgeist* in which it has been conceived and created. After all, an important aspect of the postmodern condition is a recognition that the individual and the subjective is a valid position from which to know the general and apparently 'objective'. I am avoiding using the word 'universal' because I do not think that assumptions about the 'universal' are easy to make or, in the end, hold water. So when I use 'general' I will be referring to the pluralism of present times, the network of commonalties, similarities and differences – sometimes competing, sometimes cooperating, often arguing but, above all, coexisting. If this constitutes a 'universal' without privileging any particular 'universal' promoted by interests that hold the reins of knowledge, then so be it. I prefer to speak of the relationship between the particular and individual, on the one hand, and the general and commonly held or known – even if not held 'universally' by everyone – on the other.

In summary, the resonance between Jung and the postmodern I wish this chapter to convey stems from how architecture and buildings have been understood in recent times to both shape, and be shaped by, the general life of the people who use them. Second, I have been inspired by the way architecture has been used as a metaphor of choice to say something about our postmodern times, and, third, the way buildings are made self-consciously to express or to comment on other buildings or on people's lives more as public works of art than functional spaces. Fourth, as I have said already, individual architects – like the greatest artists and psychologists – sometimes have the genius to express something about the condition of humanity for all of us when they are at their most subjective in expressing themselves, and their own vision, in their buildings.

BUILDINGS, MODERNISTS AND POST-MODERNISM

The concept of the postmodern has long been established and debated within the field of architecture and architectural criticism. It was in architecture that the term modernist was established to describe, and then identify, not only buildings designed in a certain way but buildings designed with a specific *attitude* to technology, and a *philosophy* of society and of the social function of architecture itself. Buckminster Fuller, for one, believed that by 'doing more with less' in architecture, society's problems could eventually be solved. As Charles Jencks – the architectural critic and the first to reintroduce the word 'post-modern' in the late 1970s – defines it: *'modern architecture is the overpowering faith in industrial progressivism and its translation into the pure, white International Style (or at least the Machine Aesthetic) with the goal of transforming society both in its sensibility and its social make-up'* (Jencks, 1996: 23, italics in original). There is an overwhelming anomaly with this modernism, however, as Jencks points out: 'Whereas modernism in architecture has furthered the ideology of industrialisation and progress, modernism in most other fields has either fought these trends or lamented them' (ibid.). In other modernist arts and philosophies such as those of Nietzsche, Sartre, Yeats, Joyce, Picasso and Duchamp, for example, there is a distinct lack of optimism and faith in progress amounting to nihilism and uncertainty.

So, already, we have the sense that modernism is not simply progressive and positive but also contains within itself an aspect that is reflexive and self-critical. Jung was clearly aware of this when he writes about James Joyce's *Ulysses* and the art of Picasso. He begins by asserting that *Ulysses* is no more the product of individual pathology than modern art as a whole – modern art is not produced by any disease (it is not the result of a schizophrenic perspective for example), but it is a collective expression of our time. The reason Jung seems to despair of its expression – 'an art in reverse, a backside of art that makes no attempt to be ingratiating, that tells us just where we get off' (Jung, 1932/1952, CW 15: para. 178) – is because in its abstraction and negativity, such art is (merely) surplus in its restatement of where we are already at – the modern condition. It forms part of 'an almost universal "restratification" of modern man, who is in the process of shaking off a world that has become obsolete' (ibid.: para. 179). Jung seems irritated with the fact that such art still needs to deliver such a view when the modern condition is so obvious and what it requires now is not more deconstructive nihilism, alone, but also efforts towards healing. From a perspective that was ahead of his time, Jung writes arrogantly of this modernist aesthetic, also drawing psychoanalysis into his line of fire, 'They have this in common with Freudian theory, that they undermine with fanatical one-sidedness values that have already begun to crumble' (ibid.). It is as if, for Jung, the creative destruction of modernity should begin and end with Nietzsche. We should have moved on into a deeper restoration of human values by now and not need such negative reiteration of the 'values that have already begun to crumble'. Jung's is an individual approach that, at this stage I think we find, fails to take sufficient account of the social forces ranged against such a reconstruction. Perhaps the twentieth century has needed many opportunities to shake off a world that has become obsolete. Jung is, like Nietzsche, speaking from the heights while other citizens are developing their perspective still in the foothills from which position they still require largely deconstructive texts. However, it is the legacy of Jung's psychology, if not of Jung the man as well, that is able to deliver a view that goes beyond deconstruction and critique but also offers ways forward. We might view this as the tension between the anti-modernist Jung and the postmodern: his critique of the critique that is modernist art, while appearing reactionary and damning, is in fact an impatient urge towards another era we have barely just encountered. It is significant that his review of *Ulysses* was republished in the 1950s, twenty years after it first appeared; this seems to suggest that, as with much of Jung's thought, Western culture has taken some time to realise, and has only recently achieved, conditions which are receptive to much of what he has to say.

We may regard these receptive conditions within modernity as the postmodern condition itself – which amounts to saying once again that we are dealing with contradictions, a pluralistic coexistence and an over-lapping of values rather than any simplistic periodising of 'movements' or positions. The complex relationship between the modern and the postmodern is revealed in the work of several architects interviewed by Charles Jencks, and I will be using their own words to explore the definitions of modern and postmodern begun in earlier chapters. Philip Johnson and Peter Eisenman provide interesting perspectives which convey the articulation of personality and cultural expression I am interested in, but it is Frank Gehry who provides what I think is the most compelling attitude and complex body of work in this field. It is the very complexity of the modern and postmodern in Gehry, the individual and the architect, that sheds light on an identical complexity in C. G. Jung.

In the nineteenth century, the industrialised West witnessed an unprecedented expansion of science and technology and vast material success accompanied by an increasing secularisation of society. The conquering of nature and the exploitation of its wealth, along with the theories of Darwin, Adam Smith and Marx, made the belief in God less important than Enlightenment's aim: the power of humanity to forge its own destiny through human knowledge of, and control of, the world. The 'crossed-out God' of the Enlightenment could finally be deleted. Modernism became the new religion, as perhaps the Economy is now a pseudo-religion with consumerism its ritual form of worship. In 1921, le Corbusier proclaimed: 'There exists in this world a new spirit; it is to be met with particularly in industrial production . . . We must create the mass-production spirit. The spirit of constructing mass-production houses' (quoted in Jencks, 1996: 22). And Mondrian declaimed, 'The life of contemporary cultivated man is turning gradually away from nature; it becomes more and more an a-b-s-t-r-a-c-t life' (Jencks ibid.: 25, quoting Banham, 1960: 150). In modernism the value of abstraction and of aesthetics took on an overriding importance. For example, Jencks cites the Shroeder Residence, Utrecht, designed by Rietveld in 1924, as: 'The canonic modern building – white, abstract, overlapping planes with primary-coloured accents. "Every machine is the spiritualisation of an organism" – with brilliant buildings like this, the Dutch Calvinists, for a short time, made one believe it' (Jencks, 1996: 25). Jencks likens modernism to a Protestant crusade which protested against the 'degeneracy of ruling class taste' and against different styles and ornament as 'culturally sick':

> Modernism is the first ideological response to social crisis and the breakdown of a shared religion. Faced with a Post-Christian society, the creative elite formulated a new role for themselves; inevitably a religious one . . . Here is the final legitimisation of the Protestant Crusade; the First World War. This, according to Standard Doctrine, was caused by a civilisation thoroughly corrupt, overdecorated, smug, eclectic and class-ridden. It justified total eradication . . . Corbusier called this new age 'the vacuum cleaning period'.
>
> (ibid.: 24,25)

Forty years earlier, Anna O. had used a similar phrase – albeit a low-tech version – when she described her 'psychoanalysis' with Freud's colleague,

Breuer, as 'my chimney sweeping'. The modernist urge to cleanse away the old was pervading both the individual imagination and the cultural world. Apart from their great creativity through this same period, the theories of Freud and Jung have also been understood as arising out of the social crisis and breakdown of religion in this era. In Jung's case, especially, analytical psychology has been analysed as a replacement for the individual path and social role once offered by Christianity itself (Homans, 1979). Jung's thinking was originally developed against the modernist background of Freud's psychoanalysis, but it departed radically to create a psychology with quite different emphases after the split with Freud. This splitting ushered in Jung's self-analysis, his breakdown and his breakthrough, which also coincided with the period of the First World War. Just as modernism in art, architecture, philosophy and psychoanalysis established itself against the old order of the nineteenth century, Jung began to develop a critical, anti-modernist psychology of the individual subject and contemporary culture which could be characterised as the shadow of the 'positive' modernists. This entailed a response to modernity initiated early in the twentieth century – at the same time as Joyce, Cezanne and Picasso, for example – but containing a similar critique and similar qualities to what we now regard as the postmodern position in relationship to the modern. Support for this view may be found by comparing Peter Homans's understanding of the cultural significance of Jung in his book *Jung in Context. Modernity and the Making of a Psychology* (ibid.) with the way that Jencks describes modernism as a Protestant crusade. Homans shows how Jung's personal circumstances – notably his loss of paternal idealism brought home by his pastor father's loss of faith in Christian belief – coincided with the cultural crisis of secularism experienced by European society in general. Jung's personal struggle was also the struggle of his own, and hence our own, times. Homans describes how the rise of the 'Protestant psychologic' at the end of the nineteenth century, in which Jung grew up, ushered in the century of 'psychological man'. Homans then makes the key point that Jung, in his own development and his psychological writing, 'interrupted the Protestant psychologic',

> Psychological man tends to view the social order as destructive of personal, inner integrity rather than as a means of fulfilling and completing that integrity. Consequently, he turns away from socially prescribed values and instead attempts to construct value and meaning in terms of his own self-consciousness . . . Carl Jung's life and thought exemplify this feature of psychological man in what can only be called an extraordinarily precise and all-encompassing way.

> (ibid.: 199)

It is my own interpretation that, in doing so, Jung produced a critique of the modern psyche and modern culture which constitutes a critical postmodern position highly relevant for the end of the twentieth century.

CHARLES JENCKS ON DEFINING THE POSTMODERN IN ARCHITECTURE (AND ELSEWHERE)

After its heroic, revolutionary beginnings in the 1920s, modernism, similar to other aspects of the avant-garde, proved so successful that it imploded from the margins where it had started and rejoined the bourgeoisie to end up as Sunday supplement central. As Jencks points out, 'a social shift had occurred which only became apparent in the seventies. Instead of the avant-garde being a noble, oppressed minority, as it had been for one hundred and sixty years, it was – hard to believe – the reigning taste' (Jencks, 1996: 26). Then, to coin a psychoanalytic idea, modernism suffered the fate of being condemned to repeat what will not be remembered, and reacted to post-modernism with the same vitriol that had been thrown at Corbusier and Gropius by the traditionalists in the 1920s. In 1981, under the heading (once again) 'Decadence', *Le Monde* announced that a spectre was haunting Europe; the spectre of Post-modernism (Lemaire, *Le Monde Dimanche*, 18 October 1981, p. xiv, quoted by Jencks, 1996: 27). With its reference to the 'spectre' image of an earlier time I wonder if M. Lemaire realised how postmodern he had already become with this use of reference and irony. In a lecture published in 1980, the theorist of American modernism, Clement Greenburg, attacked Post-modernism as 'aimless, anarchic, amorphous, self-indulgent, inclusive, horizontally structured and aims for the popular' (Greenburg quoted by Jencks, ibid.). The new 'movement', Post-modernism, had definitely arrived; but how was it to be defined?

Charles Jencks notes how 'An intense commitment to pluralism is perhaps the only thing that unites every post-modern movement' (ibid.: 29). He first applied the term in 1975 to various departures from modernism that had been going on since the 1960s each of which 'questioned the hegemony of modernism; its elitism, reductivism and exclusivism, and its anti-city and anti-history stance' (ibid.). Jencks stands by his (1978) definition of Post-modernism as

> double-coding – the combination of modern techniques with something else (usually traditional building) in order for architecture to communicate with the public and a concerned minority, usually other architects.
>
> (ibid.)

This may be very true of Frank Gehry's house but how could this be so of Jung's Tower which, as a building, is not concerned with the public or with architects or, indeed, how does this relate to Jung's psychology which we are seeking to contextualise? We need to slip into metaphor here so let me restate Jencks with a couple of substitutions: *Double-coding – the combination of modern techniques with something else (usually traditional wisdom) in order for psychology to communicate with the public and a concerned minority, usually other psychologists.* I offer this to help us understand how, in his inclusion of a pluralistic range of 'other' traditional wisdoms, such as Greek mythology, Gnosticism, alchemy and so on, in combination with a modern psychoanalytic attitude and language, Jung develops a radical psychology which challenges modernism in a similar fashion. What needs to be asserted is that Jung does not use aspects of past wisdoms in a reactionary or sentimental yearning for the past, for a golden age of greater humanity. On the contrary, Jung is not citing these as examples of a 'better' humanity but he is employing them in a new way. He stays with our present condition and comments on *this* by the juxtaposition of past forms. He is not comparing like with like and simply letting past traditions show us up for the impoverished neurotics we are, or how the Enlightenment has failed us. What Jung seeks with his juxtapositions is a refraction of modern consciousness and modern culture through *unlike* lenses retrieved from the desert of Western history. His concern is our psychology but he does not compare it with *psychology* of the past but with *cosmology, mythology* and *epistemology* of other eras. It is by creating such original juxtapositions and comparisons that Jung's psychology offers a counterpoint to the narrow horizons offered by modernity. His perspective extends beyond this horizon in all directions: not only where we have come from, but also what surrounds us today and what may lie ahead. If 'the past is another country', we have already emigrated but that does not mean we should forget; indeed, to forget where we have come from, and how so much of what we thought we had left behind is still with us, leaves us disoriented and map-less in hostile territory. This is the danger of modernity; and Jung seeks to allow one of the products of modernity – psychology – to become the thread that will lead us out of the labyrinth. Jung's psychology arises out of, and requires similar solutions to, the dilemma of the architects who Jencks describes as,

> necessarily caught between society at large on the one hand and a very specialised discipline on the other. The only way out of this dilemma is . . . being trained to look two opposite ways at once. Thus the solution I perceived and defined as post-modern: an architecture that was professionally based and popular as well as one that was based on

new techniques and old patterns. To simplify, double coding means elite/popular, accommodating/subversive, and new/old.

(ibid.: 29–30)

Post-modern architects were trained by modernists just as Jung was apprenticed within the modernism of Freud's psychoanalysis, and like them, from *The Theory of Psycho-Analysis* (1913, CW 4) onwards – but not forgetting the Zofingia lectures (1896) of his youth – Jung also wished to 'build and protest at the same time' (Jencks, 1996: 30). Jung's relationship to psychoanalysis parallels the postmodern architects' relationship to the context in which *they* trained, that is, 'the continuation of modernism and its transcendence' (ibid.).

MODERN, LATE-MODERN, POSTMODERN OR WHAT?

At this point it seems appropriate to ask again: why should we regard Jung as postmodern? Would it not be truer to say that Jung's psychology is more Late-modern? In answering this, an examination of such categories as they are analysed within architectural criticism proves illuminating. Jencks points out how two famous buildings – Piano and Rogers' Pompidou Centre in Paris and Norman Foster's Hongkong and Shanghai Bank – have both been erroneously categorised. In the former, 'The modernist emphasis on structure, circulation, open space, industrial detailing and abstraction is taken to its late-modern extreme, although again often mis-termed post-modern'; while Jencks regards Foster's building as 'Post-modern failure, late-modern triumph. The structure is totally designed all the way through, fairly flexible and extremely expensive. A corporate Rolls Royce it epitomises the contradictions of modernity: egalitarian and hierarchical' (Jencks, 1996: 47). Differing from Jameson, Lyotard, Baudrillard and others over the definition of 'Late'-modern, Jencks has this to say:

> It is mostly 'Late' because it is still committed to the tradition of the new and does not have *a complex relation to the past, or pluralism, or the transformation of Western culture, or a concern with meaning, continuity and symbolism.*
>
> (ibid.: 46, italics added)

Judging by this last definition, Jung is disqualified as 'Late-modern' and, within Jencks's frame, qualifies impeccably as postmodern.

I wish to consider two further views deriving from the perspective of the architect before I go on to the 'case example' of Frank Gehry and his house.

Not only do these examples unpack the relationship between modernism, Late-modernism and postmodernism, but, in passing, they also involve two additional, relevant subjects – the philosophy of Nietzsche in one case, and the experience of psychoanalysis in the other.

PHILIP JOHNSON, NIETZSCHE, TRANSVALUATION AND AESTHETICS

In an informative dialogue with the architect Philip Johnson – where, in fact, Jencks does most of the talking – Jencks begins with the anomaly of the 'Modern' as expressed by New York's Museum of Modern Art: 'If it's a museum then it's to do with the past, and if it's "Modern" then it's attacking history' (Jencks, 1990: 154). This is the contradiction normal to Modernism – once it became Establishment it could no longer persist as an adversarial culture always breaking down convention and the Establishment. This is why, in architecture, Post-modernism emerged in the 1960s to break down the hegemony of the Modern Movement – it is 'an attempt to find a new radicalism' (ibid.).

When pushed to cite the philosophical roots of his architecture, Philip Johnson regards Nietzsche as a major influence, quoting his favourite sentence: 'Art is with us so we don't perish from the truth' (ibid.: 157). It is the Nietzschean aspect of both modernism and Post-modernism that permits Jencks to come to the conclusion that in his buildings Johnson is a protagonist of both Late- and post-modernism; not only a critical and deconstructive modernist but also – in the way he has consulted history for its examples – a Post-modernist. In addition, Jencks reckons Johnson is now Neo-modern, a term he thought Johnson himself had coined, but Johnson tells Jencks flatly (twice) 'I never heard it till this afternoon' (ibid.: 158). Jencks adds, hopefully with irony, 'There's another term we could use called "modern modern"' (ibid.: 159), as he digs for further definitions beyond what we might regard as useful, to which Johnson retorts, 'everything gets labelled: that's one thing we don't have to worry about because we have Charles Jencks' (ibid.).

Somehow, within this banter important points are made. Johnson's travelling from Late- to Post- to Neo- is viewed within the 'quintessential aspect of modernism', that is: 'to tear itself up' (ibid.: 164). Marshall Berman's book on modernity, titled with a phrase from Marx – *All That Is Solid Melts Into Air* (1983) – emphasises the great project of permanent renewal that is modernity, 'the power of the bourgeoisie to destroy all the traditions that it creates in its past, even the "Tradition of the New"' (Jencks, 1990: 164). It is a text used by psychoanalytic cultural theorists like Stephen Frosh (1991) to justify the 'hope' in modernity over 'nihilism' of the postmodern and to establish Freud's value as a modernist, as I have referred to in Chapter 2. Jencks, however, identifies this aspect of modernity with a central tenet found in Nietzsche – the 'transvaluation of all values'. And he notes how this transvaluation is now made through the belief in art and culture, while, for the nineteenth century, it was made in factories and in modernisation (Jencks, 1990: 164). I will be debating the relevance of Nietzsche in Chapter 6, but here Jencks is making the important point that modernism depended on *modernisation*. Modernisation no longer exists in the West, where only 12 per cent of the population works in factories, but it now occurs in the Pacific rim countries – the factories of Japan and South Korea, and those of Mexico and Brazil. Thus, Jencks concludes, 'modernism is the Catholic orthodoxy left over from the reality which has long ago disappeared' (ibid.: 165). This is the contradiction: in the absence of economic and technological modernisation, modernism as the 'transvaluation of all values' seems to lack purchase and to lose its grip. Hence the Nietzschean stance of challenging dominant values appears to be without its original context; but does this mean it persists in a vacuum leading to a sense of it being an anachronistic irrelevance? I do not think so. This is the type of slur more commonly thrown at Jung, while, in Nietzsche, as we see in this analysis of architecture, there is discovered a contemporary relevance despite the shift in social context.

This 'rediscovery' of the relevance of Nietzschean modernism offers us yet another way of rediscovering the relevance of Jung. Again there are clues in Jung's essay on *Ulysses*. After criticising Joyce's unmitigated nihilist – 'boring' – art, Jung comes round to finding a value that was not at all apparent in the first instance. Essentially his point is that this book – and by implication this *modernism* – offers a more subtle deconstruction of modernist values. First he admits that, 'What frees a prisoner of a system is an "objective" recognition of his world and of his own nature' (Jung, 1932, CW 15: para. 182). But, specific to modernism and its belief in its own greatness, which Jung criticises as a dangerous obscuring of a fuller human potential, he then notes how the 'nihilism' of *Ulysses* has a specific critical value, 'For the man who is dazzled by the light the darkness is a blessing, and the boundless desert is a paradise to the escaped prisoner' (ibid.). The point is that a critical modernism *is* at the same time *anti-modernist*; furthermore, in the absence of modernisation itself in the West, as I was saying earlier, this critical position gains purchase against a new condition which then constitutes a new context or 'problem'. This new context, for Jung and for contemporary art and architecture, is religious and spiritual: ironically, the very sphere that Enlightenment and then modernisation thought it had overcome and could abandon. Postmodernism is the restored radicalism of modernity. But under these new conditons of the absence of modernisation *postmodernism is the depth of modernity just as the psychology of the unconscious is the depth of psychology.* (As I have said earlier, I also agree that the postmodern clearly has a 'surface' aspect, but this is only a contradiction up to the point where it is realised that *les extrêmes se touchent.*) In both cases, 'depth' refers to what has been buried, to what has been repressed and to what lies in the shadows – the shadows created by the harsh light of Enlightenment and modernity. The postmodern problematic, then, is not only a reflexive twist in modernity but it has the specific quality of drawing our attention to that which modernity, quite rightly at the time, was most keen to abandon. The life of the spirit, the symbolic life, the religious life, had disintegrated into dogma far removed from spiritual values. The 'Catholic orthodoxy' was in need of a challenge. Now this has been accomplished, *it is the challenge that is being challenged.* Ultimately, the transvaluation of all values lies not only in the social, moral and epistemological spheres but in the sphere of spiritual values.

None of this necessarily leads us back to a new fundamentalism, the 'source' or to 'God'. As I have tried to capture in my own phrase *consciousness consciousing*, this is a new spirit, not simply a restoration of pre-modernist values: when Jencks cites postmodern ideas of Derrida and Lyotard on the end of 'meta-narratives', the lack of deep foundations and on there being no direction to history, Johnson replies that, for him, history doesn't have a teleology – but while 'it has no overall "meaning"; . . . it has its own meaning. That is why I hate Plato so much and his idea of objective truth – with the Idea – capital I – having objective existence' (ibid.: 166). This position puts Johnson in strict contrast with a modernist such as 'Le Corbusier and the "religion of modernism" which did have a direction, did have a social agenda' (ibid.) precisely because he was working within the context of modernisation. Jencks finds that Johnson is modernist in a new context and is thus also postmodern with his 'constant embracing of change . . . putting creativity at the top of the agenda . . . celebrating that Nietzschean, Dionysian aspect of creativity and fashion' (ibid.: 168–169). There is a sense here in which the spirit is carried by the aesthetic – a tradition long established in sacred art. Jencks points out how, within the postmodern, aesthetics are prioritised to such a degree they become the ultimate value from which other values can be derived. Post-modernists argue that 'aesthetics has been the legitimiser of uprooting people and destruction. Look at the flip-side of this, what Nietzsche already announced as the "Destructor–Creator" – Superman. He melts things into air as does the cycle of modernisation' asserts Jencks (ibid.: 169).

For Jencks, Philip Johnson reveals a modernism pushed to the point of Post-modernism but without the irony and yet *with* a Nietzschean spirit of the transvaluation of values. I believe that the extent of this analysis is helpful when we come to think about where Jung stands in relation to the postmodern and these Nietzschean values that Jencks reserves for modernism but then somehow has to recognise as postmodern due to the change of social context from early to late twentieth century. As we will see shortly, Frank Gehry is more of a Deconstructionist, but this also means that a similar spirit of the Destructor–Creator – central to a postmodern *spirit* – is involved.

PETER EISENMAN, PSYCHOANALYSIS AND NOSTALGIA

Also in conversation with Charles Jencks, the architect Peter Eisenman agrees that his own consciousness of Deconstruction and decentring stems from his entering intensive psychoanalysis. He did this, he says, 'to become grounded . . . After analysis for the first time I was really able to deal with myself, not as the public wanted me to be, but as I needed to be . . . I knew what I had to do for myself' (ibid.: 210). Eisenman acknowledges that he has slipped in and out of Post-modernism while holding to the idea that 'Being slippery . . . is the trait of a Post-modernist . . . being slippery is part of the discourse' (ibid.: 212), thus revealing, in my view, another quality of the postmodern which affirms it while simultaneously allowing it to slip away. Eisenman's most important statements turn on the themes of the complex relationship with the past and of nostalgia once again – those themes particularly relevant to criticisms of Jung and to his revaluation within the postmodern.

For Eisenman, 'historical imagery . . . tries to move architecture away from itself – to be disjunctive with its past. It tries to move architecture to what I call "between", between its old past and a repressed present' (ibid.: 213). If we employ the substitution applied earlier and this time insert "psyche" in place of "architecture", we may begin to get an image of Jung's relationship with the 'past' – the language of other traditions which he uses to convey his phenomenology of the modern psyche. *Jung's historical imagery tries to move psyche away from itself – to be disjunctive with its past. It tries to move psyche to what I call 'between', between its old past and a repressed present.* However, when Eisenman states 'I think all continuity and tradition deals with a nostalgia for a tradition that is no longer possible . . . I think nostalgia leads to what can be called "the aestheticisation of the banal" which is what Post-modernism is also about', Jencks comes back in disagreement:

Nostalgia can be perfectly healthy or perfectly radical. In the case of the French Revolution, Roman dress and recalling Republican virtues was positive radical nostalgia. In the case of someone recalling his parents, or his background, or his race, or his Jewishness, or his position, or his memory, it's perceived as a very functional and real thing, it's talking about having a feeling for something that was and isn't now. How can memory not be involved with an element of nostalgia, why repress it?

(ibid.: 213)

Jencks points out a distinction that is especially important when it comes to any consideration of past forms, nostalgia, memory and its repression in psychoanalytic and Jungian thought. Eisenman makes the point that he is 'not against memory as a tissue of forgetting. There is a difference between this kind of memory and the sentimentalising of memory which is nostalgia' (ibid.). Jung's use of the 'past' of Greek myth, Gnosticism, alchemy or even the symbols of Christianity, has too easily been criticised as 'nostalgia for a tradition that is no longer possible'. On the contrary, I think we need to revise our opinion along postmodern lines to discover, as Jencks says, a nostalgia that is perfectly healthy and also radical. Rather than presenting a 'sentimentalising of memory', Jung's relationship with the past is far more about finding a fulcrum outside the present – the creating, in Jameson's terms, of a critical distance – a point from which a lever of critique can be operated. This is why Jung makes use of the texts and imagery of alchemy to understand the processes of individuation, analytic treatment and the transference. Jung finds nothing in modernity or in psychoanalysis that is more adequate to the task of understanding certain psychological phenomena. It is strengthening, not sentimentalising, to discover precursors – whether these be the antecedents of his theory as Jung believed of the alchemical texts, or the important strands of a biographical past, memories of past family dynamics, re-remembered as a personal narrative in an analysis.

FRANK GEHRY'S HOUSE

Frank O. Gehry is a highly singular type of architect of whom Charles Jencks writes, 'Fundamentally, architecture seeks to make the transitory aspects of life both monumental and permanent. In a sense, with his (non)architecture, Gehry reverses this role and . . . transforms permanent material into ephemeral plywood' (Jencks, 1990: 198). This is not to say that Gehry only makes insubstantial buildings – far from it. His most recent projects include the Guggenheim Museum in Bilbao, Spain and the Walt

Disney Concert Hall in Los Angeles – both of which are public buildings and constructed on a large scale. For the contemporary city, a cultural centre is 'like our present day cathedrals' (BBC, 1992) but Gehry describes the Walt Disney Concert Hall with typical modesty:

> 'We're not going to the moon – it's not that level of scientific – I wish it was but it's not. All we're doing is taking a normal stone wall veneer and curving it out so it's hanging and we're making continuous curved surfaces which certainly were done in the Renaissance.'
>
> (Gehry, BBC, 1992)

The Concert Hall takes its imagery from sailing boats, dancing Shivas and fish shapes, and has looked to some like a series of sails or a woman's hat at Ascot that is flying away. However, the tone of deconstruction and the sense of a reversal of the permanent that Jencks refers to can be clearly detected when the building is also likened, by its critics, to: 'A pile of rain-soaked cardboard; the contents of a waste paper basket; or, broken crockery' (BBC, 1992). This style or sensibility towards architecture is found to be most relevant in Los Angeles itself. The pluralist, bricoleur quality of Gehry's buildings which use a mixture of materials and technologies, from the present and the past, and which peel back surfaces as well as erecting edifices, is particularly suited to the modern urban sprawl of Los Angeles where an ethnic, economic, and aesthetic heterogeneity vibrantly persists. As one critic comments:

> 'A city is about divergence – about different views of the good life and we shouldn't try to think of ourselves as an integrated culture . . . we should have things in common but friction and difference . . . should be celebrated and also should be allowed. That's the lesson of Gehry – that he's relaxed about it. He says "I'll use ten different materials in a building to represent that heteroarchitecture – that heterogeneity".'
>
> (BBC, 1992)

It is Gehry's own house in a Santa Monica suburb that expresses most vividly the postmodern, deconstructionist, pluralist ethic – the reversal process which 'peels back and reveals, like archaeology, the botched and bungled inner layers which are hidden in any normal work' (Jencks, 1990: 198). And it is this house and, to some extent, Gehry the man – and Gehry's perspective and attitude – that I want to place beside Jung and his Tower to help gain a sense of Jung's qualities and thinking which similarly reveal a postmodern pluralism and a deconstructive ethic that is quite in contrast to the essentialism and regressive romanticism of which he is often accused.

In the analysis of the postmodern both in architecture and in the wider culture, the metaphor of psychoanalysis is often used to convey the essence of postmodern concerns. On the one hand, the metaphor describes the sense of a powerful self-scrutiny and reflection that constitutes the postmodern condition, while on the other, it gets across ideas of peeling back the surface to dissolve the illusion of homogeneity and to reveal contemporary culture and cultural forms in all their disparate heterogeneity. This is similar to how an analytic treatment addresses the fiction of a unitary personality to reveal the complexes, and the population of the inner world of the psyche the modern ego ignores at its peril. With the reversal of conventional architectural aims in Gehry's buildings, 'Like psychoanalysis, a favoured metier of the Deconstructionists, the result may be a patchwork of disconnected elements in search of a story. Analysis, whether critical or psychoanalytic, is not necessarily synthetic or meaningful. It does not unite by idea, theme or aesthetic, nor does it try to change the world for the better. It simply shows the working parts in their semi-autonomous state. As a process of design, however, this method results in an aggregation that is experienced as meaningful' (ibid.: 198–200). The postmodern problematic can partly be framed by asking: Exactly what period do we inhabit? Or, more simply, who are we? Some find the urge to self-scrutiny problematic – fearing we may become more and more 'enveloped by the couch of psychohistory' (Jencks, 1996: 12). However, Jencks takes a different view: 'This need not necessarily be depressing; Socrates, Christ and Thoreau – to name three self-questioners – made deep introspection into an art of strength. Since two-fifths of the world is now forced onto the couch, might we not learn to cultivate this strength?' (ibid.: 13). I would include Jung as a further self-questioner who, as a typical example of contemporary 'psychological man', certainly made deep introspection into an art of strength. And – to slip from metaphor to the literal for a moment – although we know Jung eschewed the couch in preference to facing his patient, his particular self-scrutiny is in line with the general self-reflexive problem to which Jencks refers. As Jung writes in just one of many revealing passages:

> Our cerebral consciousness is like an actor who has forgotten he is playing a role. But when the play comes to an end, he must remember his own subjective reality, for he can no longer continue to live as Julius Caesar or as Othello, but only as himself, from whom he has become estranged by a momentary sleight of consciousness. He must know once again that he was merely a figure on the stage . . . and that there was a producer as well as a director in the background who, as always, will have something very important to say about his acting.
>
> (Jung, 1933, CW 10: para. 332)

Gehry's house, set among ordinary suburban homes in a residential Santa Monica street expresses, perhaps like psychoanalysis, a hyper-reflexivity. But here, instead of using psyche to examine psyche – the 'impossible' task that is psychology – the play is that of architecture about architecture. We should let Gehry himself take up the story:

> 'My wife . . . found this little dumpy house and I knew I couldn't move in to it exactly the way it was. We didn't have a lot of money to spend on it so I got the idea of wrapping it with the new house and leaving the old house intact – 'cause it had an iconic presence in the neighbourhood. And somehow that play of the old and the new led to a pretty strong statement, I guess, about middle-class America and my middle-classness and my relationship to it and my neighbours.'
>
> (Gehry, BBC, 1992)

Gehry describes himself as 'An architect from California that people think of as a weirdo – and I sort of like hiding behind that appellation because it gives me a lot of freedom to do what I want to do' (ibid.). In this he reveals a celebration of, and a confidence in, his individuality that Jung endorsed in himself with remarks like 'I am not a Jungian – I am Jung!' Gehry's 'new house' wrapped around the old one was built from cheap materials juxtaposed and set at angles to each other so that window-frames, glass, wire fencing and metal sheeting created a tension of shapes and elements that disturbed local sensibilities. 'People said that it was just cheapskate and he said, Yeah, that's right. I'm building what your backyard looks like but I'm turning it into an art form' (BBC, 1992). And in an attitude that is reminiscent of the reactions to Freud's first formulations of psychoanalysis and sexuality, the public were similarly offended: '"People next door said, Hey, you can't do that! You can't turn what we don't see into a high art form. That's despicable. That's awful. It's junk." "But," (Gehry replies), "that's how you live"' (Gehry, BBC, 1992). Coincidentally, Frank Gehry, was also 'apprenticed' to a master from Vienna:

> 'I was trained quite well by a Viennese architect to make perfection. I was very discouraged . . . trying to achieve those perfections with the budgets I had. I saw Rauschenberg and Jasper Johns . . . making beautiful work out of junk; and I like buildings under construction better than buildings finished . . . I decided that I would try that route – "Maybe I should become optimistic about the wood-butcher carpentry and use it for what it is – not try to make it what it isn't."'
>
> (ibid.)

Gehry's vision, then, encompasses and transcends several oppositions or dichotomies: the monumental and the transient, the past and the present, the surface and the hidden, heterogeneity and the homogenous, perfection and patchwork, and, perhaps above all, the private and the public. The loss of public space – both in urban building and in the political sense – is a central postmodern concern, and Gehry's work addresses, and holds the tension of, this opposition between the public and the private in symbolic and practical terms. As with any life and any body of creative work, there is a context to Gehry's building that points up all these oppositions so that they become highlighted and are able to generate reflection and critique. Gehry's context is the city of Los Angeles, while Jung's context is the modern soul, but there is a parallel to be found here between the modern city and the modern psyche. Focusing on this stimulates the postmodern urge towards reflection upon relationships between the individual and the collective, and those between the personal and the political – a central concern for post-Jungians such as Andrew Samuels (Samuels, 1993). A particular aspect to Jung as architect of the modern soul – the tension between the individual subject and the collective culture – is reflected by Gehry as architect of the modern city. Similar to Jung, and to Freud before him, 'the achievement of Gehry amongst other things is he's set our condition in front of us in so many different ways . . . for good or for bad. More than any other contemporary architect I can think of he poses to us the problem of what this city really is – has become' (BBC, 1992). Architects of Frank Gehry's generation were architects of the New Deal – 'believing they would go out and be able to design amenities and neighbourhoods in a liberal America' (ibid.). At a certain point, architecture 'began to become the creation of monumental things or of fantastic private spaces and ceased to be the creation of cities and of city fabric' (ibid.) in a way that is analogous to the postmodern shift in psyche. 'That introversion in Los Angeles can actually be related to a historical turning point which was about between 1951 and 1953 when there was a hysterical struggle in this city against public housing and social housing in the name of the Cold War' (ibid.). An environment emerged where architecture danced solely to the tune of the market place – the design of buildings for private corporations or wealthy individuals. Frank Gehry himself thinks 'my politics, my upbringing, everything would suggest that I would be more interested in city planning, in urban design, than just doing houses for wealthy people. I have trouble with that. The clients that do hire me I warn them in advance' (Gehry, BBC, 1992).

Jung's Tower, like the uninvestigated, simplistic view of Jung's psychology, is a private, individual building which, at first glance, appears to have little in common with the collective sphere or with public life in the same way as Gehry's private buildings. But, referring to Gehry's houses, one commentator poses the question: 'Denied a chance to engage on a large scale with the real LA does Gehry's urbanism appear in a sublimated form even in the most private commissions?' (BBC, 1992). Judging by Gehry's comments on his own house and the design of many of his buildings this would seem to be the case. He once said he always wanted to be a politician but he thought his ideas were too strange to be accepted so he became an architect instead. 'He doesn't make political architecture and he doesn't engage in abstract urban planning – instead his buildings represent a particular vision of what the city is and how the city could be' (ibid.). Equally, there is a reflection, and a radical critique, of modernity to be found in Jung's psychology even when it appears to be presented in the form of the psychology of a private individual.

Jung's writing conveys the rich and varied expression of psyche by compiling layers of illustration, reference and metaphor from sources as diverse as Christian and Mithraic symbolism, Eastern philosophy, medieval alchemy, contemporary anthropology, quantum physics, Greek mythology, and so on. Gehry, too, builds his reflection of what 'we' are through a diverse combination of signs and effects. The Chiat/Day office building, in Venice, Los Angeles, is adorned at the front with a giant pair of binoculars designed by the artist Klaus Oldenberg. Inside,

> 'what Frank has done has made it sensuous, amusing and full of different building types. In other words, when you go in there you don't know whether you're in a home, or whether you're in the theatre, or in the downtown of a city, or in a theatrical set from Hollywood or what. It cuts across all the categories – even the sacred – so when you get inside one of his most effective rooms which is covered with cardboard, and the air changes, your pulse changes, the sound changes because it soaks up all the reverberation, you think you're in the Parthenon in Rome. It's one of the most sacred spaces I've ever been in. It's extraordinary to find it in the middle of an office building.'
>
> (Charles Jencks interviewed in BBC, 1992)

Reading Jung, or being involved in Jungian psychotherapy, can convey the same effect for many of us and, I maintain, carries a parallel postmodern expression of, and comment upon, who 'we' are, and, maybe, *how we got here and where we are heading.*

CARL JUNG'S TOWER

The nineteenth century saw the rise of professional scientific interest in two emerging disciplines – those of geology and archaeology. Together with Darwin's theory of evolution, these three fields of scientific study came to be used as powerful metaphors for expressing other aspects of human life in the new 'science' of psychoanalysis. The geological image was one of layer upon layer piled up through historical time but visible at a glance through the study of a sectional view of a rock or a cliff-face. The archaeological image also spoke of something 'buried', but in this case the image emphasised a surface layer with its 'history' hidden beneath it. Moreover, what lay buried not only had to be unearthed, but also to be interpreted and translated into a 'meaning' for the present. In several passages throughout the Standard Edition of his works, Sigmund Freud uses archaeological imagery to convey the concepts and aims of psychoanalysis. At its richest, this also involves the colonialist image of the exploration of terrain never previously visited by modern man, an image of hacking back obstacles and revealing ruined forms that then have to be deciphered and reconstructed. There is an example from *The Aetiology of Hysteria* (Freud, 1896, SE 3: 192) in which Freud makes an analogy between conscious and unconscious, on the one hand, and surface appearance and hidden meaning, on the other. In addition to this, the way the initially 'unreadable inscriptions' (ibid.) become eventually 'deciphered and translated' (ibid.), combines with the image of the analyst as a heroic explorer-detective to provide *the* grand metaphor of psychoanalysis.

What do we find when we look for Jung's version of a 'layers' model of the psyche? What is Jung's metaphor? In *Memories, Dreams, Reflections* (Jung, 1983/1963: 182–183), Jung details a dream which, he tells us, 'became for me a guiding image which in the days to come was to be corroborated to an extent I could not at first suspect' (ibid.: 185). The dream involved Jung descending through the layers of a house where each room he entered he identified as progressively older in architectural style. The upper storey had 'a kind of salon furnished with fine old pieces in a rococo style' (ibid.: 182), below this the next room dated from the fifteenth or sixteenth century, 'The furnishings were mediaeval; the floors were of red brick' (ibid.). Beyond this Jung describes his descent into 'a beautifully vaulted room which looked exceedingly ancient. Examining the walls, I discovered layers of brick among the ordinary stone blocks, and chips of brick in the mortar. As soon as I saw this I knew that the walls dated from Roman times' (ibid.). The final layer of the building is a cave – 'Thick dust lay on the floor, and in the dust were scattered bones and broken pottery, like remains of a primitive culture' (ibid.: 183). Jung dreamt this on the voyage to the USA he took with Freud and Ferenczi in 1909, and he reports it in the context of discovering how there were aspects of his inner world and his theorising about the psyche which he was finding difficult to share with Freud. Jung was struggling at the time with questions about Freud's psychoanalysis – especially the question: 'What is the relationship of its almost exclusive personalism to general historical assumptions?' (ibid.: 185). Jung tells us Freud produced a personalised interpretation of the dream, but for Jung, 'It was plain to me that the house represented a kind of image of the psyche – that is to say, of my then state of consciousness, with hitherto unconscious additions. Consciousness was represented by the salon. It had an inhabited atmosphere, despite its antiquated style. The ground floor stood for the first level of the unconscious . . . In the cave, I discovered . . . the world of the primitive man within myself – a world which can scarcely be reached or illuminated by consciousness' (ibid.: 184).

Jung's 'layers' metaphor, then, emerges as something rather different from the archaeological image coined by Freud. In the latter, the focus is on an heroic modernist enterprise of reconstruction – a discovery and a rebuilding of the 'truth' of the other: the 'truth' of an earlier civilisation and the 'truth' of the repressed contents of a personal unconscious that are hidden beneath the hysterical symptoms. For Jung, the layers of his dream building meant something quite different and distinct from Freud's model of the psyche and the original conception of the psychoanalytic project. In pondering the question of the relationship between the personal and impersonal-historical, Jung found that 'My dream was giving me the answer. It obviously pointed to the foundations of cultural history – a history of successive layers of consciousness. My dream thus constituted a kind of structural diagram of the human psyche; it postulated something of an altogether *impersonal* nature underlying that psyche' (ibid.: 185). The dream inspired Jung to return to a study of archaeology, myths and the Gnostics which, in combination with his study of the fantasies of the patient Miss Miller, eventually led to the publication of *The Psychology of the Unconscious* (Jung, 1912, CW 5) – arguably Jung's first text of analytical psychology as distinct from psychoanalysis.

Post-Jungians like Andrew Samuels criticise the Jungian metaphor of the psyche as a house – with its layers, its rooms, its ascending and descending and its hidden features. I am sympathetic to this criticism but not entirely so. Samuels's point is that such an image of the psyche tends to be hierarchical in the way 'upper' levels are privileged over the 'lower'. In postmodern times this image jars with the pluralism evident across contemporary individual and cultural life. Why should the psyche be a house or any sort of building at all? Samuels asks (Samuels, 1989: 26). He favours the image of a network where different *aspects* – not 'layers' – of psyche may predominate from time to time, not within a hierarchy, but competitively and with none privileged over the other. What is important in this view is the emphasis on the *dialogue* achieved between these aspects of psyche – the way they communicate – which has implications for, amongst other things, a more egalitarian relationship between the 'healthy', the neurotic and the psychotic parts of the psyche.

Samuels regards the dominance of the 'building' image of the psyche as the result of our hunger for structure in Western European thinking. But there is another way of looking at all this. What if, as seems to be the case with postmodern architecture I have been discussing, buildings are less about ourselves *being structured* – as was the modernists' aim – and more about a concrete expression of our humanity *deconstructed* to reveal the plural psyche in concrete – in both the individual and the cultural sense? After all, where is the hierarchy in the buildings of Frank Gehry? It is precisely this element that his architecture seeks to abandon. His buildings are sublimely pluralistic with their references to the expensive and the cheapskate, to the individual and to the collective and to the past and the present. Postmodern architecture is in fact a revolt against the hierarchy and structuring which tends to dominate the over-rationalised lives we lead. Postmodern buildings are the reverse of what Samuels finds worst about the 'house' metaphor, they are about pluralism and not hierarchy, reference rather than essentialism.

With these thoughts, I think it is possible to view Jung's psychology in a different way. Re-reading Jung's 'house' dream from our postmodern position at the end of the twentieth century, I think it is legitimate to regard it as not so much a hierarchical model of the psyche but one that is more expansive and less rational, with many spaces for consciousness to inhabit or to be inspired by. Although Jung does refer to the 'primitive', the 'deeper', the 'darker' and the 'alien', his intention is not to deprioritise these aspects by the creation of hierarchical layers but to achieve precisely the reverse. Jung, in my view, seeks to 'raise' the abandoned spaces that modernity neglects into a full and restored significance that places them, not 'beneath', or even 'above', but *alongside* all the other 'higher' aspects. His dream home, his psyche-as-a-house, is an *inclusive* model or metaphor, not a divisive, excluding one; the model includes the function of 'depth' and 'going down' with the intention of challenging that which modernity represses, that which the surface keeps hidden. To mistake this as the creation of a heirarchy in the psyche is a misinterpretation. Towards the end of his essay on Joyce's *Ulysses*, when Jung becomes more appreciative of the book's significance he offers us an image that seems to parallel what I am saying about his house metaphor. Jung imagines Ulysses as a being, a symbol of what makes up the totality of all the singularities that constitute Joyce's modernist novel,

> Try to imagine a being who is not a mere colourless conglomerate
> soul composed of an indefinite number of ill-assorted and antagonistic
> individual souls, but consists also of houses, street-processions, churches,
> the Liffey, several brothels, and a crumpled note on its way to the sea –
> and yet possesses a perceiving and registering consciousness!
>
> (Jung, 1932, CW 15: para. 198)

There is no hierarchy here but an inclusive, embracing vision of humanness
and human life that challenges the narrow discriminations of modernity
and makes *Ulysses*, 'truly a devotional book for the object-besotted, object-
ridden white man!' (ibid.: para. 201). Jung's psychology goes beyond
the challenge to modernity and brings a greater vision of healing for
the 'object-ridden white man'; Jung's books, 'have, like the doctor, some
magical incalculability, some gift to probe a wound and assuage it in the
same breath' (Sergeant, 1931: 70). Like Ulysses the symbol, and similar to
a Frank Gehry building, Jung's psychology brings us disjunctive elements
and heterogenous juxtapositions in a combination that, taken as a whole,
expresses the contemporary 'architecture' of the modern, or postmodern,
Western soul.

Jung did not only dream buildings but from very early on he had a practical
relationship to stone and construction which led to his building of the
Tower at Bollingen, on the shore of Lake Zurich in Switzerland. There
is no way I can claim this to be an example of postmodern architecture
in itself, but, if we bear in mind what has just been said about the
house-psyche metaphor, and add to this the way that Jung quite explicitly
regards the building as a manifestation of his own subjective states, the
postmodern significance of the Tower will become clear. The themes I wish
the reader to bear in mind are the combination of disjunctive elements:
subjectivity and otherness, the past and the present, the 'civilised' and the
'primitive', and the 'wrapping' of successive layers over time. Visitors
have regularly described the building as 'medieval', 'a fairy castle' and
a 'hideout' (McGuire and Hull, 1980: 64, 164, 170) and all the reports
mention thick stone walls and the great wooden door (ibid.). In *Memories,
Dreams, Reflections* (Jung, 1983/1963: 250–265), Jung devotes a whole
chapter to the building of the Tower, and to what the building and the
subsequent stone carvings he made there meant to him. He also tells us
about various experiences linked to the place which link the land, the earth
the buildings occupy, to the recent history of the place. For instance, when
he began to build in 1923 his eldest daughter exclaimed 'What, you're
building here? There are corpses about!' (ibid.: 258). This seemed fanciful
at the time but building the next stage four years later, Jung did come across

a skeleton with a rifle bullet in its elbow – 'It belonged to one of the many dozens of French soldiers who were drowned in the Linth in 1799 and were later washed up on the shores of the upper lake' (ibid.). Another time, Jung heard voices and music near the Tower which, on the one hand, he understood as the compensatory hallucination of a crowd as experienced by the hermit in solitude, but which, on the other hand, he linked to a historical event – the gathering in medieval times of young mercenaries who marched from central Switzerland to Italy where they served as soldiers fighting for foreign princes.

Apart from this tendency to refer to past historical times as he situates the Tower both in thought and in space, Jung emphasises a primitivity to the building which also appears to refer 'backwards': 'in its location and style it points backwards to things of long ago. There is very little about it to suggest the present. If a man of the sixteenth century were to move into the house, only the kerosene lamp and the matches would be new to him' (ibid.: 264). There is no electricity or running water at Bollingen and the aim of this sort of primitivity for Jung is *simplicity*. 'I chop the wood and cook the food. These simple acts make man simple; and how difficult it is to be simple!' (ibid.: 253).

In one way this 'regression' to the primitive and the simple can be viewed solely as a romantic, Walden-like effort to 'get closer to nature' with the idea that there is something fundamental that man cannot get in touch with in himself otherwise. But there is also something in this that seems reminiscent of Frank Gehry when he speaks of his own Santa Monica house, deconstructed and wrapped – rather than constructed – as a comment on the junky – for this read, 'primitive'? – and normally hidden away back yards of his neighbours in the street. In both cases it is not so much an urge to 'get back' to nature, or to simplicity, or to fundamentals, as it is *a way of challenging modernity and the present and its assumption of progress and superiority achievable through a greater and greater sophistication of technology.* Additionally, as was said earlier when considering Philip Johnson's buildings, 'reading' the Tower in a late twentieth-century postmodern context – that is, in the absence of modernisation which would have provided a frictional purchase until recently – there is an aesthetic function we need to observe. This is the spirit captured in the Nietzschean aphorism Johnson quotes: 'Art is with us so we don't perish from the truth'. In other words, as an aesthetic product of individual creativity, Jung's Tower represents and expresses his response to modernity in much the same way as his more critically explicit texts (in CW 10, for example) and his psychological concepts – such as individuation, self, the complex and the objective psyche. Far from being simply a Romantic rejection of and retreat from modernity, Jung's Tower is an aesthetic embodiment of Jung's own individuating psyche – which is itself the lived critique of modernity he formalises in his psychological writing. Jung's building, Jung's life and Jung's writing are presenting several facets – different perspectives or plains – of the same critique.

One visitor to Bollingen wrote of Jung in 1931:

> I had seen him often as a highly civilised modernist, driving a red Chrysler though the twisting streets of Zurich . . . before I came upon the primitive Jung, one rainy summer day, outside his favourite dwelling place – a grey stronghold, of mediaeval outline, standing alone and apart, surrounded by hills and water . . . Ensconced there in the shelter of the round stone tower which he had built with his own hands, dressed in a bright blue linen overall, with his powerful arms in a tub of water, I beheld Doctor Jung earnestly engaged in washing his blue jeans.
>
> (Sergeant, 1931: 65–66)

The pluralism and complexity of this image of Jung is sublime. The appearance of someone like the apron-clad cobbler from *The Elves and the Shoemaker*, but set in the far more substantial surroundings of a medieval stronghold, is simultaneously overlaid with an image straight from the modern age of production-line cars and internationally mass-produced leisure-wear. How often do we think of Jung in his Levis cruising Zurich in a red American car like a character out of F. Scott Fitzgerald? This is not a trivial question but one that highlights what the Tower, and Jung's psychology, is more about. It is not simply the case of an anti-modernist search for fundamentals in the 'past', or in the 'simple', or even in the 'primitive'; no, for Jung, reference to and connection with all these are just part of the pluralistic task Jung calls individuation – *becoming the person you were intended to be, or, becoming what one always was*. In this, past, present and future are mixed up so that there is no one-way traffic but there are flows in both directions at all times. We need to know the past in ourselves to fully live in the present and guide the future, or else we are dragged there unconsciously by events themselves with little regard for human need. This is very much a postmodern position – one that seeks to question the modernist myth of progress riding on the back of science. At times, Jung is quite unambiguous in his critique of modernity:

> we have plunged down a cataract of progress which sweeps us on into the future . . . Once the past has been breached, it is usually annihilated, and there is no stopping the forward motion. But it is precisely the loss of connection with the past, our uprootedness, which has given rise to

the 'discontents' of civilisation and to such a flurry and haste that we live more in the future and its chimerical promises of a golden age than in the present . . . We rush impetuously into novelty, driven by a mounting sense of insufficiency, dissatisfaction and restlessness. We no longer live on what we have, but on promises, no longer in the light of the present day, but in the darkness of the future, which, we expect, will at last bring the proper sunrise.

(Jung 1983/1963: 263)

For Jung, individuation, whether expressed in the stone of Bollingen or in his writing, is nothing more or less than being fully oneself. This means including parts of oneself that have been lost or neglected not only due to circumstances of personal history – parents, upbringing and so on – but have also been lost or neglected due to the collective conditions of the era and culture: for Jung and ourselves in the developed West this means the era of late-modern industrial capitalism. However, the personal and the collective, as well as the past and the present, are difficult to differentiate and separate in any final way:

A collective problem, if not recognised as such, always appears as a personal problem, and in individual cases may give the impression that something is out of order in the realm of the personal psyche. The personal sphere is indeed disturbed, but such disturbances need not be primary; they may well be secondary, the consequence of an insupport able change in the social atmosphere. The cause of disturbance is, therefore, not to be sought in the personal surroundings, but rather in the collective situation. Psychotherapy has hitherto taken this matter far too little into account.

(ibid.: 261)

Since Jung wrote this, post-Jungians such as James Hillman, Andrew Samuels (1993) and Michael Vannoy Adams (1996a), amongst others, have specifically addressed this important aspect that has been underemphasised during the period when Jungian psychology has been subsumed within the personally focused world of post-Freudian psychoanalytic psychotherapy.

Beginning in 1923, Jung built the Tower at Bollingen in several stages over a period that spanned thirty years. Far from developing within a paradigm of structure and hierarchy, the Tower spread and grew almost organically in parallel with Jung's own individuation and the needs that arose in him at different times in his life. It was never conceived, or architecturally designed as a whole – or even constructed in layers from the bottom up. It is true that Jung regards the last addition, an upper storey added after his wife died in 1955, as representing his ego-personality, thus fulfilling the 'hierarchy' criticism: 'Earlier, I would not have been able to do this; I would have regarded it as presumptuous self-emphasis. Now it signified an extension of consciousness achieved in old age. With that the building was complete' (Jung, 1983/1963: 252). However, this is not the *only* way the building expresses Jung's psyche and individuation. The metaphor has a greater plurality in this case. The building of the Tower sprang from a need in Jung 'to achieve a kind of representation in stone of my innermost thoughts and of the knowledge I had acquired' (ibid.: 250). He did not plan a proper house but just a primitive one-storey dwelling, 'It was to be a round structure with a hearth in the centre and bunks along the walls. I more or less had in mind an African hut where the fire, ringed by a few stones, burns in the middle, and the whole life of the family revolves around this centre' (ibid.). In this we notice one of Jung's many references to the *other* – not only the other of the past but the contemporary other that is the otherness of different cultures which Jung also values deeply in a fashion that eschews hierarchy and celebrates difference. But, probably realising that the ambition of a primitive hut that could 'concretise an idea of wholeness' (ibid.) was over-idealistic, Jung abandoned this as 'too primitive' (ibid.) and instead built a simple, round, two-storey house. This represented for Jung the maternal hearth and gave him a feeling of repose and renewal, but he became aware that 'it did not yet express everything that needed saying, . . . something was still lacking' (ibid.: 250–251). So, four years later, the central structure was added with a tower-like annex.

Again, after a four-year gap, the 'incompleteness' feeling came upon Jung – he felt the building 'still seemed too primitive' (ibid.: 251). He wanted a room apart entirely for himself where he could guarantee being alone (after all, although Jung is not specific about this himself, he did have five children who were inevitably producing the first of his nineteen grandchildren) – and once again Jung cites another culture for illustration: 'I had in mind what I had seen in Indian houses, in which there is an area . . . to which the inhabitants can withdraw. There they meditate for perhaps a quarter or half an hour, or do yoga exercises. Such an area of retirement is essential in India, where people live crowded very close together' (ibid.). Jung extended the tower-like annex less out idealism but for more practical reasons. He created a room which acknowledged and, literally, provided space for this stage of his individuation. The emphasis was on a deep inwardness that Jung engaged with at the same time as, and as complementary to, a busy public and professional life at the beginning of the 1930s. Here, Jung tells us, 'In the course of years I have done paintings on the walls, and so have expressed all those things which have carried me out of time into seclusion, out of the present into timelessness. Thus the second tower became for me a place of spiritual concentration' (ibid.) and, I would add, an architectural space that expressed his psyche's personal spiritual space, which itself represents the collective search for spiritual space we may witness in a variety of forms in postmodern times. After another four years, a courtyard and a loggia by the lake were constructed in response to Jung's need for a larger space open to the sky and to nature. He saw this development as the completion of a quaternity, and achieved over twelve years, thus drawing the comparison with his own individuation and contact with the self. Much later in 1955 he added the upper storey as mentioned above. 'I suddenly realised that the small central section which crouched so low, so hidden, was myself! I could no longer hide myself behind the "maternal" and the "spiritual" towers' (ibid.). It seems highly significant that Jung puts these words in quotes now – an action that suggests Jung's conscious awareness of these terms as *portmanteau* words – sliding signifiers – in stark contrast to using them as referring to something fundamental or essential. I believe it is this refusal to be weighed down by language and concepts, necessary for Jung's own expression but derived ultimately from the discourse of modernity that surrounds us, that suggests Jung is both deconstructing hierarchy while still having to think within terms that seek to include it (such as conscious/unconscious, of course). I will go into the theme of language in Jung and postmodern theory in more detail in Chapter 8.

CONCLUDING REMARKS AND OTHER POINTS OF VIEW

The aim of this chapter has been to explore the postmodern through its expression in architecture and thereby refine some of the ideas and definitions – especially those around the use of past forms, nostalgia and history – begun in the first chapter. It struck me that the idiosyncratic self-expression of Frank Gehry's house, which has aspects that are both individual and collective, could be compared with Jung's house – the Tower at Bollingen. There is a critical commentary on modernity and modern times to be found in both buildings, which, although expressed in different vocabularies, speaks with a comparable postmodern voice. Jung is seldom recognised for this aspect of his thinking and work, and I offer this playful comparison with Gehry's postmodern architecture as an approach to the recontextualising of the Jungian perspective which reveals it as so relevant for our postmodern times. Recently, other writers have also drawn parallels between aspects of Jung's thought and various qualities and themes to be found in architecture. None of these writers explore the same theme as mine above, none mention the Tower, and all pursue their themes – for example, individuation (Tyng, 1990), wholeness (Lundquist, 1990) and containment and regeneration (Levine, 1990) – in a rather globalised and essentialist manner. Although what they say is interesting, they are typical of the view of Jung that promotes the universalist ideas in his writing at the expense of his critical, more postmodern position. Tyng takes a theory about the phases of architecture expressing cycles of entropy and creativity and compares these phases to the phases of individuation that Jung describes in his later thought (Tyng, 1990). In doing so she attacks the postmodern with the usual slur of 'superficial' as if postmodern qualities could not also express the energy of the collective unconscious: 'Much of the highly publicised current architecture of this phase has lost its power in superficial and personal "historicism" split off from the archetypal energy of the collective unconscious. Perverse and too-clever witticisms of postmodernism are the limp froth of this spiral form empathy' (ibid.: 111). She excepts the Pompidou Centre and the Hongkong and Shanghai Bank buildings from this for having a level of integrity and vitality, but, as I have discussed earlier in this chapter, Tyng has not recognised these buildings for the Late-modern capitalist edifices they are and mistakes them for being a version of the postmodern.

Lundquist (1990) writes about temples, mandalas and wholeness, spending much time quoting Jung's own reports on his visits to temples and Jung's 'wholeness' dream set in Liverpool. Again the aim seems to be towards an homogenising of the human spirit, rather than recognising the plurality of the individual and collective psyche where 'wholeness' is just another perspective among many. Levine (1990) provides a most interesting paper about the architecture of Frank Lloyd Wright (died 1959) who was a contemporary of Jung and only seven years older. Levine writes about Wright's attempts to integrate 'nature' or the landscape with his buildings and his preoccupation with 'containment' and the 'original' function of buildings as shelter. Linking these themes with the tragic events of Wright's life, Levine also notes how Wright later incorporated large pots into the buildings, so both pot and building served as archetypal containing vessels for regeneration – 'the pot provided a continuous image of inside and outside at once while remaining stable and permanent in shape' (Levine, 1990: 130).

Although these examples are laudable for their linking of Jung's ideas with other cultural and individual themes in architecture, in doing so they emphasise the apparently 'essential' in Jung – a tendency that is common to too much of the Jungian commentary. My aim in this chapter has been to link cultural themes in architecture to the aspects of Jung that get under-played – those aspects which coincide with postmodern concerns around modernity, the complex relationship with the past and the other, difference, doubleness and plurality – and which make Jung and post-Jungian thinking so vital to any discussion of the individual subject and the social context at the start of the twenty-first century.

5 Postmodern Gender: Masculine, Feminine and the Other

DEALING WITH THE ESSENTIAL

Having spent many pages up till now arguing for the postmodern qualities in Jung's psychology, it is now time to consider where Jung appears far more essentialist, conformist, and, to the contemporary reader, reactionary. In a way that is quite in contrast to his radical critique of modernity and modern consciousness and rationality, Jung's perspective on the feminine, and on the psychological attributes of, and differences between, men and women strikes many as old-fashioned, irrelevant and often offensive. In Jung's psychology, women and men appear to be tied to the abstract principles of *eros* and *logos* with a rigidity that compares with Freud's more physiological emphases on the presence or absence of a penis as formative of psychological difference. Granted, there is an emphasis on the contra-sexual element to be found in the unconscious of a man or a woman which Jung formulates as the archetype of the *anima* in the first case and the *animus* in the latter. But this only serves to deepen the tendency towards essentialisms in Jung – a universalising trend that finds its ultimate expression in his theory of the archetypes of the collective unconscious, itself.

It strikes me that there are a number of ways to approach this issue: in the first place, we need to examine some of the received wisdom that says that the postmodern condition is characterised by the end of grand narratives, the demise of all essentialist concepts, and the rise in an acceptance and legitimation of small-scale 'truths' that comprise local narratives and discourses and so promote a valuation of plurality and difference. Apart from the obvious contradiction that such a view forms a grand narrative of itself and contains its own essentialism, it has also been pointed out how the whole business of the universal and the local forms a tense contradiction within late capitalism that does not resolve itself in either direction. For example, while, on the one hand, multinational enterprise and the global economy tends to result in a flattening of differences on the grand scale so we may travel thousands of miles to encounter identical products – like Coca-Cola and McDonald's – chain stores and services, on the other hand, the high street has never before witnessed such an ethnic diversity of foods, artefacts, materials and images drawn from every quarter of the globe. Before the 1970s in the UK it was difficult to find a provincial greengrocer who had heard of sweet peppers or avocado pears let alone stocked them. The same trend in world-shrinking trade results in very contrasting effects when experienced either at the global level or at the local level. One level assumes we wish to drink Coca-Cola or Heineken (I get nothing for this product placement, by the way) or watch Disney's *The Lion King* wherever our plane touches down, while the local level assumes the very opposite: that we *don't* wish to eat the same thing every night but want to vary our diet between Indian, Chinese, Thai, Italian, Jamaican, Japanese, Ghanaian cuisine every night – or at least appreciate the opportunity to do so. This is one example of the argument from the world-economy, but the end of grand narratives and universalising, essentialist beliefs refers more usually to the shift between a modern and a postmodern position on knowledge, or, to put this more accurately, *the legitimation of knowledge*. For many commentators, the postmodern is characterised by what Lyotard calls the end of master narratives, but Fredric Jameson in his foreword to Lyotard's *The Postmodern Condition: A Report on Knowledge* (1984), points out how,

> paradoxically . . . the vitality of small narrative units at work everywhere *locally* in the present social system, are accompanied by . . . a more global or totalising 'crisis' in the narrative function in general, since . . . the older master-narratives of legitimation no longer function in the service of scientific research – nor, by implication, anywhere else (e.g. we no longer believe in political or historical teleologies, or in the great 'actors' and 'subjects' of history – the nation-state, the proletariat, the party, the West, etc.).
>
> (Jameson, in Lyotard, 1984: xi–xii)

In other words, 'local', sometimes marginal, narrative truths persist throughout the postmodern scene as 'sub-narratives', if you like, which Jameson explains by positing,

> not the disappearance of the great master-narratives, but their passage underground as it were, their continuing but now *unconscious* effectivity as a way of 'thinking about' and acting in our current situation. This persistence of buried master-narratives in what I have elsewhere called our 'political unconscious' . . .
>
> (ibid.: xii)

Contemporary culture has thrown into us into a great uncertainty about unitary 'truths': moral values, the purpose of human life, the belief in human progress and, perhaps above all, the inviolable trust in scientific investigation and its ability to reveal the world's and nature's secrets. This loss of master discourses and the shift from certainty to uncertainty has produced the necessity for a greater and greater tolerance of difference and of incommensurability. Expressed in forms of 'local' narratives which do not make claim to being whole 'truths', such 'local' forms of knowledge are always in tension with the opposing tendency to cling to unitary truths. It seems that this distinction between 'local' forms and master narratives is useful when discussing gender issues under postmodern conditions. In the discussion of masculine and feminine attributes and gender roles and differences, attempts to produce definitive truths consistently keep emerging. More often than not such attempts to pin down gender differences and essentials rely on biological, evolutionary and anthropological 'evidence' as if the scientism of such investigations contains a privileged 'truth'. However, when the power of scientific rationality itself is seriously challenged in postmodern times, the establishing of questionable facts on the basis of other questionable facts proves a fruitless exercise. There arises a plurality of views and a plurality of 'truths' which are seen to be contextually dependent in the extreme. When it comes to the position of women themselves, it hardly needs pointing out how the master narratives of modernity have been literally just that – the discourse of the masters, or rather, of patriarchy. As Maureen O'Hara writes: 'When every "system of truth" . . . has concluded that women are biologically, intellectually and morally inferior, that we are at once dangerous and naturally nurturing, that we are unsuitable for public office and should be protected and subjugated – then you bet feminists have a stake in conversations about "truth" and "reality"!' (O'Hara, 1996: 147).

Any examination of the tension between the universal and the local, and between essentialist beliefs and diverse, local forms of knowledge obviously throws up problems of how we are to regard Jung's theory of archetypes and his views on feminine and masculine psychology, both of which appear highly universalising and essentialist in the grand narrative style. It is due to this that these concepts have been subjected to a good deal of criticism – not least from Jungian scholars and analysts themselves. It is with these post-Jungian writers who are the focus of the present chapter that we are most likely to come across a re-reading of Jung's psychology within the postmodern frame; this is not to excuse Jung for the essentialist aspects of his views, but, having admitted these, to then note how post-Jungians take up such important themes such as male and female psychology and the concepts of *anima/animus* in an effort to examine them for their relevance in the present. This project is no less legitimate then, and compares to, the feminist re-examination of Freud's 'dark continent' of women through Lacanian lenses, only to discover the limits of this and develop further, more individual, psychoanalytic feminist theories as have Julia Kristeva and others who I mention later. What this argument amounts to is, similar to Jameson quoted above, the recognition of a state where the grand-narratives do not disappear, but where their authority no longer holds so fast and thus renders them more malleable, more plastic in the hands of the user. To return to the metaphor of postmodern economy, the grand theories are required to become more consumer friendly or 'consumer responsive' if you like; knowledge, like everything else, becomes more consumer driven. The negative aspect of this results in a 'pick-and-mix' knowledge which tends to lose any persuasive power or weight, but on the positive side there emerges a democratisation of knowledge which retains the value of the earlier narratives or discourses while also asserting the validity of criticising these from 'local' positions that may be novel to the discourse but have the effect of expanding its frame and its 'truth'.

THE GENDER PARADIGM

In addition to the end of grand-narratives, a further defining quality of the postmodern condition is the end of a unitary, single self. It is no longer enough to *be* – the tendency towards hyper self-reflection in contemporary culture constantly prompts questions about *this being* or *that being*, questions that are ultimately about the subjective identity, or identities, of each man and woman. Psychology as a way of self-reflection is typical of postmodern times: given the degree of uncertainty around the dominant forms of rationality which have been scientific, instrumental and extra-verted, it seems inevitable that psychology should have arisen as a new perspective. Once established in culture, psychology has then fed back into self-consciousness its doubts about that very rationality and influenced its assumptions – thus changing the idea of 'knowing' and taking human culture to a different plane of self-experience. The rediscovery of the unconscious at the end of the last century arose at the height of the success of Enlightenment rationality to deliver material benefits through the achievement of industrial technology – just at the moment when such successes were beginning to be doubted. The role of psychology since then has been to help us live with the consequences – but only if it is recognised for what it is, a *critical practice*, and not mistaken for a further 'scientific truth'. This is why Jung insisted we paid the greatest attention both to consciousness and to what influences it – the rest of the psyche in the form of the personal and the collective unconscious. It need not matter so much here whether these elements, consciousness, personal unconscious, collective unconscious, are described in the language of previous sciences like biology, ecology or even evolutionary theory – what matters, and what Jung saw, was that the self-reflective attention of human consciousness to itself could no longer be ignored as if it was somehow less relevant to the world of truth and matter. Jung saw that psychology was less about an objective analysis of the human mind and more about the recognition that consciousness *constructs reality*. For some time now, post-Jungians have paid close attention to this facet of analytical psychology which Michael Vannoy Adams refers to as the 'psychical construction of reality' (Adams, 1991). These writers – more of whom we will encounter in Chapter 8 – take Jung's psychology as the starting point for addressing and deconstructing our contemporary construction of reality which is addressed elsewhere by postmodern thinkers, and along the way they do not shirk at the task of deconstructing Jung's psychology itself. This is especially so in the field of gender and the psychological theories attached to it. The post-Jungian analyst Andrew Samuels, whose work on gender will be discussed later, is explicit about where he is coming from:

> You will gather from these remarks that post-Jungian analytical psychology is part of a post-structural intellectual matrix – or, rather, that when I employ the term 'post-Jungian', I am deconstructing analytical psychology. The key terms are now interaction – of psychic themes, patterns, images, behaviour, emotions, instincts – and relativity – archetypes in the eye of the beholder, a dethroned self, and democratic individuation.
>
> (Samuels, 1990: 295)

For many years, challenges to long-held assumptions about masculine and feminine 'nature', 'identity', 'behaviour' and so on have persisted but it is perhaps more recently, over the last twenty years, that feminist discourse has formed part of postmodern critique. Some have felt that the first wave of feminist critique during the 1960s and 1970s was more typically modernist in its aims and its tone. Following Lyotard's identification of two types of 'legitimation narrative' typical of Enlightenment modernism, the feminist movement seemed to qualify as a continuation of this in two ways. On the one hand, its emphasis on women's liberation forms part of an 'emancipation narrative', while on the other, the focus on 'consciousness raising' which aimed to provide greater insight into male power forms part of the second legitimation narrative of speculative knowledge generated for its own sake. Stuck within the patriarchal discourses of Enlightenment 'women could occupy only a range of pre-given positions: they could write only as surrogate men' (Thornham, 1998: 43). Given the Western, bourgeois, white, heterosexual origins of Enlightenment discourses, the essential woman of feminist theory would then be 'as partial, as historically contingent and as exclusionary as her male counterpart' (ibid.). There has needed to be a shift away from the universalised 'woman' to an emphasis on differences between women and on the partial nature of 'knowledge(s)' around the feminine. As Sue Thornham puts it: 'once it occupies this position, feminist thought would seem to move away from its Enlightenment beginnings, and to have much in common with postmodernist theory' (ibid.: 43–44).

The feminist challenge these days, then, is not only enlightening and emancipatory, but, like postmodernism itself, it also contains implications for pluralism, for the acknowledgement of difference without hierarchy and for the questioning of a unitary self – a self that has been consistently based on a fixed gender identity. But, above all, these challenges to assumptions about gender are not only a visible result of postmodern change but *they are also the motor of further critical discourses that extend beyond questions about gender itself.* This is because gender difference, the symbolic opposition of the male and the female, has been employed as a paradigm throughout human history. On the one hand, it has been the far from neutral way of understanding human qualities within a hierarchy that privileges those qualities attributed to the male, but, on the other hand, it has also served as a way of retaining the very idea of oppositional thinking itself. As is well known, Jung uses gender differences in both these ways so it will be interesting to see where, and how, post-Jungians have begun to deconstruct gender and its applications within the postmodern frame.

The Jungian analyst Beverley Zabriskie points out how gender has been a constant throughout the ages in the way it has been used by human beings to grasp their world and to make psychological and emotional sense of it.

> The receptive and the penetrating, the near and the distant, the cyclic and the linear, the containing and the moving were manifest pairs, complements, opposites, in both the elements and creatures of nature. They were assigned gender, the most apparent carrier of difference. Gender was thus projected onto, and seen in correspondence with, humankind's external surroundings: . . . Gender informed and shaped the understanding of the universe . . . and was then extended into mythology, theology, philosophy, history, sociology, and psychology.
>
> (Zabriskie, 1990: 267)

According to Zabriskie, there now seems good evidence to suppose that, in previous eras, female attributes and feminine energies were valued and celebrated far more than they have been over the last two thousand years. The growth of civilisations in size and complexity saw a consequent change in the valuing of the feminine and the demoting of a culture and cosmology of Great Goddesses:

> As male rulers and conquerors of ascendant civilisations sought to have their agendas and appetites reinforced by male gods, goddesses in many cultures lost primary status to increasingly patriarchal and domineering father gods . . . The ascendant masculine values rigidified into patriarchal orthodoxies, self-consciously superior toward all that seemed to belong to women's contextual and emotional sensibilities.
>
> (ibid.: 269)

Zabriskie gives the example of how a general experiential quality, the principle of the receptive – once positively assigned to the feminine – has suffered under patriarchy. Women are valued for their supportive connections to others but they also tend to be placed in the position of living up to characteristics projected onto them by patriarchy and for these to be viewed as innate. Thus, Zabriskie summarises,

> womanly relatedness may be merely submission to an outer mandate or an internal compulsion – at the cost of authentic relation to the actual and potential in oneself and in another. Sadly, the fundamental, universal principle of the receptive, with its powerful and active generative energy, is then domesticized, as if transmuted and tamed within the constricting notion of availability.
>
> (ibid.: 271)

Zabriskie claims that depth psychology 'implicitly challenges patriarchal authority' by the way it suggests individuals and groups are shaped by the unconscious, but then, of course, has to admit how its late nineteenth-century founders, Freud and Jung, were steeped in the patriarchal assumptions of their times. Here we come once again upon the problem of *how can a challenge to the dominant rationality emerge with any radical force from that very rationality itself?* I think the way to look at this is that the radical challenge does not emerge fully formed to any degree at all. It will always carry the language and assumptions of the previous perspective and it is only over time and through frequent reworking in different cultural spaces that a robust enough shift will become more or less established. Even then, the new thinking will drag behind it much of the old and critics of the new departure will find it tempting to dismiss real change on the grounds of the assumptions still left over from the beginnings. I think this is the problem we have with psychoanalysis and analytical psychology and 'the unconscious'. Not only is there a problem with Freud's and Jung's views about women and the feminine, but further difficulties lie with the tendency to genderise aspects of the psyche – and then assume sexist hierarchies between these aspects – which, nowadays, strikes many analysts as quite unnecessary.

There is something powerful in the concepts of depth psychology that goes beyond the patriarchal tone of the original texts. This is why it is so important to pay more attention to the reworking of Freud and Jung by post-Freudians and post-Jungians, and why a number of feminists have turned to post-Freudian writers like Lacan. Having said this, we are still able to detect important deconstructing elements in Jung's own writing that, despite his patriarchal essentialism elsewhere, support a radical challenge to modernity when it comes to feminist concerns. As Zabriskie points out: 'Jung noted that the conscious values that had informed "civilised" Western women and men in the last two millennia were masculine: authority and dominance within hierarchical structures, penetrating and focused assertion and aggression, superiority of linear cognition and detached rationality' (ibid.: 272). And, within a way of thinking about the psyche that regarded it in tension and balanced between pairs of opposites, the unconscious became characterised as feminine: 'Insofar as he believed the unconscious to have a compensatory function in relation to the cultural dominants and the established ego, it followed that the intuitive, elliptical, contextual and emotionally charged mythopoeic language and imagery of the unconscious shared qualities and associations with those outside the prevailing order: the poets, mystics, dreamers, lunatics, lovers and women' (ibid.). Jung's personal experience was key to this understanding of the psyche of contemporary men: it was a female voice he encountered in his own imaginal self-analysis:

> I was greatly intrigued by the fact that a woman should interfere (*sic*) with me from within. My conclusion was that she must be the 'soul' in the primitive sense, and I began to speculate on the reasons why the name 'anima' was given to the soul. Why was it thought of as feminine? Later I came to see that this inner feminine figure plays a typical, or archetypal, role in the unconscious of a man, and I called her the 'anima'. The corresponding figure in the unconscious of a woman I called the 'animus' . . . It is she who communicates the images of the unconscious to the conscious mind, and that is what I chiefly valued her for.
>
> (Jung, 1983/1963: 186–187)

The idea of the unconscious and the feminine coinciding and becoming linked due to their shared position as being Other to cultural dominants which are of a masculinist, patriarchal mode of being is central to the post-Jungian view of analytical psychology as a radical response to modernity. But I wish to leave this theme at an introductory stage at the moment to go on to examine some postmodern views of sex and gender and then return to compare the Jungian position with these.

POSTMODERN SEX, POSTMODERN GENDER

Several feminist thinkers critically address a range of sexist assumptions about women and gender difference which then come to form a discourse of women's *nature*, essential qualities and attributes which are used to explain the position women find themselves allocated within culture. This is the critique of Mary Daly in *Gyn/Ecology* for whom there is an essential female nature which is determined by and is manifested through the female body. This view then notes how the uniquely female is denigrated and repressed in patriarchal culture so that women are prevented from knowing and appreciating themselves and their sister human beings. A separatist solution is recommended – one in which women should create their own institutions, symbols, religions, and so on that would reflect an 'essential feminine consciousness'. With such regressive urges, promoting some idea of a golden age of the feminine that needs to be re-found, and the retention of female essentialism, this is hardly a postmodern view. It is, however, one which has appealed to readers of Jung, who find in it a revaluation of the feminine and literalise this to mean women themselves. As I said above, it is as the Other that women are aligned with a variety of Others, via the feminine, but it is a mistake to find in this anything about what is essential in women themselves.

Carol Gilligan, like Nancy Chodorow, produces a different critique which focuses on the asymmetry in child-rearing that tends to reproduce gender asymmetries. The idea is that girls develop a connectedness to the world and others while boys must separate to individuate. Emancipation for women will only arrive once it is acknowledged that 'woman's ways of knowing are not second-rate versions of "real (read patriarchal) knowledge" but in fact speak to crucial aspects of human existence totally ignored by "male-stream" thinking' (O'Hara, 1996: 148). These ideas are more useful, especially in positing undervalued human qualities that get allocated to women, but I feel the theorising relies too much on the power of familial experiences early in life without addressing other wider and deeper sources of cultural influence. When it comes to a postmodern feminist critique, it is the French feminist writers Julia Kristeva, Luce Irigaray and Hélène Cixous who have the most to offer in the way they argue that the deepest layers of women's and men's psyches are in fact constructed within – and so form part of – patriarchal discourse. The feminist analyses above, in their emancipatory and enlightening forms, suffer from being limited by a reliance on the language of the very discourse they seek to address.

Although these three feminist writers are distinctively individual – a point they all regard as central to countering the homogenisation of women in patriarchal culture – they are frequently grouped together because of the way they understand the position of women from a postmodern perspective. Their analysis of women, culture, language and psychoanalysis forms a challenge to the dominant rationality that, on the one hand, provides a critique of modern culture that extends beyond feminist concerns, but, on the other hand, also locates the position of women as a central and emblematic field illustrative of a range of postmodern critical thinking. All of this plus their use of the concept of the unconscious in their discourse, makes a comparison with analytical psychology, despite its patriarchal roots, a real possibility, and one which I will use to shed light on the postmodern concerns common to both.

What are Cixous, Irigaray and Kristeva saying in their postmodern critique that is also feminist discourse? And what are post-Jungian writers and feminists saying that compares with this? First, similar to the Jungian view, Cixous and Irigaray emphasise how Western culture is characterised by a certain form of rationality, a product of the Enlightenment, that assumes superiority and is unconscious of its one-sided, repressive and repressed, assumptions. This form of rationality, Irigaray maintains, is male and structured by a form of identity – that is, A is A because it is not B. It is a rationality characterised by binary, either/or thinking which minimises ambiguity and ambivalence by maintaining oppositional categories like culture/nature, head/heart and so on. Jung's thinking displays such an oppositional style, it must be said, and this has been criticised by post-Jungians such as Zabriskie (1990) and Samuels (1989) – not least when Jung opposes the 'masculine' and the 'feminine'. Cixous relates this style of rationality to the creation of an opposition between 'man' and 'woman' and she also notes that such pairs always involve a hierarchy which privileges one side of the pair and represses the other. These dialectical structures powerfully influence the formation of subjectivity and thus of sexual difference. Cixous uses Hegel's Master/Slave relation to illustrate how woman becomes represented as the Other, which is necessary to the creation of identity but which then persists as a threat. This is a view of

sexual difference as a power structure where one side, the female, otherness
and difference, has to be repressed. Questioning the inevitability of structural hierarchies, Cixous, like all three writers, focuses on the space where
women are placed by culture. Irigaray points out how this is a monosexual
culture where women are marginalised and dislocated as 'defective men'.
The form of reason we live with is not neutral but gendered, and its great
discourses such as science are in fact discourses of the male subject. The
master narratives the postmodern abandons really are of the *master* who is
both male and in charge. In proposing rationality as male there is a danger
in classing *women* as irrational or as the unconscious of culture, but as one
commentator puts it: 'What is important is that rationality is categorised
by Irigaray as male, not in order to oppose it, but in order to suggest a more
adequate conceptualisation in which the male does not repress or split
off the female/unconscious, but acknowledges and integrates it' (Sarup,
1993: 117).

In one way, this is what Jung recommends in his own writing, but, as
Demaris Wehr (1988) points out, when Jung declares he is going to discuss
the *anima*, an aspect of male psychology, what he in fact does is to launch
into a description of the psychology of women. His views are fudged
between the unconscious Other of male ego-consciousness, which is
characterised as 'feminine', and the way this is described in terms of – and
as if it were identical to – the psychology of women. In Jung, the feminine
Other to 'male' Enlightenment rationality – a useful critical analysis –
becomes compounded with a sexist attempt at describing the psychology of
women which is full of all the errors that the first critique would wish to
address. It is no wonder that Jungians have been in two minds about
analytical psychology on the feminine. While it is valid to link the *anima*
and female psychology in terms of how the projection of a male *anima* onto
women contours women's self-image, to do so without a recognition of the
bias of patriarchal culture results in an essentialist view just at the point at
which Jung could be really revaluing the 'feminine'.

Thus the downside of Jung's valuing of the 'feminine' as part of a
general critique of the one-sidedness of modernity, becomes a confirmation
of women as the repressed, and inferior Other which, for Jungian feminists,
plays into women's actual experience of themselves as alienated and
inferior. Wehr cites this passage from Jung for its subliminal message that
women can find their identity through the service of a man:

> Woman, with her very dissimilar psychology, is and always has been
> a source of information about things for which a man has no eyes.
> She can be his inspiration; her intuitive capacity, often superior to
> man's, can give him timely warning, and her feeling, always directed

towards the pesonal, can show him ways which his own less personally
accented feeling would never have discovered.

(Jung, 1917, CW 7: 186)

Polly Young-Eisendrath notes how all her women patients suffer
from an evaluation of themselves as somehow deficient or inadequate,
and Demaris Wehr following Mary Daly's ideas of the internal self-hater
or 'internalised oppressor', notes how Jungian psychology may help by
offering a form of dialogue with such an internal figure – complex or
sub-personality – and thus restore a woman's autonomy and identity as
an individual. But she is more critical of Jungian methods whereby ego-
consciousness needs to reduce its dominance to allow in the influence
of other aspects of the psyche and the self. It is pointed out that under
patriarchy, it cannot be assumed that the state of the ego is similar for
women and men. When the dominant consciousness is 'male', women's
ego is compromised. The rebirth of the personality contingent upon a
'death' of the ego needs to proceed differently for men and for women,
Wehr claims. 'For example, perhaps men need to undergo the annhilation of
an ego experienced as separate and distinct from others and to be reborn
into relationality' (Wehr, 1988: 103). On the other hand, women need not so
much the annihilation of the ego but a 'need to die to the false self system
that patriarchy has imposed upon them, whatever form it has taken' (ibid.).

Beverley Zabriskie points out how we owe much to Jung for his
resurrection and revaluing of the mythopoeic and inner figures of the
unconscious and of history which contribute to a restoration of a 'feminine'
otherwise undervalued and ignored in modernity. At the level of the individual – in Jungian analytic work – attention to inner images that are either
threatening to a woman's identity – from a conventional point of view –
or are idealising of the male, can, through integration with the woman's
consciousness, offer a sense of self and a more complete personality less
subject to the influence and pressure of patriarchal society. But Zabriskie
agrees that Jung was at fault in projecting his own *anima* and personal
associations onto women and their psychology, 'It is as if the archetypes fell
into matter and reemerged as stereotypes' (Zabriskie, 1990: 276). One
result of this confusion of the unconscious feminine in himself, and other
men, with women themselves lead to the intimation that women *are* more
unconscious than men. (Something very similar could be said here about
Jung's attitude to the psyche of non-Caucasians which appears as racist
as his views on women are sexist. We find here a parallel confusion
and projection, this time on to black people, of an unconscious 'primitivity'
in Jung himself, his own 'missing layer of consciousness' he found hard to
acknowledge (Adams, 1996a).)

So, to summarise the comparison I am making between postmodern feminist theory, Jungian psychology, and its post-Jungian critique: For Jung, the modern psyche manifests as a partial, fragmented version of its potential, dominated by an overly rational consciousness, and with the tendency to project onto others and the world unconscious contents that are denied by the dominant culture. As mentioned above, this dominant style of consciousness was recognised by Jung as being distinctly masculine and coterminous with the rise of patriarchal culture over the last two millennia, an idea which led, in complementary fashion, to conceiving of the neglected aspects as feminine. What Jung saw as necessary for modern culture, the integration of the unconscious and ignored, despised aspects of psyche, was never expressed directly in terms of the position of women. For better or for worse, Jung did not see the need to address women's position as a separate concern. For Jung, we are all, men and women alike, suffering from the same loss – the loss of contact with the unconscious. In a similar way, the French feminists do not restrict their view to women alone, but note that men too suffer from a diminishment in their potential humanity. *Both men and women suffer from a lack.*

JULIA KRISTEVA, THE ABJECT AND THE *LAPIS*

In my view, Julia Kristeva theorises the psyche of men and women in such a way that closely approaches the Jungian concern for modern culture and modern consciousness, and proves useful for its amplification. Kristeva and Irigaray both affirm the archaic force of the pre-Oedipal which remains preserved but repressed in – or excluded from – the human subject. Following Lacan's position that 'masculinity' and 'truth' are bogus cultural constructions – maintained by the privileging of the phallus within patri-archal culture – for Irigaray and Kristeva the pre-Symbolic, pre-Oedipal realm of the semiotic is pre-patriarchal and therefore offers the potential for psychical experience that is free of the cultural restrictions that patriarchy imposes. (For an explanation of Kristeva's use of the terms 'semiotic' and 'Symbolic' which differ radically from the Jungian usage see Chapter 8, pp. 193–194). Together with Cixous, Irigaray and Kristeva focus on the place or position from which women can speak. In a way that helps us link these ideas with analytical psychology, Rosalind Minsky summarises how these thinkers not only see,

> women's position as the lack as marginal, dislocated, excluded, despised, abandoned and rejected but also a position which, *because it lies in the unconscious,* allows a way of speaking to women and men

beyond the reach of phallic control, in a domain which potentially offers meanings based on openness, plurality, diversity and genuine difference. *In other words, this position may offer women and men the opportunity to become themselves.*

(Minsky, 1996: 180, italics added)

In seeking to extend the feminist agenda, these theorists are keen to say something about the condition of women *and* men which amounts to a critique of culture and consciousness – a critique that I find comparable to Jung's position. Jung's psychology emphasises how, in contemporary western culture, attention to the unconscious is minimised, ignored and despised. Jung's concern is the lack and the strength to be found in the marginalisation of the unconscious, while the French feminists are concerned with the lack and the strength to be found in the marginalisation of women and the 'feminine'. The latter express themselves in psychoanalytic and Lacanian terms: the pre-Oedipal and pre-Symbolic; in contrast to Jung who, among several forms of expression, found the language and symbols of alchemy imagistically and emotionally resonant as ways of conveying the unconscious outside the dominant rationality – or outside the Symbolic Order, to use Lacan's term – which constructs a particular cultural 'reality'. When Jung is expressing himself in the metaphor or language game of alchemy, he notes how words like excluded, discarded, rejected, abandoned and despised are used to refer to the *lapis philosophicorum* or philosopher's stone. The *lapis* refers to the concept of the humble stone, which is, on the one hand, rejected by the builders – perhaps the 'builders' of mainstream culture and rationality – but, on the other hand, is valued by those who are paying attention to the neglected and marginalised aspects of their psyche and their humanity. The *lapis*, in other words, the rejected, marginalised and discarded, may then be used in achieving the goal of integrating conscious and unconscious parts of psyche. Viewed within such a frame, the passage I highlighted above – 'this position may offer women and men the opportunity to become themselves' – appears to refer to the Jungian concept of *individuation* – Jung's version of *know thyself*, or rather, *become thyself* – which is the process of such an integration. Jung tells the story of how, when he was building the Tower at Bollingen, among the stones specially cut and delivered from a quarry there was a cornerstone which had been wrongly cut: 'The mason was furious and told the barge men to take it right back with them.' But, Jung tells us, rather than get rid of the stone, he knew he wanted to keep it but did not know why. He began to work on the stone, chiselling into its faces over the years, images and words as they sprang from his unconscious. The first was a verse by the alchemist de Villanova:

Here stands the mean uncomely stone,
'Tis very cheap in price!
The more it is despised by fools,
The more loved by the wise.

This verse refers to the alchemist's stone, the lapis, which is despised and rejected.

(Jung, 1983/1963: 253)

The researcher Johannes Fabricius, in a broad-ranging psychological analysis of alchemical texts that extends beyond Jung to both Freudian and Kleinian ideas, writes about the *repulsiveness* of the *stone* – and how this primal matter is compared to the shadow (Fabricius, 1994). An encounter with the shadow is expressed by the alchemists as 'burrowing into the dung-hill', an image that compares closely with Kristeva's concept of the 'abject'. The abject is disgusting and vomit-inducing, but, in Kristeva's view, it is not a 'lack of cleanliness or health that causes abjection but what disturbs identity, system, order' (Kristeva, 1980: 4). 'The abject is what is on the border, what doesn't respect borders . . . It is neither one or the other. It is undecidable. The abject is not a "quality in itself". Rather it is a relationship to a boundary and represents what has been "jettisoned out of that boundary, its other side, a margin" (Kristeva, 1980: 69)' (Oliver, 1993: 56). Like Jung's stone, it not only falls outside structure but it also stands for and reminds us of the very existence of the structure. It reveals the possibility of marginality by its refusal to be included or excluded and yet is still excluded.

The alchemical imagery and associations to the *lapis philosophicorum* reveal further connections to Kristeva's 'abject' that root this as a concept which goes deeper than the feminist and psychoanalytic agendas from one point of view, but, from another angle, may also reveal how these have their source in the concepts that alchemy was also expressing. Fabricius points out how certain alchemical imagery depicts the perennial mystery of the birth of the human subject – which has its source in two (the male and female parents) then develops as one (the fetus in the mother) to become two (individual and mother) upon the separation at birth. He finds that the umbilical cord symbolises – and on the biological level is the embodiment of – what we call *primary identification*: the state of the subject before the existence of subjecthood, before its separation from the body of the mother. The alchemical image of the *body-phallus-cord* – which Fabricius regards as an 'equation of the unconscious at its vaginal-uterine level of organization' (Fabricius, 1994: 75) – also appears as the archetypal image of the serpent in dreams and in myths such as the Book of Genesis where it is explicitly connected to the primal act. Fabricius quotes Otto Rank's psychoanalytic finding that castration anxiety derives its affective force from an actual, earlier, and more profound event: the cutting of the umbilical cord at birth, the aggressive separation of 'one body' (the mother–baby unit pre-birth) into two. In other words, the Oedipal crisis and resolution that thrusts the infant into the world of individual subjecthood and 'separation' from mother through the threat of paternal intervention (in Freud's formulation) is a replay or reminder of the more profoundly significant separation from the mother's body upon birth. Fabricius points out how Melanie Klein's theorising of the pre-Oedipal infant in the months after birth with its fantasies and projections of aggression and retaliation, attacking and devouring, links closely to the significance of the umbilical 'castration'. The difference is that in Freud it is the Father – or patriarchy – that performs the aggressive intervention, while in Klein, it is the more Jungian and alchemical image of the 'phallic mother', the Terrible Mother pole of the Great Mother archetype, who is fantasised as responsible for the separation. As we see shortly, Kristeva's ideas bring these two 'castrations' together, the Oedipal-Symbolic both requiring but repressing the earlier maternal authority-body.

In alchemy, the potential ego or subject is conveyed by the image of the hero-knight who, like St George in the myth, encounters and battles with the dragon's fire. In this battle for birth – or rebirth – there is a secret identity between the dragon-fighting knight and his 'fetal' animal symbol the salamander; both enter the fire (of the womb and of rebirth) without being consumed by the fire. 'By "feeding" on it and so partaking of it, reveals the salamander as a symbol of primary identification' (ibid.: 77). The link with the stone or *lapis* is quite direct in the alchemical texts: 'The philosophers have called this stone our salamander, because, like a salamander, it is fed exclusively by the fire; it lives in it, that is to say, it is perfected by it, and so it is with our stone.' In other words, the *lapis* too refers to primary identification – also known as primary narcissism, the primary self or the original non-dual state. What then, you may ask, has all this medieval gobbledegook got to do with our present subject of Kristeva's 'abject' and its connection with what she calls a maternal realm of the 'semiotic'. Kristeva is theorising a place which precedes the Symbolic order of patriarchal culture from which women (and, ultimately, men) might both speak and experience without the restrictions and distortions imposed by patriarchy. If, as Kelly Oliver explains, the abject is a relationship to a boundary and represents what has been jettisoned, the other side of the boundary, its margin, it remains threatening to the social or Symbolic order.

The Symbolic is the order of boundaries, discrimination and difference. Reality is parcelled into words and categories. Society is parcelled into classes, castes, professional and family roles, etc. The abject threat comes from what has been prohibited by the Symbolic order, what has been prohibited so the Symbolic order can be. The prohibition that founds, and yet undermines, society is the prohibition against the maternal body.

(Oliver, 1993: 56)

And this not only refers to the separation from the mother expressed as Freud's Oedipal incest prohibition or Lacan's formulation of a prohibition against the mother's *jouissance*. Kristeva's emphasis is similar to Otto Rank's in that the abject has its source in the earliest, profound separation: the separation of birth itself. Fabricius notes how 90 per cent of all fetal distress is caused by the death-like choking and suffocation experienced as the umbilical cord is cut and '200 to 300 million uninflated air sacs are expanded for the first time while blood circulates to the lungs to pick up the oxygen earlier supplied by the mother's placenta' (Fabricius, 1994: 79). In this way, human birth is a death and rebirth experience. Beyond the biological fact, Kristeva is indicating how both human life and human society are initiated by this prototypical abject experience. The identity of the subject starts here for, 'Before the umbilical cord is cut, who can decide whether there is one or two?' (Oliver, 1993: 57).

Like the *lapis* of the alchemists, primary identification, the abject is pre-subject and pre-object and thus 'Abjection is therefore a kind of narcissistic crisis' (Kristeva, 1980: 14). The phallic mother re-emerges in Kristeva's formulation as the maternal authority which regulates the boundaries of the clean and unclean self and not-self through the regulation of the food the body takes in and the regulation of the faeces the body expels. In this way the abject, and boundaries and 'order', are founded on maternal authority; it is this maternal authority that the Symbolic order represses while at the same time it relies on its foundational boundary-laying. The abject persists as a threat to the Symbolic order that has to be excluded not repressed. Thus the abject and the *lapis* refer to many linked themes at the personal, social, epistemological, biological, alchemical and sexual levels of human experience. They refer to the emergence of 'twoness' from 'oneness' that is human birth – the beginning of self and other; they refer to the rejected 'unclean' and marginal that is excluded from the order of (patriarchal) rationality and is associated, because of birth from a mother, with the female; they refer to the 'problem' of the tension between avoiding separation from the mother and avoiding identification with the mother, which has to be 'discarded' for the entry into subjecthood and society to be possible. The abject, and the *lapis*, represents what is left out of patriarchal order, for the feminists, excluded from the rationality of modern consciousness for Jungians, and that which forms the symbolic (in a Jungian not a Kristevan/Lacanian sense) ground for the transformation of rebirth for the alchemists. Similarly, for the contemporary feminist and Jungian alike, the abject and the *lapis* both represent a conceptual space from which both modernity and patriarchy may be critically addressed.

Jung's narrative of the discarded stone literalises for us the abstraction of the abject, or the metaphor of the *lapis*. He writes of how he felt compelled to carve the discarded stone; the language that came to him was Latin sayings – 'more or less quotations from alchemy':

> I am an orphan, alone; nevertheless I am found everywhere. I am one but opposed to myself. I am youth and old man at one and the same time. I have known neither father nor mother, because I have had to be fetched out of the deep like a fish, or fell like a white stone from heaven. In woods and mountains I roam, but I am hidden in the innermost soul of man. I am mortal for everyone, yet I am not touched by the cycle of aeons.
>
> (Jung, 1983/1963: 254)

Linking back to what I have been saying in the previous chapter, Jung notes how the carved stone stands outside his Tower and is both 'an explanation of it' and 'a manifestation of the occupant' but one which remains impossible for others to understand. Jung's language is alchemical and medieval – and also Taoist in tone, something to be explored in Chapter 8 – but I feel it directs us to the pre-objectal, pre-Symbolic of Kristeva's abject and what she refers to as the 'semiotic'. Jung tells us how he wanted to carve 'Le cri de Merlin' into the back face, the 'cry that no one could understand' which, according to the twelfth-century legend, sounded from the forest after Merlin's death. Again I am reminded of the pre-Symbolic, the abject outside the boundary of 'meaning' which, although excluded, persists in the unconscious. Jung reckons that the secret of Merlin was taken up by the alchemists and, later, by his own psychology of the unconscious and 'remains uncomprehended to this day! That is because most people find it quite beyond them to live on close terms with the unconscious. Again and again I have had to learn how hard this is for people' (Jung, 1983/1963: 255). And although she theorises within a quite different discourse, when Kristeva speaks of the semiotic she too refers to 'the use of a specifically poetic language which, because of its close involvement with the unconscious, must always challenge the arbitrary, male-defined categories through which we experience the world' (Minsky, 1996: 179).

Kristeva, however, is not so one-sided to think that women, or any of us, can speak purely from the pre-Symbolic position. Any position, once represented, will be absorbed into language and assimilated into the Symbolic; this is why 'Kristeva does not place her hopes for women in the body and the pre-oedipal, phallic mother beyond the authority of the phallus' (ibid.: 180). Instead, she regards the meaning of the pre-oedipal mother as encompassing both 'masculinity' and 'femininity': 'masculine' because of the way the baby experiences the mother as all-powerful and phallic, and also 'feminine' because the mother in the semiotic 'lies outside the phallic imposition of meaning which asserts itself during the Oedipal crisis' (ibid.: 181). This is why Kristeva recommends that women 'should employ a *double* discourse which reflects the real state of identity which must always be fluid – at the same time both "masculine" and "feminine" – both inside and outside the boundaries of the symbolic' (ibid.). This double discourse brings to mind the double coding of the postmodern we came across in Charles Jencks's architectural analysis in the last chapter. In that case it referred to the way the postmodern is defined by a double-coding, not only in its combination of modern techniques with traditional wisdom, but also through the pluralistic inclusion of elite/popular, accommodating/ subversive and new/old. In that section I compared this pluralism to elements in Jung's psychology, but in the present case of Kristeva and post-modern feminism the *double* is that of the 'masculine' and the 'feminine'. Making such a comparison helps us to see how masculine and feminine are not only metaphors for a genderised, and also hierarchised, conceptualising of the 'real world', but they also *embody* such a dichotomising, in this culture and era, *in the actual bodies of men and of women*. Where the postmodern perspective helps us, whether it is speaking from the point of view of architecture, depth psychology or feminism, is how it admits and celebrates a pluralism – the *fluid* real state of identity in Kristeva – that addresses the limits of a skewed, modernist, 'masculinist', rationality as the only approach to the 'real world' and to 'truth'.

THE SHADOW, THE OTHER, PROJECTION AND THE SEMIOTIC

In her essay *Women's Time* (1981), Kristeva highlights a number of concerns that are to be found in Jung's work as well as that of post-Jungians such as Andrew Samuels who is discussed in the next section. Not only does Kristeva note that modernity is considered to be the first historical epoch in which humans have attempted to live without religion, but she also notes that the feminism of the 1980s seems to have gone beyond a social-political level and is situated in the very framework of the religious crisis of modernity. This leads her to question the usefulness of the dichotomy 'men' versus 'women' as being another thought-trap based on the original cutting, castrating imagery of patriarchy. She recommends, 'an introduction of its cutting edge into the very interior of every identity whether subjective, sexual, ideological, or so forth' (Kristeva, 1981, in Minsky, 1996: 286). Kristeva views women as part of a group of cultural scapegoats that includes others like the Jews under the Third Reich, thus her statement recommends that instead of scapegoating the external Other in a social-political field, contemporary feminism offers an opportunity for women to address the interiorised, rejected and oppressive Other within. This alternative amounts to nothing less than 'the analysis of the potentialities of *victim/executioner* which characterize each identity, each subject, each sex' (ibid.).

Apart from sounding similar to Beverley Zabriskie's analysis of what Jungian psychology can offer to women, Kristeva's position is generally similar to a Jungian emphasis on a need for the integration of the unconscious *shadow* – Jung's term for the 'other' in ourselves which ego-consciousness tends to reject. In the feminist discourse, each gender has the other as just one part of each individual's shadow, but the genderised other, and its rejection, is seen as a critical confrontation with which men and women should struggle in present times. The Jungian analyst Warren Colman, in his paper 'Contrasexuality and the Unknown Soul' (1998), emphasises how the gendered Other within each man or woman, the anima or animus image, represents lost parts of the personality felt to be foreign and other to the ego but which are calling for inclusion and to be in dialogue with ego. In this, Colman is one of several post-Jungians who have tackled Jung's tendency to identify the unconscious feminine other of the *anima* with an inferiorised woman's psychology; Colman does this by emphasising the disparaged Other without the need to anthropomorphise it into a woman. In line with postmodern feminist thinking, this post-Jungian perspective emphasises how what is kept for ego and what is abandoned or despised as other, is not neutral or accidental but arises as a result of what the culture will or will not support. This is why the critique of mainstream patriarchal, masculine dominated culture as discussed in feminist discourse is central not only to the improvement of women's position but for addressing much of the failure of modernity that postmodern thinking and Jung's psychology is also directing us toward. The concept of *projection* is as important in Kristeva as it is in Jung's and post-Jungian theorising of the Other and the shadow. *What* is projected differs across these views but the *mechanism* of projection itself is central to both their arguments. Kristeva's emphasis is on acknowledging the difference in ourselves – the 'stranger in ourselves' as she calls it – rather than denying this and projecting it onto others in an effort to establish our own identities.

As we have seen, Kristeva uses the concepts of the abject and the semiotic to track the tension between the pre-Oedipal and Oedipal construction of the human subject. Her concept of the semiotic refers to the pre-Oedipal position, the relationship with the mother and thus the 'repressed feminine'. The semiotic is always in interplay with, but repressed within, the Symbolic, the social order, but in times of greater cultural disruption, the semiotic can be seen to burst through. Kristeva sees this in the art of the avant-garde with their extreme challenges to the Symbolic and the world of the taken-for-granted. The semiotic also bursts through as holiness, madness or poetry, or often all three, although there is the risk that this is reconverted back into the Symbolic, its energy dissipated through the conserving, ordering power of the Symbolic. But the opposite extreme may arise: the social phenomenon of fascism, where disruptive semiotic processes energise not only a narcissistic adoration of the charismatic leader, but through this, a rigidified, hierarchical organisation that presents a dangerous parody of the previously dominant Symbolic while nevertheless succeeding to replace it.

Jung and post-Jungians write about the shadow in a way that suggests it functions like Kristeva's semiotic. The shadow not only has an individual function which manifests in the sphere of personal psychology and neurosis, but it is also emphasised how the shadow functions collectively, sometimes with devastating effects on cultural and political life. Dealing with the shadow on a purely personal level, Jung writes: 'Everyone carries a shadow, and the less it is embodied in the individual's conscious life, the blacker and denser it is' (Jung, 1940, CW 11: para. 131). Isolated from consciousness it cannot be modified or influenced and so it can burst forth suddenly or it may thwart the subject's well-meant intentions. Jung suggests we all need to find a way for the conscious personality and the shadow to live together (ibid.: para. 132). Among the shadow's tendencies, Jung includes the 'statistical criminal' in us all which is suppressed more or less consciously; the 'unconventional, socially awkward' tendencies repressed by 'looking the other way so as not to become conscious of one's desires' (ibid.: para. 129); and the 'inferior qualities and primitive tendencies . . . of the man who is less ideal and more primitive than we should like to be' (ibid.: para. 130). The shadow is also 'unadapted and awkward' (ibid.: para. 134) – a description that conveys further shades of Kristeva's semiotic: 'it contains childish or primitive qualities which would . . . vitalize and embellish human existence, but convention forbids!' (ibid.).

Beginning with her focus on the position of women, which depicts how the semiotic is subsumed under the symbolic, Kristeva ends up with a text about the repression of unconscious elements in the psyche – a focus very much shared with Jung. Jung seems to ignore any direct recognition of patriarchy in the feminist sense but there is a connection with the 'feminine' and the mother, too, quite detectable in Jung's concept of the shadow. He makes a link not only between the shadow and the anima – the 'feminine' in men – but also between the shadow and the 'earth' which Jung consistently associates with the Great Mother as in Mother Earth. As the source of our ambivalent relationship to an all-powerful but containing mother in the personal and the mythological sense something very similar to Kristeva's analysis of the repressed maternal body and maternal authority of the phallic mother is implied here in Jung's writing. He quite specifically states that the anima is resisted 'because she represents . . . the unconscious and all those tendencies and contents hitherto excluded from conscious life. They were excluded for a number of reasons, both real and apparent. Some are suppressed and some are repressed' (ibid.: para. 129).

Jung's understanding of the personal shadow is never far from his understanding of the shadow and its effects in the collective sense. In fact, this theme illustrates well the way in which Jung's thinking frequently slips between the personal and the collective, between the individual and the social and cultural. Critics often miss this vital element in Jung's work, reading him along too personalistic a line in a way that is more true of Freud's than of Jung's perspective. Jung's expression is often awkward, class-conscious and sexist to contemporary postmodern readers, but this should not distract us from noticing the importance of his cultural analysis. Writing in 1937, Jung makes an explicit connection between the shadow, the earth and the current situation of Nazism in Europe that predates a Kristevan understanding of the effect of the semiotic when it bursts through the collective:

> The educated public, flower of our present situation, has detached itself from its roots, and is about to lose connection with the earth as well. There is no civilized country nowadays where the lowest strata of the population are not in a state of unrest and dissent. In a number of European nations such a condition is overtaking the upper strata too. This state of affairs demonstrates our psychological problem on a gigantic scale. Inasmuch as collectivities are mere accumulations of individuals, their problems are accumulations of individual problems.
>
> (ibid.: para. 134)

By asserting that what is required is a 'general change of attitude' by individuals themselves, Jung is not being a psychological reductionist but is pointing out something similar to what we find in Kristeva's writing in the 1980s. That is, that when a culture or social formation cannot contain its Symbolic, its dominant conscious ordering of the world, to any degree – due to loss of faith in, and effectiveness of, symbols such as leadership, religious belief, economic power, national identity, political conventions or whatever – then the unconscious shadow will burst through, like the semiotic, and find in a charismatic leader a new form of order that may have devastating effects. Due to his interest in grand cultural myths, Jung analysed the rise of Hitler and the Third Reich, with its mythology and symbolism of an omniscient Germanic nation, in terms of this historical moment of European culture not being able to supply any other symbols for the projection of shadow contents which resulted in them being projected onto the State and its leader. The energy behind this projection comes from the personal shadow with its despised, childish, excluded contents – unintegrated, urgently seeking expression and bursting forth.

Certain post-Jungians, like Loren Pederson in his book *Dark Hearts. Unconscious Forces That Shape Men's Lives* (1991), connect the collective shadow with masculinity and the repression of the feminine, again in line with the postmodern feminists. Pederson produces a post-Jungian development of ideas about the shadow that links it specifically with the negative aspects of men and masculinity in contemporary culture:

> Rather than being able to rest with a conscious sense of superiority, he [the contemporary man] is saddled with an unconscious sense of inferiority – a sense of inadequacy vis-à-vis the creative maternal and the feminine. In this way he becomes impaired in his ability to promote life, to nurture, and to relate effectively and empathically with either men or women. The anima, then, even though it is projected, is best understood in this context as an incomplete, damaged sense of self.
>
> (Pederson, 1991: 164–165)

He goes on to note how men need women to carry the deprecated image of femininity as a projection of what is split off and denied in men, *with the result that women may be said to be carriers of an anima image that is contaminated by the masculine shadow*. This analysis pushes us a step further in our understanding and criticism of Jung's projection of his own anima onto women's psychology.

Pederson is keen to analyse Freud's idea of the death instinct and its connection with aggression and the way that this is culturally emphasised by men's behaviour, 'as if aggression and the drive for power and control were simply attributes of their sex' (ibid.). Pederson connects the death instinct with men's need for power, which itself is a function of men's predominantly extroverted approach to the world, women and themselves – 'or, stated another way, a result of their failure to incorporate the feminine in themselves. *We can surmise that men then need women as a group to carry this deprecated image of femininity*' (ibid., italics added).

Although Pederson makes no broad links with modernity, rationality and its values, these are implied in his analysis of the masculine, but this then causes his citing of the unincorporated 'feminine' to suffer from a degree of unfashionable essentialism. Despite this, his ideas provide another approach that goes some way towards bringing Jungian concepts in line with postmodern concerns as expressed in contemporary European feminist discourse.

THE FAILURE OF THE GODDESSES

More successful anti-essentialist views are to be found in the critique of the 'feminine principle' and of the 'goddess' movement which, at one time, appeared central to several feminist and Jungian positions on women. Maureen O'Hara puts the difficulty succinctly:

> The idea of ourselves as 'goddesses' or 'priestesses' is a deeply comforting antidote to the usual sense of insignificance most women experience in their daily lives. Nonetheless, I think 'goddess'-type language and affirmations of some inborn, biologically based 'femininity' in fact only perpetuate ways of thinking about human realities that themselves justify attitudes and social practices that have disenfranchised women for millennia.
>
> (O'Hara, 1996: 150)

The post-Jungian critique is led by Andrew Samuels who writes in his paper *Beyond the Feminine Principle* (Samuels, 1990 and 1989) 'The problem is that the more all-encompassing, the more utopian, the "bigger" the image, the more it devours other images, other people's images. The "feminine principle" can be such a megaimage' (Samuels, 1990: 298). Samuels is criticising Jungian feminism for the way it assumes there is something eternal about femininity; 'that women therefore display essential transcultural and ahistorical characteristics; and that these can be described in psychological terms . . . (while secondly) . . . much Jungian discourse on the "feminine" seems directed away from political and social action. Dwelling upon interiority and feeling becomes an end in itself' (ibid.: 296). Here he is hitting upon two major concerns for the postmodern Jungian: first is the tendency towards essentialism in Jung's theorising, specifically the theory of archetypes common to all humanity; second is the way that hierarchical thinking still remains in Jungian feminism in the way that celebrating the feminine has taken on an oppressive, privileged tone – in the manner of patriarchy and the phallus – 'leading to a simple and pointless reversal of power positions' (ibid.: 297). This second point seems very much in line with Kristeva's and O'Hara's anti-essentialism, and Samuels moves Jungian thinking on from the 'burdensome part of the legacy from Jung' (ibid.: 300) – the essentialism of the eternal and archetypes – to direct our thinking to the phenomenon of *difference*. Specifically, he refers to the way

> Each woman lives her life in interplay with such difference. This may lead to questions of gender role (for example, how a woman can best assert herself in our culture), but these questions need not be couched in terms of innate femininity or innate masculinity, or . . . some feminine-masculine spectrum. Rather, they may be expressed in terms of difference . . . The psychological processes by which a man becomes an aggressive business executive and a woman a nurturing homemaker are the same, and one should not be deceived by the dissimilarity in the end product . . . In the example, the difference between assertion and compliance needs to be seen as different from the difference between men and women. Or, put another way, what ever differences there might be between men and women are not illuminated or signified by the difference between compliance and assertion.
>
> (ibid.: 299)

I have already mentioned Cixous' criticism of oppositional thinking as typical of the patriarchal, masculine style of rationality we have inherited from the Enlightenment. It is problematic therefore, when I am on a path of discovering the postmodern views critical of modernity in Jung, to have to acknowledge how central to his overall theory is this very principle of opposites. It is the frame, inherited from his late nineteenth century background, that remains with Jung and is used to structure a good deal of what he says about the psyche. Samuels helps us with this, challenging Jungian ideas of wholeness as well:

> The notion of difference, I suggest, can help us in the discussion about gender – not innate opposites that lead us to create an unjustified psychological division expressed in lists of antithetical qualities, each list yearning for the other so as to become whole. Not what differences between women and men there are, or have always been . . . But rather the fact, image and social reality of difference itself – what difference itself is like, what the experience of difference is like. Not what being a woman is but what being a woman is *like*. Not the archetypal structuring of woman's world but woman's personal experience in today's world.
>
> (ibid.: 300)

As Zabriskie points out above, for Jung, the marginalised unconscious psyche gets expressed as 'female' in a metaphorical sense but this 'metaphor' then comes to have a 'literal' meaning. The 'literalness' of the comparison stems from the way that both the dominant rationality, and dominant cultural mores, define themselves as 'masculine'. They achieve this by privileging a one-sided 'male' culture and a certain style of consciousness which benefits anatomically-defined men and marginalises actual women (anatomically-defined) as well as other aspects of human psychology then labelled 'feminine'. As Andrew Samuels puts it,

> Sometimes it is claimed that 'masculine' and 'feminine' are metaphors for two distinct *weltanschauungen* . . . When we bring in either masculinity and femininity or maleness and femaleness, we are projecting a dichotomy that certainly exists in human ideation and functioning onto convenient receptors for the projections. Arguing that masculinity and femininity should be understood nonliterally, as having nothing to do with bodily men and bodily women in a social context, may be taken as an effort to come to terms with what is lost by the projection; but this has not led to a recollection of it.
>
> (ibid.: 301–302)

In this post-Jungian thinking we are also leaving behind the literal/metaphorical issue of 'biology'. That is, we are leaving behind one of the dominant paradigms that influenced Jung's – and, of course, Freud's – psychological thinking; and one we now see as the manifestation of a particularly *masculine* rationality. As O'Hara says, compared to the essentialist feminism of 'goddess' talk, 'The constructivist position is a harder pill to swallow. Its arguments leave the question of biological contribution to consciousness veiled in mystery. It is not that our biology is irrelevant but that it serves as a lower boundary condition through which and upon which we must construct symbolic reality, both internal and social' (O'Hara, 1996: 151). Samuels makes a similar point from the post-Jungian position: 'each person remains a man or a woman, but what that means to each becomes immediate and relative, and hence capable of generational expansion and cultural challenge. All the time, the question of "masculine" and "feminine" remains in suspension – the bliss of not knowing . . . ' (Samuels, 1990: 300). In his phrase 'immediate and relative' Samuels returns us to the tension between the global, grand-narrative and the local, the postmodern problematic, which was introduced as an initial approach to essentialism at the start of the chapter.

The shift detectable in postmodern feminism and postmodern Jungian psychology is one away from biology, away from opposites and also away from simplistic metaphorical assumptions that, as I have been emphasising, keep not only men and women in their opposed places, but also keep *one style of rationality* empowered over any other version of the 'truth'. In his example of the pitfalls inherent in both literal and metaphoric relations between anatomy and psychology, Samuels points out, 'The fact that a penis penetrates and a womb contains tells us absolutely nothing about the psychological qualities of those who possess such organs. One does not have to be a clinician to recognise penetrative women and receptive men or to conclude that psychology has projected its fantasies onto the body' (ibid.: 301). What becomes clear in Samuels' deconstruction of Jungian ideas is that:

> Animus and anima images are not of men and women because animus and anima qualities are masculine and feminine. Rather, for the individual woman or man, anatomy is a metaphor for the richness and potential of the 'other'. A man will imagine what is other to him in the symbolic form of a woman – a being with another anatomy. A woman will symbolise what is foreign to her in terms of the kind of body she does not herself have. The so-called contrasexuality is more something 'contrapsychological'; anatomy is a metaphor for that.
>
> (ibid.)

Samuels is making the point that metaphors – especially when referred to as 'just a metaphor' – are seductively misleading. They direct us towards positions and beliefs as one-sided as any 'literalisms'. (The predominance of the 'child' and 'infancy' in contemporary psychotherapy is similarly 'just a metaphor' which has extensive consequences in leading our thinking. I address this topic in Chapter 2.) They are the consequence of the human tendency to project a dichotomy of maleness and femaleness onto convenient receptors for the projections – such as rational/irrational, Apollonian/Dionysian, classical/romantic – which are not possible to genderise without this 'bifurcated projection' (ibid.: 302). Why do we do this? Samuels gives the psychological answer that, 'It could be because we find difficulty in living with both sides of our murky human natures. We import a degree of certainty and clarity, and hence reduce anxiety, by making the projection' (ibid.). I think this answer does not go far enough. For instance, why are we in the position of *requiring* 'certainty and clarity' to reduce our anxiety? Why is the murkiness, the ambiguity, plurality and ambivalence of our natures anxiety-inducing in the first place? What *tells us*, or, if you will, *who says* this is something to be anxious about and that this can be helped by importing 'a degree of certainty and clarity'? A broader socio-cultural and political view would suggest that we are once again encountering the hegemony of a dominant rationality, as the French feminists describe, characterised by its intolerance for ambiguity and by its single-minded, phallic assertion of Truth. In other words, we are encountering the Symbolic of Lacan which produces anxiety in anyone who cannot subscribe to its certainties and who, thereby, risks remaining disempowered in the margin. Once again, the lesson to be learnt is how, when we are employing the double perspectives of individual psychology and collective culture to deconstruct the human condition in postmodern times, it is important to be explicit about the historical and cultural contexts in which our depth psychological insights operate.

THE USE OF MYTHS: FRENCH FEMINISTS, JUNG AND CLINICAL WORK

I should like to end this chapter with a note about the use of material derived from Greek myths. Both Cixous and Irigaray use such mythology to extend their analyses of women's position and the roots of patriarchy but nowhere is it mentioned, as far as I have found, how this is comparable to the Jungian use of mythological themes. Jung places a great deal of importance on myths in his psychology having noticed that the 'psychic development of the individual produces something that looks very much like the archaic world of fable' (Jung, 1935, CW 16: para. 18). Many agree with Jung that both clinical and social analysis can benefit from such an approach because, 'Mythological ideas reach deep and touch us where reason, will and good intentions do not penetrate' (ibid.: para. 19). After sketching some French postmodern and post-Jungian feminist applications, I will conclude with a clinical vignette from an analysis with a woman client of my own which sheds light on feminist concerns through a re-examination of the Ariadne myth.

Cixous interprets the *Oresteia* myth and reads it as a narrative of the origins of patriarchy. Apollo's ruling that the woman is merely nurse to the seed while the man is the source of life is used to diminish the relative seriousness of matricide compared to the murder of a husband, a view that legitimates the development of patriarchal social relations. Irigaray has interpreted many classical myths where she has been particularly concerned with the unsymbolised mother–daughter relationship which has been bypassed, since the Greeks, in favour of the mother–son relationship. For Irigaray this results in women failing to achieve an identity in the symbolic order that is distinct from their role as mothers. Irigaray accepts the view that women have difficulty in separating from their mothers and tend towards relationships where identity is merged. Irigaray extends Cixous' analysis of the Orestes/Clytemnestra myth by pointing out how it is Athena, the father's daughter, who advises Apollo, against the chorus of women, that Orestes's matricide was justifiable. As Madan Sarup succinctly puts it, 'In Irigaray's account of the myth, patriarchy covers its tracks by attributing the justification of matricide to a woman. Athena, the father's daughter, was an alibi for patriarchy' (Sarup, 1993: 120).

Jungian psychotherapists are known for using myths and folk stories, in varying degrees, not only to resonate with and amplify the psychological material and imagery their clients bring but also to examine women's position. The British Jungian analyst Coline Covington has produced an analysis of the folk tale 'The Handless Maiden' which she entitles 'In Search of the Heroine' (Covington, 1989: 243–254). In this she contrasts the path taken by the eponymous heroine which differs from the path of the hero in this tale and in others. She argues for an equal valuation of the 'steady state', stillness and waiting rather than these being regarded as negative and thus negating women who enact these modes. She regards these 'feminine' attributes as being modes that belong to men and women alike so that both genders share the potential for the waiting of the heroine or the activity of the hero:

> The concept of hero and heroine – and their different struggles – cannot be applied exclusively and respectively to men and women. Men can be under the influence of the heroine just as women can follow the path of the hero. The anatomical difference between hero and heroine does not indicate a basic difference in the psychology of men and women; it is a metaphor of otherness.
>
> (ibid.: 252)

A woman client who I have called Elizabeth when I wrote about her in a previous paper (Hauke, 1997) frequently related to me in a way that called for a variety of mythological comparisons. The fact that I was a man and she a woman was an important aspect of the analysis which, apart from her individual need for healing, shed light on contemporary man–woman relationships in general for which the myths were very useful. In her analysis, the struggle with time boundaries were difficult for Elizabeth because each occasion I needed to remind her of these was experienced as a painful withholding, or refusal, of her by me which evoked childhood emotions experienced originally in response to her mother's unavailability. Elizabeth either always arrived on time or slightly early, and when I asked her to wait in the waiting room she felt hurt and rejected. For a period, she was consistently coming early because she had no watch and was taking the time by the church clock around the corner. I felt irritated by her urgent neediness and felt my own time was being squeezed. When I brought up the boundaries of the times of starting and finishing, again in an effort to firm up the analytic nature, and reality of our relationship – from a masculinist, symbolic position, I now recognise – she replied: 'But your boundary is like a sword'. She was expressing how cut off she felt by the boundary but at the same time she seemed to be valuing its phallic security. She went on to describe an image which seems to convey the possibility of her own phallic empowerment – possession of her animus or addressing her experience of 'lack' – which could become facilitated through my sword-like boundary keeping. The image was one of me as St George who, with his sword, was protecting the Dragon – who was 'like a negative, wicked mother' – from Elizabeth herself – no longer the 'vulnerable maiden' but one transformed into a woman with power. While this image carried a sense of her experience of the Oedipal triangle (and resonance of the rebirth expressed in the alchemical imagery I refer to above), it also felt positive in the casting of herself as a challenger and not a victim. And as if to confirm this, and the rightness of the boundaries, she forged a small, but sharp and heavy sword for me out of beaten metal and gave it as a gift between us.

The importance of this material symbol lies in it being her creation but given to me to be in my possession. I detect in this a particular form of female individuation that we find in the myth of the Minotaur, Ariadne and Theseus. Although it is the hero Theseus who finally slays the monster, his triumph is as much that of Ariadne's. It is she who advises Theseus the best time to attack the monster, she who supplies him with a sword as well as the vital thread by which he can find his way back out of the labyrinth. Through this, Ariadne enables her own escape from her oppressive father, King Minos, by sailing away with Theseus – only to be abandoned by Theseus on the island of Naxos.

Elizabeth herself felt very strongly that she needed my phallic maleness inside her to empower her and ground her in her work as an artist and in her life in general. She told me how she would imagine my presence as a phallic power within her when she had to accomplish some strenuous task in her studio, for example. This was a relationship with me that extended beyond the erotic bond often found in analytic work to one that seemed to point directly towards her experience of 'lack'. The myth, arising it seems from a period when patriarchy was well established, suggests a complicated dynamic that involves the effort of the woman to free herself from the oppressive Father, not directly under her own steam, but through empowering another male – the hero Theseus – who is there to 'correct' the father's errors. In this we should remember how it is through the hubris of King Minos that he keeps the bull lent him by Neptune, and it is through the copulation of Minos's wife, Ariadne's mother, and the bull that the

Minotaur is born. Like the father in *Beauty and the Beast* or 'The Handless Maiden', Minos features as the foolish father who makes mistakes that usher in the events that lead to his daughter's path of individuation and fate. Beauty and Ariadne, while pursuing their individuation, do so in reference to, and within the context of, the Father whose order remains. These stories confirm a state where woman, despite her own efforts in empowering the man, is trapped within the Law of the Father.

But, in addition, as I wrote at the end of Chapter 3, the Ariadne myth is rich in a greater imagery that is relevant for the affirmation of life, the development of consciousness, and, coterminously, the integration of the 'feminine' or anima. This is the Nietzschean position which, although there is not the space to go into it here, the French feminists also endorse. While still linked to her lover Theseus, Ariadne, 'is only the feminine image of man: the feminine power remains fettered in man' (Deleuze, 1986: 187). But when the god Dionysus finds Ariadne abandoned on Naxos and places a non-earthly crown of nine bright stars on her head, the feminine power is emancipated in the form of the beneficent and affirmative Anima.

Although Ariadne's, and my client's, individuation, such as it is, is accomplished within conditions that are dominated pervasively by the masculine, initially, there is a spark of hope in the *activity* displayed by the feminine in Ariadne's empowerment of Theseus. That this leads once more to Ariadne's abandonment, and not marriage to Theseus, may be viewed ambiguously as, on the one hand, a loss, or, on the other, a blessing achieved through the 'divine' marriage with Dionysus. Going beyond primary affirmation and the initial integration of heroic, phallic aspects, this second affirmation and integration of the unconscious feminine which Ariadne achieves goes further than women – and men – are able to achieve under present cultural conditions. In contrast to Ariadne, in the case of the incomplete project of gender and postmodernity – the integration of the unconscious Other – we still have some way to travel.

6   Jung, Nietzsche and the Roots of the Postmodern

Since the stars have fallen from heaven, and our highest symbols have paled, a secret life holds sway in the unconscious. It is for this reason that we have a psychology today, and for this reason we speak of the unconscious.

(Jung, 1940: 72)

Of all the nineteenth-century thinkers, Friedrich Nietzsche is recognised as having had the greatest impact in relation to postmodern thought. His criticism of essentialist ideas of truth have influenced Lyotard, Derrida and Baudrillard; his recommendation of genealogy over history has inspired Foucault; and his thinking on the failures of Enlightenment reason and Christian ethics, on aesthetics and on identity form the background for much contemporary social critique. Equally, Nietzsche was a founding influence for Jung who knew his works very well; Jung attended Basle University where Nietzsche had been professor and where the atmosphere had been full of his ideas (Jung in Evans, 1979: 46). Unlike Freud who denied his Nietzschean influence – no doubt due to the similarity and primacy of several of Nietzsche's psychological ideas (Ellenberger, 1994: 277) – Jung continued to observe and discuss Nietzschean ideas – both explicitly and implicitly – throughout his writing. At one stage in the discussion of psychological types, for example, Jung dialogues with Nietzsche's polarisation of the Apollinian and the Dionysian attitudes and concludes how Nietzsche had the characteristics of an intuitive introvert (Jung, 1920/1949, CW 6). A psychological analysis of Nietzsche's personality and psychopathology is seldom far from Jung's reading of Nietzsche; this never veils his clear admiration of the philosopher but rather represents in Jung an effort to integrate Nietzsche's ideas as opposed to worshipping the man, and it also acts against a youthful tendency to get inspired and carried away by both – just like Nietzsche was himself. The more recently published *Zarathustra Lectures* show Jung at his most thorough in plumbing the depths of Nietzsche's aesthetic-philosophical masterpiece for its psychological and spiritual richness. However, in this chapter, I do not propose to bring forward correspondences between Jung and Nietzsche to support the idea that they present a parallel influence when it comes to postmodern thinking in any direct or systematic way. Despite there being more than a page of references to Nietzsche in the general index of Jung's collected works, this would not be possible – let alone desirable – because Jung does not 'read' Nietzsche in such a direct fashion. It seems to me that Jung has absorbed Nietzschean thought from very early in his intellectual life and throughout his writing it may be detected as an influence. After several years of postmodern thinking that has clearly demonstrated a connection with Nietzschean ideas, it has become easier, when reading Jung, to spot areas of overlap between Jungian concepts and emphases and their Nietzschean counterparts that have influenced the postmodern. This chapter explores a selection of these in an intertextual fashion: the deposing of the subject or individual ego, perspectivism and complexes, genealogy and history, and, finally, the Last Man, mass-man, the *ubermensch* and individuation.

However, I have to insert a *caveat* that will apply throughout what follows. Nietzsche's thought is vast and widespread over many themes and topics; equally, it covers a span of development from Nietzsche's youth to his maturity and thus constitutes a further range that resists homogenisation. Second, the interpreters of Nietzsche – commentators, critics, scholars, devotees and enemies – again vary widely in the way that Nietzsche's ideas are understood, applied and connected to further thought. Third, both these factors also apply to Jung's thought, thus making the project of examining the relationship between the two potentially, unmanageably vast. Attempts have been made which show how such a project can extend to encyclopaedic proportions. Therefore, this present chapter will attempt to offer no more than a focused comparison of certain of Nietzsche's ideas that, on the one hand, strike me as comparable with Jung's, and, on the other hand, a hundred years later, seem to constitute a common source of what we now call postmodern thinking. In common with other discussants of Nietzsche and of Jung, the selection will be subjective and will be shaped by my own concerns and the limitations of my own epistemological field. In making this statement, I do not seek to excuse the omissions or mistakes that will inevitably arise from my attempt to compare the ideas of Nietzsche, Jung and the postmodern, but, instead, I would like the chapter to be read more as a discussion document from which to launch further arguments about the significance of both Jung and Nietzsche for postmodern thinking and for contemporary life.

NIETZSCHE AND GERMAN THOUGHT AT THE END
OF THE NINETEENTH CENTURY

Like Jung, Friedrich Nietzsche (1844–1900) was born the son of a Protestant minister. He was only eleven years older than Freud, but senior to Jung by thirty years and thus representative of a generation directly preceding Jung's own. Precociously brilliant, Nietzsche was appointed professor of classical philology at the University of Basle in 1869 at the unheard of age of twenty-five. By the time of his retirement due to ill health in 1879, he had embarked on a remarkable series of books and continued writing until 1889 when his mental and physical health deteriorated severely – leaving him in mental isolation until his death in 1900. Nietzsche's writing became extremely popular in the 1890s and was reviewed and discussed in the daily press as well as in intellectual circles. The myth of Nietzsche – first as the recluse, then as the one struck down by madness – grew after his death, giving him the status of a prophet as much of what he had asserted and predicted – such as the slaughter of World Wars – came to be true.

Up until 1880 or thereabouts, European thought was dominated by positivism, scientism and evolutionism. It had been these that had under-written the great expansion of industrial mechanisation, urbanisation and colonial exploitation that characterised the dominance of European culture throughout the world. The exploitative thrust of industrial capitalism had become harnessed to the materialistic aims of scientific discovery which contoured a particular belief in human 'progress' begun by the Enlightenment. Europeans of this period could believe their achievements represented the peak of human civilisation and the overcoming of nature, and that this achievement had been accomplished through the application of man's greatest tool – scientific rationality.

Around 1885, however, there emerged a change in the intellectual orientation of Europeans that produced reverberations throughout a variety of aspects of culture. Central to this change was the challenging of many of the assumptions and values of the dominant ideology – a challenge which amounted to the first widespread critique of Enlightenment rationality and the values it had brought with it since the aesthetic response of the Romantics a century earlier. This was not a revolution based on class antagonisms or a war fought over territorial ownership, as in previous eras, but it was a revolutionary battle all the same. This time the battle was to be fought over the embedded values and beliefs that had lain trans-parent within the assumptions that governed both the *status quo* and the revolutionary changes of the previous centuries of Enlightenment thinking.

Here is one example of Nietzsche's acidic critique of the scientism of his day that remains relevant – and perhaps even more so – in the present age:

Cause and effect. – We call it 'explanation', but it is 'description' which distinguishes us from earlier stages of knowledge and science. We describe better – we explain just as little as any who came before us. We have revealed a plural succession where the naïve man and investigator of earlier cultures saw only two things, 'cause' and 'effect' as they were called; we have perfected an image of how things become, but we have not got past an image or behind it. In every case the row of 'causes' stands before us much more completely; we conclude: this must first happen if that is to follow – but we have therewith *understood* nothing. Quality, in any chemical change for example, appears as it has always done as a 'miracle'; likewise all locomotion; no one has explained 'thrust'. How could we explain them! We operate with nothing but things which do not exist, with lines, planes, bodies, atoms, divisible time, divisible space – how should explanation even be possible when we first make everything into an *image*, into our own image! It is sufficient to regard science as the most fruitful possible humanisation of things, we learn to describe ourselves more and more exactly by describing things and the succession of things. Cause and effect: such a duality probably never occurs – in reality there stands before us a continuum of which we isolate a couple of pieces; . . .
(Nietzsche, 1882, GS 112/1977: 61–62)

This is Nietzsche the deconstructionist, the debunker and critic of modernity with its scientific 'truths' and its faith in instrumental reason. Nietzsche's views were in common with the growing anti-materialistic spirit of his times – a theme also pursued energetically by the student Jung as recorded in the *Zofingia Lectures* of 1896–1897 (Jung, 1983, CW Supp. Vol. A). Nietzsche's writing was, as his alternative title to *Twilight of the Idols* (1889) suggests, an example of *How to Philosophise with a Hammer* – but his philosophy was a radical departure from what had gone before. Well ahead of its time, it has far more in common with psychology and critical theory. It is not only modernity and its cultural, moral and scientific achievements, but also the psyche of the modern 'civilised' European which falls beneath the sledge-hammer of Nietzsche's critical psychology. These deconstructive fields are often linked as, for example, when he views the thirst for knowledge as a manifestation of mankind's self-destructive instincts, claiming that science is, 'a principle inimical to life and destructive. The will for truth could be a disguised wish for death' (*Die frohliche Wissenschaft*, No. 344, quoted in Ellenberger, 1994: 275).

Nietzsche is again the psychologist rather than the philosopher when we find him joining in with the late nineteenth-century trend of an 'unmasking' or an 'uncovering' psychology already being expressed in the literary works of Dostoevsky and Ibsen, and, of course, in the burgeoning psychoanalytic theory just being developed by Sigmund Freud. For Nietzsche, man is both self-deceiving and deceiving of his fellows – a view that predicts concepts central to depth psychology. As in psychoanalysis and analytical psychology, consciousness is relativised in Nietzsche – we are all farthest from ourselves and suffering from self-deception because it is the unconscious that is central to our being while consciousness – which modernity prizes above all – is merely 'a more or less fantastic commentary on an unconscious, perhaps unknowable, but felt text' (*Morgenrothe*, 123, quoted in Ellenberger, 1994: 273). Notice, too, how Nietzsche's use of the word 'text' predates Lacan's formulations of the unconscious as an obscured language by some sixty years. Even more significantly, it is Nietzsche, again, who first uses the term Id (*das Es* – the It – in *Also Spracht Zarathustra*) to describe the unconscious psyche, the realm of our primitive, instinct-driven natures.

THE DEPOSING OF THE SUBJECT

It is Nietzsche's attention to *das Es*, the Unconscious and the relativisation of *das Ich* – the 'I' or Ego – that provides a useful starting point from which to consider his relationship to both Jung and postmodern thought. As a philosopher, Nietzsche saw as one of his tasks the deposing of the Cartesian and Kantian view of the subject as an indispensable and central focus. Nietzsche notes that,

> a thought comes when 'it' wants, not when 'I' want; so that it is a *falsification* of the facts to say: the subject 'I' is the condition of the predicate 'think'. *It* thinks: but that this 'it' is precisely the famous old 'I' is, to put it mildly, only an assumption, an assertion, above all not an 'immediate certainty'.
>
> (Nietzsche, 1973: 28–29)

As David Macey puts it, 'Nietzsche's anti-Kantian aphorisms are an important moment in the emergence of the contention that subjectivity is an effect rather than a cause, that something – the unconscious, language – speaks through and of the individual' (Macey, 1995: 73). I have mentioned more than once in this book the common-place assertion that, similar to the Copernican revolution, Freud also decentred the subject-ego through drawing our attention to the unconscious – after which the subject of modernity could no longer consider him or herself in complete charge of the subjective psyche. However, although the evolution of Freud's ego has a complicated history, there is a sense in which it remains quite pre-Nietzschean – and hence Cartesian/Kantian – inasmuch as it retains a central orientating function between the psyche and Reality. For Freud the ego must, ultimately, remain in charge, moderating and controlling the uncivilised impulses stemming from the unconscious id:

> in its relation to the id it is like a man on horseback, who has to hold in check the superior strength of the horse; with this difference, that the rider tries to do so with his own strength while the ego uses borrowed forces . . . Often a rider, if he is not to be parted from his horse, is obliged to guide it where it wants to go; in the same way the ego is in the habit of transforming the id's will into action as if it were its own.
>
> (Freud, 1923: 25)

In pointing out how Lacan's return to Freud was aimed at deposing the hegemony of American ego-psychology and restoring to psychoanalysis the fundamental discovery of the unconscious 'which is held to subvert the conventional notions of the subject' (Macey, 1995: 74), David Macey points out the sense of the 'famous old "I"' still retained by Freud's 1923 reformulation, 'It inherits many of the characteristics of the preconscious-conscious system of the first topography. The ego controls perception and is responsible for reality testing. It is the seat of rational thought, and the agency which introduces – or attempts to introduce – a temporal order into mental processes' (ibid.: 73). Lacan's formulation of the mirror-phase of psychic development was intended to point out how the ego is formed in profound alienation to the subject. Going back to Freud's earlier work 'On Narcissism' (Freud 1914), Lacan states, 'In Freud the theory of the ego is intended . . . to show that what we call our ego is a certain image that we have of ourselves, an image that produces a mirage, of totality no doubt' (Lacan 1981: 273).

Jung's conception of the unconscious, like Nietzsche's and similar to the emphasis in Lacan, is one in which the ego, and hence consciousness and subjectivity, is utterly relativised against an unconscious which is experienced by the subject as profoundly *other*. The relationship between the ego – the centre of consciousness – and the unconscious self – the centre and totality of the whole psyche – is not one where the ego takes charge, but one in which the ego is to the self as the 'moved is to the mover'. Jung is clear about the implications of such a view for the autonomy of the subject and the idea, beloved of the Enlightenment, of 'freedom':

I have suggested calling the total personality which, though present, cannot be fully known, the *self*. The ego is, by definition, subordinate to the self and is related to it like a part to the whole. Inside the field of consciousness it has, as we say, free will. By this I do not mean anything philosophical, only the well known psychological fact of 'free choice', or rather the subjective feeling of freedom. But, just as our free will clashes with necessity in the outside world, so also it finds its limits outside the field of consciousness in the subjective inner world, where it comes into conflict with the facts of the self. And just as circumstances or outside events 'happen' to us and limit our freedom, so the self acts upon the ego like an *objective occurrence* which free will can do very little to alter . . .

. . . it is only since the end of the nineteenth century that modern psychology, with its inductive methods, has discovered the foundations of consciousness and proved empirically the existence of a psyche outside consciousness. With this discovery the position of the ego, till then absolute, became relativized . . . its freedom is limited and . . . In my experience one would do well not to underestimate its dependence on the unconscious.

(Jung, 1950, CW 9ii: paras 9,11)

As with Nietzsche, Jung affirmed that 'he' did not think but that 'thoughts think me'. In *Two Kinds of Thinking*, a paper dating from 1912 (revised 1952), Jung discusses the source of symbolic representation manifested in fantasies, myths and dreams, as lying in non-directed thinking which he opposes to the purposive, directed thinking of ego-consciousness. Of the latter he says, 'the culture-creating mind is ceaselessly employed in stripping experience of everything subjective, and in devising formulas to harness the forces of nature and express then in the best way possible' (Jung, 1912, CW 5: para. 23). This, he argues, makes modern humans rich in knowledge but poor in wisdom; the centre of gravity is now the materialistic while for the ancients it was the fantastic. Here we find Jung emphasising postmodern concerns around the critique of modern culture in the form found in both Nietzsche and his own Zofingia lectures of nearly thirty years earlier. It comes as no surprise, then, when Jung quotes Nietzsche on dreams with, 'dreaming is a recreation for the brain, which by day has to satisfy the stern demands of thought imposed by a higher culture' (Nietzsche, 1878b, *Human, All Too Human*: 24–27).

The revision and critique of enlightenment rationality and its particular assumptions, initiated for modernity by Nietzsche and his hammer blows, owes more to Jung and Lacan as the heirs of this deconstruction than it does to Freud. Especially when it comes to deposing the heroic subject of Kant and Descartes – despite important differences such as Lacan's post-structural linguistic emphases – both Jung and Lacan retain a focus on the radical concept of the unconscious. This constitutes a theme of similarity and contrast between Jung and Lacan that proves unavoidable when it comes to discussing Jung and the postmodern, and even more so when Nietzsche is examined as a precursor and influence.

PLURALISM, PERSPECTIVISM AND COMPLEXES

Closely connected with the relativisation of the subject as just discussed are the themes of perspectivism in Nietzsche, and of pluralism as found in cultural theory and post-Jungian psychology. Before Nietzsche, it was the eighteenth-century philosopher Vico who, well ahead of his time, provided a way of thinking about successive groups of humanity, civilisations, which, rather than promoting the hegemony of enlightenment views of his day, instead valued the plurality and the range of different perspectives that constituted human life. As Isaiah Berlin puts it,

> Vico seemed to be concerned with the succession of human cultures –
> every society had, for him, its own vision of reality, of the world in
> which it lived, and of itself and of its relations to its own past, to nature,
> to what it strove for. This vision of a society is conveyed by everything
> that its members do and think and feel – expressed and embodied in the
> kinds of words, the forms of language that they use, the images, the
> metaphors, the forms of worship, the institutions that they generate,
> which embody and convey their image of reality and of their place in it;
> by which they live.
>
> (Berlin 1991: 46)

Perspectivism is a metaphor of epistemology as *vision*; it is a way of addressing the problem of what is 'true' about the world that situates this issue back with the subjective observer. From the perspectival approach, how things are arises from how they are constructed by the subject experiencing them. The 'truth' of the world varies according to the various perspectives from which it is viewed. This, then, is in strict contrast to an approach, such as the scientific objectivity of classical scientific empiricism, that maintains there can be a reality that will always be 'true' independently of any observer. Perspectivism also counters the Kantian–Platonic idea that there is an unattainable 'real' world existing beyond the limitations of human senses and thought. Nietzsche addresses both these issues and they become combined in his idea of perspectivism which becomes at once both a philosophical position – by addressing Kant's transcendent – and a psychological position involving the cognitive and affective interests of the human subject. Jung, I contend, expresses this combination of epistemology and psychology in his ideas of personality and the complexes, thus developing Nietzsche's perspectivism within analytical psychology. I will use the rest of this section to justify this statement.

Nietzsche states his own position in *On the Genealogy of Morals*:

> ... let us guard against the snares of such contradictory concepts as 'pure reason', 'absolute spirituality', 'knowledge in itself': these always demand that we should think of an eye that is completely unthinkable, an eye turned in no particular direction, in which the active and interpreting forces, through which alone seeing becomes seeing *something*, are supposed to be lacking; these always demand of the eye an absurdity and a nonsense. There is *only* a perspective seeing, *only* a perspective 'knowing'; and the *more* affects we allow to speak about one thing, the *more* eyes, different eyes, we use to observe one thing, the more complete will our 'concept' of this thing, our 'objectivity', be.
>
> (Nietzsche, 1887/1967, *On the Genealogy of Morals* III, para. 12)

For Nietzsche, not only is the seer/knower always *situated*, the activity of knowing is also never disinterested but is always rooted in our affective constitution. Cognitive consciousness, *logos*, is entwined with affective constitution, *eros*, and as David Owen interprets Nietzsche, 'Our consciousness is neither disembedded nor disembodied; knowing, like seeing, is an activity which attends the embedded and embodied character of human subjectivity' (Owen, 1995: 33). Following from this is Nietzsche's second metaphor for 'knowing': 'interpreting'. All knowing about the world is necessarily an act of interpretation, a selection of certain features and a disregarding of others. We only 'know' according to our 'point of view' – our particular cognitive and affective perspective, in other words – and no knowledge, including that of so-called 'science', can be exempt from this. Moreover, we select according to our *interests*. There is no dis-interested knowing as Nietzsche himself asserts, 'It is perhaps just dawning on five or six minds that physics too is only an interpretation and arrangement of the world (according to our own requirements, if I may say so!) and *not* an explanation of the world' (Nietzsche, 1886/1973: 26, para. 14). In addition, Owen reminds us that it is important to note that the truth of an interpretation about the world 'does not exclude the truth of other interpretations of the world which serve other interests. It is an important feature of perspectivism that it rejects the idea that the truth about the world could be exhausted by any single description of it' (Owen, 1995: 34).

Why is this perspectivism not merely a relativism? Owen's answer is two-fold: he finds that Nietzsche's rebuttal of the appearance/reality distinction answers the charge that a position that does not recognise universal and necessary features of rationality is relativist. Nietzsche's progressive argument with the Kantian distinction of appearance and reality ends up where 'the real world' – appearing in quotes in the later stages of his thought – although not denied an existence, is seen as a superfluous concept and outside human interests. Nietzsche's final position is one, 'in which he recognises that rejecting the thing-in-itself entails rejecting the idea that the empirical world is mere appearance and, consequently, rejecting the idea that our human truths are illusions, which, in turn, entails recognising that truth is not independent of our cognitive interests' (ibid.: 32). In a note Owen adds, 'I think that the weakness of those who argue that our concept of rationality involves notions of non-contradiction and identity is that they don't account for how we acquired this concept!' (ibid.: 53). Second, against the charge that perspectivism is relativist because it gives us no criteria for claiming one perspective is better than another, Owen points out that all perspectives have 'equal rights to claim epistemic authority' (ibid.: 34) – i.e. truth – by which standards of rationality come into play, but this is different to saying that all perspectives claim equal authority. Philosophically, the difference may appear subtle, but psychologically – and culturally – the distinction is clear in the way it admits the importance of the contextual and affective grounding of all perspectives.

Isaiah Berlin summarises the distinction between relativism and pluralism in a parallel fashion,

> 'I prefer coffee, you prefer champagne. We have different tastes. There is no more to be said.' That is relativism ... Vico's (view) is not that: it is what I should describe as pluralism – that is, the conception that there are many different ends that men may seek and still be fully rational, fully men, capable of understanding each other and sympathising and deriving light from each other.
>
> (Berlin, 1991: 48)

Of interest to the Jungian point of view on pluralism and perspectivism, Berlin also notes how 'Intercommunication between culture in time and space is only possible because what makes men human is common to them, and acts as a bridge between them' (ibid.). This statement implies a supra-cultural possibility that gets expressed in the Jungian idea of the collective unconscious, and in Joseph Henderson's post-Jungian concept of a cultural unconscious (Henderson, 1991). The concept of pluralism itself has been taken up and applied to the Jungian psyche by Andrew

Samuels in *The Plural Psyche* (1989) and *The Political Psyche* (1993), to express both the plurality of the complexes, archetypal images and sub-personalities of the individual psyche, from a Jungian point-of-view, and the plurality of coexisting forms in contemporary political and social life. And it is the tension between these, the individual and the collective, the personal and the social-political, which I will use as the starting point for linking Nietzschian perspectivism and Jungian pluralism in what follows.

Summarising perspectivism, David Owen concludes that 'a perspective is a complex of beliefs going in the same direction!' and that 'Nietzsche's use of perspective as an (affectually bound) web of beliefs and as an (affectually bound) style of reasoning is quite coherent' (Owen, 1995: 36–37). Such a 'complex' or 'web of beliefs' or 'style of reasoning' forms the basis of Jung's theory of the complexes as elements that constitute human personality. This idea was so central to Jung's psychological theorising that not only did he regard the complex, and not the dream, as the *via regia* to the psyche, but he also considered calling his psychological theory 'Complex Psychology' before it was called Analytical Psychology as it is today. These emphases on the complex by Jung are not simply ways of distinguishing his views from those of Freud, but the concept of the complex also played a central role in the collaboration of Jung with Freud in the early years of their relationship.

In 1906, Jung sent Freud details of his experiments on word association. This record of delays in replying and changes in skin-conductivity in subjects responding to lists of stimulus words led Jung to develop his idea of the complex and led Freud to think that here was the experimental verification of his own theories of repression. In his early formulations, Jung regarded his findings within Freud's psychoanalytic frame. The complexes were indicators of the neuroses, knots of affects and beliefs unacceptable to the conscious mind are therefore repressed in the Unconscious. They were the source of the symptoms psychoanalysis attempted to treat.

> Usually there are only a few personal matters to which the disturbances of the experiment refer. Rilkin and myself have introduced for this 'personal matter' the term *complex*, because such a 'personal matter' is always a collection of various ideas, held together by an emotional tone common to all . . . Somatic states are never the real, but only the predisposing causes of the neuroses. The neurosis itself is of psychic origin, and emanates from 'special psychic contents', which we call a *complex*.
>
> (Jung, 1911, CW 2: paras 1350 – 1351)

In other words, the results of the association experiment were directly parallel to the free associations and linguistic slips revealed on Freud's couch, and led similarly to psychoanalytic insights about the repressed contents of the unconscious which were the source of neurotic symptoms.

Twenty-three years later, Jung had not abandoned the complex as he had abandoned Freud and psychoanalysis, but the concept had become revised in the direction of a general psychology rather than remaining as merely evidence of the pathological.

> The association test . . . reproduces the psychic situation of the *dialogue* . . . What happens . . . also happens in every discussion between two people. In both cases there is an experimental situation which constellates complexes that assimilate the topic discussed or the situation as a whole, including the parties concerned. The discussion loses its objective character and its real purpose, since the constellated complexes frustrate the intentions of the speakers and may even put answers into their mouths which they can no longer remember afterwards.
>
> (Jung, 1934, CW 8: para. 199)

Jung's use of the term 'constellated' refers to the way that complexes are formed which then govern the affective and cognitive perceptions and actions of the personality in a way that is outside conscious control. Here, the complex sounds much more directly in line with the Nietzschean idea of a perspective, especially when Jung emphasises the contribution of affect, 'What . . . is a "feeling-toned complex"? It is the *image* of a certain psychic situation which is strongly accentuated emotionally and is, moreover, incompatible with the habitual attitude of consciousness' (ibid.: para. 200). Jung remains ambiguous about whether the complex is still a disturbance or aberration or, alternatively, the extent to which it constitutes an unavoidable aspect of every psyche, part of every individual's personality. It seems that both positions are true – modern consciousness has an inevitable dissociated quality: it is 'normal' to be fragmented and to have to struggle with this. The postmodern attitude would be an acceptance and celebration of this, and the post-Jungian position has become informed by this in its questioning of any automatic condemnation of 'fragmentation' (see Hauke, 1995). The idea of 'sub-personalities', autonomous complexes, is widely accepted as a way of understanding both normal and troubled personalities (see, for example, Redfearn, 1985).

On the one hand, Jung notes how 'Only when you have seen whole families destroyed by them . . . and the . . . tragedy and hopeless misery that follow in their train, do you feel the full impact of the reality of the complexes' (Jung, 1934, CW 8: para. 209) while, on the other hand, he notes that 'complexes are not entirely morbid by nature but are *characteristic expressions of the psyche*' (ibid.). 'These fragments subsist relatively independently of one another and can take one another's place at any time, which means that each fragment possesses a high degree of autonomy . . . there is no difference in principle between a fragmentary personality and a complex' (ibid.: para. 202). Indeed, Jung refers to ego-consciousness itself, the same subjective consciousness that the complexes seem to auto-nomously disrupt, as a complex – an 'ego-complex' created in humans by 'later levels of conscious development' (ibid.: para. 204). It seems that, for Jung, it is aversion to our complexes that causes the greatest difficulty, not the fact of the complex itself. 'Fear of the complexes is a bad signpost', Jung warns 'because it always points away from the unconscious and back into consciousness . . . Despite overwhelming evidence of all kinds that complexes have always existed and are ubiquitous, people cannot bring themselves to regard them as normal phenomena of life'. And, in line with the challenge to the unitary rationality of Enlightenment that Nietzsche's perspectivism also provides, Jung's attitude to the complex is similarly challenging: 'The fear of complexes is a rooted prejudice, for the superstitious fear of anything unfavourable has remained untouched by our vaunted enlightenment' (ibid.: para. 211).

Finally, bringing this perspectivism squarely in line with scientific psychological investigation, and pointing out its limitations, Jung notes,

> No investigator, however unprejudiced and objective he is, can afford to disregard his own complexes . . . As a matter of fact, he *cannot* disregard them, because they do not disregard *him*. Complexes are very much part of the psychic constitution, which is the most absolutely prejudiced thing in every individual. His constitution will therefore inexorably decide *what* psychological view a given observer will have. Herein lies the unavoidable limitation of psychological observation: its validity is contingent upon the personal equation of the observer.
>
> (ibid.: para. 312)

In this, Jung is referring, amongst other things, to Freud and his psycho-analytic theorising which held emphases Jung eventually could not share, and which led to the end of their collaboration. Elsewhere, Jung is quite specific about differences in psychological theories which arise from the different personalities of the theorists, where no single theory, including his own, is the whole truth, and each perspective stands as valid as another in a plurality of psychologies. In an essay contrasting his views with those of Freud (Jung, 1929, CW 4), Jung begins emphatically by stating that all ideas, especially the psychological, are 'fifty-per-cent' subjective: 'For the purposes of psychology, I think it best to abandon the notion that we are today in anything like a position to make statements about the nature of the psyche that are "true" or "correct"' (ibid.: para. 771).

Andrew Samuels, writing in *The Plural Psyche* (1989), draws together the plurality of the psyche and the plurality of depth psychological theorising that moves the argument on further. He quite rightly makes the distinction between pluralism and 'eclecticism' and 'relativism', but although he promises to differentiate pluralism from what he calls 'perspectivalism' as well, his views seem to coincide with the Nietzschean-led theme of Jung and perspectivism I am advocating. Samuels writes:

> *My proposal* is that, from an experiential point of view, the psyche may be seen as containing relatively autonomous spheres of activity and imagery and that, over time and according to context, each sphere has its dominance. Similarly, from a more intellectual point of view, each school of depth psychology may be seen as relatively autonomous from the other schools and its theory as having its own strengths and weaknesses . . . accepting that, in some ways and some situations, the other guy has a more utilizable (more true?) theory . . . (This is) not the same as agreeing to disagree and different, too, from being 'eclectic'. For eclecticism means singing selected verses only. Eclecticism ignores the contradictions between systems of thought, whereas pluralism celebrates their competition.
>
> (Samuels, 1989: 12–13)

In other words, all perspectives have a 'validity' but not all at the same time and for the same observation. The utility, or 'reality', of perspectives will vary according to context.

This point of view has influenced more recent anthropological and philosophical discussions of 'rationalities' different from those of our own Western industrialised cultures. Tambiah (1990), Winch (1964), Horton (1967) and others have discussed the role of relativism when it comes to the beliefs and types of 'science' found in other societies, and in Chapter 11 I will be discussing the perspectival approach as it may be applied to rationalities in our own culture that are defined as 'sane' or 'mad'. But Jung's perspectivism is evident in his attitude to the beliefs and rituals of other cultures, despite the contradictory evidence stemming from a colonialist, Victorian racist bias that also emerges (Dalal, 1988). Again it is Samuels who notices how Jung promotes a type of multiculturalism in his valuing of what we in the West can learn about the psyche from the forms of thought and behaviour to be found across the world. Unlike Freud, Jung travelled widely to experience some of these himself in Africa, USA, India and elsewhere, and while Samuels does not want to 'join in knee-jerk defences of Jung' he does recognise,

> that, alongside the unfortunate excursions into racial typology, we can also discern the seeds of a surprisingly modern and constructive attitude to race and ethnicity. For example, in 1935 Jung argued against the imposition of 'the spirit' of one race upon another, referring to a Eurocentric, judgmental approach to other cultures. Here and elsewhere in Jung's writings, there is also a respect for and interest in the evolution of different cultures.
>
> (Samuels, 1993: 309)

Michael Vannoy Adams' book *The Multicultural Imagination* (1996a), and a paper of my own (Hauke, 1996b) also address post-Jungian views on race and plurality.

Lastly, it should not be forgotten how it was Jung the psychiatrist at the Burgholzi hospital in Zurich who advanced an attitude to, and a method of treating, psychotic patients that accepted their 'mad' perspectives on 'reality' and sought to heal their distress by finding value and meaning in their utterances. In contrast to prevailing views of the time that the perceptions and experiences of those suffering psychotic disturbances – later called schizophrenic illness – were purely aberrations of normal rationality caused by organic or inherited malfunctioning of the brain, Jung approached psychiatry with a fresh perspective of his own. This new attitude was not only influenced by Jung's senior, Bleuler, but also indicates a Nietzschean perspectival approach to the psyche which Jung brought to this critical area of his early experience and one which, later, contributed to his mature theories of the psyche.

GENEALOGY AND 'HISTORY'

The third major area of comparison between Jung, Nietzsche and the postmodern is that of *genealogy*. In Jung's writing there is frequently an historical emphasis, or, rather, what appears to be 'history': a tendency to refer to past forms of thought, rituals, myths and beliefs in his effort to map the contemporary, modern psyche and, above all, to analyse this psyche with all its lacks and its potentials. In this section I propose to argue that Jung's 'history-making' is not really about history as such but follows the same trajectory, and critical aim, of *genealogy* as employed by Friedrich Nietzsche in his critical philosophical and psychological writing.

Genealogy is concerned with tracing the origins and development of a phenomenon that not only asks *how* it is possible but also *why it is necessary*. Nietzsche distinguishes genealogy from history by pointing out, in *On the Genealogy of Morals* (1887) for example, that there is no linear evolution in our accepted conceptualisations – 'good' and 'evil', in this case – but that these notions have been formed in response to changing conflicts and accidental events. If the image of history is one of a series of great 'men' and great 'movements' and of one thing leading rationally to another, the image of genealogy is that of the family tree, whereby, through the accidents of marriages, births, deaths and divorces – not to mention 'illegitimate' births – a line of development proceeds haphazardly and unpredictably. In the second image, the present is still the 'result' of the past but not in any evolutionary, linear or rational sense at all but clearly as the 'result' or 'effect' of the ups and downs of human life. I will refer to Michel Foucault's analysis of the difference between the linear concept of 'history' and the disjunctive concept of genealogy as expressed in his seminal paper 'Nietzsche, Genealogy, History' (Foucault, 1971). It is Foucault's work in tracing the genealogy of madness, sexuality and marginalisation, and their relationship to power and knowledge that endorses, and employs, Nietzsche's techniques to develop a critique of modernity along postmodern lines.

In describing how what appears as 'history' and the search for roots and precursors in Jung's psychology as being more accurately read as a genealogy along Nietzschean lines, I wish to address a number of issues. One is the idea that Jung's writing seeks to establish essentials in human psychology in a fixed fashion. I think that this is a misunderstanding of Jung that can be clarified by an examination of what genealogy is and what it tries to achieve. Another is how Jung produces a critique of modernity and modern consciousness that extends beyond the aim of mapping the psyche simply for the purposes of treating psychological and emotional distress as has been the emphasis elsewhere in depth psychology. A third issue concerns the contextualising of the sufferings of the modern psyche, a way of seeing all so-called pathology and so-called 'normality' as having a 'history' that, once analysed as a genealogy, provides a perspective view that counters the essentialising tendency towards the construction of universal 'causes' in the same way as many strands of postmodern thinking counter this tendency elsewhere. These points then help us to begin rethinking concepts in Jung that appear to be most essentialist, and thereby the least postmodern, such as the concept of the archetypes.

Several times in earlier chapters I have referred to tendencies in postmodern culture and thought such as 'nostalgia', 'looking back' and 'retrogressive' that have been analysed at length by postmodern theorists

– especially Fredric Jameson and Charles Jencks. The emphasis has been that, rather than reflecting a Romantic, defensive or retreating solution to modernity, these are in fact ways in which subjects and societies orient themselves in a complex and fragmented world. 'Looking back' becomes a way of looking at the present with the intention of looking forward. As a more formal intellectual discipline, genealogy is the same thing – as David Owen summarises:

> Nietzsche's historical reflections are similarly concerned with sketching the contingent roots through which we have become what we are (namely, modern individuals) in order to provide a context of meaning within which we can recognise and critically reflect on our modernity. Thus, a provisional understanding of genealogy as a Nietzschean term of art would point to its concern with providing a history of the present in order to facilitate critical reflection upon the present.
>
> (Owen, 1995: 39)

Nietzsche's view emphasises not only how 'our reflective activity is always both historically and culturally situated and affectively structured' but also that 'the activity of critique must recognise its own contextual and interested character' (ibid.). This is Habermas's point that critique of modernity starts within, and is to an unavoidable extent, limited by the context of modernity. At first glance, Habermas's views would seem to render Jung's particular genealogical approach redundant, especially when he asserts,

> the path of restoration is barred to modernity. The religious-metaphysical world-views of ancient civilisations are themselves already a product of enlightenment; they are *too rational*, therefore, to be able to provide opposition to the radicalized enlightenment of modernity.
>
> (Habermas, 1987b: 53)

However, against this, Habermas also notes that, following Nietzsche's head-start, certain critical theorists, Heidegger and Bataille, *do* find a way 'back' that then serves to disrupt the hegemony of enlightenment reason:

> like Nietzsche, Heidegger and Bataille must reach beyond the origins of Western history back to archaic times in order to rediscover the traces of the Dionysian . . . It is here that they have to identify those buried, rationalised-away experiences that are to fill the abstract terms

'Being' and 'sovereignty' with life. Both are just names to start with. They have to be introduced as concepts contrasting with reason in such a way that they remain resistant to any attempts at rational incorporation. 'Being' is defined as that which has *withdrawn* itself from the totality of beings that can be grasped and known as something in the objective world; 'sovereignty' as that which has been *excluded* from the world of the useful and calculable.

(ibid.: 58, italics in original)

Habermas's understanding of Nietzsche, Heidegger and Bataille could easily include Jung's and Kristeva's ideas in this same trajectory. When Habermas refers to the 'other' of reason as 'what is simply unmanipulable and not valorisable – a medium into which the subject can plunge if it gives itself up and transcends itself *as* subject' (ibid.), he could be referring to Jung's concept of the unconscious self which humanity needs now, more than ever, to maintain in a dialogue with the ego-subjectivity of modern consciousness. According to Habermas, Being and sovereignty – the 'abstract terms' which are brought to life by being filled with 'those buried, rationalised-away experiences' Enlightenment ignores – constitute the Other to Enlightenment reason by their status of that which is *withdrawn* or *excluded*. While this clearly applies to aspects of Enlightenment such as Newton's alchemical researches, this understanding also resonates with Kristeva's notion of the abject which was encountered in the previous chapter as her term for what gets excluded by patriarchal rationality. Both Jung's self and Kristeva's abject are different aspects of – and different conceptualisations of – *the* other to reason: the unconscious psyche in general. By associating the unconscious with ancient source material, Jung is seeking the Other to Enlightenment reason – for him, the other to modern consciousness – either in places where such reason has not touched or in places reason has abandoned like the abandoned *lapis*, the discarded 'stone of no worth' (no 'worth', that is, as far as Enlightenment was concerned). Like Nietzsche, and subsequent critical theorists, Jung extended the idea of reflecting on the past to a broader view that encompassed past traditions and beliefs of humanity as he discovered them in ancient texts. And in addition, it is most important to note *how* Jung's scholasticism challenges Habermas's initial assertion that Enlightenment reason has the power to absorb the world-views of ancient civilisations within the language of it own rationality and thus renders them useless as a fulcrum of critique. The fact is that many of the texts that Jung found were either highly esoteric – like the alchemical works he studied – or they were newly discovered, and unavailable to the early Enlightenment, like the Nag Hammadi scrolls. Either way they had escaped incorporation and working over by an enlightenment rationality which had found little use for them or had not known about them. This would not apply to Jung's use of Greek mythology and, given the degree to which this material has been made 'too rational' over the centuries, perhaps post-Jungians should be wary of the weaker potential for the critique of consciousness that this material contains.

By 'looking back', Jung found a critical fulcrum by which he could reflect on how we are and the possibilities of what we could become. Similarly,

> Nietzsche's concern with reflecting on how we have become what we are is also a reflection on how what we are both enables and constrains what we may become. In other words, Nietzsche's concern with reconstructing the historical conditions of possibility of what we are is also directed to how what we are acts as the conditions of possibility for our being otherwise than we are.
>
> (Owen, 1995: 40)

For Nietzsche, the possible outcomes of our condition were either the *Last Man* or the *Ubermensch* – but not both. Jung developed the theories and technique of analytical psychology to help, optimistically it might be thought, towards the second outcome – the *Ubermensch*, the *Overman*, and, after exploring Foucault's analysis of genealogy, I will be examining the relationship between the *Ubermensch* and Jung's central concept of *individuation* in the next section.

In his essay, 'Nietzsche, Genealogy, History' (1971), Michel Foucault analyses the difference between history and genealogy and challenges the former's esssentialism and its assumption of 'origins'. Foucault uses what Nietzsche has to say about the limitations of 'history' and historicity to promote the idea of genealogy as a method that, centrally, 'opposes itself to the search for "origins"' (Foucault, 1971: 77). Also coming under fire from Foucault are the historical fixtures of *Herkunft* – 'stock' or 'descent' – and *Enteshung*, 'emergence'. As Foucault puts it, 'if the genealogist refuses to extend his faith in metaphysics, if he listens to history, he finds that there is "something altogether different" behind things: not a timeless and essential secret, but the secret that they have no essence or that their essence was fabricated in a piecemeal fashion from alien forms' (ibid.: 78). He quotes Nietzsche from *Human, All Too Human*: 'devotion to truth and the pre-cision of scientific method arose from the passion of the scholars, their reciprocal hatred, their fanatical and unending discussions, and their spirit of competition – the personal conflicts that slowly forged the weapons of reason' (ibid.). The genealogical emphasis is not on 'original' states or on descent in an unbroken continuity as we might find in traditional history, but on the accidents, deviations and dead-end turnings that produce the pluralistic subject and society of modernity.

> Genealogy does not pretend to go back in time to restore an unbroken continuity that operates beyond the dispersion of forgotten things; its duty is not to demonstrate that the past actively exists in the present, that it continues secretly to animate the present, having imposed a predetermined form on all its vicissitudes. Genealogy does not resemble the evolution of a species and does not map the destiny of a people. On the contrary, to follow the complex course of a descent is to maintain passing events in their proper dispersion; it is to identify the accidents, the minute deviations – or conversely, the complete reversals – the errors, the false appraisals, and the faulty calculations that gave birth to those things that continue to exist and have value for us.
>
> (ibid.: 81)

Jung's perspective can be seen to coincide with this view of life and the development of phenomena as non-linear and accidental at both the level of the individual personality and at the level of modern social forms. In 1913, on the cusp of his final break from Freud, Jung was already revising the tenets of classical psychoanalysis along his own lines using material that emerged from the clinical treatment of his own patients. I expand these ideas more fully in Chapter 7, but the point I wish to make now is how Jung emphasises that, for the individual, personality, character, and hence the way reactions to conflict in life are dealt with or manifested, arise haphazardly out of the accidental events of early life. Emotional development derives from a series of accidents and then, following the individual's particular impressions received from these accidental happenings, 'accidental events and regression form a vicious circle: retreat from life leads to regression, and regression heightens resistance to life' (Jung, 1913: para. 403). For Jung, there is no discrete 'trauma', or original 'cause', that results in a symptom or 'effect'. Psychological dis-ease is the result of accidental effects in combination with the unique and differentiated sensitivity of individuals. The search for 'origins' and any linear continuity between cause and effect is eschewed in favour of the more Nietzschean perspective expressed as, 'The iron hand of necessity shaking the dice-box of chance'. In his development of psychoanalytic ideas Jung seems in line with Nietzsche's critique of traditional history as Foucault expresses it, 'The forces operating in history are not controlled by destiny or regulative mechanisms, but respond to haphazard conflicts' (Foucault, 1971: 88).

When he is considering the individual as subject of – and subjected to – modern society, Jung is similarly critical of the tendency in modernity to favour the statistical norm – resulting in an artificial levelling and distortion of the 'haphazard'. Writing in the 1950s towards the end of his life, Jung is found struggling with the tensions between the individual and the mass, between statistical averages and individual realities in a fashion that predicts postmodern concerns, 'The doctor, above all, should be aware of this contradiction. On the one hand, he is equipped with the statistical truths of his scientific training, and on the other, he is faced with the task of treating a sick person who . . . requires *individual understanding*' (Jung, 1957, CW 10: para. 497). And in the manner of Nietzsche and Foucault, Jung reveals a clear *anti-absolutism*,

> The statistical method shows the facts in the light of the ideal average but does not give us a picture of their empirical reality. While reflecting an indisputable aspect of reality, it can falsify the actual truth in a most misleading way. This is particularly true of theories that are based on statistics. The distinctive thing about real facts, however, is their individuality. Not to put too fine a point on it, one could say that the real picture consists of nothing but exceptions to the rule, and that, in consequence, absolute reality has predominately the character of *irregularity*.
>
> (ibid.: para. 494)

Jung's warning about the 'doctor' compares with Foucault's – originally Nietzsche's – critique of the traditional historian who wishes to encourage thorough understanding, to exclude qualitative judgements and to create a comprehensive view excluding differences, in summary, 'His apparent serenity follows from his concerted avoidance of the exceptional and his reduction of all things to the lowest common denominator' (Foucault, 1971: 90–91).

It is interesting to note how Nietzsche, and then Foucault, attend to the body in their analysis of the apparent, but false, unity of experience and history. The realm of physiology – the 'marvellous motley' of fragmented body-parts – becomes a metaphor, and more than a metaphor, to express the contradiction between apparent wholeness and actual disjunctions in the subject and in history. In much of this discourse we can see the inspiration for Lacan's idea of the 'mirror-stage' whereby the infant constructs the rudimentary ego from an alienated image of the self thus replacing the anxiety of somatic fragmentation with the fiction of a unified ego. The importance of Lacan's psychoanalytic view to the present argument is how it situates the formation of subjectivity in the *particular context of modernity*: as for Jung, the modern ego or subject suffers a partial and distorted experience of 'humanity' – an experience where much has been withdrawn, excluded or levelled out. Foucault notes how Nietzsche occasionally employs the phrase 'historically and physiologically' (Nietzsche, 1889, No. 44) and then likens the perspective of genealogy – or 'effective history' – to that of a doctor who 'looks closely, who plunges to make a diagnosis and to state its difference' (Foucault, 1971: 90). This is similar to how Jung moves between individual psychology and psychotherapy treatment – the 'doctor' – on the one hand, and the wider perspective of modern consciousness and culture – the 'effective history' – on the other. What comes together in this perspective is a relinquishing of the generalisations of the 'philosopher' and his dominance of history in favour of an approach that locates the individual and the collective in the same frame. Foucault wishes to achieve this without the unifying aims of traditional history just as Jung wishes to understand the modern psyche phenomenologically and without recourse to metaphysics. When Foucault follows Nietzsche in stating that, 'History has a more important task than to be the handmaiden to philosophy, to recount the necessary birth of truths and values. It should become a differential knowledge of energies and failings, heights and degenerations, poisons and antidotes. Its task is to become a curative science' (ibid.), he is demonstrating an aim that could apply as equally to the psychological and cultural analysis that Jung has provided us with.

Jung's focus on the individual and the particular arises, like the Nietzschean critique of traditional history, within the context of, and as a challenge to, the *Entstehung* (emergence) aims of history in nineteenth-century Europe. Nineteenth-century Europe, 'the land of interminglings and bastardy, the period of the "man-of-mixture"' (ibid.: 92), was, in a manner of speaking, desperately seeking *sui-sense* – a sense of itself, an identity and a uniting sense of where it had come from – in a fashion typified by Freud's famous archaeological metaphor of psychoanalysis as a process of interpretation and restoration of meaning. Foucault points out how one root to this artificial creation of identity through the (mis)use of history is parodic. This is a view we have encountered in earlier chapters where I detailed how the contemporary creation of historical 'realities' are simulacra that, when literalised as 'historical truths' are then opposed to the theme of history as reminiscence or recognition. This latter approach is preferred by the postmodern where the need for fixed identity is abandoned along with any idea that such a singular, static identity ever existed or is ever possible. On the one hand, 'The historian offers this confused and anonymous European, who no longer knows himself or what name he should adopt, the possibility of alternative identities, more individualised and substantial than his own' (ibid.: 93). One result of this nineteenth-century historicising is the creation of the mass man, who is the focus of Jung's critique as one of the greatest risks to modern European culture. On the other hand, however, those with historical sense will see that this is simply a disguise,

> The new historian, the genealogist, will know what to make of this masquerade. He will not be too serious to enjoy it; on the contrary, he will push the masquerade to its limit and prepare the great carnival of time where masks are constantly reappearing. No longer the identification of our faint individuality with the solid identities of the past, but our 'unrealization' through the excessive choice of identities . . . Caesar, Jesus, Dionysus, and possibly Zarathustra.
>
> (ibid.: 94)

With this position we are entering the postmodern – the perspective from which all assertions of such 'truths' and identities are seen for what they are: parodic, dissociated and constructed. The trick is not to simply abandon these masks, these identities, as if there were some 'real' 'truth' behind them to be got at, but to celebrate them for what they are – a masquerade, a carnival of exchangeable images and identities to be adopted and exchanged in a fully conscious manner. At first sight this does not seem to be a view with which Jung himself would be in agreement. He had a particular theory about identities and masks which he conceptualised under the term *persona*, the archetypal, or typical, tendency for all human beings to operate behind different masks according to the variety of their relationships and roles in social life. On the one hand he regarded the persona as insubstantial and as the first aspect of the psyche to be addressed when embarking upon the task of analysis and personal individuation. On the other hand, he never believed that our masks were entirely indispensible but rather that they had to be known for what they were and consciously acknowledged as only part of the personality. Identifying with one's mask was a neurotic distortion. Foucault, in the context of European historical, collective identity, seems to be advising the same thing. So as to counter our singular identification with *one mask* he advises that we celebrate *all* our masks and abandon our ideas of a single preferred 'origin'. This does not amount to claiming that we *are* all our masks and nothing else, but it is rather a critical stance against the imposition of the *singular mask*, or identity or persona. Viewed in this way, the acceptance of multiplicity sounds more like a *perspectival* view of 'identities' and this, as we saw at the beginning of the chapter, is more in line with Jung's theory of the complexes, the sub-personalities that make up the psyche, than it is with the

Jungian notion of the mask or *persona*. By accepting the plurality of our 'origins', our collective, historical identities – as well as our individual 'multiple' personalities and *persona* – the narrow, conformist tendencies within modernity may be resisted to the greater benefit of the human spirit and the living of a collective and individual life.

TIIE *UBERMENSCH* AND INDIVIDUATION

Perhaps a better way of expressing what both Nietzsche and Jung would like to see happen is to replace the word *resisted* with *outgrown* or *overcome*: 'the conformist tendencies within modernity may be *overcome*'. Nietzsche's work is never aimed at final solutions but, like depth psychology, it is aimed at seeking out hidden presuppositions. As Kaufmann puts it, 'the result is less a solution of the initial problem than a realisation of its limitations: typically, the problem is not solved but "outgrown"' (Kaufmann, 1974: 82). In clinical work, this is often the language I – and many post-Jungians – use with clients when dealing with neurotic conflicts stemming from the complexes. The complex does not disappear, but as the treatment proceeds and the rest of the personality becomes stronger and more integrated (in the sense of it being in better communication between its 'parts', not necessarily more 'whole'), the complex loses it dominance over the rest of the personality and recedes in its power to disturb. It gets outgrown, or, to put it another way, it gets overcome by the now greater significance of the rest of the personality.

The 'problem' with modernity as Nietzsche saw – its 'symptom' if you like – was characterised as nihilism and decadence; but, just as postmodern thought a century later identifies similar qualities and does not stop with these but goes on to investigate and celebrate the potential in what it finds, Nietzsche, too, addresses modernity as 'a condition of possibility' (Owen, 1995: 105). From the criticism of modernity that sees it as nihilistic, decadent, insubstantial or depthless comes a *perspective of possibility* – a *telos* which Nietzsche, and Jung, I think we will find, expresses in the form of two possible but opposed outcomes. In Nietzsche these are either the *Ubermensch*, the Overman (frequently mistranslated and misinterpreted as the 'Superman'), or the *Last Man*. In Jung, the self-overcoming *telos* of the human individual, the *Ubermensch*, is expressed in his concept of *individuation*; the alternative possibility of the *Last Man* gets expressed in Jung's idea of the total loss of individuality found in the *mass man* of modernity. When put together by Nietzsche, these two contrasting figures represent, on the one hand, the completion of modernity (the *Last Man*), and, on the other, the overcoming of modernity (the *Ubermensch*) (ibid.).

The concept of individuation is probably one of the most central defining concepts of Jung's psychology and one that distinguishes his perspective from those of the other depth psychologies. Individuation is also of vital importance in any consideration of the relationship between Jung and the postmodern due to the fact that it involves not only the psychological development and being of the individual subject, but does so within the context of collective society. Individuation is about the dual struggle of the subject with, on the one hand, the 'inner world' of the unconscious in all its infantile, personal and collective aspects, and, on the other hand, the struggle with the 'outer world' of collective society. In modern times, this latter struggle concerns the fate of the individual under the State and its levelling effects, as Jung clearly expresses, but since Jung's death in the sixties, post-Jungians sensitive to the interface between culture and the individual have recognised other, equally powerful forces limiting the individual. As I wrote in the opening chapters, postmodern concerns now focus on the effects of the global economy, mass media representation, and the homogenisation of styles and values – governed by those of North America and Europe – which comprise equal, and to some extent, more hidden, threats to the potential for subjects to become individual men and women.

In analysing the concept of individuation within the frame of postmodern concerns and the idea of the Overman, we need to pay attention to clearly defining a number of related terms: *identity*, *individuality*, *individualism*, *individuation* and *society*. Jung was aware of this and, in trying to clarify his position, he is often contradictory, but, by reading across his texts it is possible to discover the consistency in his position on the individual, the collective, and on society and the need for individuation. I will be focusing on those found in *Two Essays On Analytical Psychology* (CW 7, 1953) and *Psychological Types* (CW 6, 1920/1949). In the first book, Jung writes at length on the possibilities for development for the modern human being. After describing the alternatives for the ego-subject of succumbing either to social conformity or to inflation by overwhelming material stemming from the unconscious, Jung proposes this alternative,

> There is a destination, a possible goal, beyond the alternative stages dealt with in our last chapter. That is the way of individuation. Individuation means becoming an 'in-dividual', and, in so far as 'individuality' embraces our innermost, last, and incomparable uniqueness, it also implies becoming one's own self. We could therefore translate individuation as 'coming to selfhood' or 'self realization'.
>
> (Jung, 1953, CW 7: para. 266)

In overcoming tendencies and temptations to become absorbed in mass social values, on the one hand, or in world-denying primordial imagery on the other, the human subject has the possibility of 'over-growing' (*uberwaschen*) both to produce a different outcome and a different subject. But why is not Jung's 'self-realisation' simply some 'narcissistic', apolitical path that simply abandons the collective in favour of personal self-gratification? As Jung puts it, 'Self-alienation in favour of the collective corresponds to a social ideal; it even passes for social duty and virtue . . . On the other hand, self-realization seems to stand in opposition to self-alienation' (ibid.: para. 267). In other words, is not self-realisation selfish and anti-social? Why should it be a goal for the individual who remains within collective society? Jung answers,

> This misunderstanding is quite general, because we do not sufficiently distinguish between individualism and individuation. Individualism means deliberately stressing and giving prominence to some supposed peculiarity rather than to collective considerations and obligations. But individuation means precisely the better and more complete fulfilment of the collective qualities of the human being, since adequate consideration of the peculiarity of the individual is more conducive to a better social performance than when the peculiarity is neglected or suppressed. The idiosyncrasy of an individual is not to be understood as any strangeness in his substance or in his components, but rather as a unique combination, or gradual differentiation, of functions and faculties which are in themselves universal.
>
> (ibid.)

What Jung is doing here is removing that hard and fast line between the 'individual' and the 'collective'. What he emphasises is that the very characteristics that constitute the unique *difference* of the individual *are all collective characteristics themselves*. Therefore, the denial or suppression of individual characteristics is not only limiting and distorting of individuals (as in the extreme case of Stalinism or fascism) but it also impoverishes the social collective of accessing the full range of human possibilities. There is no gain for collective humanity by the repression of its individuals' distinctive differences – not unless, that is, there is a 'third' force abroad – let us call it, for the sake of argument, feudalism, catholicism, capitalism, protestant ethic or suchlike – which *requires* the repression of the majority of subjects to create a 'society' in which a small minority holds 99 per cent of the power and usually the wealth too. From the point of view of this type of society, for any change to occur it is politically necessary that the power balance is swung in the other direction by the (revised) collective force of the majority. However, although this may redress the balance – and the outcome may be more favourable to more subjects – there still persists a state where 'the tail wags the dog' and the individual remains restricted – albeit with different restrictions. History offers us little optimism when it comes to such shifts in the collective organisation of individuals (from feudal to industrial, monarchy to republic, feudal to communist, communist to capitalist, for example) a point which Jung, from his perspective of individual psychology, criticised as a sequence of exchangeable '-isms'.

In a parallel fashion, serious criticism has been levelled at postmodern thinking for its inability to offer leverage towards social and political change. I think this is a mistake that arises from a failure to recognise the importance of the individual for the collective within a paradigm that remains stuck with the oppressive power of collective society in the form of capitalist forces. I do agree that much psychological thinking – especially Jung's – underestimates the pervasive and subtle power of capitalist forces, but, on the other hand, the contradictions of late capitalism – for example, its denial of individual taste while simultaneously seeking to please every kind of different consumer with its products, or its need for both monopoly *and* competition – have left it exposed to challenge. In the present era there are grounds for seeing this challenge as arising less from collective movements – thus repeating the stale pattern – than it does from the cumulative effect of a multiplicity of individual voices. This challenge is not complete or ubiquitous, of course, but it *is* present as a new counter-force.

Jung, with his disparaging of the '-isms' clearly had little good to say of political movements. He had lived throughout the twentieth century and witnessed Europe's spectacular failures when it came to the mass reorganisations of national societies. But it would be an error to assume that this bias in Jung meant that he was not as passionate about the future of European society and the West in general, as he was about the psychological state of modern humankind. The fact is, as we have started to see, for Jung there was little need for distinction between the two. Far from denying the importance of society or the collective in favour of a predominately individualistic inner focus, as he is often read, Jung is at pains to clarify the relationship between the subject and society; Jung felt that, just as man cannot exist without oxygen and water, neither can he live without society, it is 'one of the necessary conditions of his existence' (Jung, 1941, CW 16: para. 224).

It is true that Jung does not pay as much attention to social forces as analysed sociologically as he does to the individual subject as analysed psychologically. This is why a post-Jungian revision and debate, of which this book is a part, is necessary (cf. Samuels, 1993). But his concept of individuation is clearly as much a cultural project as it is a psychological project; as the following quotation asserts, the fate of the individual and the collective is intertwined.

> Individuation is a natural necessity inasmuch as its prevention by a levelling down to collective standards is injurious to the vital activity of the individual. Since *individuality* is a prior psychological and physiological datum, it also expresses itself in psychological ways. Any serious check to individuality, therefore, is an artificial stunting. It is obvious that a social group consisting of stunted individuals cannot be a healthy and viable institution; only a society that can preserve its internal cohesion and collective values, while at the same time granting the individual the greatest possible freedom, has any prospect of enduring vitality. As the individual is not just a single, separate being, but by his very existence presupposes a collective relationship, it follows that the process of individuation must lead to more intense and broader collective relationships and not to isolation.
>
> (Jung, 1920/1949, CW 6: para. 758)

This ethic of an individuation which is simultaneously an embracing of – and an expression of – the collective has implications for Jung's concept of *identity*. Jung warns how we need to guard against being swept away by the loss of self that arises from identity with the mass, as well as the loss of self which arises from identity with archaic imagery arising from the unconscious. 'Identity is primarily an unconscious conformity with objects . . . Identity is responsible for the naïve assumption that the psychology of one man is like that of another, that the same motives occur everywhere' (ibid.: para. 742). Therefore, in Jung, there are clear warnings about the dangers of identification that is seen to diminish individuality. This is at odds with a postmodern view that sees multiple identities as inevitable and as another form of individual expression. For Jung, 'Identification is an alienation of the subject from himself for the sake of the object, in which he is, so to speak, disguised' (ibid.: para. 738). On the other hand, Jung refers to those who have 'one highly differentiated function' which they identify with as a necessary transitional stage on the way to individuation. Here, Jung is referring to creative individuals whose individuation proceeds through their focus on their best developed function. Here is a good example of how the individual through such a subjective concentration contributes most fully to the whole of culture and collective life. In this there is no contradictory polarisation of the individual on the one hand and the collective on the other. How else could our own culture have been collectively enriched by the visual art of Michelangelo, Cézanne, Howard Hodgkin, or Jackson Pollock, for example, or the music of Beethoven, Parker, Coltrane and the Beatles, or the science of Madame Curie or Galileo, or the literature of Shakespeare, Beckett and Nietzsche, and the politics of Martin Luther King and Gandhi, if the *individuals* behind the creative products that comprise our culture had not dedicated themselves to their individual paths. Their very uniqueness in the culture – their *passionate individual dedication to being 'themselves'* – produces aspects which constitute *collective culture 'itself'*. It should not surprise us, then, when we return to Nietzsche's concept of the *Ubermensch* we find him saying this,

> *One thing is needful*: To 'give style' to one's character – a great and rare art! It is practised by all those who survey the strengths and weaknesses of their nature and then fit them into an artistic plan until everyone of them appears as art and reason and even weaknesses delight the eye.
>
> (Nietzsche, 1974, #290)

Here, the character of the Overman is conveyed by Nietzsche as a type of self-mastery. Nietzsche presents this in terms of 'making oneself a work of art'. In other words, 'becoming what one is can be likened to the process of creating a work of art' (Owen, 1995: 111). And just as Jung's individuation is defined succinctly by the same 'becoming what one is', equally we may be justified in describing the self-affirmation of the Overman and the self-realisation of individuation not only as 'making oneself a work of art', but also by the more familiar psychotherapeutic idea of 'making a narrative of the self'.

Closely aligned to Nietzsche's idea of the Overman is his concept of *amor fati* which 'represents love of life because Nietzsche posits the fateful character of existence' (ibid.: 109). (This is not a philosophical claim of determination over freedom because Nietzsche rejects the freedom/determination antinomy as tied to the metaphysical realist position.) Like individuation for Jung, *amor fati* 'is an expression of the idea of becoming what one is (*applied to both the individual and the cultural community*)' (ibid., italics added). Equally, 'becoming what one is' is not a solitary activity as it might first sound, but, for the contemporary interpreter of Nietzschean values, 'my actions and reflections take place in the context of my relations with both my self and others, that is, within a dialogic context of intersubjective relations' (ibid.). At this point I note, once again, how Owen's contemporary explanations of Nietzsche's Overman and *amor fati* echo Jung's notion of individuation despite there being not a single reference to Jung or to individuation in the index of his excellent book. I can only hope that my present efforts will go someway towards calling attention to Jung's highly accessible psychological expansion of Nietzschean themes which otherwise might rest unapplied and unaccessed on the philosophy shelves.

I will finish with Owen's summary of Nietzsche's argument which links individual fate with the fate of the collective. From the perspective of the *ubermensch*, of self-overcoming and self-realisation, 'the piece of fate that I am' is identical to what Jung means by *individuation*:

> one is fated to act as one does because how one acts is what one is. Human beings are pieces of fate. Thus, to love one's fate is to love one's life, to affirm the relationship of the self and the world . . . However, in the same way that we talk about the character of a person, we also talk about the character of a culture, of humanity and of the world. Indeed, the piece of fate that I am is a part of the piece of fate that my culture is, which is a part of the piece of fate that is humanity, which is, in turn, part of the fate of the world.
>
> (ibid.: 109–110)

I do not think I could find better words with which to conclude this excursion into the thoughts and aims of Friedrich Nietzsche and Carl Jung, and their articulation with postmodern concerns.

7 Nietzsche, Power and the Body, or, Jung and the Post-Hysteric

Far from contemplative reflection, philosophy is a consequence of the drive to live, to conquer, a will to power that is primarily corporeal. Philosophy is a product of the body's impulses that have mistaken themselves for psyche or mind. Bodies construct systems of belief, knowledge, as a consequence of the impulses of their organs and processes.

(Grosz, 1994: 126)

AT THE SALPÊTRIÈRE

On 6 May 1877, Blanche Wittman, a young girl of fifteen entered the Salpêtrière Hospital in Paris to work as a nurse and to receive treatment from the great neurologist Charcot. Her background was common to many of the great French hysterics of the 1870s. She was the eldest of nine children of whom only four made it into adulthood. Her father went mad and ended his days in an insane asylum. At two years of age Blanche experienced convulsions, paralysis, mutism and deafness. 'She was undoubtedly nervously tainted from birth, Charcot and his followers thought when they collected her history' (Drinka, 1984: 123). Her childhood and adolescence up to entering the Salpêtrière was a tale of poverty and of threatened, if not actual, sexual abuse at the hands of her employer. And although Marceline, Genevieve and Louise had a certain fascination and greater photogenic qualities, it was Blanche who turned out to be a real 'find' for Charcot. It is she who is depicted fainting into the arms of the master in the famous painting 'A Clinical Lesson of Dr Charcot at the Salpêtrière'. She was the star hysteric of the Salpêtrière.

Under hypnosis Blanche, like other hysterics, would fall into a catalepsy.

The experimenter would move the limbs of the patient in different directions, and the patient would hold the pose for long periods of time. Also, when the hypnotist shaped the hysteric's hand into a fist, suggesting anger, or opened and placed her hand above her head, suggesting surprise or fright, this would cause the rest of the body to assume a pose of anger or fright. The teeth would grit, the hands would clench, the eyelids would narrow in anger; or the eyes would grow saucer-wide, the mouth would open as in fright.

(Drinka, 1984: 135)

There are two elements to this sort of hysterical pose that have a particular relevance. Not only does Drinka note that, 'Like a film producer, Charcot possessed the ability to make breathtaking "finds"' (ibid.: 124), but the poses Blanche was able to strike with such conviction must have appeared very much like snapshots – or 'stills' from Charcot's movie-making – indicating they were clearly influenced by the widespread, powerful and new medium of photography. In addition, Ellenberger tells us how, in the absence of movies and TV in the nineteenth century, a major influence on social presentation and interpersonal behaviour was the theatre. Theatrical performances from the most sophisticated through to the 'tabloid' music-hall were hugely popular, and were a great influence on social behaviour in the cities. As Ellenberger points out,

the theatre had an enormous importance. Great actors enjoyed immense popularity . . . A publicity industry as it exists today was hardly known at the time, so that every man had to make his own publicity either through journalistic acquaintances, salon gossip, or by making himself conspicuous in some other way. Hence the theatrical way of life, poses, verbal violence, public quarrels.

(Ellenberger, 1994: 256)

Just as with film media nowadays, emotional expression was influenced and conventionalised partly in response to what was witnessed at theatrical performances and their extension into public daily life. This might be thought of as the beginnings of 'the medium is the message' – a concern I have mentioned before in connection with Princess Diana and the hegemony and distortion of the photographic image. It is, of course, purely a coincidence that it was also the Salpêtrière hospital where Diana was taken after she met her fate, and where she died.

Of all the hysterics, Blanche's induced paralyses and expressions of fright or anger, generalised throughout her body, were the most astonishing seen at the Salpêtrière. She was photographed and painted and, by the late

1880s, dubbed the Queen of the Hysterics. Years later – in the 1920s – she was interviewed about the Charcot period and I will return to Blanche and her fate at the end of this chapter.

It strikes me that, despite its contemporary absence as a diagnostic term in psychiatry, hysteria remains a vital concept for psychoanalysis. For a start, its importance lies in its historical function – by which I mean how the treatment of patients diagnosed as hysteric in the late nineteenth century eventually led Breuer and Freud to formulate the seminal theory and method of what became known as psychoanalysis. It is hard to imagine psychoanalysis becoming formulated without the hysteric patient and her symptoms. As we know, it was from the treatment of Anna O., Dora and others that terms and concepts such as the unconscious, repression, putting into words, transference love, and the importance of the sexual instinct, childhood experience, trauma and fantasy were developed – and still form the conceptual background of the psychoanalytic project for many today.

On the other hand, the symptoms that were the hallmark of the hysteric of that era seem to have all but vanished from the contemporary psychiatric scene. This can be partly accounted for by the way we now have far more diagnostic categories. Kraepelin did not distinguish dementia praecox from manic-depressive insanity until 1883 and it was not until 1911 that Bleuler coined the term schizophrenia. The hysterics of the Salpêtrière and Freud's cases exhibited symptoms, such as hallucinations, that might classify them as psychotic, suffering from a schizophrenic illness, these days. Epileptic and Tourette's-type symptoms, internal fantasies, obsessions, eroticised and other unadapted social behaviour, all seem to have featured in the symptomology of the nineteenth-century hysteric. So, in one way, hysteria is still around, but we have simply ceased to call it that. I think this view only goes so far, however, and in this chapter I would like to focus on two *specific* features of hysteria that seem to have particularly characterised it in the past, and which also seem present in certain, parallel pathological conditions of the present day. These two features are *power* and *the body*.

However, in delineating these two aspects of the hysteric, I wish to discuss something far wider than the so-called pathology of hysterical and post-hysterical symptoms. I use *power* and the *body* as the axes of a view of modern consciousness which is not only found as a perspective of Nietzsche's, but which is also to be found in the theorising of Freud and Jung. I outline Nietzsche's idea of *life as will to power* – this time as a perspective that powerfully influenced Freud's and Jung's concepts of psychic energy or libido, the psychology of the *inner*. I compare the view of Elizabeth Grosz who uses Nietzsche and others to theorise about the body as a surface inscribed upon from the *outside*, the social and the cultural conditions it inhabits. Noting Freud's concept of a body-ego (*The*

Ego and the Id, 1923), I follow this with Jung's revision, after the split with Freud, of what he thought hysteria, 'aetiology' and 'trauma' were really all about in his book *The Theory of Psychoanalysis* (1913, CW 4). I will say something about individual differences and how varying cultural contexts may encourage or inhibit symptoms, and comment on the relationship between the body and its environment – especially how, despite human need and the power of the conscious psyche, fate, in the form of the environment or the unconscious, still holds overwhelming power. I conclude with some further thoughts around Nietzsche's ideas of the *Ubermensch* and self-overcoming which I link to the task of analysis and Jung's idea of individuation. I will finish with the fate of Blanche Wittman – as, indeed, it finished with her.

THE WILL TO POWER

Nietzsche's doctrine of the will to power is not some Darwinian self-preservative instinct but should be regarded as more the 'expenditure of energy itself' (Patton, 1993: 152) – or 'expanded reproduction'. This sounds like the precursor for Freud's concept of libidinal psychic energy except for one important difference. What is fundamental about this energy for Nietzsche is not the satisfaction of some aim or desire as it is for Freud: 'the fundamental principle is not the goal but the process, not the momentary stasis attained by the satisfaction of need or desire but the expenditure of energy itself' (ibid.). For Nietzsche, 'What is great in man is that he is a bridge and not a goal' (Nietzsche, 1883–1885, 1961: 44) – in other words, the energy vented is 'life as the will to power' and this power is not object directed. Consequently it seems to resemble not Freud's (or even Adler's) conceiving of libido but more the generalised psychic energy of Jung's formulation. Especially relevant for our discussion of the body of the hysteric, this general conception of power, 'includes all forms of activity directed at the maintenance or increase of the power of the body in question, as well as forms of activity which might lead to its destruction or its transformation into a different kind of body' (Patton, 1993: 153). In addition, will to power and the transformation of the body become linked through the specifically human phenomenon of *consciousness*, 'for Nietzsche one of the ways in which humanity is transformed by the operation of will to power is through the development of consciousness . . . With this transformation of the human animal into a historical being, that is, a being characterised by consciousness, the character of human will power is also changed' (Owen, 1995: 43).

Once consciousness has developed into the highly differentiated form experienced in modern times, humanity manifests a drive to increase the *feeling* of power rather than maximise any actual increase in the *quantity* of power itself. Moreover, with the development of consciousness 'the feeling of power becomes *mediated through meaning*' (ibid.: 44, italics added), so that there is a 'self-conscious, interpretative element in every human act of will' (Patton, 1993: 155).

For our purposes in discussing hysteria, what is noticeable about the individuals diagnosed as having hysterical symptoms is their powerlessness – for reasons of class or gender or both. I think this applies to men as well as women, to sufferers in the nineteenth century and in the present day (I will detail what I mean by contemporary hysteria presently), and to instances in cultures outside the European.

For example, George Drinka reminds us how the female hysterics under Charcot at the Salpêtrière – such as Genevieve, Louise and Blanche with their distinctive physical symptomology expressed in their bodies – were poor, displaced, cruelly treated, powerless and sexually abused women who found shelter and some safety within the walls of the hospital. Did they also find safety, and a *feeling* of power, within the walls of their symptoms? In some cases, the male hysterics revealed a parallel diminishment in feelings of power for rather different reasons. The men at the Salpêtrière seemed to have all suffered some shock in the face of an overwhelming aspect of the mechanical world. One such is the man named Pin, 'a labourer who had stood transfixed with fear before a rolling barrel that had broken loose from a pulley. (The barrel had not touched him)' (Drinka, 1984: 101). Industrial capitalist society ushered in its own psychopathology: the railway and railway trains were a common cause of profound trauma – resulting in what we would now call post traumatic stress disorders, but at the time such trauma seemed to arise from a sense of powerlessness in the face of threatening, and inhuman, machinery and from the mechanical world in general. The *feeling* of power generated by subjective meaningfulness is often inversely connected to *actual* power,

> For a human being to experience his or her *self* as powerful requires that s/he experience being in the world as meaningful. We can note two significant consequences of this conception of human agency. Firstly, it entails that an increased feeling of power may denote a decrease in actual power and *vice versa*. In other words, my way of rendering my experience meaningful may generate an increased feeling of power, yet this may undermine my actual capacity for autonomous agency.
>
> (Owen, 1995: 44)

David Owen notes how this is essentially Nietzsche's objection to Christianity which was regarded as 'the philosophy of slaves' – a belief system and an ethic constructed to deal with the powerlessness of subjects enslaved within the Roman Empire.

In non-Western cultures, it is often those who are without power who seem to express hysterical symptoms – whether these are regarded as pathological or, as I. M. Lewis details in his book *Ecstatic Religion* (Lewis, 1971), they are labelled as possession by spirits. In the anthropological example he cites, women in the *sar* spirit cults of North Africa and the Middle East are subordinated within a highly rigid patriarchal system. To get what they wish for in terms of material goods requires the co-operation of men who control financial power. The *sar* cult of the women allows for a culturally legitimated possession by the spirit which is expressed through the body in the form of an ecstatic dance reminiscent of the nineteenth-century European hysteric's body state. Not only are woman able to make demands 'as' the spirit – or as the hysteric – they are also known to 'roundly upbraid the husbands in terms that would not be tolerated were they expressed directly by the women themselves' (ibid.: 79). This example brings to mind the function of *seduction* as an aspect of the body in the subject's experience of *power*. Baudrillard has analysed how seduction can replace the need for force; it is a point of view that has been criticised for its sexist implications but it is perhaps also indicating a postmodern approach to power and change from which we can learn. It is certainly central to any understanding of what the hysteric may be trying to achieve through their body.

As I have been suggesting, I think we find contemporary forms of hysteria in our present day Western culture which can also be understood within the idea of the will to power. Both anorexia and self-harm (self-mutilation) have been conceptualised as involving the sense of power. For the anorexic, feeling power through conquering hunger, the instinctual urge to eat becomes linked to a feeling of power over the body form as it becomes transformed into one that is thinner. With this comes a feeling of power over the environment – especially all the other individuals who are concerned for and involved with the anorexic. The individual who cuts him or herself may experience similar 'self-overcoming' and power over the body's experience of pain as well as power over other's attention to them and their body. Of course, both cases may well be involving the creation of feelings of power over the body to deal with – in a compensatory way – overwhelming loss of power and control over inner emotional pain and/or uncontrollable external circumstances.

This brings me to my parallel theme: the body of the hysteric.

HYSTERIA AND THE BODY

As I have already mentioned, the symptoms of hysteria in the late nineteenth century covered a wide range and many symptoms can be classified more precisely these days within other categories. Once this has been done, what is left over, broadly speaking, is a very particular range of symptoms that are being *directly expressed through the body of the hysteric*. In the classic literature these range from swooning and rigidity, a specified sequence of body convulsions (which may be viewed as expressing the forms of seductive and erotic or passionate worshipping behaviour), squint, anaesthesia and paralysis of limbs, and the somatic dramatisation of emotions in a theatrical fashion.

What has classical psychoanalysis to say about this body which, to be frank, has been rather ignored in the literature? Compared to earlier views of the nineteenth century, one of the achievements of the dynamic psychology of Freud and Jung has been the differentiation of the 'organic' from the 'psychological'. In contrast to the time when all mental dis-ease was seen as having an organic, material cause, the age of 'psychological man' has tended to err in the opposite direction and neglected the body. So it is with interest that we find in Freud's *The Ego and The Id* a footnote which first appeared in the English translation of 1927 but does not, according to Peter Gay (Gay, 1995: 637) appear in the German edition. Freud writes,

> The ego is first and foremost a bodily ego; it is not merely a surface entity, but is itself a projection of a surface. [*The footnote says*], 'i.e. the ego is ultimately derived from bodily sensations, chiefly those springing from the surface of the body. It may thus be regarded as a mental projection of the surface of the body, besides . . . representing the superficies of the mental apparatus.
>
> (Freud, 1923 quoted in Gay, 1995: 637)

Freud's assertion of the direct link between the ego and the body, I believe, provides us with an initial perspective by which to understand the body of the hysteric. Under particular circumstances – power I have mentioned, but also conditions arising from cultural specifics and individual differences – some individuals may be found expressing, or even existentially *being*, an ego-self almost solely through the body. The way this idea seems to reverse the direction Freud writes of where ego is derived *from* the body surface – i.e. from the outer to the inner – may have implications for the Lacanian idea of the mirror stage whereby a fragmented body achieves coherence as ego, but an ego that is forever alien to the subject. With the hysteric, the body appears to be the stage, the actor and the drama that communicates the ego. It is as if the order of language gets replaced by the order of the body. On the one hand, this may be seen as a regression and a failure but, on the other hand it could be seen as an achievement: *a refusal of the order that is imposed upon the subject – a refusal of the Symbolic order of mainstream culture.* This would make sense in terms of the way the hysteric seeks feelings of power not otherwise available to them as actual power – for reasons of patriarchal culture and the shock of 'the railway god' in the past – and for additional reasons of more complex inter-personal breakdown in the present day.

For *some* men and women, the body may take over expression of the ego and its very being. For others, part-body expressions may arise as forms of psycho-somatic illness which is more widespread. Individual differences are important to acknowledge in all this. We should remember that although it has been remarked how the diagnosis of hysterics went up from 4 per cent to 17 per cent in the Saltpêtrière under Charcot, it is also of interest that it was *only* 17 per cent at its peak. There were clearly many other conditions and symptoms not classed as hysteric. We might also note how, in the present day, the cultural legitimation of symbolic forms not normally regarded as pathological, such as slimming, body piercing and tattooing, offer the channels (or grammar) of body 'language' used by the anorexic and the self-mutilator respectively. Ian Parker connects such 'fetishisation' of pierced body parts with a postmodern attempt to mark parts of the body as a reference point, 'a mark of identity in a shifting world of signs' (Parker, 1997: 179), as well as making a connection with the retrieval of a world lost to modernity through the association of such body-piercing with the 'membership' practices of other, non-Western cultures.

In her book *Volatile Bodies: Toward a Corporeal Feminism* (Grosz, 1994), Elizabeth Grosz provides a different perspective on the body and the subject – one which also derives from a reading of Nietzsche. Grosz begins by noting how Nietzsche questions the primacy of consciousness or experience in conceptions of subjectivity and focuses on the body as a sociocultural artefact rather than as a manifestation of what is private, psychological and 'deep' in the individual (ibid.: 115). Grosz's alternative perspective is one which sees the body as a surface inscribed on from the outside, and she vividly illustrates this with Kafka's story of a literal, tattoo-like inscription of the body by a special machine as a punishment and a bringer of consciousness and conscience in the piece called 'In The Penal Settlement'. In this writing,

> Kafka explicitly describes the machine as an instrument of writing, as a material means of inscription through which propositions, texts, and sentences are etched onto the prisoner's skin, and through it, his

subjectivity. This writing machine is the mechanism of transfer through which an abstract, or rather a textually based, law is rendered incarnate, living.

(ibid.: 137)

But when Grosz emphasises 'surface' effects in this way of looking at the body she is clear to note that even though Nietzsche, Deleuze and Foucault 'focus on the body as a social object, as a text to be marked, traced, written upon by various regimes of institutional . . . power' (ibid.: 116), the result is not merely *superficial*. She uses the analogy of the Mobius strip which, due to a single twist, makes marks inscribed on the outer surface appear on the inner and *vice versa*. The 'surface' and the 'depth' coincide through the manipulation and rotation of the flat plane. The Mobius strip – and its more esoteric mathematical cousin the 'three-dimensional' Klein bottle (Rosen, 1995) – are key images for deconstructing strict, either–or models within depth psychology and the postmodern frame. In a statement that particularly brings to mind what I am suggesting about the body of the hysteric, Grosz, following de Certeau's thinking, states how 'the subject is marked as a series of (potential) messages or inscriptions from or of the social (Other). Its flesh is transformed into a body organised, and hier-archized according to the requirements of a particular social and familial nexus' (Grosz, 1994: 119).

Grosz notes that Nietzsche does not have a coherent theory of the body although, as we have seen in the last chapter, he frequently refers to it. Unlike for Foucault where 'the body is penetrated by networks and regimes of power-knowledge that actively mark and produce it as such' (ibid.: 122), Nietzsche has a conception of the body that is considerably more positive and productive: the body is an active source and site for the will to power. Similar to the interpretation of the will to power, derived from David Owen, outlined earlier, Grosz describes the relationship between will to power, consciousness and the body thus,

Consciousness can be regarded as the direct product or effect of reactive forces in the governance of the body. For Nietzsche, consciousness is a belief, an illusion: on one hand useful for life, a convenient fiction, and on the other hand an effect of the inwardly inflected, thwarted will to power or force that, instead of subduing other bodies and forces, has sought to subdue itself.

(ibid.: 124)

This statement might now be considered in the light of what has already been said about the formation of the ego, and the hypothesis I propose later.

This suggests the hysteric suffers a twist in her or his 'inwardly inflected, thwarted will to power' with the result that consciousness, or the 'I', remains still tangled up with the 'reactive forces in the governance of the body' rather than going on to become a 'speaking' 'I'. I also propose that the body itself serves as a communication in the absence of a sufficiently developed capacity for language – again the result of a thwarted will to power and the consequent lack of ego development. Grosz points out the connection between language and the body in Nietzsche's thinking which helps us understand how the most sophisticated achievement of humans, the linguistic, still has the animal body at its base and so may rely on it (or, 'regress' to it?) when will to power does not achieve its expression as full ego-consciousness:

> language itself, he suggests, is at base corporeal. Words are doubly metaphorical: they are transcriptions or transpositions of images, which are themselves transpositions of bodily states. For Nietzsche, bodily forces underlie language and its possibility of representation.
>
> (ibid.: 126)

At this stage I will leave Grosz's Nietzschean analysis of the will to power, and its relationship to consciousness and the inscription of the body, until the significance of this perspective is picked up again in my concluding remarks about the body of the hysteric. I now turn to Jung's theory of hysteria and trauma which, we will see, differs a good deal from Freud's aetiology in the way that it relies more on the functioning of a generalised libido or will to power, and less on 'causes' in the 'past'.

JUNG AND THE STAGE-MANAGEMENT OF HYSTERICAL SYMPTOMS

In 1913, Jung published *The Theory of Psychoanalysis* in which he provided a revision of Freud's original formulations around the aetiology of hysteria and developed his own trauma theory. Jung details the case of a young woman who, upon leaving a farewell party with a group of friends, produced a hysterical reaction in response to a coach and horses that came charging towards the party as they stood in the street. Her friends swiftly stepped out of the way, but the woman in question ran along in front of the horses, unable to avoid their path, until they reached a narrow bridge where she would have leapt off into the water had someone not managed to grab her out of the way at the last minute.

In analysis with Jung, the woman produced a recent memory of a parallel incident when she had found herself confronted by armed soldiers advancing towards her in the street in St Petersburg during the uprising of 1905. On this occasion she had acted with swift rationality and ducked out of the way into a safer place. The woman also produced a childhood memory which seemed linked to the hysterical incident. She recalled how, as a child of seven, she had been travelling on a coach when the horses ran out of control and were heading towards a ravine. The coachman urged her to jump off with him and the patient, aged seven, just managed to achieve this before the horses plunged over the edge to their death. Jung's question to himself is: Why was there no hysterical reaction on the occasion of the real danger from the soldiers, while the hysterical incident – where she could have as easily stepped out of the way – led her to 'freeze' into perpetuating the danger as if it was inescapable?

There seems to be a relationship between the childhood trauma and the present incident but is it necessarily a causal relationship? Jung does not think so and prefers to focus on the *present conflict* in the woman at the time of the hysterical reaction. He theorises that '*the cause of the pathogenic conflict lies mainly in the present moment*' (Jung, 1913, CW 4: para. 373, italics in original.). Psychic or emotional conflict in the present causes the libido to split, in Jung's words, between its fantasy desires and the inability to carry them out in the present conditions. An 'infantile' reaction occurs – a childish solution of a conflict by libido being invested in a fantasy belief rather than in real action. This can take the form, as in the case he discusses, of the use of reminiscence for 'staging an illness' – a process Jung calls '*regression of libido*' (ibid.: para. 365).

The woman was involved in a difficult love triangle with Mr A and his wife. The occasion of the farewell party was that of Mrs A's departure, a time that offered the opportunity for meeting with Mr A – although this would still have been illicit. Jung points out how the patient felt impotent – that is, *without a feeling of power* – and shrank from the opportunity to get herself alone with Mr A; but, unconsciously, the libido – her will to power, I suggest – still carried out her desire in the form of the embodied hysterical behaviour. The incident led to her ending up being comforted by Mr A at his house as she had wished. The patient told Jung that, when the horses were approaching her, her feelings were 'as if something inescapable now had to happen' (ibid.: para. 366). The relationship to the incident in the past is not causal. Instead, Jung hypothesises that, 'The theoretical gain from this story is the clear recognition that an unconscious "intention" or tendency stage-managed the fright with the horses, very probably using for this purpose the infantile reminiscence of the horses galloping irresistibly towards disaster'. (ibid.: para. 364). In this, we notice Jung taking full cognisance of the theatrical, communicative quality of the body of the hysteric as cultural conditions permitted, but, in addition, the sentence I italicise below suggests how the hysteric produces an urge towards *feeling power* precisely when environmental conditions deny her *actual power*.

> The fright and the apparently traumatic effect of the childhood experience are merely staged, but staged in the peculiar way characteristic of hysteria, so that the *mise en scène* appears almost exactly like a reality. *We know from hundreds of experiences that hysterical pains are staged in order to reap certain advantages from the environment* . . . from the psychological point of view the pains are just as real as those due to organic causes, and yet they are stage-managed.
>
> (ibid., italics added)

When Jung notes that 'libido retreats before the obstacle it cannot surmount' (ibid.: para. 383) he draws our attention to the issue of powerlessness and the will to power which is libido's primary condition. To suggest why this reaction to a life conflict occurs for some and not for others Jung cites the accidental events of early life and the sensitivity of certain individuals: 'accidental events and regression together form a vicious circle: retreat from life leads to regression, and regression heightens resistance to life' (ibid.: para. 403). But Jung is not so pessimistic about this state of affairs – the condition of a regression of libido also has a helpful and preparatory tendency. Paradoxically, this view compares with Freud's idea that neurosis is an unsuccessful attempt at self-cure despite the fact that Freud also regarded regression as purely a retreat from reality. In this contrast it is possible, once again, to spot a theme we have encountered several times before in the present book. This is the theme which maintains that looking to the past, or regression, is not merely defensive or avoidant of reality as it might be for the modernist, but, on the contrary, it has a creative, deconstructive function. For Jung, it is mistaken to deny the teleological value of the apparently pathological fantasies of the neurotic or hysteric; they are, in fact,

> the first beginnings of spiritualization, the first groping attempts to find new ways of adapting. [The neurotic's] retreat to the infantile level does not mean only regression and stagnation, but also the possibility of discovering a new life-plan. Regression is thus in very truth the basic condition for the act of creation.
>
> (ibid.: para. 406)

In the case of some manifestations of hysteria it might seem that the regressive fantasy being staged is that of an infantile absence of power and control with the focus entirely on the body. The absence of any ordering by language and the employing of the 'body-order' to communicate to the environment points to an early regression of libido to a pre-verbal position, prior to the mirror-stage of ego development. The behaviour of the hysteric has a distinctive communication function – it reaches out to the environment and is noticed, even if the message being displayed is not, and perhaps never can be, that clear. It cannot be 'read'. In fact, if the communication concerns life's urge to a feeling of power that is not being satisfied in any other way, this is so imprecise a 'message' in terms of discreet content that it is no wonder that the symptoms of the hysteric are so baffling. The message simply conveys: 'I am powerless. I am feeling my power'. Individual difference, accidental events and cultural conditions will then provide the script and the setting for the stage management and dramatisation of this primal urge of life affirming itself.

SELF-OVERCOMING, INDIVIDUATION AND *TELOS*

As I discussed in the previous chapter, a key concept in Jung's psychology is that of individuation whereby a human being has the inherent ability to fully become the person they have the potential to be. The first task of this life-long process is to become an 'I'. Only after the ego has achieved for the subject a degree of separation and autonomy from the parental matrix – a degree of individuality or self-identity – can the ego then itself be realised as relative: as only a partial version of the self it represents. It is ironic that only a robust enough ego is able to tackle such reflection and to humble itself in a relationship with the rest of the personality – a dialogue that becomes empowering as the limitations of the narrow ego boundaries are overcome. A weaker ego is fully occupied with the daily struggle of self-survival and ego-strengthening – an issue that has important implications when it comes to cultural inhibitions on ego-development and empowerment. We have come across post-Jungian feminist criticisms of this issue as regards women and Jungian therapy in Chapter 5.

On the one hand I have been suggesting that the hysteric suffers an acute lack of ego development so that the subjective sense of an 'I' is barely experienced, if at all. The hysterical symptoms, I suggest, may then be viewed as an attempt to create 'I', a meaningful self derived from the feeling of power, but, here, staged as a drama involving the whole body. In this sense the symptoms seem to compensate for a weak or missing sense of 'I' or ego; in Nietzschean terms, will to power remains with the governance of the body having failed to spawn ego-consciousness. But, if we take up Jung's teleological perspective, then the hysteric is not so much lost in a pathological regression but is attempting to solve his or her fate – 'the first groping attempts to find new ways of adapting . . . the possibility of discovering a new life-plan', as Jung puts it (Jung, 1913, CW 4: para. 406). This is not to imagine that the hysteric has a *solution* – the hysterical condition or incident is barely a beginning – but the emergence of the hysterical body does seem in many cases to mark the break between the old fate and the new fate, the previous life and the future becoming – becoming an empowered 'I' and then, with luck, proceeding on the path of individuation to fulfil their human potential. Anna O., for one, we are told, went on, as Berthe Pappenheim, to become a leading social worker and feminist.

I detailed in the last chapter how Nietzsche's concept of the *Ubermensch* or the Overman is a universal ideal version of a process which he also recommends as a possibility at the *individual* level. Nietzsche's 'making of oneself a work of art' can also be expressed as the making of *a narrative unity of the self*, nowadays a fairly common way of expressing part of the aims of analytic treatment, which is how several commentators – Lou Andreas-Salome for example (Ellenberger, 1994: 277–278) – are able to make the link between the concept of the Overman, self-overcoming and the task of analysis. (In making this connection between Nietzsche's *Ubermensch* and an essentialist and progressivist concept such as the 'goal' of the 'narrative unity of the self' we are, once more, up against the degree to which Enlightenment values and language persist in Nietzsche's thought, as indeed they do in Jung's. In this I take the view that no postmodern, deconstructive critique is complete in itself and divorced from Enlightenment. But this does not mean that a challenge and a critique is superficial, or is merely nihilistic, or is not proceeding in any sense at all. Why should the idea of basic values or of a sense of progress be commandeered by Enlightenment alone? Perhaps it is not so much the case that Nietzschean and postmodern critique denies such concepts but they now constitute attempts at repossessing them for alternative, non-Enlightenment, aims.)

In classical psychoanalysis, the conscious ego is confronted with its regressions, resistances and retreats that prevent the subject's optimal adaptation to life and social reality. In the classical form of Jungian analysis, a strong enough ego is assumed and the self-overcoming takes the form of a deeper integration of the psyche and the potential personality that has both a collective and a personal dimension. The narrative fiction of ego-identity can here become absorbed in the wider myth of self-knowledge. A key aspect of this process of self-overcoming is the withdrawal of projections that the subject has previously been thrusting out onto the environment, the world of 'others'. Other people and groups have up till then been distorted by psychic contents of which the subject has been hitherto oblivious. I have speculated how the hysteric may be attempting to create an 'I' with the body. For this to happen would mean that an aspect or an action of the psyche is being projected onto the body of the subject – just as it might otherwise be projected onto another person. In this projection, the body supplies an 'I' alienated from the rest of psyche but one which can provide a feeling of power. This process seems to be an attempt to regain control over abuses or conflicts arising out of an unbearable environment which the rudimentary, barely forming 'ego' is too weak to bear. The hysteric seems to be attempting a self-overcoming of the unsuccessful rudimentary ego using this technique of the 'projected' body-'I'. The aim is noble but the method is faulty. The value of classical psychoanalysis as an aid to self-overcoming lay in its close attention to and use of *verbalisation* in helping the 'I' establish itself psychically instead of being driven into a part-body or fully somatic expression. Further individuation can be facilitated in Jungian analysis once the conscious 'I' is able to start integrating difficult contents and conflicts deriving from both the inner and the outer environment.

In attempting to overcome the insufficient, powerless and abused 'I' and to reinvent one that carries the feeling of power, the hysteric, as in any individuation, always involves the world beyond the body, beyond the skin boundary. In this way, the acting upon the body of the self-mutilator and the anorexic appears symbolic of the reshaping of the body-as-ego which is their desire. In addition, this always presents a *message* to the environment – the visible body-state that is the hallmark of the hysteric. As we have noticed, there tends to be a stage-managed, theatrical quality to these symptoms. But what if, once the hysterical presentation is unconsciously adopted, the environment takes over, so to speak, and dictates the course of the condition – what the subject becomes – in other words, the subject's 'fate'. In the 1920s, Dr A. Badouin who had been one of Charcot's young disciples, sought out Blanche Wittman in his effort to discover why the grand hysteria that had been so prominent in the 1870s to 1890s had disappeared by 1910. I will let George Drinka take up the end of the story:

> Blanche had never left the Salpêtrière. No longer a patient, she had become a radiology technician. X-rays had just been discovered by the Curies, and Blanche found herself a niche in which she could be somewhat productive. Badouin wrote that Blanche had ceased to have her crises 'when the time had passed in which these experiences were a la mode'. However, as her ill fortune would have it, she had become

a victim of her new profession. She had contracted the 'abominable cancer of the radiologist'. As the cancer had spread, her limbs, one by one, had been amputated.

(Drinka, 1984: 150)

Blanche seemed to die as she had lived. An abused girl with a fragmented ego, only partly healed through the ego-body of the hysteric, and sublimely fated to have that body, too, literally fragmented at her death.

8 Image, sign, symbol: representation and the postmodern

> All this discussion would be superfluous in an age or culture that possessed symbols.
>
> (Jung, 1940: 72)

MEANING

From the outset, three key concepts have characterised psychoanalysis and analytical psychology: the 'image', the 'symbol' and the 'meaning'. Freud sought the latent meaning 'behind' the manifest images of dreams and found many such images to be 'symbolic' of fundamental instinctual processes operating within the unconscious. Similarly, the symptoms of hysterics and neurotics constituted further symbolic material that would lead Freud to the interpretation of their underlying 'meaning', hidden and repressed in the unconscious. 'Meaning' could not exist alone in this epistemology – an interpreter, the analyst, was always required. Jung's early psychiatric work led him to pioneer a new attitude to the imagery and experiences reported by psychotic patients. The new perspective on their delusional material – hitherto regarded by psychiatry as meaningless babble – was to find it had an intrinsic meaning. On the one hand, such meaning was quite personal and subjective for the patient, but far from 'meaningless', as it was in the case of the young woman who 'lived on the moon' (Jung, 1983/1963: 150). But on the other hand, Jung claimed the images his patients brought revealed evidence of a collective 'meaning' in that the imagery had impersonal, historical, mythological and cultural precedents of which the patients were unaware. As in psychoanalysis, the imagery and symbols produced by the psyche are deemed to hold 'meaning' for Jung, and in his initial work as a psychologist he casts himself as investigator and interpreter of such imagery as Freud did with the imagery and symbols he 'discovered'.

To a great extent, then, we have here the most modernist attitude of depth psychology. One in which the master discourses of the 'great men' of depth psychology dictate the meaning of symbols and imagery and dictate the unitary 'truths' that lie 'behind' manifest appearances. Jung, for example, attributes certain symbolic imagery to the activity of the archetypes, an activity that lies, ultimately, 'behind' or 'beneath' all human behaviour. For Freud, it is the drives that are being symbolised in psychic images. This is the aspect of psychoanalysis that has been so parodied in the second half of the twentieth century, where Jungian correspondences between circular shapes or the number four and 'wholeness' or 'the self' are as subject to criticism and ridicule as are the interpretation of snakes and tower-blocks as penises, or handbags and purses as vaginas.

Although it is true that, from time to time, Jung exhibits an Aristotelian 'nothing but' attitude to images, symbols and their meaning that casts him as utterly modernist, there is also another Jung who offers a completely different meaning to 'meaning' which can only be viewed as postmodern (Miller, 1989). In this chapter I intend to detail this reading of Jung using the work of several post-Jungians whose commentary and analysis cover a range of postmodern concepts and issues in linguistics, semiotics and epistemology and concepts to be found in the work of Derrida, Lacan and Kristeva (Adams, 1991, 1992, 1995, 1996a, 1996b; Casey 1990; Casey *et al.*, 1990; Hillman, 1990; Kugler, 1978, 1979, 1982, 1983, 1990a, 1990b, 1993; Miller, 1989, 1990a, 1990b). In doing so, I hope to show how postmodern concerns with signs, symbols and representation provide a context within which to read Jung's psychology as a text which, far from simply exhibiting an irrelevant modernism, Romanticism or individualism, contributes to the discussion of the subject and his or her location in postmodern culture. Up till now I have been focusing on an attitude to Jung and the postmodern that emphasises the 'outer' radicalism of Jung in the way that his psychology challenges modernity in culture and society. The last two chapters on Nietzsche and the position of the 'hysteric' as an individual and as a cultural phenomenon have already begun to bridge the apparently 'inner' and 'outer' worlds we inhabit. The writers I will be referring to approach Jung with an attitude that deconstructs assumptions about how modern subjects re-present the world of modernity and postmodernity to themselves. Their approach is phenomenological and psychological but not simply so. In mapping both the modernist and structuralist elements in Jung's thought, they also reveal the post-structural and the postmodern. Whether this is 'purely' their own perspective or Jung's authorial 'intention' is also included as an element of their discourse – one which goes some way to helping with the continuing issue of the extent to which Jung 'is' postmodern and the extent to which post-Jungians interpret him as such. I expand on their ideas to find links with the work of the psychoanalyst, James Grotstein – who points out the importance of the unrepresentable – the ineffable Other – in the concepts of Winnicott and Bion. I also draw the parallel with Taoist texts where, in another way, the writers are trying to find ways of expressing and representing that which is beyond language or image or any form of representation and is thus the very Other of consciousness itself.

'SEMIOTIC' AND 'SYMBOLIC'

One very important point to note at the outset is how what we understand by the terms semiotic and symbolic has altered considerably over the period between Jung's formulations and the analyses of representation we find today. The definitions Jung worked with could be summarised as follows: If an expression stands for a *known* thing, even if this expression is commonly called 'symbolic', it is not a symbol but a *sign*. If an expression stands for an *unknown* something, which, therefore, by definition cannot be expressed or represented more clearly in any way, then such an expression is a *symbol*. For Jung, the *semiotic* refers to representations of *known* things, while the *symbolic* refers to representations of the *unknown*. Jung gives the example of how the custom of 'handing over a piece of turf at the sale of a plot of land might be described as "symbolic" in the vulgar sense of the word, but actually it is purely semiotic in character. The piece of turf is a sign, or token, standing for the whole estate', adding lightheartedly, 'The winged wheel worn by railway officials is not a *symbol* of the railway, but a *sign* that distinguishes the personnel of the railway system . . . Thus when the badge of a railway official is explained as a symbol, it amounts to saying that this man has something to do with an unknown system that cannot be differently or better expressed than by a winged wheel'! (Jung, 1921/1971, CW 6: para. 814).

However, these days, the meaning of the *semiotic* and the *symbolic* has reversed. The symbolic, as David Miller puts it, 'has veered away from the unknown in the direction of the known . . . which leaves the sign world to be the locus of the unknown' (Miller, 1990a: 328). This is why the semiotic of Julia Kristeva I referred to in Chapter 5 was found to be more comparable to the unknown, shadowy and unconscious in Jung's conceptualisation, whereas the Symbolic, as conceived by Lacan, refers to the collective, cultural ordering and thus what is known – 'symbolic perspectives assimilate psyche's images to secondary processes, predictive synthesis, and judgment' (ibid.). Miller discusses this reversal in the context of the

#1 and the #2 personality of Jung (Jung, 1983/1963), which he equates with a 'knowing' modernist Jung, and an 'unknowing' postmodern Jung, respectively, with the latter particularly deserving our attention:

'If Jung were alive today, would he not have to be a semiotician rather than a symbolist? Would he not be nearer to the French Freudians than to the American Jungians', Miller asks, 'what Jung called the symbolic, and recommended for the soul, is . . . the paratactic, "gappy", unknowing that is today called semiotic' (Miller, 1990a: 328).

I will go into Miller's ideas and the development of postmodern theories of representation as expounded by Paul Kugler in the course of this chapter, but the point here is that semiotics, symbols, image and representation are, like everything else, slippery terms in postmodern times.

STRUCTURALISM, POST-STRUCTURALISM, DECONSTRUCTION; PLUS THE SOCIAL CONSTRUCTION OF REALITY

For those who are more familiar with Jung than they are with some of the -isms I will be referring to I thought it wise to offer some brief definitions of these terms to help with understanding their use by postmodern Jungians. In short, they are all ways of analysing how human beings represent reality in their minds and communicate these representations between themselves. Cynics might point out how these theoretical frames are merely the ways in which academic intellectuals represent reality in *their* minds, but, despite this, these ideas have been highly influential across a range of intellectual activities including the study of linguistics and language aquisition, mythology, social anthropology, literary criticism, philosophy, the history of ideas and psychoanalysis.

Structuralism is a method of analysis which may be applied to the data accumulated for analysis within a number of fields of enquiry. As a method it has its roots in, and derives its lexicon of ideas from, the structural linguistics of Ferdinand de Saussure (1875–1913). Saussure saw language as a system of signs and analysed signs into their two components: the sound, utterance or written mark – the material manifestation of language – he called the *signifier*, while the notion or mental idea it refers to Saussure called the *signified*. The actual object or event that the idea or signified refers to in the 'real world' is left out of the picture; this is a method for analysing how humans build up and communicate their apperceptions of that world, it is not about that world in a physical scientific sense. There can be no signified without its material partner, the signifier; a concept cannot be deemed to exist without a linguistic signifier. This system of signs also applies to significations outside language. As we saw in an earlier chapter, Roland Barthes applied such a system to a variety of cultural signs – visual signifiers such as the Roman hair curl or brow-sweat – that signify cultural concepts and general meanings that those in the cultural group recognise. The point is that this method of analysing phenomena is not about the 'reality' of the phenomena, but, like sentences and words in a given language, human life consists of a system of signs and significances quite apart from the 'things themselves'. For instance, these days, a red rose tends to signify the new Labour Party in Great Britain; in another era it signified the House of Lancaster. A wreath of flowers used at a funeral signifies an expression of condolence; the etymology of the sign is not the point so much as the way it functions as a communication in a system of signifiers. Most importantly, the significance – or meaning if you like – is determined by the culture inhabited by the sender and receiver who employ the sign and not by the nature of the signifier itself. Claude Lévi-Strauss, the structural anthropologist, particularly emphasised how the 'natural' and the 'cultural' should never be confused. An antelope in the wild is one thing, but when it is killed and transformed into food by cooking it becomes a cultural object or signifier; moreover, when the cooked body is divided up as portions of meat, the choice and distribution of the parts of the animal's body become further cultural signifiers that have meaning and significance – a code – for the group.

Structuralists also emphasise how the relationship between a signifier and the signified is *arbitrary*; in other words, there is no necessary relationship between the two. In English we have the sound/mark FLOWER for the general concept this signifies. This sound and word has no necessary relationship to the idea of a flower; German speakers use a different sound/ word BLUMEN but within each language-using group the relationship between signifier and signified is agreed and communicates. We saw above how a red rose has signified different ideas in a quite arbitrary way. The point being established here by the structuralists is how there is nothing essential about the relationship between the two aspects of signs but that signs only achieve communicable meaning derived from the context in which they are used. The last word in a sentence makes a crucial difference because it completes the context, e.g.

> Johnny is going to the toilet.
> Johnny is going to the dance.
> Johnny is going to the dogs.

Here it even shifts the significance of the word 'going' as well as the sort of person signified by the word 'Johnny'. As Saussure famously put it,

'Language is a form and not a substance'. What signifiers do is to delimit *difference*; they set up a system of differences and distinctions, both in terms of sounds and written words, which then make meaning.

Saussure made the important distinction between *langue* – a whole language system – and *parole* – speech, or the portion of that system being employed at any one time. The first consists of the underlying structures and relationships that make up a language code, while the latter is the communication that is created on the basis of the underlying structure. In linguistics and the study of language and the brain, Noam Chomsky established the idea that there are deep structures to human language which are universal; languages that differ widely on the 'surface' – Chinese, French, Bantu, Inuit and Xhosa, for example – all have the same 'deep' rules. This has been accounted for by positing a universal similarity to language structures in the brain of homo sapiens. This results in universal forms of linguistic structuring – the *structural relationships between signifiers* – while allowing for an infinite *variety of forms* that the signifiers themselves might take. The most universalising of the structural theories are those of Lévi-Strauss and Jacques Lacan. Lévi-Strauss extended insights on the structural relations between signs in the field of cultural anthropology where he pointed out 'underlying' structural relationships between various elements in myth – especially the Oedipus myth – and other elements of culture such as kinship relations, magic and dietary rules and behaviour (Lévi-Strauss, 1977). Lévi-Strauss also turned his attention to psychoanalysis where he revised Freud's structural model of the psyche along linguistic lines, into a 'preconscious' which contained personal memories and imagos, and an 'unconscious' which was 'empty', its sole function being the imposition of structural relations (rather like Chomsky's 'deep structures' for language). As Lévi-Strauss puts it:

> We might say, therefore, that the preconscious is the individual lexicon where each of us accumulates the vocabulary of his personal history, but that this vocabulary becomes significant, for us and for others, only to the extent that the unconscious structures it according to its laws and thus transforms it into language . . . The vocabulary matters less than the structure.
>
> (ibid.: 203)

The similarity between this and Jung's archetypal model, where the archetypes of the collective unconscious, empty of any 'content' of their own, have a similar structuring function on the personal unconscious and consciousness, is emphasised by post-Jungians such as Paul Kugler, whose work will be examined shortly.

Jacques Lacan used structural methods to re-read Freud and psycho-analytic theory. He emphasised how all human beings eventually have to communicate and represent themselves through the Symbolic – the linguistic system of signification that the culture (in Lacan's emphasis, a patriarchal culture of the Father) imposes on every individual. As a result of this, personal desire and individuality gets repressed in the unconscious and leaves the psyche of men and women with a sense of loss or lack. As I have mentioned before, for Lacan, the ego is a false construct necessary for the functioning of the Symbolic but alienated from the individual subject. This conceptualising of a gap between the insubstantial ego and a fuller sense of subjectivity, leaving subjects with a compulsion towards a 'wholeness' or completion of themselves, compares with Jung's emphasis on the relationship between the ego – the centre of consciousness – and the self which is defined as the largely unconscious and therefore largely 'potential' entirety of the personality.

As you might imagine, there has been a good deal of argument against structuralism due to its emphasis on deep, underlying structures which govern mental processes and cultural life. These ideas have come to be regarded as authoritarian and essentialist; such predetermined structures left no space, and no accounting, for individual expression or for the operation of chance. The ideas that challenged structuralism – *deconstruction* and *postmodernism* – have come to be grouped under the generic term: *poststructuralism*. Deconstructive ideas prefer to emphasise differences rather than similarities within and between systems: the gaps and paradoxes that are evident as we witnessed with Foucault's genealogical methods in Chapter 6. Derrida's deconstructions pointed out internal contradictions in texts previously regarded as coherent; he argues against any idea of fathoming an author's 'intention' and the validity of new readers (re)reading texts under new circumstances. Language precedes its author and so he or she has no priority over the 'meaning' of a text; language has powers beyond our control and so, as Humpty Dumpty said, 'It all depends on who is to be the master'.

Jungians vary in their understanding of deconstruction and the extent to which deconstructive ideas are evident in Jung and applicable to his psychology. Polly Young-Eisendrath sees deconstruction as 'a skeptical philosophy of doubt and criticism of established methods and theories in many diciplines' and consequently she finds 'little resonance between Jung and deconstruction' (Young-Eisendrath, 1995: 5). For her, deconstruction has a nihilistic quality just as the postmodern has in general – a view that I challenge throughout this book. I think the problem lies in distinguishing *what deconstructs and what is deconstructed*. There are other views that regard certain Jungian psychologies as profoundly deconstructive. Michael

Vannoy Adams criticises Young-Eisendrath by asserting that Jung's conception of the unconscious is one that directly deconstructs consciousness. I am quite in agreement with this view that sees Jung's overall project as one of deconstructing modern consciousness – it is, in fact, the pivotal perspective of this present book and central to the idea that Jungian psychology has many parallels with the postmodern. As Adams puts it, Jung's view is that the function of the unconscious is to compensate the conscious while Derrida would say that the unconscious deconstructs the conscious; either way, 'A compensatory or deconstructive unconscious would serve a similar purpose, which would be to expose the partial or prejudicial conceits, transvaluate the unviable values, of the conscious' (Adams, 1995: 7).

Adams is also one of the few to have written at length about the deconstructive thrust of one particular form of Jungian psychology – the imaginal psychology of James Hillman. As we will find later in this chapter, many post-Jungians prefer to stay with the images that arise into consciousness – through dreams or whatever – and to help clients to analogise and amplify these rather than to translate or decode them into 'meaning' as has been the psychoanalytic method. Not only does this empower the client in the relationship by deprioritising the 'master discourse' of the analyst as 'the one who knows', but this technique also has implications for the relationship or heirarchy between concepts and images – in structuralist terms, between the *signified* (concept) and the *signifier* (image). Deconstructive philosophy challenges both the *opposition* between signifier and signified and the *privileging or hierarchising* of the signified (concept) over the signifier (image). In this comparison, Hillman's technique of allowing the image a life of its own, so to speak, is equivalent to Derrida's emphasis on the autonomy of language; both image and language precede the subject and have an autonomy which needs to be respected at that level – the level of the signifier – and not distorted by a reductive translation or interpretation. We cannot completely abandon our concepts but Hillman's reversal of priorities is perhaps, 'a strategy necessary to counteract the iconoclastic tendencies of analysts . . . to remind analysts (who have forgotten or repressed the fact) that the concept needs the image just as much as – or more than – the image needs the concept' (Adams, 1992: 248). The emphasis changes from 'this *means* that' – which is both Freud's and Jung's position from the early days – to one in which 'this is *like* that'. The emphasis is on 'patterns of similarities, without positing a common origin for these similarities' (Hillman, quoted in Adams, 1992: 246). As Adams explains, if the image is that of a big black snake, for example, the idea would be to pursue the image for what it is *like* – to analogise it – rather than reduce it to a concept such as evil, sin, death, sex and so on.

Lastly, we need to note a different approach – one which is not derived from linguistic theories – taken by Peter Berger and Thomas Luckman in their book *The Social Construction of Reality* (1971). Here they set out in detail the way that humankind (denoted as 'Man' when they were writing) actively and collectively constructs social reality through the processes of habitualisation and institutionalisation. Although the social world derives from 'man's' biological equipment, the social world is entirely the result of human activity – it is 'man-made' not 'natural'. This includes the habitual ways that humans have of conducting themselves ('there I go again' eventually becoming 'This is how things are done'), rules and institutions like the 'family' and the incest taboo, and including the various forms of language. Vital to the argument is the way the authors emphasise that it is only once the social world is transmitted to a new generation which is born 'into' it, that it can be called a social world. The child is presented with human social forms, social institutions and language, as 'the way things are' in such a way that there are as opaque and unquestionable as the rest of the world (the world of 'nature'). Only later is a distinction realised and that social institutions may be investigated and challenged. Despite being a human invention, the institutions of social reality have an objective existence that precedes human subjects and will go on after them, despite the variable desires of individual subjects. The social world of humanity gets erected as a 'second nature' over the first.

The way that Berger and Luckman describe how the human environment, with the totality of its socio-cultural and psychological formations, becomes established through repetition and 'a reciprocal typification of habitualized actions by types of actors' (ibid.: 54), sounds similar to the way that Jung explains how archetypes arise as structuring tendencies in the human psyche, 'There are as many archetypes as there are typical situations in life. Endless repetition has engraved these experiences into our psychic constitution, not in the form of images filled with content, but at first only as *forms without content*, representing merely the possibility of a certain type of perception and action' (Jung, 1936/1937, CW 9, 1: para. 99). The comparison extends to the way in which archetypes, or, rather, manifestations of archetypes are also not biological in themselves although they derive from our biological nature. The archetypes are as specifically human as the social reality we create; furthermore, they are not 'fixed' just as the social environment is not fixed, but both have an objective existence that each new generation encounters and experiences as 'reality'. Michael Vannoy Adams argues that Jung's conception of collective psychology is one that is need of reconsideration and perhaps reformulation. He speaks of *the psychical construction of reality*, by which he means that, the individual vision of external reality is mediated – that is *psychically constructed* – by schemata, categories, or 'types' (be they archetypes or stereotypes), which, if not naturally inherited, are so culturally ingrained in the unconscious that they might as well be.

(Adams, 1991: 253)

In his reformulation, Adams advocates a *psychology of knowledge* which helps us see how the archetypes of the collective unconscious participate in the formation of human social reality in much the same way as Berger and Luckman describe its formation from the perspective of the sociology of knowledge. This might lead us to investigate not more *similarities* in some essentialist structuralist effort (of which the Jungian use of archetypes is often accused) but, on the contrary, to seek out 'difference', 'to develop a deliberately *contrastive method* and apply it to contemporary issues of collective psychology – for example, to the topics of diversity, pluralism, and multi-culturalism' (ibid.: 255).

IMAGE, IMAGO, WORD: IMAGINATION AND LANGUAGE

Whenever I have been required to teach Jungian psychology at an introductory level, I have always begun by emphasising that the unconscious is *really unconscious*. Nothing can be assumed to be known about the unconscious, it is *really the not-known*. The concept that is signified by our term *the unconscious* is a negative, a not-something, the not-conscious. The unconscious is an absence, a lack, a *not*. When we think we are knowing something about it, such knowledge is conscious knowledge and therefore no longer unconscious. Such conscious knowledge not only includes the images of dreams and fantasies, but it also includes all our speculations about the unconscious dynamics 'behind' behaviour and all our 'theories' about the unconscious – its 'contents' and its 'processes'. Ultimately, all these so-called *unconscious contents and unconscious processes are all, and always, unknown*. While emphasising this to beginners in the study of depth psychological ideas, this view, I believe, also needs to be emphasised at every step of the way in the study of Jung's psychology and in the training of therapists. All too frequently, the practitioners of analysis and therapy forget they are dealing with the unknown, a forgetting that leads to widespread assumptions within psychotherapy which become ossified as the dogma of depth psychological theory – the social construction of a psychotherapeutic reality, if you like – where the tendency is to regard hypotheses as 'truths', or even the 'nature', of the unconscious. As we work within a paradigm whose focus *is* this unconscious, it is important to recognise that we work within a paradigm of *not knowing*. This, in a nutshell, is the attitude to Jungian depth psychology that locates it as postmodern. This is in contrast to a modernist attitude, still prevalent throughout the psychoanalytic psychotherapies, which maintain that the unconscious, like any 'object of science', can be known and talked about descriptively, analytically and deductively, using a wide variety of 'truth statements'.

The post-Jungian Paul Kugler adds a corollary to the problem I have set out above: the relationship between the unconscious and consciousness,

> To arrive at a knowledge of something unconscious, that content must first be psychically *represented* to consciousness as a word, an image, an emotion, or inscribed in the flesh as a psychosomatic symptom. These (re)presentations in consciousness constitute the textuality of our psychic life and are the primary focus of depth psychology.
>
> (Kugler, 1990a: 307)

Paul Kugler is one of several postmodern Jungians who has been influenced by structuralist and post-structuralist textual and linguistic models in his understanding of Jungian psychology. Kugler points out how we are both 'author' and 'critic' – or 'reader' – of our own texts. We read our 'own' psychic images as 'other'. When we consciously recall our dreams, we relate the images and the narrative back to ourselves as if it were an objective text like a novel or a film. This leads him to ask, 'Who *is* the author of our psychic text? Who *is* the intended reader? And, furthermore, on what "principle" will we "ground" the act of analytic interpretation?' (ibid.: 307–308). This is the sort of question that has been approached elsewhere in literary theory and Kugler uses developments in this field to inform his postmodern reading of Jungian psychology. Kugler notes three effects of the acquisition of 'language' (i.e. , the psychic capacity for representation). First, lived experience is symbolised and replaced with a text; this textual realm mediates the object world and self-experiences 'by establishing a self-representation in language through use of the first-person pronoun "I"' (ibid.). This makes self-presentation possible in conscious thought and symbolised in a dream – which Kugler also refers to as a 'text'.

Second, as a consequence of the subject representing him or herself through language, 'the personality is divided into an *experiential self* and a *textual self*' (ibid.: 312). Following this, the speaker identifies with the textual self through the pronoun 'I' which is only 'a stand-in, in the realm of language – for the more primary self of experience, excluded from the realm of representation' (ibid.). This is why Lacan can affirm that speaking subjects exist in a condition of profound alienation – the ego, the 'I' of *re-presentation* is identified with, but it is distanced from the *experience* of being. There is forever a gap between experience *of* the subject and its representation *in* the subject. Challenging the Cartesian – therefore, Enlightenment – proposition of 'I think, therefore I am', Lacan asserts: 'I think where I am not, therefore I am where I do not think' (Lemaire, 1977: 166) or, as Madan Sarup puts it: 'I think where I cannot say I am' (Sarup, 1993: 10). Finally, the exclusion of the experiential self from the represented self leads to a third effect of language acquisition: an unconscious order of experience. 'Although mediation is necessary for consciousness and self-consciousness, the price paid for textual mediation is the creation of a certain unbridgeable distance between text and original lived experience. The realm of unmediated experience is the realm of the unconscious' (Kugler, 1990a: 312).

An often quoted example of this process derives from Freud's vivid description of his grandchild as a baby playing with a cotton reel on a string in his pram. The infant would throw away the reel out of sight over the edge of the pram uttering the syllable *fort* – the German for *gone*. The child would then retrieve the reel on its thread so it was back in the pram with him uttering *da* – German for *there*. This is the famous *fort/da* where the infant psyche has achieved both representation and language. What goes on in this psychological development is best understood when it is divided into three parts: first, it is thought that the infant is dealing with a critical emotional situation in its young life – the presence and absence of mother. Mother's presence or absence is an event in the world over which he ultimately has very little control. To cope with this he uses the cotton reel as a replacement for mother, a representation of mother which also goes and comes back, but, this time, to his delight, under his own volition. This is the first stage of representation. The second stage of representation is the introduction of a verbal signifier to represent the first representation: *fort* for 'gone', *da* for 'there'. Thus the 'experience' – mother's presence or absence – is doubly removed: first by representing her as the cotton reel, second by language. What gets left over, what is left out and missing and so consigned to the unconscious is the original issue: mother's going and returning and the affects and fantasies around that core event. We do not live in a world of 'presentations' but one of re-presentations that are further re-represented in linguistic forms; we are doubly alienated from experience.

This alienating quality of language and representation would seem to pose a problem to clinical psychological work that relies on verbal exchange and interpretations. Kugler finds that the shift to a philosophy of *deconstruction* – which is *the* shift into the postmodern – offers a way forward in our thinking about depth psychology, representation and interpretation. Kugler describes the problem of interpretation in clinical work by noting how depth psychology approaches its material from certain 'first principles' – certain absolutes or 'God principles' that seem to lie outside the material itself. 'If the therapist is committed to *a priori* ultimates, the significance of the case material comes about through a reduction to such absolutes as drives, the Oedipus complex, archetypes, biochemistry, the environment, family systems, childhood traumas, the analytic frame, and so on' (ibid.: 313). All these absolutes are temporally located in the past but other approaches, including the Jungian, have *a posteriori* absolutes located in the future. The clinical material may be interpreted as referring to ultimates such as the self, archetypes, wholeness, soul, death and so on. As Kugler sees it,

> For these first principles to perform their explanatory function, they cannot be implicated in the very system of thought and language they are being used to explain; nor can their meaning have the same semantic status as the other meanings within the system. Their semantic status must be something like the 'meaning of meaning' or the 'metaphor of metaphors'. These *a priori* and *a posteriori* 'god' terms function as the linchpins for our Western theories of clinical interpretation . . . Here we experience how language has subtly trapped us inside the logic of the 'origins' metaphor, unconsciously elevating the term ['self' for Jungians, 'drives' for classical Freudians] to a transcendental status that now attempts to account for all the other terms. The originary, explanatory principle explains everything except itself and therefore is not the *ultimate* explanatory principle.
>
> (ibid.: 313–314)

The roots of the deconstructionist perspective lie with Friedrich Nietzsche: in *The Gay Science* Nietzsche declares 'God is dead' – by which he means that modernity has created the position where all such authorities, or first principles, the 'god' terms of Kugler's discourse, are untenable and we are left floating in space as if we have, as Nietzsche puts it, 'unchained the earth from the sun'. The contradiction of contemporary thinking which involves the coexistence of, on the one hand, a modernist trust in originary principles and, on the other, a postmodern deconstruction of all 'fundamental' truths might be illustrated by the old joke about graffiti found on the lavatory wall of Basle University. Initially, the graffiti read:

`God is dead.        Nietzsche.`

Several years later a further inscription appeared:

Nietzsche is dead.   God.

As I have been pointing out elsewhere in this book, the postmodern condition is characterised by a style of consciousness that has proceeded from a simple reflectivity which still held trust in, and felt grounded by, the existence of 'ultimates', 'absolutes' or 'truths', to a state of accelerated *hyper-reflexivity*. Part of this shift has been the realisation (or is it the 'admission'?), that our very means of knowledge and expression – notably language, but including a range of representation creating analogous systems of signs and symbols – is trapped within the limitations of human representation itself. No longer can we assume an impartial, objective understanding or interpretation of phenomena. All such efforts are now seen to be contoured by the means of representation itself which is predominantly, but not exclusively, linguistic. From Wittgenstein through to Derrida, we are now assailed with the need to confront our assumptions about what we can *safely say*, and, not least in the field of depth psychology and its clinical applications, we have to take on board the implications of this postmodern 'crisis' in epistemology. 'The reader of any text is suspended between the literal and the metaphoric significance of its words, unable to choose between the two meanings and thus thrown into the dizzying semantic indeterminacy of the text' (ibid.: 315).

This appears to be an anxiety-provoking position for the late twentieth-century subject to find him or herself in – especially if they are an analyst meant to be fostering psychological understanding for the purpose of psychic and emotional healing. Fears, and accusations, of nihilism spring up in the face of the challenge to our ideas of representation as they have done from the days of Nietzsche's deconstructions through to those of the contemporary postmodern. By now, it should be evident that I, myself, do not hold with the criticism of nihilism and, equally, find myself not nervous but relieved at the scope and potential this position offers: the freedom from having to adhere to fundamentals. The world, its human beings and their psychologies, are infinitely more complex than any system of interpretation, or any *method* of interpretation can ever grasp. Rather than relying on this or that psychological position, understanding or interpretation, there is now an opportunity – if not to float away in space, which *would* be scary – at least to feel free to move in the spaces between this and that *apparent*, but in the end, *fictional* assumption or certainty. It strikes me that the accusations of nihilism stem from those made anxiously uncomfortable by the idea of proceeding without a 'solid', 'anchored' or 'earthed' set of beliefs. To those I say two things: Of course retain these beliefs, but notice how they are *fictions* – useful fictions but all 'as if' just the same. Realising they are fictional and mutable does not mean they are nihilistic or destructive of any meaning whatsoever. Their fictional status does not dilute their *usefulness*. Second, and implied by this, feel free to *move between* these 'beliefs', or positions; we never escape language or representation, it is the atmosphere we inhabit, but to stay 'safely' – meaning *positivistically* – in a fixed 'established' position seems equivalent to a psycho-somatic emphysema where one is deluded into believing that by taking even a few steps at a time, one will be collapsing into breathless panic. I am in the same frame as Paul Kugler when he writes,

> Postmodernism with its intense focus on the problematics of self-reflection, textuality, and the process of psychic representation has revealed that these unquestionable 'absolutes' are not the eternal, archetypal structures we once thought them to be, but are rather *temporal and linguistic by-products* . . . In therapeutic analysis we still must, on one level, *believe in* our god term and use it *as if* it were the ultimate explanatory principle. But on a deeper level, we also know that it is not. And it is precisely this deeper level of awareness that prevents our psychological ideologies from becoming secular religions and differentiates professional debates from religious idolatry.
>
> (ibid.: 316, italics in original)

KNOWING AND THE UNKNOWN: ANCIENT WISDOM AND MODERN REPRESENTATION

At this point in the examination of postmodern epistemology and Jungian thought it is critical to return to the statement I made at the beginning about how *the unconscious is really un-conscious*. The unconscious is always and 'absolutely' *not-known*. From what has been said above it should be coming clear that it is this *not-knowing that requires the concept of the unconscious*, and it is the quality of *not-known* that is the criteria for what is unconscious. Put this way, then, as I have said, the 'unconscious' sounds like a negative entity, a 'not-something', an *absence*, a *lack* of something, and not the rather concretised entity depth psychology is always referring to as if it was a *something*. The postmodern realisation lies very much in this idea of a not-known, as we have noted briefly above when it was said that 'The realm of unmediated experience is the realm of the unconscious' (ibid.: 312). In other words, between the realm of conscious, textual representation and 'original lived experience' lies the not-known: *neither the representable*

nor the experience, or, to put it another way, not the represented and not the
experienced.

I intend to elaborate on this idea of the not-known unconscious with reference to the work of David Miller (1989, 1990a, 1990b) and James Grotstein (1998) and discussions between Miller, James Hillman, Edward Casey and Paul Kugler (Casey et al., 1990) where Jung's emphasis on the not-known in his psychological ideas is contrasted both with other, more positivistic, modernist psychologies, and with the modernist strands in Jung's own thought which are to be found aplenty. The point is not to underestimate the modernist Jung, but to rediscover the 'later' or 'other', postmodern Jung where the *not-known* receives full importance. In doing so we shall see how it becomes difficult to avoid offering illustrations from a system quite different to the mode of Western thought that has been referred to up till now; this alternative discourse, with an emphasis on the *not-known*, is to be found in the Taoist philosophy of Ancient China, and in its hybrid, the Zen system of China and Japan.

For a minority of commentators throughout the 1990s, the implications of depth psychology have been viewed for their potential to be linked with Eastern concepts of human consciousness and non-dualistic thought – a Real beyond representation of 'reality'. For the majority of the more scientifically minded psychologists – 'scientific' in the Western, positivistic sense – this linkage seems to have been an embarrassment. The result has been that the implications within analytical psychology, and especially within psychoanalysis, for making connections between Western thought and Eastern philosophy and psychology have been ignored. In this respect, depth psychology is behind the times with its cautious, unconfident approach to the implications held within its theories and findings. For many years, the discourse of physics, especially that of sub-atomic physics, has recognised how its findings seem to correspond with ancient systems of thought stemming from the East and elsewhere (e.g. Capra, 1975; Bohm, 1983; Peat, 1995), while physicists at the other end of the scale, those who study the astronomical matter of the universe, are more likely to endorse some idea of a creator God than they have ever been since the last two centuries over which classical physics found little need for such a concept. As the author Peter James notes, 'In 1920, 44 percent of scientists believed there was some intelligence behind the forming of the cosmos. This year it was still 44 percent. The only shift was that fewer biologists believed it but more mathematicians did' (James, 1998: 186).

Jung himself was rather tentative when it came to expressing the implications of analytical psychology in this connection until the end of his life. This needs to be understood in two ways. One is the tendency, shared with Freudian psychoanalysis, to frame much of the discourse and discoveries of analytical psychology within prevailing modernist ways of thinking in an effort to help legitimate the new 'science' of depth psychology. David Miller notes how this tendency may be understood as the discourse stemming from Jung's '#1 Personality' which Jung describes in *Memories, Dreams, Reflections*. This is the Jung of 'our Jungian concepts and categories' (Miller, 1990a: 326), the Jung who is happy to differentiate and name all the Jungian 'essentials': concepts such as archetypes, collective unconscious, ego, self and so on. The second way to understand Jung's reluctance to embrace the Eastern thought implied by his own psychology is his emphasis on the importance for Europeans of the Christian heritage as a symbolic system and a path of development for the human soul. Despite his great interest in researching connections between his ideas and the East – exemplified by his collaboration with Richard Wilhelm on Chinese texts, his endorsement of the *I Ching* and his introductions to books such as the *Tibetan Book of the Dead* and other texts on Zen and Yoga – Jung came down firmly on the side of Christian theology and symbolism. This view is connected with Jung's particular attitude to the modern Western psyche – its 'barbarous one-sidedness' which first requires what analytical psychology offers: a way of integrating unconscious contents, thereby expanding consciousness as the East has already achieved. Jung is clear about his admiration for Eastern techniques and insights, and just as clear about how we in the West are not ready for them and should develop our own methods:

> If I remain so critically averse to yoga, it does not mean that I do not regard this spiritual achievement of the East as one of the greatest things the human mind has ever created . . . The spiritual development of the West has been along entirely different lines from that of the East and has therefore produced conditions which are the most unfavourable soil one can think of for the application of yoga. Western civilization is scarcely a thousand years old and must first of all free itself from its barbarous one-sidedness. This means, above all, deeper insight into the nature of man. But no insight is gained by repressing and controlling the unconscious, and least of all by imitating methods which have grown up under entirely different psychological conditions. In the course of the centuries the West will produce its own yoga, and it will be on the basis laid down by Christianity.
>
> (Jung, 1936, CW 11: para. 876)

Despite this emphasis in Jung, analytical psychology of course contains a great deal that is 'non-Western' and this has been its main attraction to many of those who read and practice Jungian psychology today. I, for one, came to Jung in my late twenties after several years of studying and practising Buddhism – an effort which got me nowhere with myself although, at the time, I attributed this to the more 'outer' understanding that a Western urban environment was not conducive to an Eastern practice, rather than to Jung's insight that a Western psyche, on the whole, is not ready for such a practice. Despite the attraction of this non-Western aspect of Jung's thought – the aspect that Miller aligns with the '#2 Personality' of Jung – there has been, until recently, a great fear of endorsing and thinking in terms of this, most important, side of Jung. In our thinking about what the genius of depth psychology can offer, it is as if we are still at the same stage as Freud was in 1910 when he warned his young collaborator Carl Jung that, as regards the sexual theory of psychoanalysis: 'we must make a dogma of it, an unshakable bulwark . . . Against the black tide of mud . . . of occultism' (Jung, 1983/1963: 173). Jung reckons that what Freud meant by 'occultism' was virtually everything that philosophy, religion and parapsychology had learned about the psyche. He goes on to speculate that Freud was gripped by the *numinosity* of sexuality, 'regarded from within, sexuality included spirituality and had an intrinsic meaning. But his concretistic terminology was too narrow to express this idea. . . . In his own words he felt himself menaced by a "black tide of mud" – he who more than anyone else had tried to let down his buckets into those black depths' (ibid.: 175).

There is nothing like damning with faint praise to undermine another's position, especially when Jung knows the reader knows that Jung himself let down *his* buckets even further! But the point remains that the modernist fears that Freud was expressing have not gone away. Just the other week, at an academic board meeting in my own University, there was great concern being expressed that the University was offering a short course in Astrology. Those at the meeting required reassurances about the 'intellectual content' of such a course. 'Black tide' alarms emerged with concerns about 'What next? Black magic studies?' – while others like myself pointed out that the University of Edinburgh in fact offers a Chair of Parapsychology (funded by the estate of the late Arthur Koestler).

Referring specifically to this problem in Jung's psychology, David Miller asks:

> Why is it that so many persons are astonished, empowered, amazed, inspired, provoked and overwhelmed by Jung's so-called Personality #2? But the same persons quote, believe in, explain, and expatiate upon the jargon from Personality #1! Was it not Jung's view that the deep self provides the *tremendum*, the awe and insight and power? But it is ego's

explanations and ideas that have been the *fascinosum*, fascinating, fastening and fixating Jungians? Why can there not be a truly 'Jungian' (#2) psychology? – that is, one that is not Jungian (#1)?

(Miller, 1990a: 325)

What is striking about Miller's introductory paragraph that immediately lets us know we are in postmodern territory is his last question asking why we cannot have a 'Jungian' psychology that is not Jungian. Miller is taking full advantage of postmodern style and discourse to address, on the one hand, the inadequacy of the modernist, authorial approach to Jung's psychology, while, on the other hand, using a Jungian distinction between ego and self, to point out the alignment of the authorial approach with ego discourse, thus revealing the insufficiency of the ego's point of view – and how it narrows our understanding of what depth psychology has to offer. What I wish to emphasise here is how throughout contemporary culture, but especially in the field of depth psychology, the postmodern perspective is far from being destructively nihilistic but in fact offers the opportunity for what Andrew Samuels calls 'the resacralization of culture' (Samuels, 1993). This is not to imply a newly-found belief in God or even gods, this shift can equally be atheistic. What is at stake is a certain Otherness which may counter our dominant style of ego-conscious; it is in a secular world such as ours that such Otherness is represented as spiritual. *Postmodern views offer depth psychology the chance to restore its Otherness, its spiritual and religious element which was always the ground from which it sprang but which became lost through depth psychology clinging to, rather than continuing to challenge, the modernist values within which it emerged.* Psychoanalysis has embodied this clinging tendency most fully, no doubt due to 'black tide of mud' warnings, but even here, in James Grotstein's view, to be discussed shortly, psychoanalytic developments such as those of Lacan and Bion, and even Winnicott, are now recognised as offering a spiritual dimension to psychoanalysis that has been ignored or underplayed by the psychoanalytic establishment. Of course, Jung was specific about the spiritual dimension of the psyche and depth psychology, and distinguished himself from Freud in this respect, but, as David Miller is saying, Jung has still been read within twentieth-century thinking and practised within a medicalised paradigm which privileges the ego-based, modernist aspects of analytical psychology. With the arrival of the 'new paradigm', or 'ethic', or discourse of the postmodern, both psychoanalysis and analytical psychology – who I view as twins cruelly separated at birth, or shortly after – are now able to be read for the fuller, in fact the *vast*, implications depth psychology offers, and secretly always offered, for the expansion of modern human consciousness and human Being.

As I have been suggesting, and as Jung knew, Eastern thought has had many centuries of discovering and expressing, often in quite poetic and enigmatic ways, many of the insights implied by the Western psychology of the unconscious. It has probably been the very poetic and 'unscientific' style of expression of the East that has deterred the modernist, rational mind from paying more than scant attention to these forms of expression except in the margins of Western thought. A comparison with European encounters with the Other in the form of colonisation becomes more than a metaphor here. Grotstein describes Freud's retreat from the implications of his discovery of the unconscious thus:

> once he realized what he had come across . . . he . . . beat a modernist retreat to the safe ground of atheistic, scientistic negativism; i.e. he did with the *id* what Toynbee stated the British did when confronted with primitive, third-world cultures: 'they colonized them and then gave them pants and bibles'. In other words, he fled to the more acceptable, gentrified ego.
>
> (Grotstein, 1998: 42)

It is not merely coincidental that the late nineteenth-century peak of European colonisation of human Others, operating within a general thrust towards triumph over Nature, was paralleled by the European (re)discovery of the Other of consciousness – the Unconscious of depth psychology (cf. Hauke, 1996b), itself destined to be swiftly colonised as Grotstein indicates. Eastern thought, with its contrasting, respectful attitude to both 'inner' and 'outer' Nature – as Western dualism would have it – expresses the Other in forms unfamiliar and alien to the modernist thinking of the West. It is this Other of Eastern forms of expression that best conveys what Miller is driving at with the #2 Personality psychology of Jung, and which he also emphasises in his title: *An Other Jung and An Other* (Miller, 1990a).

Paul Kugler graphically conveys a parallel point about 'meaning' when he contrasts the unconscious as that which is 'known' but hidden – the modernist 'detective story' of classical psychoanalysis – to the unconscious as *unknown*, a position where 'the meaning is bracketed by doubt and an attitude of not knowing' (Kugler, 1990b: 332–333). To do this, Kugler relates a Taoist story to emphasise the 'postmodern meaning of meaning' which he compares to the well-known fable of Moses and the Khidr which Jung uses to illustrate the 'importance of transcendental meaning (the self) in the establishment of psychic significance' (ibid.: 332). Jung's story has all the qualities of a detective mystery in which Moses is shown a series of seemingly meaningless, tragic events but which are, in the end, all revealed as having an inner logic that 'makes sense' in a positive, but non-obvious, fashion. The contrasting Taoist story is one in which a farmer with a son and a horse experiences a series of disasters which are followed each time by good fortune. The farmer's neighbours come around time after time, commiserating with him over his 'bad luck' on some occasions, then congratulating him on the 'good luck' on the other occasions, and asking him what he makes of the events. Every time the farmer, after some thought, always gives the same reply: 'I don't know'. In the Moses and Khidr story where all the distressing events are revealed to Moses as having had a hidden future significance, 'there is a personification (Khidr or, in Jung's psychology, the self) who "knows" (signifies) the meaning of the future, whereas in the second story there is no such personified teleological knowledge. There is only a farmer who questions the neighbours' tendency to fix a specific interpretation to an event' (ibid.: 333–334). Kugler is making the point that we can either go for the attitude that there is significance to be found in events if only we 'knew the whole truth' or we can take the Taoist position in which there is really no 'significance' available to us. Any understanding, transcendent or not, is still man-made and subject to our representations. It is not the *not* that is the unconscious. Indeed, *this is the knot that is the not of the unconscious.*

Before proceeding with some of Miller's and Grotstein's analyses of depth psychology which seem to offer comparisons with Taoist and Zen thought, I should like to supply some brief examples of the Eastern thinking I have in mind. The fullest philosophico-religious texts are to be found in the many translations of Buddhist sutras available, but the most accessible expressions of this sort of thinking can be found in the translations of ancient Chinese seers such as Lao Tse (Lau, 1963) and Chuang Tzu (Merton, 1970). Their contributions take the form of anecdotes, prose-poems and poetry, aphoristic in style. As his translator, Thomas Merton points out, 'Chuang Tzu is not concerned with words and formulas about reality, but with the direct existential grasp of reality in itself. Such a grasp is necessarily obscure and does not lend itself to abstract analysis. It can be presented in a parable, a fable, or a funny story about a conversation between two philosophers' (ibid.: 11). Here are some examples:

Tao

Beyond the smallest of the small
there is no measure.
Beyond the greatest of the great
There is also no measure.

When there is no measure
There is no 'thing'.

In this void
You speak of 'cause'
Or of 'chance'?
You speak of 'things'
When there is 'no-things'.
To name a name
Is to delimit a 'thing'.

. . .

Does Tao exist?
Is it then a 'thing that exists.'
Can it 'non-exist'?
Is there then 'thing that exists'
That 'cannot not exist'?

To name Tao
Is to name no-thing.
Tao is not the name
Of 'an existent.'
'Cause' and 'chance'
Have no bearing on Tao.
Tao is a name
That indicates
Without defining.

Tao is beyond words
And beyond things.
It is not expressed
Either in word or in silence.
Where there is no longer word or silence
Tao is apprehended.

(ibid.: 150–152)

The emphasis here is the limited nature of language. When it comes to expressing the Other, the Real or Void, Western thought, through Kant and then Wittgenstein, is still in its infancy. Wittgenstein, in particular, saw his purpose in philosophy was not merely to distinguish what can be said from what cannot be said in language, but also to understand the structure of what can be said and to plot the limits of language. Such a limit of language is not a single continuous boundary which is found to be impassable, but it consists of 'a maze of boundaries which can be understood only by those who have felt the urge to cross them, have made the attempt and have been forced back' (Pears, 1971: 17). This offers a way of viewing Jung's position, when he expresses the struggle to 'integrate conscious and unconscious' in terms of the limits of language, image and representation for the human mind:

> I know people for whom the encounter with the strange power within themselves was such an overwhelming experience that they called it 'God'. So experienced, 'God' too is a 'theory' in the most literal sense, a way of looking at the world, an image which the limited human mind creates in order to express an unfathomable and ineffable experience . . . Names and words are sorry husks, yet they indicate the quality of what we have experienced.
>
> (Jung, 1933, CW 10: paras 330–331)

The *Tao Te Ching*, attributed to Lao Tzu an older contemporary of Confucius (551–479 BC), uses a poetic form to warn about the limits of naming when it comes to apprehending 'reality':

> The way is for ever nameless.
> Though the uncarved block is small
> No one in the world dare claim its allegiance.
>
> . . .
>
> Only when it is cut are there names.
> As soon as there are names
> One ought to know that it is time to stop.
> Knowing when to stop one can be free from danger.
> The way is to the world as the River and the Sea are to rivulets
>   and streams.
>
> (Lau, 1963: 91)

The 'way', the 'uncarved block', Tao and 'no-thing' are analogous to 'God' and the 'unfathomable and ineffable' of Jung's usage. We will see shortly how Grotstein finds further analogies in post-Freudian psycho-analytic concepts such as Bion's 'O' and Lacan's Real. In passing, it is interesting to note how the final metaphor about rivulets and streams brings to mind Jung's lifelong fascination with streams and rivulets which he played with literally on the shores of Lake Zurich and, metaphorically, as did Freud, as a way of describing the differentiation of psychic energy or libido.

At this stage, it might seem reasonable to ask 'What is the *use* of all this stuff about the Tao or the Unconscious if, when it comes down to it, it is either "no-thing", or, if "anything", it is completely beyond the grasp of human cognition and language anyway?' The ancient Chinese were fond of answering this concern – which they must have encountered as often two and a half thousand years ago as the Western mind does today. My favourite response is again to be found in the *Tao Te Ching* where Lao Tse points out the usefulness of 'nothing' – his word for the empty spaces which are essential aspects of four familiar objects: wheels, pots, windows and doors.

> Thirty spokes
> Share one hub.
> Adapt the nothing therein to the purpose in hand, and you will have the use of the cart. Knead clay in order to make a vessel. Adapt the nothing therein to the purpose in hand, and you will have the use of the vessel. Cut out doors and windows in order to make a room. Adapt the nothing therein to the purpose in hand, and you will have the use of the room.
> Thus what we gain is Something, yet it is by the virtue of Nothing that this can be put to use.
>
> (ibid.: 67)

Chuang Tzu puts a similar point more dramatically:

> Hui Tzu said to Chuang Tzu:
> 'All your teaching is centered on what has no use.'
>
> Chuang replied:
> 'If you have no appreciation of what has no use
> You cannot begin to talk about what can be used.
> The earth, for example, is broad and vast
> But of all this expanse a man uses only a few inches
> Upon which he happens to be standing.
> Now suppose you suddenly take away
> All that he is not actually using
> So that, all around his feet a gulf
> Yawns, and he stands in the Void,
> With nowhere solid except right under each foot:
> How long will he be able to use what he is using?'
>
> Hui Tzu said: 'It would cease to serve any purpose.'

Chuang Tzu concluded:
'This shows
The absolute necessity
Of what has "no use".'

(Merton, 1970: 153)

Granted, the *no-thing* of ancient Chinese thought is not identical to the *not* that the modern concept of the unconscious represents. If you recall, the unconscious of psychoanalytic thinking has been described more in terms of that which has been abandoned or left behind or excluded. This implies that it was there in the first place. The Tao is not something that was ever 'there' in that sense. Such texts do, however, help direct us towards further implications of our concept of the unconscious that go beyond its modern conception. Where both realms of thought – depth psychology and the ancient Chinese – *do* coincide is in their attempt to grapple with the limitations of human *consciousness* and its Other.

THE SUBJECT, THE OTHER AND THE NECESSITY OF THE UNKNOWN

The Freudian James Grotstein and the Jungian Paul Kugler both approach the unknowable unconscious through a consideration of the 'Subject' – also written as the *'subject of S(s)ubjects'* in Grotstein's work. Kugler's thesis concerns 'the study of dreams where the paradox arises that the human subject is not only the object but also the "subject" of our investigations' (Kugler, 1993: 1). Kugler seeks to examine the implications for depth psychology of the 'death' of the postmodern subject and, as we have seen above, does so in terms of the consequences that arise for human beings from the acquisition of language. It may be worthwhile to recap his conclusions. Referring to Lacan's idea of the *stade du miroir* whereby the ego is formed in alienation as a 'reflection' of 'itself', Kugler writes:

> The capacity for the ego to see 'itself', its representation, at a distance is the result of the originary alienation taking place during the mirror stage. This originary alienation between consciousness and representation leads to the second consequence of language acquisition: the creation of an inner sense of Otherness. . . . While psychic images are representations experienced in the sphere of consciousness, the realm of unmediated experience is the realm of the unconscious. And about this subject we cannot speak . . .

(ibid.)

This is the 'subject' of Lao Tse, and it is also the Unknown subject of depth psychology; a subject Jung was also aware of: 'I am quite conscious that I am moving in a world of images and that none of my reflections touches the essence of the Unknowable' (Jung, 1952/1954, CW 11: para. 556).

In his pursuit of the psychoanalytic Subject, James Grotstein, a Freudian training analyst of the Los Angeles Psychoanalytic Society writing in the international Jungian *Journal of Analytical Psychology* (Grotstein, 1998), focuses on the implications of several post-Freudian concepts and, in doing so, demonstrates how the late 1990s are witnessing the expansion of postmodern perspectives in American psychoanalysis following the impetus from post-Jungians a decade earlier. Grotstein's thesis seeks to distinguish the *immanent subject* – which we may take as our ego/self-representation – from the *numinous Subject* described as, 'the Subject *in* and *of* the Unconscious . . . the Subject of subjects, not unlike the Gnostic sense of the "God" within us' (Grotstein, 1998: 43). Grotstein develops a thesis that compares closely with Jung's distinction of ego and self, when he finds it necessary to delineate the two dualistic 'subjects' of the subject. He points out how Freud, through assigning prime agency to the drives 'not only eclipsed the unconscious subject but he also conflated . . . the drive as the *signifier* of distress with the drive as the distressful *signified*, a distinction upon which the fate of psychoanalysis became fundamentally imperiled' (ibid., italics in original).

Grotstein cites Bion's 'transformations in "O"', Lacan's 'Subject of analysis' and 'Register of the Real', Matte-Blanco's 'infinite sets of the Unconscious', as well as Klein's 'infant of analysis' and Winnicott's 'being' infant, as the concepts that have, since Freud, restored the Subject to psychoanalysis:

> The point is this: the psychodynamic *explanation* of what has or had happened to the patient must be totally differentiated from how the infantile aspect of the patient (the Subject) believes that it had *created, caused,* or *personalized* the event – in order to claim *psychic agency* – in order to render the event into a *personal experience*. To me, psychoanalysis is the unraveling of our personal mythic *creationism*, not a historicized 'murder mystery' of 'who done it'.
>
> (ibid.: 44)

Before Grotstein goes on to detail the postmodern psychoanalytic contributions he inevitably has to acknowledge Jung's perspective by noting that Jung was the only psychoanalyst for many years who dared explore the religious roots of the analytic Subject – until Bion. Summarizing Bion's work, Grotstein draws our attention to Bion's discoveries around the transformations that took place in analytic transferences. These consisted of transformations not only in personal consensual reality ('K') but also in 'O' *Absolute Reality*. 'When Bion uncovered "O", he not only stepped outside the known world of logical-positivistic science, he went beyond an inviolable perimeter of classical and Freudian understanding. He had done the unthinkable by invoking mysticism, religion and God' (ibid.: 48).

Whoops! There goes the neighbourhood! It's that old black tide creeping back again – and so no wonder that the British Psychoanalytical Society, according to Grotstein, celebrates Bion's work up to but *excluding* the 'transformations in "O"' (ibid.). 'O' is the *ineffable*, more like the Tao or the Way of the Chinese texts; it is called 'O', because, 'Psychologically it represents that incomprehensible, inconceivable, unimaginable and unsymbolizable experience which can only be understood as numinous' (ibid.). But words, as Jung wrote, are indeed sorry husks when it comes to expressing all this. Grotstein points out how Lacan avoided the spiritual dimension or implications in his own rereading of Freud, but, by noting the limits of language and its role in the formation of personality and subjectivity, Lacan also conceived of an 'O' – his *Register of the Real*. For Lacan, the Real is that which lies outside the capacities of the *Imaginary* (imagos, internal objects) or the *Symbolic* (the order of the Culture, or the Word of the Father – of what can be *said*) to apprehend or represent. 'O', or the Real, is '*a domain without an object. . . . It is what Freud did not realize that the unconscious consisted of when he chose the drives to be its privileged signified elements in lieu of being merely signifiers of the ineffable infinity and eternity of the unconscious*' (ibid.: 49, italics added). And, as if this was not revolutionary stuff enough for psychoanalysis, amounting to a restoration of the 'DNA' it shares with analytical psychology, so to speak, Grotstein also reveals similar perspectives in the work of Klein and Winnicott: 'Klein's clinical conception of the *analytic infant* . . . a "virtual infant", one that has the quality of the "once and forever infant", not merely the infant of time but mostly the ongoing infant of Being . . . Certainly this infant qualifies as an important way of clinically addressing the Subject of analysis' (ibid.: 59).

Jungians will also recognise the archetype of the Child here, a concept Jung uses to refer to the 'infancy' of, not the individual, but of *consciousness itself*. Post-Jungians and others have also pursued this 'other' child in an effort to understand the 'infanto-centric' tendencies in depth psychology since the 1940s (Hillman, 1975; Hauke, 1996a; Samuels, 1985). Following Klein, Winnicott developed the distinction between the '*being infant*' and the '*doing or object usage infant*' – the latter corresponding to the Kleinian infant. This psychoanalytic discourse parallels not only the Jungian concept of a self-ego dialogue where each intrinsically needs the other, but it is also reminiscent of the relationship between nothingness and form in the Taoist texts and of the relationship between God and mankind in the Judeo-Christian tradition. Grotstein points out how Freud had borrowed the term '*das Es*' from Nietzsche and Groddeck but failed to ascribe the same numinous significance Nietzsche and Groddeck had ascribed to it, and he concludes,

> I believe that there exists a 'Siamese-twinship' or Janus-faced conception of the transpersonal, collective (intersubjective) Subject, as posited by Jung and Lacan and an hereditary, individual Subject (not in the sense of Jung but in the sense of Freud and Klein) . . . Ultimately I believe that the human search for God is but another way – in part, albeit – to search for his/her own Unconscious and for the Subject of Subjects that is its prize occupant.
>
> (Grotstein, 1998: 61, 64)

And, I would add, *vice versa*. But also, *neither: not this, not that*.

After this excursion into the discourse on the Void via Eastern texts and the rereading of Freudian psychoanalysis, I should like to leave them both in the 'black tide of mud' – which, I believe, will not swamp them but, on the contrary, prove fertilising like the dark alluvial plains of the Nile delta which have been the source of the greatest cultural riches. We need to bring such excursions back to how we started with the image, sign and symbol and their attendant qualities of meaning, knowing and unknowing as they feature in postmodern Jungian psychology.

THE POSTMODERN MEANING OF 'MEANING'

Grotstein's two S(s)ubjects of depth psychology are elsewhere conceived as ego and self, or, conscious and Unconscious, or, in David Miller's formulation, Jung's #1 and #2 Personalities (Miller, 1990a). Miller draws our attention to the concepts of *plaisir* and *jouissance*, and uses Barthe's contrasting perspectives where *plaisir* – the experience of pleasure – 'contents, fills, grants euphoria', but 'it is linked to what is comfortable' and 'does not break with culture' (Barthes, 1975: 14). This is compared with *jouissance* which is not the same as *plaisir*. 'Jouissance really refers to the female experience of orgasm, waving and weaving and polymorphous, rather than pointed and focused in a historical moment' (Miller, 1990a: 326). In Kristeva's terms such 'bliss' is an experience that 'imposes a state of loss . . . discomforts . . . unsettles assumptions' (Kristeva, 1978: 36). This distinction leads Miller to liken jouissance to the postmodern Jungian attitude to clinical material, a notion of weaving, the weave in which the texture of the textile, and what Paul [Kugler] called the textuality, is in the effect of the whole. There is no call for a filling in in a way that the rational mind or the conscious ego can make sense of it. One can feel the texture, or one can sense the body of the weave, whether it is in a text or a dream. It is paratactic. It may look to us like it makes a Gestalt as a whole, but it is like a fine tapestry. When you look at it closely, it begins to dissolve. It is 'gappy' . . . but the body of it, the texture of it, is felt nonetheless.

(Miller, 1990b; 331)

David Miller is reimagining a different type of meaning and of 'knowing' in depth psychology – one in which wholeness or completeness is not forced upon or expected of the material: '*discontinuous images are juxtaposed richly without forcing a point, without insisting upon symbolic connections . . . It is jouissance that is the play of the postmodern. It is the bliss of not-knowing*' (Miller, 1990a: 326, italics added). In a few words Miller captures what this present chapter has been attempting to convey. This is the way that postmodern Jungian psychology allows the play of images without the need for any 'this means that' symbolic equations; this is rather the play of signs, the floating signifiers, that in their freedom and richness open the soul to *jouissance*, no-thing and the unknown Unconscious.

When it comes to revaluing 'meaning' itself, Miller points out how it is just as one-sided, or 'neurotic', to assert meaninglessness as it is to assert meaningfulness. One should not dismiss the 'myth of meaning' but rather explore consciously all of our *myths* of meaning, (Miller, 1990b: 334). Edward Casey adds:

Merleau-Ponty said that meaning arises at the edges of signs . . . in the way that strings of signifiers interrelate. This is also true of strings of 'symbols', and we can certainly still go on using that word, just as we are using the word 'meaning', now under a kind of double quote or 'erasure', as Derrida calls it. We can go on using these words, but now the interest is in how the particular group of signs configurates, such as those . . . in the two parables given . . . by Paul Kugler, rather than in something like an overarching sense or significance.

(Casey *et al.*, 1990: 334)

What is under discussion here is more than a simple opposition of the 'literal' and the 'metaphorical'; as Ed Casey points out, within the postmodern there is a change in the function of this concept 'the literal'. The literal does not equate with 'obdurate fact',

> Fact does not seem to have a place anymore, though there is a place
> for the unknown and there is a place for the literal as it is inscribed
> within the system of signs, a sliding system of signs . . . slipperiness,
> *glissement*. The literal slides all over the place. There is nothing to get
> stuck to or to get stuck on anymore.
>
> (ibid.: 338)

Paul Kugler maintains that the important contribution of archetypal
psychology, through Hillman especially, has been to expose the fictional
'grounding' of all theory including its own. James Hillman says of his and
Charles Boer's *Freud's Own Cookbook*, which shifts the psychoanalytic
explanatory system from sexuality to orality, 'It is using the oral in
imitation of Freud's use of the genital so as to deconstruct, showing the
whole Freudian construct as a fantasy' (Hillman, 1990: 337).

Here we come again upon the perennial criticism of Jungian psychology
which, as I promised, keeps reappearing throughout the present book. There
appears to be a Jungian discourse – call it #1 Personality or whatever – that
is full of 'essentials' and overarching, fundamental truths and one that
seems quite at odds with the postmodern position which identifies the
end of 'grand narratives' and singular 'truths'. The post-Jungians above
find the non-essential Jung through applying an understanding derived
from post-structural linguistic theory; they are educated in and aware of
postmodern issues and their application to Jungian psychology – both as
it stands and as it needs to be reformulated.

Since these discussions, a more recent contribution from Polly Young-
Eisendrath (1997) offers a perspective on 'essentialist' Jungian ideas such
as the archetype and the complex which provides a way of understanding
them within the postmodern frame. In what amounts to a perspectival
approach (see Chapter 6), Young-Eisendrath asserts the particularity of the
human world as one among many possible realities which not only coexists
with the different realities of other living creatures but also coexists with
anomalies in 'realities' in the human sphere such as those Oliver Sacks
reports in *The Man Who Mistook His Wife For A Hat* (Sacks, 1985). Within
the human 'reality', moreover, she points out the huge variety of
particulars, such as emotional patterning, both between cultures and among
individuals. Although the definition of 'self' might be widely different
across individuals and cultures, 'all people have some symbolic means to
represent the experience of individual subjectivity; the experience of being
an individual subject is universal, even though the forms that express that
subjectivity are diverse' (Young-Eisendrath, 1997: 640).

In Young-Eisendrath's perspective, the postmodern themes of
uncertainty and the *Unknown* are seen to pluralistically coexist alongside

the apparent 'essentials' of Jungian psychology – self, complex and archetype. Her particular Jungian attitude to the work of therapy, and to everyday life, is one in which all certainties, all our emotional approaches to 'reality' as constructed by the complex and the archetype, far from being 'fixed' like the idea of the complex/archetype might imply, are in fact brought into creative questioning through, 'an openness to an on-going process of discovery, based on a dialectic of subjective and objective factors of experience. Because people are loath to give up their old meanings, on which they base reality and a sense of self, analytical psychotherapy must provoke uncertainty about the value of old constructions, whole worlds of meaning' (ibid.: 642).

Although it is guided by theory, knowledge and expertise, and supported by rituals of time, space and fee, the therapeutic relationship, Polly Young-Eisendrath reminds us, is *paradoxical*. Although, as we saw above, she regards the postmodern (as she understands it) as nihilistic, her therapeutic perspective unwittingly reveals a postmodern attitude which is valuable in helping us get a handle on the relationship between the modernist 'basic truths' employed in Jungian psychology, on the one hand, and the post-modern doubleness, complexity and paradox of our times, on the other. For Young-Eisendrath, the therapeutic relationship is full of contradictions that undermine any tendency towards singular viewpoints. It is, 'impersonally personal, empathically non-gratifying, erotically non-sexual, provocatively non-aggressive' (ibid.). Despite this, due to the prevailing style of consciousness, both client and therapist are likely to get entrenched in their previously established orders,

> A person coming for help, already in distress, is likely to want to create order – an old order – in such a paradoxical environment. The analyst or therapist, in response to what the patient imposes, is just as likely to impose an old order, in the form of theory, expertise, authority and his or her own psychological complexes.
>
> (ibid.)

Analytic psychotherapy resists this, however, and Young-Eisendrath's reframing reminds us of Foucault's comparison between traditional history and *effective* history or genealogy: 'The *effective* therapeutic relationship,' she affirms, 'in contrast, is like a Zen koan for both participants: it invites and defies old interpretations' (ibid.).

The therapeutic relationship *invites and defies old interpretations*, says the Jungian therapist – just as Charles Jencks describes the postmodern architect as *wanting to build and protest at the same time, and to confirm and subvert simultaneously*. Postmodern Jungian therapy has much in common with these aspects of postmodern culture – '*Post-Modernism has the essential double meaning: the continuation of Modernism and its transcendence*' (Jencks, 1996: 30).

We have certainly travelled some distance in this chapter. From an initial consideration of the concepts of image, sign and symbol it has been necessary to get involved in a broad discussion about representation and language itself. In this, the postmodern developments in epistemological theory taken up by Lacan and Derrida after the inspiration of Saussure's structural linguistics have been seen to influence several post-Jungians in recent years. Their considerations led to confronting the nature of the Unconscious as the truly Un-known: no-thing and ineffable like the Tao of Ancient Chinese thought. The way psychoanalysis, albeit in the margins, is beginning to catch up with these implications of the Unconscious through the ideas of Lacan and Bion has been described using the recent work of James Grotstein. Finally, David Miller's and Polly Young-Eisendrath's perspectives seem to bring a postmodern position firmly back into the consulting room as well as into everyday life with a double-coding of the 'essentialist' Jung, one the one hand, and the paradoxical, Unknown, Jung – his #2 Personality – on the other. The postmodern, and the 'Eastern' implications of this perspective persist till the end. On the last page of *Memories, Dreams, Reflections*, at the end of his life, Jung, too, quotes Lao Tse, saying,

All are clear, I alone am clouded.

(Jung, 1983/1963: 392)

9   Affect and modernity

> It is safest to grasp the concept of the postmodern as an attempt to think the present historically in an age that has forgotten how to think historically in the first place.
>
> (Fredric Jameson, 1991: ix)

DEATH AND SEX

My original idea for this chapter was to attempt a consideration of affect through history. I thought I would be able to track historical differences in one or two affects like 'love' or 'fear', perhaps, comparing the expression of emotions found in texts from the medieval, Renaissance, eighteenth and nineteenth century right up to the present psychoanalytic era. I had wondered, for instance, what had been the emotional experience at a public execution in any of these eras, and how had emotions experienced by subjects at such an event changed over the centuries. At a more local and contemporary level, I was interested in the passage in Nick Hornby's novel *High Fidelity* (Hornby, 1996) where the narrator ponders how his father felt, a generation earlier, about sex, love, and the attendant anxieties and emotions, compared with what the narrator experiences in the late 1980s.

> 'Dad, did you ever have to worry about the female orgasm in either its clitoral or its (possibly mythical) vaginal form? Do you in fact know what the female orgasm is? . . . What did "good in bed" mean in 1955, if it meant anything at all? . . . Aren't you glad that you've never had the "You might be right-on but do you clean the toilet" conversation? . . . And what would he say, I wonder, "Son, stop whinging. The good fuck wasn't even *invented* in my day, and however many toilets you

clean and vegetarian recipes you have to read, you still have more fun
than we were ever allowed." And he'd be right too.'

(ibid.: 102)

The attitude I had planned to take would have been that affect, like
sexuality, gender and other previously transparent 'essentials' of 'human
nature', is a *construct*, a particular categorising of part of human experience.
Objectively it is a bounded concept, and subjectively an experienced state,
but one that is always delineated and *defined against what it is not* – which
is usually 'rationality'. Affect, as a construct, is subject to cultural and
historical shaping which varies from time to time and place to place. So
it seems especially important for European psychological thinking to pay
attention to the *genealogy of affect* – its family tree – so we may know what
we are talking about and what we are not talking about when it comes to
affect as a general concept in psychology. But I realised this subject could
not be tackled so simply. Interesting as this unborn essay would have been,
I rapidly saw that it was not possible to track human affect across history.
To be sure, I could find all sorts of literary references to love, courtly love,
the passions, the humours and moods but these did not seem to amount to
anything I could compare to what we nowadays refer to as affect or emotion
(I will use both these words synonymously in this chapter, but not the word
'feeling' which I will come to later). Why was this so? There is a long
answer, I believe, and there is a short answer. The short answer is that until
the arrival of psychology and psychoanalysis in the late nineteenth century
– respectively, the heir of Enlightenment and its late-modern, most reflexive
manifestation – affect had never been purified out of its matrix in Being.
As the ideal of a value-free science under the scrutiny of an objective
observer had taken grip with such success in other endeavours guided by
instrumental rationality, so did these sciences – those of the physical,
chemical and biological portions of purified Nature – then offer a model and
a practice for the examination of the human psyche in a similar fashion.
Affect has simply been a later result of the modern practice of fragmenting
the world and the creation of objects.

That is the short answer. The creation of affect as a distinct 'object' – and
why I find this move untenable – is the long answer and the main theme of
the rest of this chapter. Once I had had my intuition about what the concept
of affect might entail, I had the good fortune to get hold of a book by Bruno
Latour called *We Have Never Been Modern* (Latour, 1993). Reading
Latour's work has helped me to tackle the coarseness of the idea that *affect
as an object is some sort of modern invention*. His answer to this type
of position is that we have never really broken from the past or from other
styles of humanity – we have never been modern, there has been no such

linear moving on and development. For Latour, our big mistake as moderns is the exclusive focus on each pole of our modernising to the exclusion of the other: the purification of the world into discrete objects on the one hand, or the mediating or networking of all these parts, on the other. What Latour points out as missing in our conceptualising of what we are up to, is any sense of a *mediating between these two poles themselves*. The entire dynamic is built upon that bedrock of modernist rationality – the reliance upon *oppositional thinking*, a style of theorising that also underpins both Freud and Jung. For my part, I think I can see how psychology and psychoanalysis carry both trajectories – first due to the classical object-making of all phenomena in which we regard bits of ourselves, our psyche, in the same way that we regard bits of the world. And then, second, because, in the case of psychology, it is a matter of the *Enlightenment observer self-observing*, the same process ushers in a mediation or hybridisation of the phenomena under scrutiny which psychology tries, at the same time, to keep as separate bits.

Latour's book argues how critical theory, semiotics, postmodernism and the focus on language, have all failed to address this element of modernity. I will be suggesting that psychology offers a field in modernity where this problem may be viewed and the concept of 'affect' may reveal this. The perspective will vary, of course, from theory to theory so I will briefly track the genealogy of affect in psychological science from Darwin through James to Schacter, and, in psychoanalysis, from Freud's repression and Jung's complex to the oppositional pairing of affect and intellect in modern psychotherapy with a brief comparison between Klein and Lacan. In the main, this essay is about affect as an object, but it is also about the abandoning of objects in the subjectivity of psychoanalytic practice.

CHARLES DARWIN, WILLIAM JAMES AND THE THEORISING OF EMOTION

Locke and Descartes valued conscious rationality above all else. For them, the idea of the unconscious was an unnecessary absurdity. Locke asserted that it was, 'Nonsense to teach that the mind thinks even when it is asleep and unconscious' (quoted in Yrjonsuuri, 1995). The affectual aspect of the human mind also received pretty short shrift. For Enlightenment thinkers the emotions were quite surplus to the requirements of an objectifying consciousness which sought to examine the world or 'nature' as a thing apart – and preferably at the end of a microscope or a telescope. When it came to the self-examination of late modernity, the affects had become cast as a thing apart – phenomena detached from human rationality; affects were an anomaly in the otherwise rational human mind, to the point of being regarded as a 'mistake'. For the nineteenth century this meant that the emotions could be grouped with that general area of human experience that, while still found in the human, was deemed of the order of the 'animal' or of 'nature'. What made this thinking possible, in part, was the idea of Evolutionary theory that humanity had evolved from the animal and still bore its traces. Charles Darwin published *The Expression of the Emotions in Man and Animals* in 1872, in which he delineated specific, fundamental emotions in humans and animals that had a visible, external behavioural form. The emotions in humans could be viewed as both linked to the animal and also as irruptions into 'normal' rationality. In both ways they belonged to the non-rational aspect of the human mind. In 1884, William James asked *What is an Emotion?* and shifted the thinking considerably. He maintained that the outward emotional expression is the *result* of a prior emotional, neural signal and, more specifically, that, 'our feeling of the (bodily) changes as they occur *is* the emotion' (Gregory, 1987: 218). In other words, we blush and *then* we experience – or 'read' – ourselves as 'embarrassed' rather than the other way round. This idea was supported by the Danish physician Lange, and the James–Lange theory of emotion persisted through the first half of the twentieth century in academic psychology. It rests on strictly conscious cognitive foundations which teach that an individual's perception of their own bodily responses – an autonomic response like streaming tears, for example – constitutes the emotion that is experienced. Others such as Cannon in the late 1920s criticised this position by pointing out the vagueness of the bodily responses and the lack of regular 'fit' between them and the range of emotions. The question hung suspended: 'Do we grieve because we cry, or do we cry because we grieve?' (ibid.: 219).

In the late 1960s, Schachter bridged the argument by maintaining that a general visceral arousal was necessary for experience of emotions, but an individual will describe the emotions in terms of the information, cognitively processed, available at the time. Interestingly, the idea of emotions as *interruptions* in rationality re-emerges at this time – here in the effort to explain the persistence of emotion-tinged memories predominating in the individual. The visceral arousal, it is thought, arises from some cognitive or perceptual '*discrepancy* or conflict between the state of the world and the expectations which the individual brings to the situation' (ibid.: 220).

I imagine the reader is already putting together these ideas with what has been added to them by psychoanalysis and its attention to mental life from the perspective of the unconscious. Academic psychology has theorised the emotions without calling upon the concept of the unconscious – unless this is regarded as no more than the activity of the autonomous nervous system.

In their theorising, the conscious cognition of affect is what is important. We might reverse this direction in thinking by pointing out how psycho-analytic attention to the emotions made a theory of the unconscious *necessary*. The question arose: How is it that affects may surprise us and catch us unawares? Is this just due to the activity of the nervous system or does it not imply there is a form of mental activity going on below the threshhold of consciousness? The issues and problems thrown up by nineteenth-century theorising on the emotions – hampered by the idea of the 'rational unitary subject' – appears to have required the return of one of Enlightenment's original 'rejects' – the concept of an unconscious mind. The opposing of the *rational* and the *emotional* gets overlaid by the opposing of the *conscious* and the *unconscious*. What has to be watched out for in this sort of oppositional thinking is the tendency for each side of the opposed pairs to become equated as with unconscious/affect versus conscious/cognitive – a mistake which arises from the imposition of oppositional thinking itself.

In one fell swoop two categories rejected by the Enlightenment – the unconscious and the affects – were brought back into focus and importance at the end of the nineteenth century with the theories and empirical discoveries of Freud and Jung. (And, incidentally, with Jung, but not with Freud, the crossed-out God of the Enlightenment became undeleted too.) Initially it may be helpful to track just where the psychoanalytic project hit upon the link between emotions and the unconscious. This will involve us in how different theoretical approaches and methods – especially the differences between Freud and Jung – contributed to a concept of affect. Echoes of this dialectic between affect and the unconscious, on the one hand, and rationality and consciousness on the other persist in the biases and preferences found in psychoanalytic psychotherapy today – in what psychotherapy thinks it can achieve: its objective, as well as its objects.

REPRESSION, THE COMPLEX AND AFFECTS

It is impossible to imagine the beginnings of psychoanalysis without the concept of affect. It is as essential a foundation stone as the uncons-cious mind, the mechanism of repression and the hysterical symptom. Surprisingly, perhaps, I would place sexuality, instincts, pleasure and the woman patient as the second layer of the mansion that Freud built. The symptoms of hysteria pre-existed psychoanalysis of course, but it was Freud's genius to explain these in terms that brought together the already familiar and the mysteriously new. Affects, emotions and their expression in behaviour were a recognised, if still problematic, aspect of humanity, but for psychoanalysis to formulate a theory which explained how these same affects may also become repressed, dammed up and rechannelled into behavioural expression that appeared disconnected from the original affect, was something new. Freud's original method was also novel: it was suggested that, through the manipulation of a cathartic re-experiencing of repressed emotions, the symptoms connected with them would cease to have a function and would then disappear. The major emotion involved seems to have been the one labelled *anxiety*, and, in the early formulations where some sort of sexual trauma was thought to be the environmental cause, anxiety was linked to fear, shame and disgust which, while repressed, could provide the fuel for neurotic and hysterical symptoms. The concept of affect and its repression was, and is now, central to what many think psychoanalysis is all about.

Elsewhere at this time, affect was beginning to reify itself as an explanatory tool of the new science of psychology via the Word Association experiment and, in particular, via what the psychiatrist C. G. Jung made of his results in the light of Freud's theory of repression. Now, given the importance of the link psychoanalysis made between affect, free-association and what interrupts free-association, we should look back along this branch of ideas. In doing so we come upon the figure of Sir Francis Galton (1822–1911).

Situated in the mid-nineteenth century at the peak of mechanistic materialism, Galton displays what was best and worst in the splitting tendencies promoted by a faith in human scientific rationality. Such a faith in human objectivity had led to a thirst for phenomena to investigate which began to *create* objects while still imagining it was 'discovering' them in the world. 'Nature' became science's most general object, but, I believe, 'affect' too was created as an object within the investigating subject himself. This particular act of purification, as Latour would call it, had the function of not only creating a new object – *affect* – for psychological investigation, but also, by such a separation, the 'purity' of the scientific observer's objective *rationality* was preserved.

Enlightenment had crossed-out God as a precursor to its objectifying of Nature and its contents, and Galton's earlier experiments – on the effectiveness of praying to God – had been 'ingenious but controversial studies which showed, to his own satisfaction, that prayer was ineffective in bringing about the events that were prayed for' (Gregory, 1987: 283). His seminal experiments in free association which followed these studies on prayer were aimed at discovering whether people may 'freely' choose what they think (he concluded against 'free will'). Galton was a cousin of Darwin and had an overwhelming faith in the eventual understanding of evolution and hereditary in entirely materialistic and deterministic terms. The dark side of this project led to his ideas on eugenics, but we also have him to thank for the modern weather map (which first appeared in *The Times*, 1875) – which, rather like academic psychology itself, also presents an expert 'scientific' version of what already appears obvious to the 'lay' community through their ordinary, non-scientific, perception.

The same rationalist atmosphere of the late nineteenth century that encouraged Galton in his grandiose faith in techniques that would measure a vast range of individual and social human qualities, also encouraged Freud, in *The Interpretation of Dreams* (1900) to display a parallel rationalism. Pursuing similar goals of a value-free objective science applied reflexively to mankind itself, Jung had taken up the association experiment after Galton as a diagnostic instrument that might predict and reveal groupings of powerful emotions, which he called complexes, that were influencing the bizarre behaviour and beliefs of his patients at the Burgholzi Hospital in Zurich. It is not surprising that it was the objectifying of unconscious emotions as complexes which interrupted 'normal rationality' that brought Jung's psychology directly in line with Freud's psychoanalysis. Before he had met Freud for the first time, Jung wrote in *Association, Dream and Hysterical Symptom* (1906), 'the interferences that the complex causes in the association experiment are none other than the resistances in psychoanalysis as described by Freud' (Jung, 1906, CW 2: 353). At this stage, Jung was at one with Freud and nineteenth-century scientism in making a cornerstone of their thinking the casting of affect as scientific object. It strikes me that this very process – the splitting off of the 'emotional' from the 'rational' and thus creating affect as a distinct 'object' – can itself be viewed as, so to speak, *modernity's own complex*. The degree to which this objective reification of affect has been retained, revised or critically addressed will be the topic of my next section.

THE LIFE AND DEATH OF AFFECT AS AN OBJECT

Freud expanded his ideas from the consideration of repressed emotions in hysterical patients to construct a theory of mind where affect became tied to the more biological (and therefore more 'scientific') idea of the *instinct* and, through this, became regionalised in an unconscious characterised by the ultimately objectifying name of the 'It'. Instinct and affect resided in the 'It', in contrast to the region of the 'I', which was characterised by its rational, organised aim of adaptation to 'reality'. Let us not quibble about the transparency of the historical and cultural construction of the 'reality' being assumed at the time – this pales into insignificance beside the primary assumption of a rational–emotional oppositional split in the first place.

There is no question here of blaming Freud for bad science or distorted thinking, but the point being made seeks to underline how *this sort of psychology arises from, and tries to heal, a specifically modern consciousness with a specifically modern pathology*. To a certain extent, we have need of a *psychology based on such a split because we are so split these days*. The danger, or mistake, lies in the tendency to universalise this position in ignorance of historical and cultural differences. Where psychotherapy may go wrong is to forget this and, in its own terms, fail to be conscious of the relative nature of its profoundest assumptions. In other words, to mistake what are helpful perspectives for universal human essentials.

Freud developed the theory of psychoanalysis in a trajectory that begins with hysterical trauma and the repression of affect, proceeds to a theory of sexuality and the Oedipus complex, and eventually the meta-theorising of the Life and Death instincts. In this Freud displays an effort to reconceive a psychoanalytic science that is less reliant on the rational/emotional split of its beginnings. However Freud, as with many of his supporters, is constantly tempted to revise and correct old ideas as if they can always be squeezed into the new thinking, rather than admitting they have little use-value in the light of the latest thinking and data and should be abandoned. This reveals another complex: reliance on the authority of the master narrative, which leads us to relieve our anxiety by turning to the master discourses with repetitive acts of revision rather than to risk the inevitable insecurity which results from revolution and the critical deconstruction of ideas – the alternative position of a critical postmodern psychology.

It was this latter path, I would suggest, that Jung himself pursued after his break with Freud just before the Great War. It is significant that the historical moment of the First World War is cited as the vital break with the nineteenth century, the dismantling of Victorian values and the start of our present postmodern era. Jung's was a risky trip which led to personal psychological breakdown and not just a change of ideas. It was as if Jung had to deconstruct his own modern consciousness so as to discover and theorise about human psychology with a fulcrum placed some distance from the nineteenth-century scientific rationalism of his roots. This led to his reflections on the psyche and its relationship to a new object, modern consciousness itself, which Jung attempts to formulate using a pluralistic range of 'non-' or 'other-rational' ideas such as those derived from alchemy, Native American and African ritual and belief and Eastern esotericism as I have mentioned. In doing so, the 'universalism' of psychoanalysis becomes confronted with historical and cultural difference while remaining honest about its European, modernist roots.

Following up the genealogy of affect in Jung what do we find? In line with the differentiating of his own ideas from those of Freud, Jung's downplaying of the sexual instinct in favour of, on the one hand, a generalised psychic energy, and, on the other, a promotion of the religious or spiritual 'instinct' in the human psyche, led to a different conceptualising of affects and their function. Like Freud, Jung's thought led him towards a general theory of the mind, but one which led away from the focus on individual mental pathology and led to quite different conclusions about the nature of the human psyche. Through this the role of affect changed from the hot-to-handle culprit always opposed to and ready to interrupt a much-cherished rationality which, alone, had defined humanity for nineteenth-century Europeans. In Jung's mature thought, affect becomes far less of an 'object' and, consequently, far more integrated into a general model of the psyche: affect appears alongside, rather than opposed to, perception and thinking. But Jung's psychology goes further than this when he shows affect to have a significance in the psychic economy which is as central to what it is to be human as rationality was once thought to be.

Jung achieves this repositioning through his theory of the archetypes. Jung's archetypes are the structuring principles of the human psyche; they are empty of specific content or form until they encounter the individual and cultural environment of a human life. This encounter results in a dialectical process whereby a human psyche is, on the one hand, determined according to the structuring expectations of the archetypes, but, on the other hand, reveals an almost infinite variety of expression, a range of vast differences across individuals and cultural groups that, nevertheless, retains a distinctive human quality. But the theory of archetypes not only bridges the universal and the individual, it also bridges what modernity distinguished as either Nature or Culture. Jung's vision is heir to the seminal critique of modernity found in Nietzsche's assertion that 'man is a bridge and not a goal . . . he is a *going-across*' (Nietzsche, 1883–1885, 1969: 44). As mentioned in Chapter 6, Nietzsche's theory of perspectives has a parallel in the idea of the complex in Jung's psychology and both share, and are characterised by, an affectual tone. Our 'way of seeing things' is intimately linked with our affectual response to things. Jung still retained the psychoanalytic idea of complexes and the repression of affects as dynamics of the personal unconscious, but he also made a link between these and the functioning of archetypes of the collective unconscious. The complex was seen as deriving its particular significance as a vortex of emotional energy from the functioning of archetypal activity in the psyche. *This perspective places affect or emotion centrally within the dynamics of the psyche and not in contrast or opposition to so-called 'rationality'.* For Jung, the archetype is especially known by its affectual tone which accompanies the imagery, cognition and behaviour manifested by archetypal activity. Emotions are the way human beings know themselves and the world and in this respect are equal to the role played by rational thought. In Jung's view of the psyche, affect seems to become the subjectively experienced equivalent of what is otherwise described by the abstract terms of psychic energy or libido. There can be no rationality without an accompanying emotion, they are part of the same process despite modernity's prioritising of rational activity alone. (Perhaps this is where Jung's ideas come close to those of Schacter mentioned earlier, where visceral arousal is thought to arise from the perceptual discrepancy or conflict between the environment and the expectations which the individual brings to the situation. The 'expectations' in Jung's theory would be the life-forming urge of the archetype meeting environmental conditions with each individual.)

Because common English usage finds the words 'affect' and 'emotion' interchangeable with the word 'feeling', it is important to note the particular, and different, use of this word in Jung's psychology. In his theory of psychological *types* and the *four functions* of consciousness, Jung analyses conscious psychic activity into the four functions of thinking, sensation, intuition and feeling. In contrast to how it is often used in English, Jung's use of the word 'feeling' is not as a synonym for emotion or affect. In the four functions, sensation tells us that a thing *is*, thinking tells us *what* it is, intuition informs us what it may *become*, while feeling is the activity that *judges and evaluates* a perceptual object. It is true to say that *affect* may accompany any of these functions.

THE HYBRID, PERSPECTIVES AND THE OBJECT OF PSYCHOTHERAPY

This contrast between the Freud branch and the Jung branch of the genealogy of affect may be viewed as an example of what Bruno Latour refers to as a hybrid. The hybrid is a function of Modernity that combines what is previously, or elsewhere, kept apart. There are two angles here: if we emphasise 'previously' we are conceptualising change, and linkage, in terms of linear time – modern, late-modern or postmodern 'periods'. If we emphasise the term 'elsewhere' we are talking spatially using concepts of the 'margin' as opposed to the 'centre' of the culturally dominant thinking. I am in favour of the perspectival approach to conceptualising these shifts. In this analysis – which is Thomas Kuhn's approach to shifts in scientific rationalities (Kuhn, 1962) – paradigm shifts occur via a process of including more and more of that which is at the edge of the field of vision. As our vision relaxes its concentration on the centre point of the horizon which delimits a particular perspective, so the boundaries, those edges on the margin of vision, come more into focus and, eventually, determine a completely different point of view. This is the process of the paradigm shift which contains the seeds of radical change (to utterly mix these metaphors) located in the defocused margins of what went before.

How does this sort of understanding help us with our topic of the significance of affect in psychotherapy today? In the main, by which I mean in the *centre* of dominant perspectives, I think we find that affect has been reified to become the prime object of concern in that applied form of psychoanalysis known as psychotherapy treatment. Powerful emotions in the patient and in the therapist, emotions experienced and denied, projected and introjected, emotions in the transference and the countertransference are repeatedly regarded as the main, if not the only, focus of this style of treatment. This prioritising of affect as the major object of treatment then determines its 'other'. The 'other' of affect and the loosely named feeling approach to therapy is, of course, the 'intellect' and the 'intellectual approach'. As I have mentioned, and as Jung was quite specific about, this split is needed to address the specific historical and cultural condition of the modern Western mind that displays a skewed, over-rational approach and neglects the full range of human capacity, in which the emotional is significantly undervalued. To simply privilege affect, in depth psychology, is a pointless reversal of the problem. Jungians are often guilty of privileging affect over thinking. As Michael Vannoy Adams has put it, 'Jungians are always talking pejoratively about someone being "up in his head". They never criticise anyone for being "down in his body" – unless it were "down in his penis". A few years ago James Hillman gave a talk entitled "Getting in Touch With Your Thinkings". The ironic oddity of the title just proves how unthinkable it is for Jungians to be in touch with thinking' (Adams, 1998, personal communication)! What is needed is more of this irony – which may lead to a fuller integration of all sides of our natures: the emotional and the intellectual, the conscious and the unconscious, the cognitive and the affectual.

Despite what has just been said, a further irony lies in how the marginalisation of Jungian thought at the edges of a hegemonic Freudian psychoanalysis, has caused it to suffer, by comparison, both the accusation of being too 'intellectual' and, in an odd contradiction, the other modern slur of 'mystical'. Jung's alchemical researches have been accused of both by those whose vision stays narrowly focused on a particular horizon. In a different way, and for different reasons, Jacques Lacan's influential reading of the psychoanalytic project suffers from a similar accusation that he, too, neglects the emotional dimension through his over-intellectual approach. This is in contrast to Melanie Klein who is regarded as having replaced emotional engagement back into the practice of psychoanalysis which, by the 1920s, was suffering from the intellectual positivism found earlier in *The Interpretation of Dreams*.

I would like to comment briefly on this contrast between Lacan and Klein. First of all, it is striking how, despite an emotional sincerity and engagement with patients which is clear from her clinical reporting, Klein somehow manages to construct theoretical conclusions with a highly intellectual, speculative quality. I compare this to the work of Winnicott, where we find great emotional engagement but without nearly so crisp a theoretical expression. Perhaps this is because affect and intellect were more entwined and integrated in him than in others who adopt a positivistic Enlightenment style. In psychology, I believe the easier and less contradictory the expression of an idea, the less accurately does it reflect or describe the complexities of human experience, and *vice versa*.

Lacan's work is indisputably intellectual, but, in the field of psychoanalysis, his is another marginal hybrid, an offshoot arising from the cross-pollenation of psychiatry, psychoanalysis and structural linguistics. When Lacan rereads Melanie Klein reporting on the autistic little boy Richard, he reveals the structuring, ordering function of Klein's empathic, emotional understanding of the child's inner world: 'Dick – little train, Daddy – big train . . . The station is Mummy; Dick is going into Mummy . . . ("You want to fuck your mother")' (quoted in Felman, 1987: 105–128). Yet this is no intellectualising at the neglect of the emotional: on the contrary, I believe affect is implicit in Lacan's analysis. Not only does Lacan note how Klein's intervention sows the seed of the Order of the Symbolic as if this was some separate, discrete cognitive act, but, for Lacan, what Klein says to Richard also provokes the kindling of anxiety, the emotional dimension of the experience of distinguishing self from environment – the experience of a 'lack', the initiation of Desire, the beginning of individuality and the relationship between self and other. Resulting from his anxiety, Richard's *Call* to his nurse – an act that is both rational in its differentiation of her from him and, at the same time, emotional in the affect that is brought about by making this differentiation – reveals the embeddedness of the cognitive and the affectual that characterises the human psyche.

It is at the margins of psychoanalytic thinking like Jung's and Lacan's that we will find a postmodern perspective that employs intellectual tools not simply to divide and objectify but also to bring together and heal. This is a perspective on the psyche and psychotherapy that advances Freud's late modern formulations which themselves had previously provided a radical challenge to the persistence of Enlightenment thinking with the concept of the Unconscious.

In conclusion I offer no recommendations for addressing either the over-emphasis on affect in psychotherapy or the equally present criticism of an overly intellectual practice. Both criticisms arise from the fallacy that modernity, the matrix of all our so-called 'modern' thinking including psychoanalysis, is just one perspective and one that is an advance on what went before and has been left behind. It is not and it has not. Bruno Latour puts it bluntly in his book's title: *We Have Never Been Modern*. Modernity, we are coming to realise, is multi-perspectival. Newtonian mechanics exists alongside the behaviour of electrons studied by sub-atomic physics despite them contradicting each others' 'rules of nature' which cannot 'logically' coexist. This does not stop us, however, from building computers that rely on the mutual cohabitation of both these worlds of matter. Modernity *contains* Enlightenment, the modern, the late modern and the postmodern. It also contains the Ancient in 'irrational' practices such as the bringing of a green tree into the house at Christmas, as Jung was fond of reminding us.

In summary, what I am suggesting with this approach to psychoanalysis, analytical psychology and the place of affect is this: as with any perspective, it all depends on where you are standing. A shift to the left or right, up or down, and the view will change. What was near will now be far, what was hardly visible at the edge of your field will now loom large. And none of us are standing still. We move between the Ancient, the Enlightenment, the Modern and the postmodern daily. We move between them sometimes in a single analytic session, I think you will find. Modernity oscillates between its splitting or 'purification' and its re-linking or 'networking' tendencies (Latour, 1993). I think we should acknowledge this, and incorporate *this perspective* in our Ancient/postmodern practice of psychoanalysis. Upon reflection, we may then see how it has always been there.

10 Mind and Matter: Jungian psychology and postmodern science

> Do we really have to make this tragic choice? Must we choose between a science that leads to alienation and an anti-scientific metaphysical view of nature? We think such a choice is no longer necessary, since the changes that science is undergoing today lead to a radically new situation. This recent evolution of science gives us a unique opportunity to reconsider its position in culture in general. Modern science originated in the specific context of the European seventeenth century. We are now approaching the end of the twentieth century, and it seems that some more *universal message* is carried by science, a message that concerns the interaction of man and nature as well as of man with man.
>
> (Prigogine and Stengers, 1984: 7)

POSTMODERN SCIENCE: READING THE DATA

Throughout this book there have been many references to how the postmodern position is one that questions fixed ideas of Reality or Truth; how it deconstructs modernist certainties and metanarratives and promotes a plurality of perspectives against singular views. Fair enough, some say, we all know there can be different points of view on a variety of phenomena, but how can this postmodern perspective possibly apply to the realm of science and scientific knowledge? Surely, science is about *facts*; it is about the study of *nature*; and, to qualify as *science*, it is, above all, *objective* and therefore immune to any simple varying of opinions and views. And indeed, scientific thinking, research and assertions do still present themselves and their work in such a fashion. Any individual with access to newspapers, TV or radio is now bombarded with a great deal more 'scientific knowledge' than they have been in any previous era. With the volume of such information, the individual subject is confronted with several unavoidable realisations: the contradictory quality of scientific assertions and the competition between them for asserting their Truth as the only truth, the way that such science knowledge is clearly linked to interest groups, the reliance on mechanical and on statistical forms of measurement that establish the Truth only to get overridden by subsequent results, and the culture of the Expert who is presented as the legitimate Authority on a scientific subject.

This is not an exhaustive list, and the concerns of postmodern science cover further issues. As a UNESCO report noted in 1974, 'For more than a century the sector of scientific activity has been growing to such an extent within the surrounding cultural space that it seems to be replacing the totality of culture itself' (UNESCO, 1974: 15–16, quoted in Prigogine and Stengers, 1984: 30) – the danger lies in the dehumanising effect of scientific activity. Thomas Kuhn's *The Structure of Scientific Revolutions* (1962) opened up the natural sciences to sociological examination and analysis and was the first to coin the idea of *paradigm shifts* as a way of conceiving how scientific world-views have changed throughout history. Since then, postmodern concerns have focused on several areas. One is the way in which scientific knowledge is driven as much by the concern for profit-making technological applications of such knowledge as it is by a desire to understand the world. The activities of drugs manufacturers who will only invest the millions needed for research and development as long as there is a guarantee that the medication produced will sell profitably like any other commodity, are a case in point. Medical science, and scientific activity in general, has been criticised by feminists for being male-dominated. There has been a tendency, for example, for women in childbirth to be restricted and controlled by the medical establishment; and while a male contraceptive pill has been ignored as a non-runner despite its being as effective as the commonly used female pill, a drug to promote male erections has been sold extensively all over the world.

The objectivity of scientific investigation is often called into question these days, not so much from the point of view that science is failing to achieve its own standards but from the view that realises that a totally objective position is impossible to achieve. Any human examination of a phenomena must always involve human intervention into that phenomena which leaves it in a different state from before. A simple and succinct example is the way we measure pressure in a car tyre: we are never able to measure the exact pressure because the introduction of the measuring instrument – the tyre pressure guage – requires losing a little pressure for it to register. However, the degree of such a change can be calculated exactly and then be compensated for in the final calculation. This is true in general for classical physics. The difference is trivial under these circumstances but the same principle might have far larger consequences for other phenomena under other conditions. Discoveries arising from Chaos Theory (Gleick, 1988) and Complexity Theory now draw our attention to the highly complex interaction of phenomena as well as subtle regularities in seemingly random phenomena – like the shape of a coast-line or the behaviour of the weather – that only reveal themselves through the very large scale sampling and analysis now made possible through the use of powerful computers. In this case the system needs a potentially infinite amount of data for a full definition. Any intervention changes the system in a totally deterministic way, but because of extreme complexity we cannot compute the amount of the disturbance.

Last, but not least, science in postmodern times is in thrall to the filmic and photographic image in the same way as every other aspect of culture. Stephen Hawking wrote the best-selling scientific book ever, *A Brief History of Time*, but is best known to millions not through his theories but through the image of his wheelchair-bound body and his computer-generated voice. He has recently been on British TV advertising spectacles. We see him gazing out of a capsule gliding past the planets of the solar system in a science-fiction image of space travel. As he passes the planets his familiar, and yet impersonal, computer voice tells us how his eyes are so important to him. In other words, the scientist who 'gazes' into the farthest reaches of space to seek out theories of the beginning of time and the universe is being used to endorse the qualities of a pair of spectacles we can go out and buy in the high street. This is also the postmodern vision.

This chapter does not reach so far and will restrict its concerns to a particular aspect of the postmodern deconstruction of science: the way that classical science, in its investigation of natural phenomena, has always assumed that the tool of investigation – the experiment and experimenter – constitutes a variable whose effects on the system can be considered as 'negligible' or, if they are significant, then their effects can be calculated exactly. The idea of the presence of an observing mind itself was completely outside the discourse of physics – it was never considered. The study of psychology, and especially the psychology of the unconscious initiated by Freud and Jung, coincided with extraordinary developments in twentieth-century physics which challenged the assumptions of classical physics of the previous 500 years. The challenge began with Einstein's theories of relativity which emerged as a constraint on such assumptions of pure objectivity and gave science a definite 'human' quality, as Prigogine puts it. Nevertheless, Einstein firmly believed in the objectivity of nature. While the phenomena he considers may appear different to observers under different conditions of observation – gravitational fields, or frames of motion – the underlying laws are identical; they are totally objective and independent of the observer.

However, at this point we should start to consider the role of *theory* and theorising. In other words, the way in which data, observations, experiments, concepts and so on all undergo some sort of *reading* – in the postmodern sense – and that this reading implies a constraint upon 'objectivity' which brings in the importance of *interpretation* when it comes to making assertions about the *realities* of physics. I agree with David Peat when he affirms that science does have the yard-stick of experiment and that experiment does, in a certain sense, give us objective data about the world. *But the way that the experiment is performed and the way that the data is read are all determined by the theory which, itself, is partly founded on observation and partly on imaginative readings* as I will expand on shortly. When the young scientist Werner Heisenberg was trying to work out how to account for the mass of observations made by the early quantum experiment, Einstein told him that it is the theory that suggests the observations, and not the other way round. The theory suggests what should be observable, and on the basis of the theory one then constructs experiments. Text book accounts of relativity begin with the Michelson–Morley experiment to show the constancy of the speed of light and other experiments, but Einstein's idea arose out of a creative act of intuitive perception which he developed into a theory. It was then this theory that suggested how to make experiments and how to read the data and not the other way round. This is the vital point that Heisenberg took and used to help him construct Quantum Mechanics (Peat, 1999, personal communication). Further discoveries about the behaviour of light and sub-atomic matter from Planck, Pauli, Heisenberg, Neils Bohr and others added to the paradigm shift in classical science.

Strangely enough – but as is often the way with synchronous events – just as I reached this point in my redrafting of this chapter, I happened to step outside and speak to my neighbour who runs an engineering company. Our conversation – which was only quite short – led to him relating a story that illustrates the exact points I am making, that is, how the apparent objectivity of classical physics is subject to interpretation and human need which, while not overriding the laws of nature, certainly presents brand new facets which from previous perspectives would be regarded as 'impossible'.

The story concerns two anchors. When semi-submersible rigs were required for off-shore oil drilling in the North Sea, these rigs were so large that the anchors required to keep them in place had to be so gigantic and heavy that they presented extreme problems of manufacture and delivery. The efficiency of an anchor – according to the theorising available – depended entirely on its weight. Until then, no one had come across any other way of making an anchor more efficient except by adding more weight. But at a marine exhibition in Amsterdam my neighbour noticed an anchor of a new design and within two weeks had bought the licence. This new anchor was so successful in bypassing the increased weight problem without losing its efficiency that he eventually manufactured it and sold it all over the world making its inventor a millionaire in the process. What made this anchor able to overcome the constrictions imposed by the weight-efficiency formula of the old theory? What the inventor had done was to apply a different theory from a completely different field to that of anchors stabilising objects in water. His insight was to apply aerodynamic theories concerning the way that aeroplanes stay *up in the air*, through the surface area and resistance of their wings, to the reverse task – the function of keeping an object *down in the water*. He found that, instead of having to increase the *weight* of the anchor, its efficiency could be improved as equally by increasing the *surface area* of the anchor. But how could he increase the surface area of an anchor without increasing the weight? He simply made the vast anchor in two halves, and, weight not being an issue now, left the inside hollow. A classical law that related the efficiency of the anchor to its weight alone was thus overcome without disturbing the laws of physics. The anchor and the problem was simply taken out of one set of beliefs or rules or theory, and had another set applied to it. Nothing in Nature had changed, but in the human sphere, something had changed profoundly. It is at this level of the 'objectivity' of classical science that we need to consider the vital importance of the human factor, the mind that gets applied to the phenomena.

Neils Bohr, in replying to Einstein's objections about the apparent lack of objectivity in quantum theory, pointed out that scientific theories suggest particular ways of reading phenomena which then provide parameters for observation. He used the phrase 'The disposition to make an observation', meaning that once you have decided to observe the system in one way, you then construct a certain type of experiment and nature is forced to answer in one particular way. As the Nobel Prize winner Ilya Prigogine puts it, 'we are moving away from our rather naïve assumption of a direct connection between our description of the world and the world itself. Objectivity in theoretical physics takes on a more subtle meaning . . . Whatever reality may mean, it always corresponds to an active intellectual construction. The descriptions presented by science can no longer be disentangled from our questioning activity' (Prigogine and Stengers, 1984: 54–55). Therefore, given that *mind* is present in the constructions of imagination we call our scientific theories, it looks as if the Cartesian split between matter and mind, ground zero of the Enlightenment view of science, needs considerable revision. But before we look at the significance of this development in connection with analytical psychology it may help to survey the genealogy of the mind–matter split.

Any examination of the history of early science and technology in Europe over the last 500 years will reveal how this period has witnessed an erosion of the experience of reality as *an engagement of the mental and the material*, in favour of a promotion of the idea of *detached observation*. The science of the Enlightenment, in seeking to objectify the world through privileging the tools of observation and measurement, succeeded in creating a 'world of objects' where the 'detached observer' floats like a 'ghost in the machine'. By relying on the Cartesian dichotomy that consciousness is always *of something other* than the observing consciousness itself, classical science – centrally, the science of Sir Isaac Newton – came to regard as its object a world where the observing mind is, to all intents and purposes, absent or ghostlike. Such a position extended into the values of Western culture in general, due to the way that modernity links science, technology and economic activity – that is, human activity, governed solely by the profit motive – and thus abstracts and alienates human consciousness even further. How then did such a fundamental split in consciousness arise? Ironically it was the *joining together* of the human representatives of the material and the mental worlds – the craftsman and the scholar – that led to the reinforcement of the mind–matter split. Up until the late medieval period, skills in the material world – the knowledge of mass, shape and force – were the prerogative of the craftsman. The craftsman (who was most commonly but not entirely male) knew about the properties of matter from his intimate involvement with the materials of his craft. For the medieval scholar, however, the material world was regarded as too base for his concern and his practice was devoted to the manipulation of thought and a knowledge of and a relationship with the spiritual world. At the end of the Middle Ages, these two extremes of relating to the world met and began to inform each other. Craftsmen were becoming literate, reflecting on and publishing their knowledge at the same time as scholars were beginning to take an interest in the material world. The mathematics of the scholars, for long regarded as a reflection of spiritual truths, began to be used to illuminate the laws at work in matter that, up till then, had been non-abstracted – contained and passed on through the craftsman's know-how. The gap between matter 'out there' and mind 'in here' was initially bridged by measurement, but, as time went on, the act of measurement itself became more and more a source of alienation. Tools of measurement became less and less connected to the phenomena under scrutiny leading to increasingly theoretical formulations.

Prior to the inception of classical science, medievals such as the alchemists and the astrologers looked into the *world* to understand themselves; the seventeenth-century European mind, however, looked into *itself* to understand the world. The internal, idealistic designs conceived by scientific minds developed into scientific rules and abstractions; this process was then accelerated through ignoring the intuitive constraints of practical craftsmen to create, by the nineteenth century, thought experiments that then led to the application of scientific principles in technology. The method of idealization proved fruitful, for instance, 'Sadi Carnot imagined an ideal heat engine which could in practice no more be realised than Galileo's frictionless inclined planes' (Edelglass et al., 1992: 58). This idealising method, apart from providing important design criteria, then led to new concepts of which the most important was the concept of energy – originally conceived in the effort to understand mechanical processes. Since then, the concept of 'energy' and the first and second laws of thermodynamics which governed the conservation of energy entered the world-view of the nineteenth century. 'It was a universe in which the future resulted from the present following the necessity of entirely mechanical laws. For the educated person of that time, this was how the world really was' (ibid.: 59).

When Maxwell introduced the concept of the electromagnetic 'field', he found a way of unifying the apparently quite different forces of electricity and magnetism. A field cannot be seen or touched, it is not available to the senses, although the forces involved are quite real. This is an example of how scientists were forced back on using their imagination to describe the forces involved in matter by making analogies to the world of the senses – all of which were mechanical analogies. At the end of the nineteenth century the world picture of classical physics consisted of *matter, electromagnetic waves*, and *energy*; a view which relied increasingly on mathematics and imaginative faculties to create an image 'in here' – the mind – which might accurately represent the reality 'out there'. Ironically, this method of depicting the world – the process of scientific understanding – bears a striking resemblance to how the understanding or world-view of 'the ancients' or 'primitives' comes about. For Jung, premodern consciousness or 'reality' is the result of psyche projecting itself upon the world of matter and taking the resulting picture as objectively 'real' – as if, for example, the random, irregular scattering of the stars in the night sky really are existing in the form of constellations of the Fish, the Archer and so on, and not just unpatterned, random phenomena being *constellated by* the human mind, the observer, in a search for meaning and coherence.

As scientific materialism – the fullest extension of Enlightenment rationality – reached its peak in the nineteenth century, it found itself challenged from two different quarters which together began to constitute the paradigm shift we are still experiencing in the present day. From one direction came philosophical challenges to the European confidence in scientific rationality from the Romantic movement, Friedrich Nietzsche, the growing attention to psychology – the scientific observation of the observer himself – and other reflexive, critical theories like those of Marx and Engels. From a different quarter, physicists investigating problematic issues, notably classical scientific theories about the behaviour of gravity and of light, were coming to conclusions that did not accord with the common-sense understandings derived from mechanistic theories of classical science which all educated people assumed to be 'reality'.

The physics that gave rise to materialism also signalled the demise of materialism, and this demise appears to arise from the very success of Enlightenment rationality. In creating imaginative and mathematical models of reality, materialist science made the fateful mistake of forgetting what it had done by taking such a model, which is a *description* of reality, to be reality itself. The concept of energy is an example of this: we cannot see or touch 'energy', and yet we accept that it really exists because we are so used to talking about it as a way of understanding a variety of processes. Whatever it is that the word 'energy' refers to – and there is no doubt that what it refers to is a reality – the concept itself is an imaginative construct. It is a mistake to let the concept, let alone the word itself, kid us into believing we know more about the *something in nature* it refers to than is possible.

In his book *Wholeness and the Implicate Order*, the quantum physicist David Bohm points out how since time immemorial, human beings have used their thinking to divide the world up for the purpose of reducing practical problems to manageable sizes. But he warns against the extension of this tool of thinking beyond its range of usefulness,

> Being guided by a fragmentary self-world view, man then acts in such a way as to try to break himself and the world up, so that all seems to correspond to his way of thinking. Man thus obtains an apparent proof of the correctness of his fragmentary self-world view though, of course, he overlooks the fact that it is he himself, acting according to his mode of thought, who has brought about the fragmentation that now seems to have an autonomous existence, independent of his will and of his desire.
>
> (Bohm, 1983: 2–3)

Bohm then goes on to develop his theory of the Implicate and Explicate Order in which our fragmented experience of the world, the Explicate Order delivered through our minds and senses, is regarded as embedded in a unified Reality – the Implicate Order. The implication of this idea is that our minds and senses are categorically unable to know reality – the Implicate

– as it actually is, but, contrary to the claims of Enlightenment science, the consciousness of humans is always limited to a partial and ultimately inaccurate world picture. In this way, although coming from a different epistemological tradition, Bohm's Implicate parallels Lacan's concept of the Real.

Critical to these quantum phenomena is the fact that, completely opposite to the conditions of classical physics where the scientific observer and tools of measurement are deemed to have no effect on the experiment – the conditions of the experimental equipment in quantum science have been found to have an influential effect that *is not mechanical or causal* but which, nevertheless, constitutes an intimate part of the phenomena. Physical science now has to account for the way that, at the quantum level, the conditions of observation seem intimately connected to sub-atomic matter. Briefly, the quantum phenomena I am referring to are *non-locality*, *wave-particle duality*, the *Uncertainty principle* and *Probability theory*. Non-locality effects were always inherent in quantum theory but explicitly discovered through those experiments following the famous Einstein–Podolsky–Rosen experiment which, by the 1980s, had observed the counter-intuitive – meaning non-common sense – phenomenon that, when two particles that had originally been correlated together are separated, it is discovered that this correlation persists even at very large distances *without there being any causal link, or any transformation of information or signals of any kind between them*. This principle implies that the particles are somehow part of the 'same system' which is not related by cause and effect, and that they are correlated together in a way that cannot be reduced to any sort of localised connection in space and time. It implies that, as Bohm argued years ago, *concepts* like space and time are classical in nature and cannot be imported wholeheartedly into the quantum domain. This has implications for psychological theories of both the archetypes and synchronicity which I will go into later.

Similarly, Heisenberg's *uncertainty principle* establishes that it is impossible to know both the *position* and the *momentum* of a quantum particle *simultaneously*. If you measure one at all accurately, you lose information about the other completely. This principle goes beyond the idea that the conditions of observation limit the outcome of what is observed and claims that, *in principle*, the very concepts of position and momentum are ambiguous within quantum theory; and, moreover, that a quantum particle cannot be said to 'possess' a position as can a classical particle like a rock. In the macro world of matter, according to classical science, all objects possess these, but in the micro-world a particle seems to be hardly an 'object' at all but needs to be conceived of more in terms of a *process* or a manifestation of fundamental symmetries.

The phenomena of the *wave-particle duality* refers to experiments with light where it is found that light, or for that matter, electrons, will behave *either* as waves *or* as particles – a 'double-coding' of matter which includes mutually exclusive elements not permissible according to classical laws of science. Which form the light takes for the observer depends, moreover, on the way the experiment is set up. Heisenberg had the idea of a sub-atomic particle as existing as *potentia* or *potentialities* and that it is only when a measurement is made that the wave function of a particle 'collapses' and a single actuality is achieved. This idea cannot be accounted for in quantum theory itself but this may be what Pauli meant by 'the irrationality of matter' (Peat, 1999, personal communication). This idea of 'reality' not as fixed and solid but as *potential* is important to bear in mind as we begin to bring these ideas beside the ideas of Jungian psychology. As Paul Davies, Professor of Mathmatical Physics, puts it, 'quantum physics presents a picture of reality in which observer and observed are inextricably interwoven in an intimate way. The effect of observation is absolutely fundamental to the reality that is revealed, and cannot be either reduced or simply compensated for' (Davies and Gribbin, 1992: 208–209). When it comes to sub-atomic matter – but with the possibility of wider implications – quantum science restores the significance of the 'subjective' observing mind as an unavoidable aspect of any human examination of the world 'out there'.

Originally, psychoanalysis thought it could proceed with the assumed objectivity of a classical science even though its object of investigation, the unconscious–conscious psyche, was itself also the very tool of that investigation. Nowadays the practice of psychotherapy has to acknowledge its inter-subjective basis rather than making claims for a distanced, impartial objectivity. (This is in spite of the fact that the rest of psychology as practised in the Universities still proceeds by controlled experimentation and statistical proof along the lines of classical science as if the psychological phenomena under scrutiny were completely independent of any influence from the investigating mind and social context to any significant degree.) The reflexive development in depth psychology owes much to Jung who emphasised how both the therapist and the client were 'in' the treatment and subject to mutual influence and change. This is not at all the situation with quantum physics, of course, but what *is* analogous between the two practices is the way that any idea of a detached, impartial observation has had to be abandoned. The observer and the observed are now, in postmodern times, regarded as being in relationship to each other – although the consequences of this vary widely from the peculiar pheomena of the quantum world to the interpenetration of thoughts and feelings experienced by both therapist and client in the consulting room. It would be a huge over simplification to reduce interpersonal psychological phenomena to something like the quantum effects I am sketching, but, nevertheless, as we shall see, there is something seductive about comparing such effects primarily because, in many aspects, neither of them are able to be accounted for by the laws of classical science. There are probably quite different ways of comprehending each set of phenomena which have not been discovered or formulated yet, and just because they share the position of being unexplainable by known laws of classical science does not necessarily predict that they will have anything else in common. But from the perspective of a critique of the dominant rationality, they both share a position that challenges Enlightenment assumptions and so both offer the chance to rethink ourselves and the world. This is exactly the position that Jung took in his thinking about psychology and 'nuclear' physics. In a filmed interview in 1957 Jung notes how he does not have the mathematical talent to dialogue with the new physics but how he does have

> a certain relation with it on the epistemological questions . . . I have often discussed this with Professor Pauli. He is a nuclear physicist, and to my amazement I found that they have terms which are used in psychology too, and simply on account of the fact that we are entering a sphere – the one from without, and we from within – which is unknown. That's the reason for the parleys between pychology and higher mathematics.
>
> (Jung, 1957: 306)

As A. N. Whitehead wrote referring to the disjunction between classical physics and discoveries about the quantum world, 'a clash of doctrines is not a disaster, it is an opportunity' (Whitehead, 1967: 186)

OTHER SCIENCE

From another point of view – that which regards scientific knowledge as a type of contemporary mythologising – an extra-terrestrial anthropologist investigating our belief system might conclude that the concepts of 'energy' and 'particles' are not so much scientific 'facts' about 'reality', but collectively agreed upon, imaginary concepts which then construct an important aspect of 'reality' for the culture that subscribes to the belief. In this way, our 'science', which, we believe, constitutes the most hard-headed and reliable knowledge about ourselves and the world, is not so very different from the mythological beliefs of human beings in other places and other times: the knowledge and beliefs of the Other – the so-called 'ancients' and 'primitives'. In his book *Blackfoot Physics* (1995), David Peat notes how the idea of the *experiment* is central to the belief of Western scientific rationality that this is the most accurate and valid means of investigation of phenomena. Experiments are 'objective' and, 'are designed to exclude or control external influences and to emphasize a few key variables, or conditions, which can then be studied in a repeatable fashion. In its extreme form one finds echoes of Hans Eysenck's dictum "if it cannot be measured, it does not exist"' (Peat, 1995: 250). Francis Bacon, with all the gung-ho enthusiasm of early Enlightenment science, said we should put nature on the rack and force her to reveal her secrets. Later on, the poet Goethe had pointed out the artificial nature of scientific experiments for, 'in their retreat from the fullness of phenomena, they have the effect of isolating and tricking nature' (ibid.: 251). Non-Western science fails to meet the isolating, objective criteria of the *scientific experiment* and is thus deemed inaccurate, impressionistic and mistaken. Peat points out how the 'knowledge' of Eastern mystical traditions which is sublimely subjective in character, is in fact gained not through any haphazard introspection but through 'the employment of instrumentation, experimentation, and observation in their meditative and mystical practices. Within the mystical traditions these disciplines are considered to be scientific precisely because they are disciplined and reproducible' (ibid.). In addition to this, we should take note of the growing usefulness, success and validation of a variety of alternative perspectives and treatments that are not amenable to methods of classical scientific experimentation and validation. I am thinking here of acupuncture, Chinese herbal treatments, homoeopathy, certain forms of osteopathy, and even psychodynamic psychotherapy itself which, although there have been attempts to account for their theories and effects along the lines of classical science, still remain obscure to any such 'explanation'. While a good deal of research has established the efficacy of alternative non-drug treatments for a variety of conditions ranging from pregnancy sickness to coronary heart disease (Conway, 1988: 29–36), most of this is ignored as it does not fit the mechanistic, reductionist paradigm of medical science and the drugs companies. Nevertheless, this has not prevented such treatments from functioning pluralistically alongside conventional medical treatment, and, indeed, from sometimes being found in the same hospital or surgery.

Peat also points out how Laws of Thermodynamics, vital in the development of classical physics in the industrialised West during the nineteenth century, arose out of the social and political needs of Europeans at the time. Carnot's motivation was to put the French ahead of the newly industrialised English, with whom they were at war, with more efficient engines and machines; Rumford began to figure out the equivalent of heat and work by observing the heat that was generated when cannons were bored. Although connected with such practical concerns as the efficiency of machines, the laws of thermodynamics gave rise to concepts like entropy. Entropy is a totally objective fact of the universe – no matter what we want to believe we cannot change this. But, as an Indian physicist has pointed out, the Indian view of efficiency would be related to monsoons that transport vast amounts of water for irrigation from the Indian oceans; or it might just as well be about small machines like spinning wheels. The point is that an Indian thermodynamics would read the world in a radically different way. It would come up with totally objective data and observations – but these would be of quite a different order than European thermodynamics (Peat, 1999, personal communication and Sardar, 1984).

In summary, there are other ways of doing science that differ from and may not be inferior to the form developed in the last 500 years of European civilisation. In fact, as we have seen, Western science has been experiencing the limitations of its methods, assumptions and beliefs to such an extent that a paradigm shift in the conception of mind, matter, knowledge and reality has been under way for some time. Such a shift coincides with other aspects of the postmodern critique of Enlightenment certainties, and also constitutes an important area of Jungian and post-Jungian psychology that has long been involved in the challenge to conventional scientific assumptions.

THE *UNUS MUNDUS*: ARCHETYPES, THE *PSYCHOID* AND SYNCHRONICITY

As we have seen elsewhere in this book, there has always been a love–hate relationship between Jungian psychology and classical science. The latter has tended to represent the overly rational style of consciousness that Jung believed was the source of danger for the modern psyche. However, in recent years, increasing attention has been paid by Jungian theorists to the relationship between the new physics and psychology. This relationship had been a concern of Jung's since he was meeting with Einstein in Zurich between the years 1909 and 1913. As Jung said,

> Professor Einstein was my guest on several occasions at dinner ... These were very early days when Einstein was developing his first theory of relativity, it was he who started me off thinking about a possible relativity of time as well as space, and their psychic conditionality. More than thirty years later, this stimulus led to my

relation with the physicist Professor W. Pauli and to my thesis of psychic synchronicity.

(Jung Letters, Vol. 2, 1974, quoted in Card, 1991a: 26)

The pregnant phrase 'their psychic conditionality' refers to areas of Jungian psychological theory that have been receiving more attention since Jung's first formulations due to the evidence arising from quantum science. These areas are the theory of the archetypes, the concept of the psychoid unconscious, the *unus mundus*, and the theory of synchronicity. It was Jung's contact with the physicist Wolfgang Pauli that became central to Jung's theorising on mind and matter, and which led to his developing the concept of the *unus mundus*. Jung knew Pauli both as a patient whose analysis he supervised, and as a scientist with whom he could discuss parallels between the phenomena being revealed in modern physics and in analytical psychology. Together they wrote *The Interpretation of Nature and the Psyche* published in 1955. The *unus mundus* is the term Jung used to describe the transcendent, unitary existence that underlies the duality of the mind (*psyche*) and matter (*physis*),

> the *unus mundus* contains all of the preconditions that determine the form of empirical phenomena, both mental and physical. These preconditions are archetypal in nature and therefore completely non-perceptual, pre-geometrical, and pre-logical. Only when they reach the threshold of psychic perception do they take on specific representations in the form of images of geometric or numerical structures. Consequently, archetypes are the mediating factors of the *unus mundus*. When operating in the realm of *psyche*, they are the dynamical organisers of images and ideas; when operating in the realm of *physis*, they are the patterning principles of matter and energy.
>
> (ibid.: p. 29)

Perhaps it can be seen how the *unus mundus*, the idea of a non-dualistic reality is parallel to David Bohm's idea of an Implicate order, which, like the archetypes, is not able to be known to the conscious mind directly. Archetypal theory is the formulation of a concept that has been revived in modern times by Jung and Pauli; and of which Pauli, speaking as a physicist, said, 'As *ordering* operators and image-formers in this world of symbolical images, the archetypes thus function as the sought-for bridge between the sense-perceptions and the ideas and are, accordingly, a necessary presupposition even for evolving a scientific theory of nature' (Jung and Pauli, 1955, in ibid.).

Jung noted how mathematics and psychology used similar language when it came to approaching what was difficult to represent in classical terms. Terms like the 'transcendent function' – a mathematical term for the function of irrational and imaginary numbers and a psychological term for the unconscious function of bridging oppositional polarities in consciousness – led him to speculate on their implications for the link between matter and mind:

> Since psyche and matter are contained in one and the same world, and moreover are in continuous contact with one another and ultimately rest on irrepresentable, transcendental factors, it is not only possible but fairly probable, even, that psyche and matter are two different aspects of one and the same thing
>
> (Jung, 1947, CW 8: para. 418).

As I have mentioned before, in expressing his theory of the archetypes, Jung employed an analogy with the electro-magnetic spectrum in which the portion of the spectrum that is visible light corresponds to those psychic processes capable of reaching consciousness. At the lower 'psychic infrared' end of the spectrum, 'the biological, instinctual psyche, gradually passes over into the physiology of the organism and thus merges with its chemical and physical conditions . . . the archetype describes a field which exhibits none of the peculiarities of the physiological and yet, in the last analysis, can no longer be regarded as psychic, although it manifests itself psychically' (Jung, 1947, CW 8: 420). Jung reasoned that just as the instincts are grounded in the somatic processes of the neural system, the archetypes similarly possess a non-psychic 'psychoid' basis where matter and mind are not differentiated as in the assertions of classical science: 'If so, the position of the archetype would be located beyond the psychic sphere, analogous to the position of physiological instinct, which is immediately rooted in the stuff of the organism and, with its psychoid nature, forms the bridge to matter in general' (ibid.).

Jung was led to investigate the psychoid and the *unus mundus* further due to two influences – his study of alchemical symbolism as it appeared in his patients' material as well as in ancient texts, and his repeated encounters with synchronistic phenomena which he saw as evidence that psyche and matter were two aspects of the same thing. 'The synchronicity phenomena point, it seems to me, in this direction, for they show that the nonpsychic can behave like the psychic, and vice versa, without there being any causal connection between them' (Jung, 1946, CW 8: para. 418). As Charles Card notes, 'The most revolutionary consequence of the archetypal hypothesis is the possibility that archetypes functioning in both mental and physical realms give rise to synchronistic (acausal) connections between them' (Card, 1991b: 60).

Jung has defined synchronicity in several ways, but each definition retains the idea of acausality, that is, phenomena which display a similar meaning, orderedness or symmetry *without the presence of any causal link, or any mechanism of cause-and-effect.* Jung wrote that synchronicity is when an objective situation coincides with an unconscious image which has come into consciousness directly, or indirectly via a dream, idea, or premonition,

> I am therefore using the general concept of synchronicity in the special sense of a coincidence in time of two or more causally unrelated events which have the same or a similar meaning . . . Synchronicity therefore means the simultaneous occurrence of a certain psychic state with one or more external events which appear as meaningful parallels to the momentary subjective state – and, in certain cases, vice versa.
>
> (Jung, 1955, CW 8: para. 849–850)

Moreover, if archetypes act as the mediating principle for synchronistic phenomena in the narrow sense – the meaningfulness of the coincidental mental and physical events – Jung conjectured the archetypes are also acting as the mediating principle in *general* acausal orderedness. 'Thus the psychoid nature of archetypes extended beyond a neuro-physiological basis into the general dynamical patterns of all matter and energy' (Card, 1991a: 28).

With the discoveries in modern physics that established acausal phenomena in quantum physics as unarguably real, Jung found an opportunity 'to defend his concept of synchronicity – itself a radical departure from a causal world-view – by associating it with the acausal orderedness of quantum phenomena' (ibid.: 28). The most famous example of quantum acausality is the non-locality effect demonstrated by the Einstein–Podolsky–Rosen experiment I sketched earlier:

> Non-locality implies a type of behaviour that remains outside the limits of comprehension set by the classical scientific world-view of Western culture. When considered from within the confines of that world-view, it does appear to be magical. It is remarkable that the potentiality for non-local behaviour in the physical world has already been anticipated by Jung when he discussed acausal connections as 'synchronicity in a wider sense' more than 40 years ago.
>
> (Card, 1991b: 65)

As Jung said, citing such a comparison, 'It is only the ingrained belief in the sovereign power of causality that creates intellectual difficulties and makes it appear unthinkable that causeless events exist or could ever occur' (Jung, 1955, CW 8: para. 966).

Psychotherapists frequently encounter synchronistic phenomena that arise out of their work with patients. The last two of the four examples I will present here from my own experience seem to differ from other remarkable coincidences that occur in people's lives because they seem to be occurring in a purely psychic sphere. We all know of stories where we are thinking about a certain individual and then they either ring up the next minute or a letter from them arrives through the door or, against all the odds, they appear around the corner when it has not been known that they were even in the same country. These form a category of 'it's a small world' coincidences which, although highly unlikely as chance occurrences with high odds against them, are certainly not impossible to understand as such. Two examples of this type stem from my relationsip with David Peat the physicist and writer with whom I have discussed these matters over several years. At one time I was drafting a letter to him on these matter–mind issues and I had got to three-quarters the way down the page when my telephone rang. I thought immediately 'Wouldn't it be interesting if this is David, ringing just when he and these ideas are on my mind'. Well, it wasn't him, but it proved just as curious a coincidence. It was a TV researcher asking me to be on a panel of skeptics for a new series of programmes called *The Paranormal World of Paul McKenna* which was to consider UFOs, psycho-kinesis, telepathy and ghosts (McKenna is a famous British stage and therapeutic hypnotist). In her ignorance, the researcher had assumed that an 'Analytical' Psychologist would be most skeptical so I had to let her know that analytical psychologists are Jungian and are likely to be *more* sympathetic to these ideas. I suggested she find a cognitive-behavioural psychologist and also suggested she contact David Peat and Rupert Sheldrake herself. I felt the programme might lack seriousness if the producers were not already in touch with some of those who are writing about this material. As it turned out, David was engaged to appear on the programme which was broadcast later that year.

The other event occurred shortly before this after I had been having dinner with David and his wife, Maureen, at their home. I had mentioned that in an earlier career I had worked as a musician and spent many months in London's West End and on tour with the hit show *Elvis, The Musical* playing stand-up bass and bass guitar. At dinner, David had joked with his wife about Elvis impersonators which she knew something about and, as I had also been an actor at times, I think he had thought I was playing the part of Elvis rather than being one of the musicians. When I got home, I turned on the TV and watched a spoof detective show called *Hammer* which is made in the US. The whole story was about Elvis impersonators – they were being murdered one by one and Hammer had to disguise himself as one to investigate the killings. (It also struck me that that same day, 17 August, might be the anniversary of Elvis's death; it is very close at any rate). Both events are peculiar coincidences but still remain within chance probability. The two examples that follow are not as verifiable as they occurred for me as spontaneous images – one in a dream, one as a fantasy that suddenly appeared in my mind – but they similarly coincided with phenomena stemming from 'outside' me – in this case, two different psychotherapy clients of mine.

The more recent incident concerns the client I have referred to as Elizabeth in Chapter 5 with whom the frequency and intensity of synchronous events between us seemed to reinforce an erotic and therapeutic connection. On one occasion, as I walked up to my office door quite early in the morning before our session, an image remembered from the David Essex film *Stardust* came clearly to mind. In the scene, the rock-star character played by David Essex is in bed with two lovely, naked young women who are identical twins. At that time of the morning, walking across the cobbles of the covered market in Greenwich with the cafes opening up and putting out their tables I thought this an odd image to pop up and could not find any relevant association within myself or round about me. We began the therapy session and about half-way through – some 55 minutes after my fantasy – Elizabeth recalled a dream of a 'David Essex-looking guy in an art class who had an identical twin' and how she was aware of relating differently to the different person 'underneath the identical outside'. There were other aspects to the dream, but Elizabeth associated David Essex with Jesus Christ. Later, after she had said her children call me 'the funny man' who mummy goes to see, and her son had said 'I wish I could go and see a clown every morning', I recalled that David Essex had played Christ as a clown in the musical *Godspell*. The 'funny man' linked also with the previous day's dream when Elizabeth was going to see 'John Cleese' – also JC – realising that this was at the same time that she had an appointment with me. So far, the 'twins' and the 'David Essex' images had coincided but in a different combination. There were no twin girls in her dream but Essex himself was twinned. Then Elizabeth added a further personal dimension that recalls the 'young girls' aspect when she told me she had met David Essex when she was 13, 'but I must have looked a lot older', she said. It was at a wedding and other girls were asking for the singer's autograph but she did not want one. Essex called her 'blasé' at the time and, in the session, Elizabeth understood her behaviour as a way of hiding and defending herself against needy feelings by adopting a self-sufficient pseudo-maturity. She was concerned that I, too, might be convinced by this and that I might then tell her: 'You are too adequate to let me help you'. I never revealed my fantasy to her, but you can imagine how struck I was by hearing all this shortly after I had mysteriously recalled the image from the film.

My last example differs in that, rather than involving a fantasy of my own and a dream reported by the client, it concerns a dream of my own which was then echoed by what a client, who I had not even heard of at the time, described several months later. In the dream, which I discussed with my analyst at the time I dreamt it, I was riding my motorbike up to a customs post on a border where there were guards who spoke German. Outside the post was a Native American Indian woman who was clutching a child wrapped in a shawl to her breast. I spoke in faltering German to the guards inside, asking how far it was to the other side and also asking what was the story behind the refugee-looking woman and child outside. The guard told me 'They are Sioux' – at least, when he uttered 'Soo' I took it to mean the Native American Indian group. Once outside, I was getting to drive on when the woman let the shawl drop and I saw that the child had a long scar stretching from her sternum down to her stomach.

Several months later I had begun work with a new client whose name happened to be Susan or Sue. Our early conversations were giving me a picture of her early life and especially of her younger sister – who I will call here Mary – who had had a profound effect on the family as she had been born with critical heart problems which had required major surgery. My client spoke of how she had 'been carrying Mary ever since' and then, with a dramatic gesture of her hand which crossed her chest from top to bottom, she revealed how Mary 'had a scar from here to here' – exactly as with the child the 'Sioux' was carrying in my dream.

There can be no cause and effect relationship between these incidents, but in the case of the work with clients they both had a profound linking effect that reinforced my engagement with the work. Such phenomena bring to mind analogies with the non-local effects found between particles in sub-atomic physics where there is also a complete absence of any causal link to connect the events. In a later section I will come back to how therapy regards these events in ways which compare to and also contrast with analogous phenomena in the quantum world.

If they are not to be dismissed as purely coincidence – and surely, the odds against these being chance occurrences must be extremely high – and are, equally, not to be regarded in a cause and effect fashion, what such phenomena do reveal may be formulated in terms of a sort of mirroring or symmetry between events. In his book *Synchronicity: The Bridge Between*

Matter and Mind (1987), David Peat, speaking as a physicist, agrees with Heisenberg that it is the *symmetries* in particle physics, and not the particles themselves, which are the fundamental aspects of nature which physics should investigate. Peat then hypothesises, 'These fundamental symmetries could be thought of as the archetypes of all matter and the ground of material existence. The elementary particles themselves would be simply the *material realizations* of these underlying symmetries' (ibid.: 91). Charles Card comes up with a parallel statement, 'If there is a general lesson to be learned from non-local phenomena it is that the primacy of symmetry principles over space–time localization may indicate that, in nature, *symmetry is ontologically prior to space and time*' (Card, 1991b: 65).

The physicist Neils Bohr asserted that there is no quantum world but only an abstract quantum description. Thus David Peat comes to assert that matter does not represent a 'fundamental reality' but rather is the *manifestation* of something that lies beyond the material domain. For him, synchronicity entails an encounter with this domain that is not quite mind and not quite matter but 'beyond' both – a domain which we hardly have the tools to investigate, let alone the language with which we might make assertions as we do with the macro-world of physical matter. 'Within the conjunction of coincidences is enfolded something truly universal that lies at the heart of all creation' (Peat, 1987: 112). Hard pressed as we are to grasp this view with the tools of classical physics, quantum physics or depth psychology, theorists like Jung have been led back to comparisons with the concepts, formulations and imagery of the alchemists and the *perennial philosophy* of the pre-rational era.

THE LINK WITH ALCHEMY

It is ironic how developments in modern physics reveal a 'reality' that does not fit with our common-sense view of the world we have developed over the last 500 years. Jung's response to this was to search for what may be learnt from pre-Enlightenment, pre-scientific ways of thinking. Jung turned to alchemical texts partly because of the images emerging from the unconscious which he encountered in his consulting room, and partly in an effort to discover an historical precursor to the concepts of analytical psychology.

In a book that traces the alchemical view of reality, Titus Burckhardt points out how, in earlier times, matter, symbolised by the earth, represented the passive principle of all visible things, whereas heaven represented the active and generating principle. These two principles, the active and the passive, were not only inseparable but also, beyond all visible manifestation, the first and all-determining poles of existence. In this view, matter remains an aspect or function of God . . . not separated from the spirit . . . (Matter) is no more than *the potentiality of taking on form*, and all perceptible objects in it bear the stamp of its active counterpart, the spirit or Word of God . . . It is only for modern man that matter has become a thing and no longer the completely passive mirror of the Spirit.

(Burckhardt, 1971: 58–59, italics added)

It is possible to see a comparison between this view and the perspective of modern physics which regards matter, not as some final end-point in itself but as a 'manifestation' or 'realisation' expressing something beyond the material domain and beyond direct perception itself. As Jung puts it, 'What or who, indeed, is this all-powerful matter? It is the old Creator God over again, stripped this time of his anthropomorphic features and taking the form of a universal concept whose meaning everyone presumes to understand' (Jung, 1931, CW 8: para. 655).

The perennial truth contained in such so-called 'primitive', pre-rational views was brought home to me from another source. When he was five years old, my eldest son came out with a parallel statement: 'Daddy, there are two Gods. One who has the idea of a thing and calls it a name, and another one who makes the thing'. To his young mind, still able to think flexibly outside our 'common-sense' views, it seems natural to suppose that there are two complementary aspects to creation – the material form and the Idea, or Word, or Spirit that has shaped it so. An analogy would be the architect's plan in relation to the actual building. The plan is not a building but simply 'in-formation' – vital to the concrete manifestation but not present, only implied, in its material structure.

The word 'Form' can mean the outward shape of an entity (its *substance*) and, in this material sense, the opposite to this is the 'form-giving cause' (that which forms) which impresses its stamp on matter and which constitutes spirit or *essence*. 'Of *materia prima*, the primordial substance, one can only say that it is receptive with regard to the form-giving cause of existence and that at the same time it is the root of "otherness", for it is through it that things are limited and multiple' (Burckhardt, 1971: 63). For the alchemists, the common basis of the four elements (Earth, Air, Fire and Water) is the *materia prima* of the world – but the four elements do not proceed from it directly but from its first determination. Burckhardt explains how this cosmology links matter and mind by citing Hindu texts, 'where corporeal elements that pertain to the material world . . . are matched by the same number of "essential measures" . . . which are contained in the cognitive subject' (ibid.: 68). The idea is that there are two groups of 'primordial determinations' – 'in matter' and 'in mind', respectively – but both derive ultimately from *prakriti* which is also known as the *materia prima* in alchemy. It is our human ego-consciousness – which is not 'mind' itself, please note – that provides a filter for these, with the result that these primary groups become divided into the subjective and objective poles of the manifested world.

I think the reader may agree that this vision of reality, which is the same as the Hermetic view of the original alchemists, bears a striking parallel to what Jung has to say about the archetypes, the psychoid and the principle of acausal orderedness. Modern psychology uses the concept of the unconscious to refer to the 'mind' aspect of the mind–matter gestalt out of which consciousness constructs a 'reality' – largely through the effects of language, it must be said – arranged around the polarity of an objective, material, outer-world on the one hand and a subjective, immaterial, inner-world on the other.

PSYCHOTHERAPY, EMPATHY AND *PSI* PHENOMENA

But let us return now to the synchronistic phenomena that arises between individuals – and epecially between therapists and their clients. In a long neglected book called *New Dimensions of Deep Analysis: A Study of Telepathy in Interpersonal Relationships* (Ehrenwald, 1954), the psycho-analyst Jan Ehrenwald details a number of cases in his practice where the patient would report a dream which contained detailed correspondences to events, scenes and places happening in the analyst's private life, but which were totally unknown to the patient. Ehrenwald develops his own theory about this phenomena describing how 'the *psi* level of functioning is closely related to the dynamics of the Freudian id – or, for that matter, to the dynamics of the Jungian Collective Unconscious' (ibid.: 123). In a footnote on the same page, Ehrenwald explains how Jung's 'new theory of "synchronicity"' has just been published (*Naturerklarung und Psyche*, Zurich, 1952), but that Jung's publication reached him only after he had finished his own book.

Coming from a psychoanalytic background, Ehrenwald cites the importance of *empathy* – a factor later regarded as central to the concept of the self and how psychoanalytic treatment works and which was developed by the theories of Heinz Kohut in the late 1960s. Ehrenwald theorises that the 'telepathic' events which a Jungian might call synchronicities, are special and deep forms of empathic contact between people; these can be of a neurotic nature or part of normal development – such as the empathic contact that occurs between mother and child. In addition to *empathy*,

Ehrenwald mentions *enkinesis*, a form of empathy which manifests as somatic symptoms, that is, not just in the emotions and thoughts of the empathiser, but in their material body. He gives the example of the person who, after watching a long performance of a Wagner opera, goes home with a sore throat as though he had been straining his *own* voice.

It has been remarked upon by several people that the close study of synchronicity tends to be accompanied by an increase in synchronistic events for the individual, and, strangely enough, directly after reading this material for an initial draft of this chapter, I believe I may have been subject to such an experience. It involves my eldest son, again – perhaps an indication of my normal fatherly empathy with him. While driving to his music lesson he complained of an irritation in his left eye. While he had his lesson I waited in another room, reading the Ehrenwald book. Driving back home, he complained more about his eye. When we stopped at traffic lights, twice I had a close look at his eye but could not see any grit or eyelash that could be causing the irritation. This led to a detailed conversation about the sensitivity of the eye and how he should not rub his eye with dirty hands and so on. I expect you can guess the rest. The next morning I awoke with a virulent conjunctivitis in my own left eye. I have only ever experienced this infection after or during a head-cold, and so its arrival in the absence of a cold is all the more sudden and unusual. The trivial nature of this event, though, is rather typical of the synchronicities we experience, and often of those synchronicities in the literature. I think synchronicities are best understood by the emotional valency they carry for the person involved rather than by their outer detail.

Related to empathy, though not usually linked with synchronicity, are the clinical phenomena of *countertransference* and *projective identification*. Andrew Samuels takes up James Hillman's use of the concept of the *mundus imaginalis* which 'enables us to speak of the location of the archetypal' (Samuels, 1989: 162). This is a concept derived from Henry Corbin, the French philosopher and scholar, which is defined as 'an in-between state, an intermediate dimension', and is therefore relevant to an understanding of countertransference phenomena. Such phenomena are also intermediate – being not only in between patient and analyst, but also in between the analyst's conscious and unconscious. Samuels's use of Corbin's idea involves, 'the suggestion that *two persons, in a certain kind of relationship, may constitute, or gain access to, or be linked by, that level of reality known as the mundus imaginalis*' (ibid., italics in original).

Samuels focuses on countertransference experiences, especially those experienced in the body of the analyst, as visions – 'disturbing spectacles' – in the same sense as does Jung. But there is also a more down-to-earth way in which Jung grapples with the function of the human psyche which seems both mysterious and ordinary at the same time. He points out how the philosophical positions of the nominalist and the realist argument – that things are 'only' in-here or are 'really' out-there – are quite insufficient. Ideas and things both come together in the human psyche which holds the balance between them. 'What would the idea amount to if the psyche did not provide its living value?' Jung asks, and, on the other hand, 'What would the thing be worth if the psyche withheld from it the determining force of the sense-impression?' (Jung, 1921, CW 6: para. 77). In Jung's view, living reality arises from the actual, objective behaviour of things and the formulated idea *as they are in combination in the living psychological process*. Only through a specific vital activity of the psyche do sense impressions and ideas gain the intensity and force of living reality. This autonomous activity of the psyche is a continually creative act. 'The psyche creates reality every day. The only expression I can use for this activity is *fantasy*' (ibid.: para. 78). It is fantasy that, for Jung, denotes the specific activity of the psyche but which also contains far-reaching implications,

> It is, pre-eminently, the creative activity from which the answers to all answerable questions come; it is the mother of all possibilities, where, like all psychological opposites, the inner and outer worlds are joined together in living union. Fantasy it was and ever is which fashions the bridge between the irreconcilable claims of subject and object, introversion and extraversion. In fantasy alone both mechanisms are united.
>
> (ibid.)

Jung then goes on to point out how, in the world of science, fantasy is just as much taboo as feeling and that the whole underlying opposition that polarises 'in-here' and 'out-there' needs to be realised as a psychological activity. Furthermore, fantasy is involuntary and often, in common with the dream, directly opposed to consciousness. Jung brings us squarely back to the concerns of this chapter when he states how, 'The relation of the individual to his fantasy is very largely conditioned by his relationship to the unconscious in general, and this in turn is conditioned in particular by the spirit of the age' (ibid.: para. 79).

Here we find Jung, thirty years before his theory of synchronicity, grappling with the themes of subject and object, matter and mind and looking for a formulation in psychological terms, and not in terms of physics or philosophy. Countertransference communications between separate individuals seem to be both images and bodily visions which give further meaning to the concepts of 'incarnate' and 'embodied'. Samuels illustrates his ideas with researched, clinical examples and admits his conclusions tend away from the 'scientific' towards the mystical much as do the conclusions of quantum physics. 'In the countertransference experience, the image is being made flesh. Where that means that the Other (the patient's psyche) is becoming personal (in the analyst's body), I would conclude that an analyst's countertransference may be further understood by regarding it as a religious or mystical experience . . . These connections between mysticism and analysis need not seem surprising. Psychology and religion cannot simply let go of each other' (Samuels, 1989: 165–167). No more than physics and religion can let go of each other nor can our theories of representation and religion let go of each other, as we saw in Chapter 8.

A popular concept in post-Jungian psychology which is linked to the phenomena of unconscious communication and is derived from classical and quantum physics, is the idea of the 'interactive field' in Jungian analysis. This involves the concept of a *third area* between analyst and analysand which, as Nathan Schwartz-Salant reminds us, is connected with parallel concepts found in Winnicott's and Ogden's writing and which centres on the 'combined subjectivities of analyst and analysand' (Schwartz-Salant, 1995: 1). Schwartz-Salant explains how, in his clinical work, he opens to the field 'as to an object'. He finds that, 'Experiencing the field and being changed by its process is a way of transforming internal structures' (ibid.: 9). Illustrating his views with several short clinical examples, Schwartz-Salant concludes, similar to Nathan Field below, that the interactive field is, 'a space with its own processes not identical to the combined projections of analyst and analysand. . . . (it is) beyond the three-dimensional notion of container–contained focused on the projective and introjective processes' (ibid.: 33). In other words, the field approach, 'is akin to a fourth dimension that complements the more usual three-dimensional model of analysis' (ibid.).

There are difficulties with the concept of the 'field', however, due to the fact that, as David Peat explains, it refers to some sort of structure founded on classical notions of space and time by which – even in conventional quantum theory – we are able to define properties at specific points in space-time. The field concept is still embedded in classical notions of space, separation, distance, transmission, interaction and so on. Peat prefers the non-local notion of *correlation* whereby things are co-related without any need for transmission *across* space (Peat, 1999, personal communication), but these ideas are still very much undeveloped at the present stage of thinking.

In a further paper titled 'Pouring old wine into a new bottle: a modern alchemical interpretation of the ancient hermetic vessel' (Rosen, 1995), Steven M. Rosen asserts that the 'field' is something far more complex and non-ordinary than some other writers, and mainstream analysis, assume. It is not a question of something 'between' the analytic couple, neither is it a 'third' element in addition to them; crucially (and I use this word in its full sense of the cross which depicts the intersection of two, opposed dimensions), it is the manifestation of something normally beyond conscious experience and only to be grasped at 'in theory' with the inadequate tools of language. This is because the field signifies not a further addition to our dyadic, exchange-based experience, but a further *dimension*, a fourth dimension, to 'reality' or 'consciousness'. Rosen writes from a point of view of the modern mathematics which deals with the qualitative properties of surfaces. The Mobius strip – an image, you may remember, we have encountered before from Elizabeth Grosz in Chapter 7 – is a cylindrical 'two-sided' surface made by a strip of paper given a 180° twist before fastening the two ends. Its mysterious property is that it is also, paradoxically, one-sided. This can be demonstrated by drawing an ink-line on just *one* surface, only to find both surfaces 'inside' and 'outside' have the mark once your pen has completed the circle. Locally, the strip has two sides – your thumb and forefinger touch each surface when you pick it up – but *as a whole* the Mobius is one-sided. With the Mobius strip, 'in-there' is not differentiated from 'out-there', and so constitutes an image which Rosen has used to explore the integration of *psyche* and *physis* (mind and matter, subject and object). This image of the Mobius strip may well serve to symbolise the *complexio oppositorum* in the objective world, but human psychological activity brings to the three-dimensional space of matter 'a fourth, intensive, subjective realm' (ibid.). What is needed to incorporate these inner depths of the psyche is a higher level model – not a two-dimensional body enclosed as an object in three-dimensional space, but a three-dimensional body standing open to the fourth dimension that is psyche. Rosen's approach is to use mathematical models, as opposed to linguistic concepts, to achieve a formulation of the way psyche combines to produce our 'living reality' as we saw in Jung's conceptualisations, above, which focused on *fantasy*. The theoretical body that satisfies this requirement to be a kind of three-dimensional Mobius strip is known, believe it or not, as a Klein bottle – not after Melanie but after the German mathematician who devised it. Like the Mobius strip, it too has an inside and outside that interpenetrate as *one*, and for this reason it cannot be physically constructed in our three-dimensional space as the two-dimensional Mobius strip can. 'When the sides of the Klein bottle fuse, they do so without *con*fusion, without losing their distinctiveness (this was also noted for the sides of the Mobius surface, the bottle's lower-dimensional equivalent). By means of the Klein bottle, outside and inside, *physis* and *psyche*, are sealed off from one another in such a way that, paradoxically, they totally mesh (ibid.: 137).

It is a particularly synchronous joke that the name of the Klein bottle, the paradoxical hermetic vessel that ushers in analytic and alchemical imagining of the true 'fourth-dimensionality' of analytic work and of matter and mind, is also the name of the psychoanalyst who, in Britain particularly, tugs our thinking in the opposite direction – that of the two-dimensional, dyadic, either–or world of the 'good' or 'bad' breast, of love or hate, subject *or* object, and of life *or* death.

Finally, I should mention a paper by Jungian analyst Nathan Field (since expanded into a book *Breakdown and Breakthrough: Psychotherapy in a New Dimension*, 1996) in which he brings thoughts about matter, mind, quantum physics and synchronicity to bear on the psychoanalytic concepts of introjection and projective identification – whose actual 'mechanisms' are not discussed in psychoanalytic literature. This omission is telling because in fact, these concepts contain assumptions that do not accord with classical science's 'common-sense' view of everyday reality. Field asks how it is possible that, according to the psychoanalytic formulations, 'an unwanted bit of one person's psyche can lodge itself in the psyche of another? How does that bit get across the intervening space? How can the recipient acquire the conviction that the feeling is his . . . ? And once the introject has been neutralised, how does it make its way back to its rightful owner?' (Field, 1991: 94).

Field cites cases where poltergeist phenomena appeared in the consulting room (Williams, 1963) and research that has revealed correspondence between patient's chains of associations and the analysts' own (Dieckmann, 1976). Field hypothesises that,

> it is not simply that we can enter into states of merger, but that we already exist in a state of merger. From the viewpoint of consciousness we appear separate individuals with a regrettable tendency to lapse into fantasies of fusion; but if we look through the other end of the telescope we will see that the fact of our connection is primary and that our sense of separateness is sustained by a system of defences that differentiates us from one another.
>
> (Field, 1991: 97)

This idea seems to accord with what Burckhardt wrote about the filter of ego-consciousness dividing 'reality' into subjective mind and objective matter (see pp. 255–257). Field goes on to emphasise how psychotherapy may be operating in a 'fourth dimension', one not normally part of our everyday reality. He compares this idea to Winnicott's 'transitional space' and asserts that the only point of importance in any session is the unknown. Field quotes Schwartz-Salant:

This space of (unconscious relations) is a transitional area between the space–time world . . . and the collective unconscious, what Jung also called the pleroma . . . In its pathological form, this dynamic invades the conscious personality in primary process thinking. But in its creative form the pleroma is the source of all healing through experiencing the numinosum, that which Jung believed was the essence of the therapeutic process.

(Schwartz-Salant, 1988)

The shift in consciousness required to accept the view of reality revealed by these aspects of psychotherapy phenomena – and those of quantum physics – is as great, Field points out, as that required in former times when humanity had to shift from a geocentric, flat-earth view, to one that was heliocentric and which saw the earth as a sphere – despite its persisting 'common-sense' flatness!

Without going into a great amount of detail that is beyond the scope of this book, this chapter has sought to bring together the postmodern challenge to classical science that has arisen from developments in physics throughout Jung's lifetime. The way that these discoveries have challenged the assumption of a hard and fast division between mind and matter has persistently caught the attention of analytical psychologists. By making analogies between psychological phenomena observed in the clinical situation and in general between people, and scientific views that challenge prevailing orthodoxies, a dialogue between depth psychology and the new physics has got underway. The association between the two remains largely at the level of metaphor at present, but there is growing evidence that Jungian theorising has much to offer the new scientific vision of the material world as Jungian analyst Anthony Stevens reported at the Royal Society of Medicine in 1993 (Stevens, 1995). It is encouraging that there are Jungian psychological theories that can meet the challenge, but it is then all the more important that the phenomena encountered – in psychology and in the physical sciences – that cannot be understood within mechanistic theories, are not more or less ignored or reduced to commonly accepted formulations, but courageously followed up within new paradigms.

11 'I'm OK, You're Mad' : Sanity, Psychosis and Community

Life is crazy and meaningful at once.

(Jung, 1954, CW 9,1: para. 65)

THE PSYCHIATRIST

I need to begin this chapter with an anecdote. It dates from when I was just starting to prepare myself for analytic training many years ago. I had had three years of analysis and was spending a morning a week with a consultant psychiatrist in his hospital out-patient clinic to observe the range of psychiatric illnesses that came through his door and how they were assessed and treated. On this occasion he was called out to the home of a couple in their late fifties and I accompanied him. The husband had rung the clinic as his wife had been up all night going about her business in the home in a manic fashion. She was known to the consultant as a sufferer of what is diagnosed as manic-depressive illness. At the house, the psychiatrist said he would go and speak with the husband to get a picture of what had been going on and that I should stay with the woman and let him know afterwards my opinion of her condition.

So, while the psychiatrist talked entirely to the 'sane' referring husband, I stayed with the 'manic' wife. She was in her bedroom and busy tidying away shoe boxes of photographs and also various pairs of gloves and so on. She was quite intense in her focus on these tasks and, like anyone interrupted in a task they want to get finished, she did not pay very much attention to my presence. I am sure she knew the doctor and knew why we were there but she was concentrating on matters more important to her. When we left, the consultant turned to me and asked what I thought. I had to say that I really did not think that she was that bad – meaning I did not think that her behaviour or attitude deviated so far from the acceptable or a norm. The consultant said he was 'not impressed' with my assessment and the woman was taken to hospital that same afternoon.

As you can imagine, this was a bit of a blow to the self-esteem of a budding 'mental health professional' but considering this chapter has required me to think again about the incident. At least three issues come to mind and it will be these that I intend to develop here. First, it seems that, partly due to my inexperience and partly due to my personality, my calibration of what was 'normal' and what was 'abnormal' seemed to be different to that of the psychiatrist and the woman's husband who referred her. But, more precisely, it was not that I did not see her behaviour as deviating from the expected, but more that I did not think it deviated so far that *something had to be done about it*. This brings in my second point. The consultant and the husband had experience of this woman's condition, they had seen it before and seen its pattern. Moreover, the consultant also had experience of many such patients and text-book cases that led his thinking and expectations within a particular rationality – the rationality of the psychiatric profession. In his culturally ascribed role he was of the profession who *know* about such matters and the recommended way of treating them. In addition, of course, the husband is aware of the psychiatrist's authority in this way – as I was too. It is just one aspect of the shared system of meanings that constitute modern culture. The psychiatrist, similar to the judge in the legal portion of society, is the legitimate authority when it comes to the particular social deviancy called 'mental illness'. This leads to my third point. The referring husband did not appear to have any recourse to alternative forms of help. Even if there had been other family members or a community group who he could have called instead of the psychiatrist, it would have been difficult for him to keep his wife within that system of care for her and aid for him. This is because the very existence of a conceptual and social system that includes expert knowledge, authority over others in law, the psychiatric ward, professional carers and psychotropic drugs exerts a certain pressure on individuals that is difficult to resist. This is all the more so when the particular form of rationality that forms the base for such a system also forms the *weltanschaung* that decides who the clients shall be – that is, those who exhibit other 'rationalities' – or discourses, or language games – categorised as deviant, abnormal or insane.

'Insanity' in our present era tends to disempower and remove the subject from the community of the 'sane' majority just as unemployment and economic marginality removes the subject from the community of the economically empowered. In fact, in a culture where material consumption is viewed as highly rational behaviour, 'insanity' and poverty often go hand-in-hand. But the sufferers of mental dis-ease do not wish to be excluded. As Foucault points out, their forced exclusion is a double punishment and a Greek friend has told me how a sufferer of schizophrenia in his home village told him he welcomed the attention he attracted – even if it was confrontational and teasing it was far better than being ignored: at least he could feel included in his community, even if it was as a buffoon. Different cultures and other eras vary in the degree to which they develop structures to *include* their 'marginal' members be they eccentric by way of rationality, of sexuality or whatever. This creative attitude is in contrast to that of the industrialised West where we simply find their *difference* a problem to be got rid of. Moreover, it is far from irrelevant that this vignette shows three men dealing with a woman who is expressing the abnormal psychology. We also happened to be all European Caucasians in this case, but both ethnic and gender differences are important when we come to talk about the scope of rationality and the forms it takes across the human range.

When it comes to psychosis and 'abnormal' psychology in general, as I see it, there are four main issues at stake: First, the *identification* of non-rational, deviant and abnormal psychology and of those subjects seen to manifest it; second, the historical contours of the dominant styles of rationality in Western industrialised nations; third, the lack of homogeneity to these styles of rationality and the power factors that hold them in place; and, lastly, the forms of treatment society offers the subject and how this varies across different cultures and different eras. My aim in this chapter is to apply the conceptual tools developed in social anthropology to a discussion of the relationship between psychosis and the dominant culture. In this, I am indebted to the work of Harvard anthropologist Stanley Tambiah (Tambiah, 1990) on the scope of rationality, and I will be sketching perspectives derived from Wittgenstein, Levy-Bruhl, Julia Kristeva and Alfred Schutz. Next, I bring in the Jungian psychologist James Hillman for his original and fully psychological views on both the *necessity of abnormal psychology and on the fantasy of normalcy* itself. Finally, I end with an anthropological report which concerns the communal response to a case of mental breakdown in a young woman. This illustrates how a traditional society, while providing the conditions for the woman's breakdown through its circumscription of acceptable behaviour, was also able to provide a 'cure'. This was enacted through the community's own indigenous concepts and structures which were used to restore the woman to her community and to her fuller self in a way that contrasts sharply with Western psychiatry.

I conclude with a comment on how we might view this attitude to psychosis as an ethical effort by the community as a whole – in contrast to our own parenthesising of psychosis as individual suffering – and thereby begin to develop what might be regarded as a postmodern, pluralistic attitude to so-called sanity and madness.

THE SCOPE OF RATIONALITY

If, as the old joke goes, neurotics build castles in the air while it is psychotics who live in them – what, I wonder, do the 'normals' do? I guess the answer would be – the normals build castles on the ground and live in *them*. In other words what is rational will be what is *grounded*. However, leaving the joke aside, in historical and cultural terms rationality will invariably be that which is found within the castle walls. Outside the walls are the barbarians, the Other, Not Us. This metaphor is not so much of sky and earth, but one of In and Out. In this image, what is inside the boundary will be what is rational (and probably 'good' and 'right') for that society – or community of beliefs – and all that is outside the boundary will be not just 'other' but non-rational (and probably 'bad'). In fact, it will not be anything about rationality itself that lets you know what is rational or not – that would be like the eye looking at itself – but it will be the *boundary*, the reassuring mass of the castle walls, that lets the subjects know where they stand: inside and included or outside and excluded.

Different societies, like different people, will have different shaped castles and these may last for thousands of years in the same form. But elsewhere, walls can come down and be rebuilt in a different place – boundaries are revealed to be not so permanent after all. This can result in anxiety and call into doubt the confident delineation of the rational and non-rational that had prevailed up till then. In one case the boundary may change to rapidly include what was previously deemed irrational. Examples that spring to mind are the rediscovery of the unconscious once rejected by Descartes and Locke, and for classical science the 'irrationality', in Newtonian terms, of the discoveries of quantum physics, as explored in the previous chapter. Alternatively, boundaries may change to exclude and restrict what was previously held to be rational. Examples of this may be the abolition of belief in ghosts and spirits of dead ancestors or the loss of a particular rationality based entirely on Christian belief which prevailed in Europe up until the sixteenth century.

My position, then, is in line with thinkers Tambiah calls the 'splitters' – those for whom there is no *one* reality or rationality. This position contrasts with the 'unifiers' or 'lumpers' for whom there *is* one rationality while the rest are deviations or mistakes. But this is not simply a case of the relativist versus the essentialist or, in anthropological discourse, cultural relativism versus European ethnocentrism. The fact is that there are plural rationalities, not only across cultures and eras, but also found side by side with dominant rationalities. In the West, the dominant culture's attempt to sustain an illusion of homogeneity results in the 'fragmentation' experienced within modern industrial society. And if 'our' rationality in the industrialised West is no yardstick for human culture as a whole – a fact only fully taken on since the end of colonial domination earlier in the twentieth century – perhaps it is time to examine the dominance of, and the basis for, the particular rationality which, by contrast, defines what is 'irrational', or 'magical' and, ultimately, 'insane'.

The comparison between, on the one hand, discriminating the rational from the insane in the industrialised West, and, on the other hand, the anthropological problem of the comparative assessment of 'rationality' across different cultures, may prove more than a useful metaphor. Just as it is some time since it has been legitimate to regard the behaviour of other human groups outside 'ourselves', as savage, childlike or primitive in evolutionary terms, dominated by magical thinking or plain 'wild', so perhaps we are working through a time when, within our own culture, we are beginning to revise assumptions about our own dominant rationalities and our own 'ratiocentricity' if you like. Anthropology has already ventured further down this path and so it has developed some tools we may find useful. In addition, as these tools have been developed by the dominant rationality of the industrialised West, thus making suspect their use with culturally different groups, it becomes no less legitimate, and probably a good test of them, to employ them within the dominant culture with its own, internal, 'otherness'. Again, since the end of colonialism, 'ourselves' can never be the homogenous monolith it pretended to be. A unitary rationality is already breaking down as Western culture adjusts to a new plurality of people, customs and values. Part of that adjustment must involve a revision of the scope of rationality and thus of the position and treatment of those marked by it as psychotic or insane. If we have begun to accept the legitimacy of the concepts 'culturally other' and 'ethnically different' why should we not be thinking about the 'rationally other' or 'differently rational' (as opposed to an awful PC term like 'rationally challenged'!)? Finally, as Habermas points out when it comes to much of postmodern thought, we do still have to think, write and work within the dominant rationality that is at the same time under challenge. To that extent this discourse is all still part of that same rationality. But to use it *reflexively* to challenge and undermine *itself* – that is the trick and the point of the exercise. In other words, not to bolster and refine something that is, to be frank, a bit worn out, but to revitalise it through its deconstruction.

MULTIPLE ORDERINGS OF REALITY: LEVY-BRUHL, WITTGENSTEIN, PEIRCE AND SCHUTZ

To a certain extent I believe it is possible to see in contemporary psychiatry, in both its neurophysiological and its psychoanalytical manifestations, an emphasis rather similar to that found in Victorian anthropology. From its imperial heights, Victorian anthropology took as its task the observation and analysis of the erroneous beliefs of 'simpler', more 'primitive' peoples. 'But it was at the same time desired to demonstrate,' as Needham remarks, 'that the errors were reasonable ones, understandable in the circumstances . . . and which could be more speedily eradicated as the savages copied European standards of observation and discourse' (Needham, 1972: 180). Such imperialist views were epitomised by Tylor and especially Frazer whose key text was *The Golden Bough*. Levy-Bruhl, in *How Natives Think*, proposed a radical challenge to the idea that so-called primitive thought was irrational or misapplied. He demonstrated, first of all, how the thinking of natives he studied in fact had its own characteristic organisation that was in contrast to the rational-causative orientation of the West. This different organisation was the 'law of participation' – 'the association between persons and things in primitive thought to the point of *identity* and *consubstantiality*. What Western thought would think to be logically distinct aspects of reality, the primitive may fuse into one mystic unity' (Tambiah, 1990: 86). Levy-Bruhl's mature thinking, stemming from the 1930s, emphasises two highly influential views when it comes to considering 'other' rationalities. One is that other cultures, or epochs, with their strikingly different categories and systems of thought, place great demands upon our powers of empathy, insight and translation. The second conclusion, in Levy-Bruhl's own words, is that,

> In every human mind, whatever its intellectual development, there subsists an ineradicable fund of primitive mentality . . . It is not likely that it will ever disappear . . . For with it would disappear, perhaps, poetry, art, metaphysics, and scientific invention – almost everything, in short that makes for the beauty and grandeur of human life. (It) represents something fundamental and indestructible in the nature of man.
>
> (Levy-Bruhl, 1949/1973 quoted from *Les Carnets*, cited in Needham, 1972: 186)

Jung, amongst others, was highly influenced by Levy-Bruhl's ideas of a different, mystical ordering of reality that coexisted with our dominant consciousness and which helped to 'explain' some of the phenomena arising from the unconscious, not only in the case of neurosis and psychosis but for so-called normals as well. In Jung, however, there remains the Victorian legacy of an evolutionary 'layering' and hierarchising of the different mentalities which immediately imposes a superior/inferior dichotomy. When we come to Wittgenstein, who also commentated in detail on *The Golden Bough*, it is possible to start thinking in more diachronic terms of, as Tambiah puts it, not so much, '"mentalities" but "multiple orientations to reality" or "orderings of reality" so as to avoid any undue stress on "innatedness" and to include the social construction of meanings and systems of knowledge' (Tambiah, 1990: 93). Wittgenstein's critical reflections on Frazer's *The Golden Bough* prefigure his later conceptions of different apperceptions of reality as so many 'forms of life' or 'language games'. The emphasis here is on it not being possible to view reality, truth and knowledge outside the frame of reference in which they have their existence. An existence, moreover, which is socially, culturally and, especially, linguistically located.

Jung expressed the unity of the human psyche across all mankind in his concept of the collective unconscious. In a different way, Wittgenstein, in challenging Frazer's Victorian colonialist emphasis on the 'errors' of the primitive, also aimed to demonstrate how the so-called 'civilised' and 'savage' are very much alike – especially when it comes to their distinctly human linguistic and cultural constructions. In doing so he brings up an important factor that seems to be of direct interest to my purpose here in locating psychosis within the dominant rationality. This is how, 'the translation of another's cultural conceptions into our linguistic categories necessarily implies a "shared space", a "bridgehead of understanding" between the two' (ibid.: 63). There is, I believe, exactly the same tension between the modalities of universality and particularity found in Wittgenstein – and later anthropological analyses of 'rationality' such as those of Malinowski and Winch – as we now need to struggle with in our considera-tion of the phenomena labelled 'psychosis'. To what extent are we, just as the Victorians with their 'savages', reading the semiotics of psychosis as merely full of error – to be cured partly by education, but mostly by chemical correction?

The discourse on rationality we might share with anthropology offers further views when it comes to differences in representation. Rather than finding one form of representation simply superior to another, it seems truer to say that any sign system can have multiple representational capacities and communicative functions. The semiotic categories developed by Peirce suggest not the dichotomisation of signs and meanings but a full continuum ranging from the signs used in a particular context for their referential capacity to transmit information in a scientific mode to, at the other end, signs used to communicate sensory (or emotional or transcendental) effects in a presentational or participatory mode. Put this way, perhaps we can see how the range of expression between, on the one hand, the psychiatrist explaining a diagnosis to colleagues, falls in to the first area (referential/ scientific), while, on the other hand, the person in treatment speaks a discourse from quite another place on the continuum (the sensory/ emotional). Furthermore, the psychiatrist at prayer, or in love, or enraptured by an aesthetic experience may find himself sharing some of the 'madness' of this end of the continuum – thus emphasising its ubiquity rather than its marginality.

It was noted in the previous chapter how we are particularly accustomed to, and adhere to, the dominant reality and criterion of 'truth' derived from the discourse of empirical science. But Alfred Schutz (1962), following on from William James and Bergson, points out that, not only is all reality never *given* but has to be *constructed*, it is also the case that, 'multiple realities arise because of the variety of needs of consciousness and schemes of interpretation that link the two' (Bellah, 1970: 242). Or as William James said: 'each world whilst it is attended to is real after its own fashion; only the reality lapses with the attention'. Schutz advances the view that all these 'worlds' – the world of dreams, the world of art, the world of religious experience, the world of scientific contemplation – are 'finite provinces of meaning' which we may find incompatible and which may have to be moved between with a leap and not by transition. In particular, Schutz regards *scientific contemplation as much a leap from the reality of everyday life as religious experiences are* – a position from which we may well want to reflect upon the 'leap into psychosis'.

To conclude this sketching of multiple orderings of reality, there is an important feminist approach to the analysis of different human discourses which seeks to address the tendency towards hierarchy. Gilligan (1982), recalling the discussion on postmodern gender in Chapter 5, writes about different orientations to reality for men and for women. She contrasts the masculine focus on individuation and the definition of self through separation or autonomy, to the female 'morality of responsibility' where relationship and connection with others is the primary focus. Julia Kristeva, as has been noted already, finds fault with such a division along strict gender lines. Kristeva's emphasis on the *individuality* of women in the feminist debate could also provide the text for all individuals – including the so-called psychotic – who are placed in the margin by the dominant discourse. As she puts it, a woman can fit herself,

> to the dominant discourse – theoretical discourse, scientific discourse – and on the basis of that find an extremely gratifying slot in society,

but to the detriment of the expression of the particularity belonging to the individual as a woman. On the basis of this fact, it seems to me, that one must try not to deny these two aspects of linguistic communication, the mastering aspect and the aspect which is more of the body and of the impulses, but try, in every situation and for every woman, to find a proper articulation of these two elements . . . I think that the time has come when we must no longer speak of all women. We have to talk in terms of individual women and of each one's place inside these two poles.

(Kristeva, 1984: 123)

ARCHETYPAL PSYCHOLOGY AND THE NECESSITY OF ABNORMAL PSYCHOLOGY

I now wish to take a swift, temporary diversion away from the multiple ordering of realities of these anthropological and philosophical discourses and dive right into the psyche and its own multiplicity as expressed by Jungian analyst James Hillman within the frame of archetypal psychology. After this we will resurface to consider an example of psychological collapse and healing in a traditional cultural setting. I hope that these ideas of Hillman's will supply a bridge between the two modes of experience of psychosis and psychopathology – that of the inner world of the individual subject and that of the outer world of the collective culture. In the Jungian view, the unconscious *psyche* encompasses both worlds.

Hillman takes a contrasting view to positions that see psychopathology as either secondary and illusory (humanistic, transcendental views), or as an accident of historical, social or political institutions (Foucault, perhaps, certainly Laing, 1959, 1967 and Deleuze and Guattari, 1972) or, quite un-related to the soul of the individual as in psychiatry. All these perspectives derive from outside psyche itself; Hillman's focus, instead, tries, 'to base pathologising wholly within the psyche and to show its necessity for the psyche' (Hillman, 1980: 2). What can he mean – that psychopathology is *necessary* to the psyche? His cue lies with Jung's 'The gods have become diseases' (Jung, CW 13: para. 54): 'our psychic illnesses are not *imaginary*, but *imaginal* (Corbin). They are indeed fantasy illnesses, the suffering of fantasies, of mythical realities, the incarnation of archetypal events' (Hillman, 1980: 2).

Hillman points out how the figures of myth, with their quarrelling, cheating and killing, 'must be classified under criminal pathology, moral monstrosity, or personality disorders' (ibid.: 3). In addition, some say the 'world of the Gods' is anthropomorphic, an imitative projection of ours, including our pathologies. But one could start as well from the other end, the *mundus imaginalis* of the archetypes (or Gods), and say that our 'secular world' is at the same time mythical, an imitative projection of theirs, including their pathologies. What the Gods show in an imaginal realm of myth is reflected in our imagination as fantasy.

(ibid.: 3)

And just as the pathologising in a myth is intrinsic and cannot be removed without deforming it, Hillman states,

If we assume that the necessary is that which occurs among the Gods, i.e., that myths describe necessary patterns, then their pathologizings are necessary, and ours are necessary to the mimesis of theirs. Since their *infirmitas* is essential to their complete configuration, it follows that our individual completion requires our pathologizings.

(ibid.: 4)

In connection with such pathologisings, the idea of Necessity becomes central to Hillman's argument. He points out that '*necessity in Greek mythical thought is spoken of and experienced in pathologized modes*' (ibid.: 5, italics in original). The word for necessity in Greek is *Ananke* – which is connected to the concepts of narrow, throat, strangle, embrace, chain and suffocation from linguistic roots in Egyptian, Syriac and Arabic. The Latin for ananke is *necessitas* with the notion of 'close bond' and family ties. But necessity and pathology are not solely linked to a negative stranglehold or kinship tie. There is also the idea that Zeus rules the world through close collaboration with Ananke. Ananke (also called Adrasteia),

is his wet-nurse and, by suckling at the breast of necessity, he draws his power and wisdom with that milk. In some contexts his nurse Adrasteia is his daughter, so that the bind is expressed in the close tie of kinship, of family obligation, even of incestuous love. This Orphic image reveals the possibility of a loving and nourishing connection with necessity. Here the relation with her power is imagined less as oppressive servitude than as dependency upon the milk of the daughter–mother soul.

(ibid.: 7)

Hillman further links *pathology* with necessity using two other themes: *compulsion* and *images*. Psychological suffering, its compulsion and the hope for therapeutic remedy are brought together in a section from Euripides *Alcestis* which Hillman quotes:

I myself, in the transports
of mystic verses, as in study
of history and science, have found
nothing so strong as Compulsion [*Anagkas*],
nor any means to combat her,
not in the Thracian books set down
in verse by the school of Orpheus,
not in all the remedies Phoebus has given the heirs
of Asclepius to fight the many afflictions of man.
She alone is a goddess
without altar or image to pray
before. She heeds no sacrifice.

(Lattimore, trans. 1955)

In this passage, Hillman draws our attention to how the language being used for dealing with *ananke* is that of therapy: 'remedies of Asclepius – and there are none. Nor are mysticism, orphicism, history, science, a match for her force. Is this because she has no image, no altar to pray before?' (Hillman, 1980: 9). It may appear a familiar idea to those treating mental dis-ease, especially psychosis, that for some patients,

necessity is experienced when one is compelled and there is no image of what is occurring. It is if there were a relation – even an inverse proportion – between images and drivenness: the more the image and altar, the less the blind necessity.

(ibid.)

Jung conceives the archetype as spanning a continuum between the body, instinct and materiality – at the compulsive end – and images at the other end of the continuum. For Hillman what this means is that 'Necessity seizes us through images. An image has its own inherent necessity, so that the form an image takes "cannot be otherwise" – whether we paint, move a line of verse, or when we dream' (ibid.), or, I would say, when we fantasise or are deluded or hallucinating.

Thus, as our psychopathology and its necessity works in every image – 'what drives us are images' – it is to images, to our spontaneous fantasies that we need to turn. The Jungian view holds that as 'reality' for humans is primarily psychic, and reality is only so if it is *necessary*, then, 'Images are primordial, archetypal, in themselves ultimate reals, the only direct reality that the psyche experiences. As such they are the shaped presences of necessity' (ibid.: 10). Hillman is not referring to the active images we move around inside us but to the images of our spontaneous fantasies. This point is critical to the argument I am developing here about multiple realities, and the inclusion of the psychotic reality within this, both culturally and personally. Hillman is referring to the images that 'arise' of themselves, independent of ego – which makes them like the images that arise in the most 'pathologised' of our community – the psychotic, the mad. This carries an implication that the 'mad' are in fact more in touch with psychic reality than those of us who do not entertain these images and divert ourselves through involvement in ego's operations and engagements directed towards the outer world – producing our so-called rational behaviour. In fact, such an intolerance to psychic images may well be vital for preserving the dominant rationality itself which, in our culture, is valued as a desirable psychological position for the mature, sane adult. In Freud, we find the apostatising of what he called the Reality Principle, in the service of which fantasy has to be avoided and discouraged as it is *'reality rejecting'*. Just as in dementia – the schizophrenia of his day – so too in fantasy, the libido is directed *away* from 'reality' and, Freud asserts, that way madness lies (Freud, 1914).

But let us consider this: it may be that such a 'reality' (i.e. Freud's and our own world of modernity and late-Enlightenment rationality) is not *reality* per se but more a particular *perspective* – and one among many at that. This might mean, then, by its exalting itself to unitary status, such a reality might be just as 'mad' – that is, solipsistically out of touch with the wider *range* of 'realities' – when it is viewed in contrast to the conventional 'madness'. That is, the 'madness' of those who are compelled to allow in the experience of *fantasy* – the *via regia* of ultimate psychic reality with all its compulsion and 'pathology'.

Hillman turns to Plato to give us the final twist. For Plato the first principles of the system of the universe are two: *Nous* – reason, order, intelligibility, mind, and *Ananke* – Necessity. In Plato's *Timaeus* he states that 'Reason overruled Necessity by persuading her . . . towards what is best' but the very fact that this had to happen brings in the concept of the Errant Cause. This *planoumene aitia* – the 'variable cause' or 'erratic cause' – is translated by such terms as rambling, digressing, straying, irrational, deviating (like I am doing with this excursion into archetypal psychology) – and, we are told, *'Planos* can refer to the wanderings of the mind in madness and to the fits of a disease. Such is the way Plato speaks of *ananke'* (Hillman, 1980: 13). Personally, I can see how many of the challenges to classical science – Quantum theory, Chaos and Complexity – are beginning to unveil this principle – but not without the difficulties that arise from having to accept their degrees of 'irrationality'. The Errant Cause is, 'The indeterminate, the inconstant, the anomalous, that which can be neither understood or predicted. It is Force, Movement or Change, with the negative attribute of not being regular, or intelligible' (Grote, quoted in Hillman, 1980: 14). Does this not sound like the *psychosis* that troubles us so? For the human psyche, the resulting irrationalities arising from Necessity are what we regard as the deviations of abnormal psychology, and, Hillman states, 'this creating activity I have called pathologizing' (ibid.). Hillman makes a point about Freud that is parallel to my own mentioned earlier. He says that, 'As Freud's "starting point", the symptom, is conceived to be different from and foreign to the rational ego, so this "starting point" (*arche*) of Plato, the errant operation of *ananke*, is equally alien from the realm of reason' (ibid.).

In case we feel lost taking this diversion let me summarise what I have brought together here. My theme has been to promote the idea that there are multiple realities or rationalities so that we can think again about the strict 'otherness' or 'deviance' of psychosis as we currently view it. I began to discuss this by borrowing a paradigm from social anthropology and philosophies applied to it which discuss the idea of 'rationality' when confronted with human practices and beliefs which are extremely distant from rational, causal, scientific views of the industrialised urban West. I felt we could learn something from anthropology's attempts to deal with its own bias against the Other that might inform us about our biases against the 'other rationality' of the mad. In using Hillman's ideas of the Necessity of psychopathology I have attempted to bring the issue of the deviant, irregular and non-rational back from being simply a socio-cultural issue to seeing it as embedded in the ground of our being, embedded in psyche and the nature of the world. 'Pathologies', other rationalities and non-rationalities outside the castle walls are part of all of us and part of the world. By paying attention to this, and to the images of our fantasy that express this, we will be in a better position to tolerate, include and benefit from psychotic realities at the same time as we are caring for the patients' distress. A distress which is arising out of their exclusion, perhaps, more than anything else.

MADNESS IN CONTEXT: AN ANTHROPOLOGICAL CASE OF PSYCHOTIC BREAKDOWN

Finally, as promised, I should like to finish with a piece of ethnographic participant-observation – an equivalent of the clinical case example from the discourse of social anthropology which illustrates these points. It shows how a culture may drive an individual mad, but then how the same culture may also contain within itself the resources to help return the individual to a happier state through a process which involves the entire community.

The anthropologist Benjamin Paul was engaged in field-work in a Guatemalan Indian lakeside village when he and his wife got to know Maria, the subject of the 'madness', and observed the events that followed. Maria's traits, we are told, suggested an affinity with masculine rather than feminine standards in a village society where there were sharp distinctions between the behaviour prescribed for men and that prescribed for women. She retained her Spanish language (it is significant that language, her 'voice', is pointed out) as the men do for commerce with the city, unlike the women who tend to turn back to relying on their native Mayan once school is finished. Maria also 'used her charm to attract men, but her attitude toward them was essentially competitive and hostile. By local standards she was immodest and aggressive' (Paul, 1953: 153). Maria had split from two husbands and was now living back with her parents when she came to work as a part-time domestic helper and informant for the anthropologists. Paul says, 'In our house, where she could escape the protective vigilance of her kinsmen, she had the rare opportunity of meeting the men who came to visit us' (ibid.: 154). It so happened that Maria eloped with one of these men, José, leaving not only her family and job but also her unweaned baby daughter. The elopement pattern was the dominant form of marriage at that time in Maria's village but, following this, Maria's father demanded her punishment in the village court house for causing him anger and humiliation and, above all, for abandoning the baby. The court imposed a fine on the couple (which José's father paid) and the court also gave the baby over to the care of the relatives of the child's biological father who had offered a wet-nurse available in their family. Paul informs us that, 'People in the village spoke ill of Maria . . . for deserting her baby . . . it is generally assumed that a baby under one year of age has a poor chance to survive if separated from its mother' (ibid.: 155).

'Having alienated nearly everybody else, Maria could still count on José and his parents – but not for long' (ibid.). Maria quarrelled with her mother-in-law who objected to Maria's bossiness and, a month into their marriage, José accused Maria of flirting with another man; Maria reviled José and his parents and he responded by beating her. 'She in turn suffered a violent attack of *colera* (rage) a culturally patterned syndrome consisting . . . of symptoms of gasping and suffocation. It gives the appearance of being a kind of adult temper-tantrum with screaming generally suppressed, and some of the anger directed at the self. The local culture frowns on the expression of overt hostility' (ibid.: 156), Paul says, which makes me wonder about how male violence seems an exception to this.

Later that night, Maria, 'lapsed into a state of unconsciousness which turned out to be the onset of a dissociated episode' (ibid.). José and his father tried to rouse her and were frightened that José may have mortally harmed her. They enlisted the aid of one of the village shamans who was reluctant to intervene because he did not want to be held responsible as 'She already looks so serious'. Then Maria 'began to wail that spirits of the dead were surrounding her and were trying to take her to the realm of the dead. This heightened the fears of those present . . . Maria was in a state of fugue . . . walking about the house talking and arguing, but only with the spirits' (ibid.: 157). All realised now she was *loca* (crazy) – a state of affairs which required the appropriate shaman. This happened to be Manuel – Maria's father: 'Now in the role of a critical specialist and not in the role of the injured father.' Manuel swung into action and the breach between the families of José and Maria was remedied. He advised seeking the help of a more powerful shaman and so all the parents plus José and Maria (who had to be taken forcibly) set out by canoe at 2 am and arrived in the next town at dawn.

This shaman's diagnosis and insight was critical to what followed in the families. 'Maria had fallen victim to the power of malignant supernatural forces. The cause lay in a history of sinful behaviour on the part of any or all of the following: Maria, her father and mother; her husband José, his father and mother' (ibid.). The first step in the course of treatment had to be a ritual whipping administered to all six by a senior relative (the only living grandparent) and this was enacted back in the village – more as a gesture and a symbol rather than as a punishment. This was the first of a series of actions undertaken to placate the spirits which involved all the family members in a pattern of interpersonal activity making Maria aware, 'that not she alone but a group of people (her kinship circle) were locked in battle with the threatening forces' (ibid.: 158).

Maria recovered over time and was able to report some of her hallucinations which had involved a number of dead ancestors and, in particular, demands on her to stay and help nurse the babies of women who appeared to her but who, in reality, had all died in childbirth. Paul identifies three significant implications arising out of Maria's episode – two of which seem pertinent to my argument today.

First, it seems clear that for a woman such as Maria, 'who was unconventional for reasons of predisposition or socialization or both', the narrowly prescribed and rigid roles available to her as a woman led to a need to escape. She tried this by marrying a succession of culturally marginal men who might have had the means and the motivation to leave the village. Stuck in her village however, 'she could only rebel, and eventually break with reality when the battle became unbearable' (ibid.: 162). Five years later Maria had succeeded in breaking away and was raising a family with José in Guatemala City where, no doubt, she benefited from the relatively greater opportunities available to her as a woman. I was glad to read that Maria was not simply returned to a greater conformity by the whole episode.

Second, Paul also makes the point about secondary guilt in mental patients in our own culture that Foucault documents – in *Madness and Civilisation*, published 14 years after Paul's paper – arising from the emerging moral responsibility imposed on the mentally ill as European society reordered itself in the early industrial era (Foucault, 1967). The judgement of society and the guilt of the sufferer can only exacerbate mental dis-ease, but the Guatemalan village culture mitigates this in two ways. On the one hand,

> hallucinations are not culturally defined as products of fantasy. Sights and sounds of ghosts are regarded by most normal people in Maria's village not as fears and fancies but as real occurrences. It was never doubted by others that dead women actually surrounded Maria during her illness . . . Maria was sick in the eyes of her neighbours *not because she imagined visitations, but because she was host to visitations.*
>
> (Paul, 1953: 163, italics added)

Paul compares this to our own culture's belief in a sick person being host to microbes, which are invisible to the naked eye but present on the basis of our own particular cultural information.

On the other hand, Maria was also *spared secondary guilt* within her culture because of – as Paul awkwardly puts it – 'the merciful ambiguity of the blameful agent in bringing on Maria's sickness' (ibid.). Although Maria's village culture holds with the idea that spirits are sent for bad behaviour, it was highly ambiguous who out of all the family members and their recent ancestors was the most blameworthy malefactor. With the cultural idea of ghostly vengeance, Maria could function as, and experience herself more as an innocent bystander rather than the guilty mental patient of our own culture where such 'non-rational escapes' have been discredited.

It seems as if all those involved in Maria's psychosis were afforded the opportunity to examine their consciences. This made the episode less a method of treating mental illness and rather more like a restructuring of the ethical values and relationships of all those involved.

Perhaps this is what R. D. Laing (1959, 1967) was implying in his views on the families of schizophrenics. That is, far from an emphasis on blaming the family for one member's madness, his views point towards the discovery of a deeper significance in the incidence of psychosis in any cultural group. Regarded from this anthropological perspective, what is significant is the ethical tension that arises out of the situation which mobilises the possibility of both cultural challenge and cultural cohesion at the same time.

This then is my conclusion. By atomising the 'other rationality' of psychosis as a deviance – and, consequently, excluding from society the human subject who experiences psychosis – we have perhaps completely missed the point. With our focus on the psychotic individual we fail to appreciate the broader cultural function of psychosis which is always embedded in its cultural context. Once seen in this way, 'insanity' really does begin to look more like it has something to offer the revaluation of values and the resacralisation of culture which modernity has thirsted for. Equally, with our focus on psychopathology as something to be cauterised out of existence by all sorts of 'methods', we fail to appreciate the significance of abnormal psychology as integral to the individual soul, to our culture and to the world.

12 'The gods are with us. And they want to play'

I have now completed the interpretation of the dream.
[*Footnote added 1909*:] Though it will be understood that I have not reported everything that occurred to me during the process of interpretation.
(Freud, 1900/1909: 118)

THE PAINTINGS OF DAVID SALLE

A few days before I finished this book, I came upon the paintings of David Salle exhibited in their entirety (almost) for his first retrospective at the Stedelijk Museum of Modern Art in Amsterdam. Apart from what I have written about Frank Gehry, I have, quite deliberately, excluded saying anything about postmodern art and aesthetics. I felt all along that there was no space to do it justice. In this brief concluding chapter, I do not wish to start on an analysis of postmodern art in any general way at all, but there is something about Salle's work – in the way I understand it, the way his critics understand it and the way Salle, himself, understands it – that struck me as highly relevant for what I have been saying about Jung and the postmodern.

Just to give you a brief idea of what they are like, Salle's pictures are huge, most of them as big as one wall of your living room, but probably taller. Reproductions in catalogues completely fail to do them justice. The paintings consist of recognisable representations, images of people, rooms, nudes, objects, still life fruit, fish, glassware, and also painted versions of consumer packaging and magazine advertisements. On the one hand they have a photographic quality with all the realism of the technically produced image; on the other hand the paintings contain large and small-scale references to other paintings throughout history – here a Picasso, there a Gericault, early Renaissance scenes and other figures in the style of Van

Gogh or Bernini. I say contain because these gigantic canvases are also collages; some consist of two or three panels, 'separate' paintings that go side-by-side. Most of Salle's paintings hold smaller canvases implanted in the larger picture which then frames them. A painting of a room, for example, has a still life of fruit inserted into it. In addition to this, sketchily drawn images, seemingly dashed off with one or two dips of the brush, float on the surface of the more carefully crafted image that dominates your initial view and these ghost-like impressions emerge only gradually as the eye relaxes its focus to take in the different layers. The overall impression is of a range of different images juxtaposed not only in terms of their sources and their references – advertising, pornography, the history of painting, bourgeois suburbanism, sculpture and African art, for example – but also in terms of their intensity and presence – some leaping out vividly to grab the eye, while others are barely apparent and float like afterthoughts. These seem to appear as 'interruptions' that emerged as the painter went about his composition but which Salle then allows to be included rather than choosing to leave them out for the sake of some pre-established coherence.

It is precisely this quality, Salle's recognition, acknowledgement and, ultimately, celebration of the range and depth of the images – from the substantial and full to the vague and transparent – that flows through him as he paints, that makes his work not only postmodern but also psychological in the sense that I have examined in this book. Many view the postmodern as anything but psychological, as being about surfaces and interchangeable shallow imagery as opposed to the complexity, layered depths and juxtapositions which we find in the psychology of the unconscious–conscious mind. The postmodern painting of David Salle manages to confound such a split view. Some commentators have said that viewing his paintings is like zapping through the TV channels catching glimpses of what flicks across consciousness. For me, this is a mistaken interpretation that seems to ignore that here is a psyche – a human being – who has produced this work from the imagination. Surfing TV channels may well be one way of analogising our conscious observation of successive imagery emerging in the psyche, but to opt for this as an analogy of Salle's paintings is to rob them of their psychologically imagistic and human qualities which are clearly evident and far from shallow.

This is not to deny that Salle is also oriented outward to the world, in very much the same way as Jung, in an effort to reach a position that is not only 'about' his own subjectivity but is also pointing towards a transcendence of the inner world–outer world polarity:

> If I walk in a street seeing all those things on display in the shop, the
> events on the street are real and mirrored in the window all at the same

time, that is a certain way of looking. I am aiming to get that into my paintings. I think the point is that the juxtapositions aren't random, but it is hard to describe what governs them. It has to do with the self-conscious but also transcendental nature of seeing. There is a feeling that if we could describe the glue holding those things together, that would decode a secret. The metaphor of the reflection in the window implies that one's point of view is specific to a moment – and in the next moment as you move, it changes.

(Salle, 1999a: 6–7)

In this we are again coming across the perspective view, concretised, naturally enough, from a painter's point of view but one which also directs us towards a reflexive, postmodern *psychological* position that we find in Jung and post-Jungian psychology. Furthermore, while some may see a degree of alienation in such a juxtaposition of images – a view that may also apply to the present book, for some, just as it does elsewhere in culture – Salle agrees that although 'the ingredients might speak to that alienation', he is not promoting alienation: 'just the opposite; I am interested in connection' (ibid.: 8). This is similar to how, in Jungian analysis, the variety and sheer otherness of the imagery that can emerge from the unconscious may be experienced as alien to the ego, but the aim is always to make a connection with such imagery, to accept it as one's own, no matter how foreign it may seem.

Salle is clearly conscious of the psychological implications of his postmodern painting when he tells of how his subject is the self he finds revealed in the juxtaposition of images. 'It's a fragmented self constructed through un-programmed juxtapositions, a self that stays experiential. There is art that reflects the singular self, and there is art that reflects the non-singular, fragmented self. Obviously I am an example of the latter' (Salle, 1999b: 19). This is the subject of Jung's psychology too – the fragmented self that has little option to be otherwise despite a desire for the fantasy of wholeness. Like Salle, we might prefer to be singular, reductive artists, but, like he says, 'I don't have it in me, so I approach it the other way round' (ibid.). This is not a matter of achieving coherence in self through art or wholeness of self through psychology, but it is a matter of *revealing self in the juxtaposition of images – and revealing a self, moreover, that stays experiential.*

Throughout this book I have had to struggle with the tension between the essentialist, modernist Jung, and everything that strikes me as postmodern in his psychology. Recently a colleague – for whom Jung is rather too essentialist in the main – summed up what I have been aiming at with this ironic comment, 'He is obviously so essentialist that, these days, you have to understand postmodernism to understand Jung!' (Tessa Adams, 1999, personal communication). Nowadays, our psychology is so differentiated, complex and pluralistic that we hardly recognise who we are. As Jung himself asserts, 'Since self-knowledge is a matter of getting to know the individual facts, theories are of very little help. For the more a theory lays claim to universal validity, the less capable it is of doing justice to individual facts' (Jung, 1957, CW 10: para. 493). Universal or essentialist descriptions of 'human nature' are bound to be inadequate. This is not a bad thing. It is how things are. The difficulty arises when we try to ignore this fact and retreat into Enlightenment-type essentialist ideas of who we are, as every psychological theorist does, rather than be frank about the complexity and plurality we now encounter in all our psychologies. Jung was stuck half-way between these positions. Sometimes he was stuck fully in an Enlightenment universalising, but elsewhere – like with complex theory and his referential use of past forms – he is keen to emphasise our psychological differentiation in modern times.

We will always find it difficult – maybe for generations to come – to completely abandon our tendency to universalise our condition and our psychology. As David Salle, in his own field, puts it, 'There is a Dionysian current in contemporary art which always has to be couched in the grammar of some mainstream proposition'. (Salle, 1999b: 19). Even the idea of the postmodern – as an explanatory or a descriptive mode of understanding – forms a grand narrative of itself. It seeks to unify a vast range of phenomena under one heading. To many, Jung seems anything but postmodern with his apparently essentialist psychological ideas such as the self, the archetypes, *anima* and *animus*, and so on. But in the same way that Jung stands just over the brow of the Enlightenment, and begins to dip down the other side into contemporary times, the postmodern, too, stands at the edge of modernity looking both backwards and forwards at the same time. As with Jung, I think the postmodern does not constitute a discourse of itself – hence the accusations of 'thinness' – but is *acting as a presence by which we are able to reassess ourselves with less constraint than ever before*. When Salle talks about what artists *do* he says, 'It is about things in between the obvious things. That is the way someone really makes work' (ibid.: 20). In a similar way, the postmodern reading of Jungian psychology enables us to be reflexive without coming to 'conclusions', to be thoughtful without being told what to think, to love and to desire without prescription and, above all, to *imagine* what we want to be and where we want to be, despite the past, because of the past and even, instead of the past.

There are several other themes in David Salle's work that resonate with what I have been saying throughout this book and, in turn, shed light on what Jungian psychology can say to us. The art critic Arjen Mulder reminds us how for twenty- or thirty-thousand years, every image on earth was produced by a human hand while it is only over the last 160 years that we can speak of images produced by machine with no human hand involved at all. By reappropriating the photographic image, the advertising image, the printed package, and representing these in paint within larger paintings, David Salle restores a humaness to such imagery. He gives it a depth and a significance that mechanical reproduction tended to rob. Old meanings and non-meanings are neutralised through Salle's combination and arrangement of otherwise easily readable pictures to give his pictures a 'compellingly enigmatic character' (Mulder, 1999: 25). And it is through his conscious–unconscious painterly involvement in such a process, I would argue, that he depicts a psyche at work and in play with its own imagery. Not simply personal imagery, although that might be one interpretation, and not only collective cultural imagery as in the pop paintings of Warhol and Lichtenstein, although these are sometimes present too. Beyond these obvious things, in the gap between them, at the edges of these, there is something else which is a mystery. There are shapes and echoes of shapes, there are cartoon sketches that do not seem to 'fit' in anywhere. These are the bits of dreams that we cannot interpret. The bits between the meanings we assign. When Mulder tries to describe this quality he could as easily be talking about working on the images of a dream: 'That which was meaningless becomes meaningful; that which was full of meaning becomes free of sense: such painting hovers above these two unfathomable depths' (ibid.: 27).

The paintings of David Salle seem to have all the postmodern elements of surface, juxtaposition, disconnected imagery, reference, irreverence, consumerism, and yet they are so rich in humanity, intensity and sincerity at the same time. This book has been about how we should understand the significance of this postmodern presence. It has been about how a postmodern approach to analytical psychology offers a purchase on revaluing contemporary culture in the twenty-first century. It suggests that postmodern fragmentation is no negative and destructive attack on modernity and its values, but is the consequence of a psyche differentiating in these accelerating times and seeking an expression of and a revealing of itself to itself in ways that seem alien and challenging to that modernity. The creativity of the unconscious, it seems, has found the conditions to make itself known in cultural forms, not necessarily with any aim in view – or any goal in the modernist sense – but more as *an activity entirely for itself, for its own celebration*. Returning to his theme of human painting *versus* technically reproduced imagery, Mulder suggests how David Salle overcomes such a split and, in doing so, how he challenges the view of a shallow postmodern 'entirely' in thrall to the insubstantiality of the photographic image – one of the triumphs of modernist science. By refusing to reject either form of representation and by incorporating them both into his individual creative and imaginative process, Salle restores psychological meaning and humanity to postmodern painting. Mulder's choice of words are so reminiscent of Jung's that it becomes even clearer how analytical psychology, whether we acknowledge it or not, has already permeated our cultural understanding,

> Whatever science and technology say, the immortals have never left us. Though they seem to have been driven beyond space and time by technical images, they can be retrieved easily, as long as one approaches them in the proper manner. They are still in our midst, in the interiors of the parallel world that David Salle never tires of painting. They stolidly guard the continuity of the imagination, whose product they themselves are. The gods are with us. And they want to play.
>
> (ibid.: 29)

Let's make sure we are in when they call.

References

Adams, Michael Vannoy (1991) 'My Siegfried problem – and ours: Jungians, Freudians, Anti-Semitism, and the psychology of knowledge' in A. Maidenbaum and S. A. Martin (eds), *Lingering Shadows: Jungians, Freudians, and Anti-Semitism*, Boston and London: Shambala, pp. 241–259.

—— (1992) 'Deconstructive philosophy and imaginal psychology: comparative perspectives on Jacques Derrida and James Hillman' in Richard P. Sugg (ed.), *Jungian Literary Criticism*, Evanston, IL: Northwestern University Press, pp. 231–248. (Originally published 1985 in *Journal of Literary Criticism* 2(1): 23–39.)

—— (1995) 'Jungians and deconstruction', letter published in *The Round Table Review of contemporary contributions to Jungian psychology*, V. III, No. 1, Sept.–Oct., pp. 3 and 7.

—— (1996a) *The Multicultural Imagination 'Race', Color and the Unconscious*, London: Routledge.

—— (1996b) 'Flowers and fungi: archetypal semiotics and visual metaphor' in *Spring*, 59, pp. 131–155.

Adorno, T. W. (1950) *The Authoritarian Personality*, with Else Frenkel-Brunswik, Daniel J. Levinson and R. Nevitt Sanford, New York: Harper & Row.

Adorno, T. W. (1984) *Aesthetic Theory*, G. Adorno and R. Tiedemann (eds), trans. C. Lenhardt, London: Routledge.

Adorno, T. W. and Horkheimer, M. (1944) *Dialectic of Enlightenment*, trans. J. Cumming, London: Allen Lane, 1973.

Alford, C. Fred, (1989) *Melanie Klein and Critical Social Theory*, New Haven, CT: Yale University Press.

Alister, Ian and Hauke, Christopher (eds) (1998) *Contemporary Jungian Analysis. Post-Jungian Perspectives from the Society of Analytical Psychology*, London: Routledge.

Anderson, Perry (1983) *In the Tracks of Historical Materialism*, London: Verso.

Ashley, D. (1990) 'Habermas and the completion of the "project of modernity" in Bryan S. Turner (ed.), *Theories of Modernity and Postmodernity*, London: Sage, pp. 88–107.

Banham, Reyner (1960) *Theory and Design in the First Machine Age*, London: The Architectural Press.

Barnaby, K. and D'Acierno, P. (eds) (1990) *C. G. Jung and the Humanities. Towards a Hermeneutics of Culture*, London: Routledge.

Barthes, Roland (1973) *Mythologies*, trans. A. Lavers, London: Paladin.

—— (1975) *The Pleasure of the Text*, trans. R. Miller, New York: Hill and Wang.

Baudrillard, Jean (1994) *Simulacra and Simulation*, trans. S. F. Glaser, Ann Arbor: University of Michigan Press.

Baumann, Z. (1989) *Modernity and the Holocaust*, Oxford: Polity Press.

BBC (1992) *The Late Show: Frank Gehry*, dir. Tim Kirby, London: BBC TV.

Bell, Daniel (1979) *The Cultural Contradictions of Capitalism*, 2nd edn, London: Heinemann.

Bellah, Robert N. (1970) *Beyond Belief*, New York: Harper & Row.

Berger, P. and Luckman, T. (1971) *The Social Construction of Reality*, Harmondsworth: Penguin. (Originally published in 1966).

Berlin, I. (1991) 'The idea of pluralism' in Walter Truett Anderson (ed.) *The Fontana Postmodernism Reader*, London: Fontana (1996), pp. 42–48.

Berman, Marshall (1983) *All That Is Solid Melts Into Air. The Experience of Modernity*, London: Verso.

Bjork (1995) *Post*, Mother Records TPLP51CD.

Bohm, D. (1983) *Wholeness and the Implicate Order*, London: Ark, Routledge.

Burckhardt, Titus (1971) *Alchemy: Science of the Cosmos, Science of the Soul*, Baltimore: Penguin. (Originally published 1967).

Capra, F. (1975) *The Tao of Physics*, London: Fontana.

Card, Charles (1991a) 'The archetypal view of C. G. Jung and Wolfgang Pauli', Part 1, *Psychological Perspectives*, 24, Spring–Summer, pp. 52–69.

—— (1991b) 'The archetypal view of C. G. Jung and Wolfgang Pauli', Part 2, *Psychological Perspectives*, 25, Fall–Winter, pp. 16–33.

Casey, Edward S. (1990) 'Jung and the postmodern condition' in K. Barnaby and P. D'Acierno (eds), pp. 319–324.

Casey, E. S., Hillman, J., Kugler, P. and Miller, David L. (1990) 'Jung and postmodernism: symposium' in K. Barnaby and P. D'Acierno (eds) (1990), pp. 331–340.

Clarkson, Petruska, (ed.) (1997) *On the Sublime in Psychonalysis, Archetypal Psychology and Psychotherapy*, London: Whurr.

Colman, Warren (1998) 'Contrasexuality and the unknown soul' in Ian Alister and Christopher Hauke (eds) (1998), pp. 198–207.

Conway, A. V. (1988) 'The research game: a view from the field', *Complementary Medical Research*, 3(8), pp. 29–36.

Covington, Coline (1989) 'In search of the heroine' in *Journal of Analytical Psychology*, 34(3), pp. 243–254.

Crews, Frederick et al. (1997) *The Memory Wars. Freud's Legacy in Dispute*, London: Granta.

Dalal, F. (1988) 'The racism of Jung', *Race & Class*, 29(3), pp. 1–21.

Davies, P. and Gribbin, J. (1992) *The Matter Myth. Beyond Chaos and Complexity*, Harmondsworth: Penguin.

Deleuze, G. (1986) *Nietzsche and Philosophy*, trans. Hugh Tomlinson, London: Athlone Press.

Deleuze, G. and Guattari, F. (1972) *Anti-Oedipus: Capitalism and Schizophrenia*, New York: Viking.

Diamonstein, B. (1980) *American Architecture Now*, New York, pp. 43–44.

Dieckmann, H. (1976) 'Transference and countertransference', *Journal of Analytical Psychology*, 21(1).

Docherty, T. (1993) 'Postmodernism: an introduction' in T. Docherty (ed.) *Postmodernism. A Reader*, Hemel Hempstead: Harvester Wheatsheaf.

Drinka, G. F. (1984) *The Birth of Neurosis. Myth, Malady and the Victorians*, New York: Touchstone/Simon and Schuster.

Eco, Umberto (1985) *Reflections on The Name of the Rose*, New York and London: Minerva.

Edelglass, S., Maier, G., Gebert, H. and Davy, J. (1992) *Matter and Mind: Imaginative Participation in Science*, Edinburgh: Floris.

Ehrenwald, Jan (1954) *New Dimensions of Deep Analysis. A Study of Telepathy in Interpersonal Relationships*, London: George Allen & Unwin Ltd.

Ellenberger, H. (1994) *The Discovery of the Unconscious. The History and Evolution of Dynamic Psychiatry*, London: Fontana Press. (Originally published 1970.)

Elliott, Anthony (ed.) (1998) *Freud 2000*, London: Polity Press.

Elliott, A. and Frosh, S. (eds) (1995) *Psychoanalysis in Contexts. Paths Between Theory and Modern Culture*, London: Routledge.

Evans, Richard I. (1979) *Jung on Elementary Psychology. A Discussion between C. G. Jung and Richard I. Evans*, London: Routledge & Kegan Paul.

Fabricius, Johannes (1994) *Alchemy. The Medieval Alchemists and their Royal Art*, London: Diamond Books.

Faithfull, Marianne, with David Dalton (1995) *Faithfull*, Harmondsworth: Penguin.

Felman, Shoshona (1987) *Jaques Lacan and the Adventure of Insight. Psycho-analysis in Contemporary Culture*, Cambridge, MA and London: Harvard University Press.

Field, N. (1991) 'Projective identification: mechanism or mystery?' *Journal of Analytical Psychology*, (36)1, pp. 93–110.

—— (1996) *Breakdown and Breakthrough: Psychotherapy in a New Dimension*, London: Routledge.

Flax, Jane (1990) *Thinking Fragments. Psychoanalysis, Feminism, and Post-modernism in the Contemporary West*, Berkeley and London: University of California Press.

Foster, Hal (ed.) (1985) *Postmodern Culture*, London: Pluto Press.

Foucault, Michel (1967) *Madness and Civilisation*, trans. R. Howard, London: Tavistock.

—— (1971) 'Nietzsche, genealogy, history' in Paul Rabinow (ed.) *The Foucault Reader. An Introduction To Foucault's Thought*, London: Penguin (1984).

—— (1982) 'Afterword: the subject and power' in H. L. Dreyfus and P. Rabinow (eds), *Michel Foucault: Beyond Structuralism and Hermeneutics*, Chicago: University of Chicago Press, pp. 212–234.

Freud, S. (1900) *The Interpretation of Dreams (First Part)*, Vol. IV in The Standard Edition (SE), trans. J. Strachey, with A. Freud, A. Strachey and A. Tyson, London: Hogarth Press.

—— (1914) *On Narcissism: An Introduction*, SE, Vol. XIV.

—— (1923) *The Ego and the Id*, SE, Vol. XIX.

Fromm, E. (1942) *The Fear of Freedom*, London: Routledge.

—— (1968) *The Revolution of Hope*, NewYork: Harper & Row.

Frosh, Stephen (1987) *The Politics of Psychoanalysis. An Introduction to Freudian and Post-Freudian Theory*, New Haven and London: Yale University Press.

—— (1991) *Identity Crisis. Modernity, Psychoanalysis and the Self*, Basingstoke: Macmillan.

Gay, Peter, (ed.) (1995) *The Freud Reader*, London: Vintage.

Gehry, Frank (1992) *The Late Show: Frank Gehry*, dir. Tim Kirby, London: BBC TV.

Gellner, Ernest (1985) *The Psychoanalytic Movement, or, The Coming of Unreason*, London: Paladin.

Gilligan, Carol (1982) *In a Different Voice. Psychological Theory and Women's Development*, Cambridge, MA: Harvard University Press.

Gleick, James (1988) *Chaos. Making a New Science*, Harmondsworth: Penguin.

Gregory, R. L. (ed.) (1987) *The Oxford Companion To the Mind*, Oxford University Press.

Grosz, Elizabeth (1994) *Volatile Bodies: Toward a Corporeal Feminism*, London:

Grotstein, J. (1998) 'The numinous and immanent nature of the psychoanalytic subject', *Journal of Analytical Psychology*, 43(1), 41–68.

Habermas, J. (1972) *Knowledge and Human Interests*, London: Heinemann.

—— (1975) *Legitimation Crisis*, trans. T. McCarthy, Boston: Beacon Press.

—— (1987) *The Philosophical Discourse of Modernity: Twelve Lectures*, trans. F. Lawrence, Cambridge, MA: MIT Press.

—— (1987b) 'The entry into postmodernity: Nietzsche as a turning point', extracted from Habermas (1987) in T. Docherty (ed.), *Postmodernism. A Reader*, Hemel Hempstead: Harvester Wheatsheaf, (1993) pp. 51–61.

Hassan, Ihab (1985), 'The culture of postmodernism' in *Theory, Culture and Society*, 2(3), pp. 119–131.

Hauke, C. C. (1995) 'Fragmentation and narcissism: a revaluation' in *Journal of Analytical Psychology*, 40(4) pp. 497–522.

—— (1996a) 'The child: development, archetype and analytic practice' in *The San Francisco Jung Institute Library Journal*, 15(1), pp. 17–38.

—— (1996b), 'Racism, incest and modernity: everyone is now a stranger among strangers' in Martin Stanton and David Reason (eds) *Teaching Transference. On the Foundations of Psychoanalytic Studies*, London: Rebus Press (1996), pp. 159–183.

—— (1997) 'The phallus, alchemy and Christ: Jungian analysis and the sublime' in Petruska Clarkson (ed.) (1997), pp. 123–144.

—— (1998) 'Jung, modernity and postmodern psychology' in Ian Alister and Christopher Hauke (eds) (1998), pp. 287–298.

Henderson, J. L. (1991) 'C. G. Jung's psychology: additions and extensions' in *Journal of Analytical Psychology*, 36(4) pp. 429–442.

Herrigel, E. (1972) *Zen in the Art of Archery*, London: Routledge.

Hillman, James (1975) *Loose Ends*, Dallas: Spring.

—— (1980) 'On the necessity of abnormal psychology: Ananke and Athene' in J. Hillman (ed.), *Facing The Gods*, Dallas: Spring, pp. 1–38.

—— (1983) *Healing Fiction*, Barrytown, New York: Station Hill Press.

—— (1990) speaking in E. S. Casey, J. Hillman, P. Kugler and David L. Miller (1990) 'Jung and postmodernism: symposium' in K. Barnaby and P. D'Acierno (eds) (1990), pp. 331–340.

Hollway, Wendy (1997) 'Teaching psychoanalysis to psychology undergraduates' in *UAPS Newsletter*, Issue 6, Spring.

Homans, Peter (1979) *Jung in Context. Modernity and the Making of a Psychology*, Chicago and London: University of Chicago Press.

Homer, Sean (1998) *Fredric Jameson. Marxism, Hermeneutics, Postmodernism*: Oxford: Polity Press.

hooks, b. (1991) *Yearning: Race, Gender and Cultural Politics*, London: Turnaround.

Hornby, Nick (1996) *High Fidelity*, London: Indigo.

Horton, Robin (1967) 'African traditional thought and western science' in B. Wilson (ed.) *Rationality*, Oxford: Blackwell (1970), pp. 131–171.

Jacoby, Russell (1975) *Social Amnesia: A Critique of Conformist Psychology from Adler to Laing*, Boston: Beacon Press.

James, Peter (1998) *Personal Computer World*, London: VNU Publications.

Jameson, Fredric (1991) *Postmodernism, or The Cultural Logic of Late Capitalism* London: Verso.

Jencks, Charles (1990) *The New Moderns. From Late to Neo-Modernism*, London: Academy Editions.

—— (1996) *What is Post-Modernism?* (4th edn), London: Academy Editions.

Jung, C. G. Except where a different publication or translation is noted below, all references are, by volume and paragraph number, to the hardback edition of *C. G. Jung, The Collected Works* (CW), edited by Sir Herbert Read, Dr Michael Fordham and Dr Gerhard Adler, and translated in the main by R. F. C. Hull, London: Routledge.

Jung, C. G. (1911–1912) *Psychology of the Unconscious: A Study of the Transformations and Symbolisms of the Libido*, trans. Beatrice M. Hinkle, Supp. Vol. B of the Collected Works of C. G. Jung, London: Routledge & Kegan Paul, Princeton, NJ: Princeton University Press (1991).

—— (1940) *The Integration of the Personality*, trans. Stanley Dell, London: Kegan Paul, Trench, Trubner & Co., Ltd.

—— (1983/1963) *Memories, Dreams, Reflections*, London: Fontana.

Jung, C. G. and Pauli, W. (1955) *The Interpretation of Nature and the Psyche*, New York: Pantheon. Bollingen Series 51.

Kaufmann, Walter (1974) *Nietzsche: Philosopher, Psychologist, Antichrist*, 4th edn, Princeton, NJ: Princeton University Press.

Kovel, Joel (1988) *The Radical Spirit: Essays on Psychoanalysis and Society*, London: Free Association Books.

Kristeva, Julia (1978) 'Within the microcosm of the "talking cure"' in J. Smith and W. Kerrigan (eds), *Psychiatry and the Humanities. Vol. 6: Interpreting Lacan*, New Haven: Yale University Press.

—— (1980) *Pouvoirs de l'horreur*, Paris: Seuil. Translated as *Powers of Horror* by L. Roudiez, New York: Columbia University Press (1982).

—— (1981) 'Women's time', trans. A. Jardine and H. Blake, *Signs*, (7)1, pp. 13–15. Extracted in Minsky (1996), pp. 282–287.

—— (1984) in Elaine H. Baruch and Perry Meisel, 'Two interviews with Julia Kristeva', *Partisan Review*, 51(1), pp. 128–132.

Kugler, Paul (1978) 'Image and sound: an archetypal approach to language', *Spring*, pp. 13–51.

—— (1979) 'The phonetic imagination', *Spring*, pp. 118–129.

—— (1982) *The Alchemy of Discourse. An Archetypal Approach to Language*, London and East Brunswick, NJ: Associated University Presses, Inc.

—— (1983) 'Involuntary poetics' in *New Literary History. A Journal of Theory and Interpretation*, Vol. 15, 1983–1984,

—— (1990a) 'The unconscious in a postmodern depth psychology' in K. Barnaby and P. D'Acierno (eds) (1990), pp. 307–317.

—— (1990b) speaking in E. S. Casey, J. Hillman, P. Kugler and David L. Miller 'Jung and postmodernism: symposium' in K. Barnaby and P. D'Acierno (eds) (1990), pp. 331–340.

—— (1993) 'The 'subject' of dreams', *Dreaming*, (3)2, June, Association for the Study of Dreams, New York: Plenum Press.

Kuhn, Thomas (1962) *The Structure of Scientific Revolutions*, Chicago: University of Chicago Press.

Lacan, J. (1981) *La Seminaire. Livre III. Les Psychoses*, Paris: Seuil.

Laing, R. D. (1959) *The Divided Self*, Harmondsworth: Penguin.

—— (1967) *The Politics of Experience and The Bird of Paradise*, Harmondsworth: Penguin.

Lash, Scott (1987) 'Modernity or modernism: Weber and contemporary social theory' in S. Whimster and S. Lash (eds) *Max Weber, Rationality and Modernity*, London: Allen & Unwin.

Latour, Bruno (1993) *We Have Never Been Modern*, trans. C. Porter, Hemel Hempstead: Harvester Wheatsheaf.

Lattimore, R. (trans.) (1955) *Euripides I*, Chicago: Chicago University Press.

Lau, D. C. (trans.) (1963) *Tao Te Ching*, Harmondsworth: Penguin.

Lemaire, A. (1977) *Jacques Lacan*, London: Routledge & Kegan Paul.

Levine, Neil (1990) 'The image of the vessel in the architecture of Frank Lloyd Wright' in K. Barnaby and P. D'Acierno (eds) (1990), pp. 124–137.

Lévi-Strauss, C. (1977) *Structural Anthropology*, Harmondsworth: Peregrine/Penguin.

Levy-Bruhl, L. (1949/1973) *Les Carnets de Lucien Levy-Bruhl*, Paris: Presses Universitaires de France (1949). Translated by Peter Riviere as *Notebooks on Primitive Mentality*, Oxford: Blackwell (1973).

Lewis, I. M. (1971) *Ecstatic Religion*, Harmondsworth: Penguin.

Lundquist, John M. (1990) 'C. G. Jung and the temple: symbols of wholeness' in K. Barnaby and P. D'Acierno (eds) (1990), pp. 113–123.

Lyotard, Jean-Francois (1984) *The Postmodern Condition: A Report on Knowledge*, trans. G. Bennington and B. Massumi, Manchester: Manchester University Press.

—— (1993) 'The sublime and the avant garde' in T. Docherty (ed.) (1993), pp. 244–256.

Macey, David (1995) 'On the subject of Lacan' in A. Elliott and S. Frosh (eds) (1995), pp. 72–88.

Malcolm, Janet (1982) *Psychoanalysis: The Impossible Profession*, London: Pan.

Marcuse, H. (1955/1966) *Eros and Civilization*, Boston: Beacon Press.

Masson, Jeffrey (1990) *Against Therapy*, London: Fontana.

—— (1992) *The Assault on Truth. Freud and Child Sexual Abuse*, London: Fontana.

McGuire, W. and Hull, R. F. C. (eds) (1980) *C. G. Jung Speaking. Interviews and Encounters*, London: Picador.

Merton, Thomas (1970) *The Way of Chuang Tzu*, London: Unwin Books.

Miller, David L. (1989) 'The stone which is not a stone. C. G. Jung and the postmodern meaning of "meaning"' in *Spring*, 49, pp. 110–122.

—— (1990a) 'An other Jung and an other . . . ' in K. Barnaby and P. D'Acierno (eds), (1990), pp. 325–330.

—— (1990b) speaking in E. S. Casey, J. Hillman, P. Kugler and David L. Miller, 'Jung and postmodernism: symposium' in K. Barnaby and P. D'Acierno (eds) (1990), pp. 331–340.

Minsky, R. (1996) *Psychoanalysis and Gender*, London: Routledge.

Mulder, Arjen (1999) 'Images that come from outside. The experiential paintings of David Salle' in *David Salle: Stedelijk Museum Amsterdam*, Ghent and Amsterdam: Ludion.

Needham, R. (1972) *Belief, Language and Experience*, Chicago: University of Chicago Press.

Nietzsche, Friedrich. All references to Nietzsche's work are from the Penguin editions with translation by R. J. Hollingdale, Harmondsworth: Penguin unless noted otherwise.

—— (1878) *Human, All Too Human*, extracted in *A Nietzsche Reader*, 1977.

—— (1878b) *Human, All Too Human*, trans. Zimmern and Cohn, quoted in Jung, CW 5: para. 27.

—— (1883–1885)(1961) *Thus Spoke Zarathustra*.

—— (1882)(1977) *The Gay Science* extracted in *A Nietzsche Reader*.

—— (1974) *The Gay Science*, trans. W. Kaufmann, New York: Random House.

—— (1886)(1973) *Beyond Good and Evil*.

—— (1887)(1967) *On The Genealogy of Morals*, trans. R. J. Hollingdale and W. Kaufmann, New York: Random House.

—— (1889)(1968) *Twilight of the Idols*.

—— (1906) *Die frohlich Wissenschaft*, no. 344 in *Nietzsches Werke*, VI, 301, Taschen-Ausgabe, Leipzig: Naumann.

—— (1906) *Morgenrothe* in *Nietzsches Werke*, V, No. 119,123, Taschen-Ausgabe, Leipzig: Naumann.

Noll, R., (1996) *The Jung Cult. The Origins of a Charismatic Movement*, London: Fontana.

O'Hara, Maureen (1996) 'Constructing emancipatory realities' in Walter Truett Anderson (ed.) (1996) *The Fontana Postmodernism Reader*, London: Fontana. pp. 147–151.

Oliver, Kelly (1993) *Reading Kristeva. Unraveling the Double-bind*, Bloomington and Indianapolis: Indiana University Press.
Orbach, S. (1996) 'Couching anxieties' in S. Dunnant and R. Porter (eds), *The Age of Anxiety*, London: Virago, pp. 149–166.
Owen, D. (1995) *Nietzsche, Politics and Modernity*, London: Sage.
Pagels, E. (1979) *The Gnostic Gospels*, New York: Random House, Harmondsworth: Penguin (1982).
Parker, Ian (1997) *Psychoanalytic Culture. Psychoanalytic Discourse in Western Society*, London: Sage.
Patton, P. (1993) 'Politics and the concept of power in Hobbes and Nietzsche' in P. Patton (ed.), *Nietzsche, Feminism and Political Theory*, London: Routledge, pp. 144–161.
Paul, Benjamin D. (1953) 'Mental disorder and self-regulating processes in culture: a Guatemalan illustration' in R. Hunt (ed.), *Personalities and Cultures. Readings in Psychological Anthropology*, New York: The Natural History Press (1967), pp. 150–165.
Pears, D. (1971) *Wittgenstein*, London: Fontana.
Peat, F. David (1987) *Synchronicity: The Bridge Between Matter and Mind*, New York: Bantam.
—— (1995) *Blackfoot Physics. A Journey into the Native American Universe*, London: Fourth Estate.
Pederson, Loren (1991) *Dark Hearts. The Unconscious Forces That Shape Men's Lives*, London: Shambhala.
Prigogine, Ilya and Stengers, I. (1984) *Order Out of Chaos: Man's New Dialogue With Nature*, New York: Bantam.
Redfearn, J. W. T. (1985) *My Self, My Many Selves*, London: Karnac.
—— (1994) 'Movements of the I in relation to the body image', *Journal of Analytical Psychology*, (39)3, pp. 311–330.
Richards, Barry (ed.) (1984) *Capitalism and Infancy. Essays on Psychoanalysis and Politics*, London: Free Association Books.
—— (1989) *Crises of the Self. Further Essays on Psychoanalysis and Politics*, London: Free Association Books.
—— (1994) *Disciplines of Delight. The Psychoanalysis of Popular Culture*, London: Free Association Books.
Rieff, P. (1959) *Freud: The Mind of the Moralist*, New York: Viking Press.
—— (1966) *The Triumph of the Therapeutic*, New York: Harper & Row.
Rosen, Steven M. (1995) 'Pouring old wine into a new bottle: a modern alchemical interpretation of the ancient hermetic vessel' in Murray Stein (ed.), *The Interactive Field in Analysis, Vol. 1*, Wilmette, IL: Chiron Publications, pp. 121–142.
Sacks, Oliver (1985) *The Man Who Mistook His Wife for A Hat*, London: Picador.
Salle, David (1999a) 'A conversation with David Salle', with Dorine Mignot, in *Bulletin Stedelijk Museum Amsterdam*, Amsterdam.
—— (1999b) 'At the edges: an interview', with Frederic Tuten, in *David Salle: Stedelijk Museum Amsterdam*, Ghent and Amsterdam: Ludion.
Samuels, A. (1985) *Jung and the Post-Jungians*, London: Routledge.

—— (1989) *The Plural Psyche. Personality, Morality and the Father*, London: Routledge.

—— (1990) 'Beyond the feminine principle' in K. Barnaby and P. D'Acierno (eds) (1990), pp. 294–306 (also in A. Samuels 1989).

—— (1993) *The Political Psyche*, London: Routledge.

Sardar, Z. (ed.) (1984) *The Touch of Midas: Science, Values and Environment in Islam and the West*, Manchester: Manchester University Press.

Sarup, M. (1993) *Post-Structuralism and Postmodernism*, 2nd edn, Hemel Hempstead: Harvester Wheatsheaf.

Schutz, Alfred (1962) *Collected Papers 1. The Problem of Social Reality*, M. Natanson (ed.), The Hague: Martinus Nijhoff.

Schwartz-Salant, N. (1988) 'Archetypal foundations of projective identification', *Journal of Analytical Psychology*, (33).

—— (1995) 'On the interactive field as the analytic object' in Murray Stein (ed.), *The Interactive Field in Analysis, Vol. 1*, Wilmette, IL: Chiron Publications, pp. 1–36.

Sergeant, E. S. (1931) 'Doctor Jung: a portrait in 1931' in W. McGuire and R. F. C. Hull (eds) (1980), pp. 65–70.

Shamdasani, Sonu (1995) 'Memories, dreams, omissions' in *Spring*, 57.

Shweder, Richard (1996) 'Santa Claus on the cross' in Walter Truett Anderson (ed.), *The Fontana Postmodernism Reader*, London: Fontana, pp. 68–74.

Smart, Barry (1990) 'Modernity, postmodernity and the present' in Bryan S. Turner (ed.), *Theories of Modernity and Postmodernity*, London: Sage, pp. 14–30.

Stephanson, Anders (1988) 'Regarding postmodernism – a conversation with Fredric Jameson' in A. Ross (ed.), *Universal Abandon? The Politics of Postmodernism*, Minneapolis: University of Minnesota Press, pp. 3–30.

Stevens, Anthony (1995) 'Jungian psychology, the body and the future' in *Journal of Analytical Psychology*, 40(3), pp. 353–364.

Sulloway, Frank J. (1979/1992) *Freud, Biologist of the Mind. Beyond the Psychoanalytic Legend*, Cambridge, MA and London: Harvard University Press.

Tambiah, Stanley (1990) *Magic, Science, Religion, and the Scope of Rationality*, Cambridge: Cambridge University Press.

Teilhard de Chardin, Pierre (1965) *The Phenomenon of Man*, London: Fontana.

Thornham, Sue (1998) 'Postmodernism and feminism' in S. Sim (ed.) *The Icon Critical Dictionary of Postmodern Thought*, Cambridge: Icon Books Ltd.

Toynbee, A. (1954) *A Study of History*, London: Oxford University Press.

Tyng, Anne Griswold (1990) 'Individuation and entropy as a creative cycle in architecture' in K. Barnaby and P. D'Acierno (eds) (1990), pp. 104–112.

UNESCO (1974) *La Science et la diversité des cultures*, Paris: UNESCO, PUF.

von Franz, Marie-Louise (1972) *C. G. Jung: His Myth in Our Time*, trans. W. H. Kennedy, New York: G. P. Putnam's Sons.

Wehr, Demaris S. (1988) *Jung and Feminism. Liberating Archetypes*, London: Routledge.

Whitehead, A. N. (1967) *Science and the Modern World*, New York: The Free Press.

Williams, M. (1963) 'The poltergeist man', *Journal of Analytical Psychology*, 8(2), pp. 123–144.

296 *Jung and the postmodern*

Winch, Peter (1964) 'Understanding a primitive society' in B. Wilson (ed.), *Rationality*, Oxford: Blackwell (1970), pp. 78–111.

Young-Eisendrath, P. (1995) 'Struggling with Jung. The value of uncertainty', *The Round Table Review of contemporary contributions to Jungian psychology*, V. II, No. 4, March–April, pp. 1–7.

—— (1997) 'Jungian constructivism and the value of uncertainty' in *Journal of Analytical Psychology*, 42(4), pp. 637–652.

Yrjonsuuri, M. (1995) 'How did mental representation take place before the Cartesian Theatre was opened?' in P. Pylkkanen and P. Pylkko (eds), *New Directions in Cognitive Science*, Helsinki, Finland: Finish Artificial Intelligence Society, pp. 148–156.

Zabriskie, Beverley D. (1990) 'The feminine: pre- and post-Jungian' in K. Barnaby and P. D'Acierno (eds) (1990), pp. 267–278.

Index

As references to and quotations by Jung appear throughout the book only the major quotations by him are indexed.